Her War Story

HER WAR STORY

Twentieth-Century Women Write about War

Edited by Sayre P. Sheldon

SOUTHERN ILLINOIS UNIVERSITY PRESS

Carbondale and Edwardsville

02 01 00 99   4 3 2 1

Library of Congress Cataloging-in-Publication Data

Her war story : twentieth-century women write about war / edited by Sayre P. Sheldon.
    p. cm.
Includes bibliographical references and index.
1. War—Literary collections. 2. Literature—Women authors. 3. Literature, Modern—20th century. I. Sheldon, Sayre P., [DATE].
PN6071.W35H45 1999
808.8′0358—dc21
ISBN 0-8093-2245-5 (cloth : alk. paper)   98-44169
ISBN 0-8093-2246-3 (pbk. : alk. paper)   CIP

The paper used in this publication meets the minimum requirements of
American National Standard for Information Sciences—Permanence of Paper
for Printed Library Materials, ANSI Z39.48-1984. ⊗

CONTENTS

PREFACE

My reasons for producing this anthology begin early in my childhood. Any person whose life has spanned a good part of the twentieth century has memories deeply marked by war. The hours I spent in my grandfather's library with a set of volumes of World War I photographs—the Belgian children with their hunger-bloated stomachs come back as clearly to me as any image of suffering in our newspapers today. Hearing Neville Chamberlain's declaration of war in a hotel room in Rotterdam, where my family was waiting to board our ship for the United States after visiting my mother's relatives in Germany, I tried to understand why the adult faces were so somber when we children felt only excitement. On the trip home, sleeping with clothes next to our beds in case the ship was torpedoed—we went off course to pick up the crew of a freighter that had been torpedoed. Other memories of World War II are strong—particularly the frustration of being too young when my older sister could at least be a nurse's aide and release actual nurses to wartime duties. My father, rejected for active service, spent three years on Pacific islands, growing food for American troops. My mother's sadness over losing contact with her German family—she later learned of the destruction of their homes in Allied bombings. My marriage to a veteran of four years with the navy in the Pacific meant hearing his stories of the days he spent sewing the bodies of marines killed on Tarawa into canvas bags for sea burial.

In the 1960s, working to end the Vietnam War, I knew that I would hide my son rather than let him go to a war I believed to be morally wrong. In the 1980s, afraid once more, now for the survival of grandchildren in a nuclear arms race, I met with antinuclear leader Helen Caldicott and helped her found a national women's organization for nuclear disarmament, which continues working today to reduce and contain the world's nuclear weaponry.

Meanwhile, through teaching literature at Boston University, I found another approach to war. Searching for a theme in a required course on modern literature, I read Paul Fussell's *The Great War and Modern Memory* and based my course on the changes in literature after World War I. Students, I found, quickened to the theme of war and its testing of the limits of human behavior. The wealth of women's war writing was opened to me; soon, I was teaching a course using only women authors and finding committed students, male and female. It seemed both natural and necessary to make women's war writing more accessible to readers and students in an anthology.

I chose the twentieth century for this collection of women's war writing because women's roles in war have changed dramatically in this century. Women have written about war as long as there has been writing—before that, they probably scratched pictographs of war on cave walls. A Sumerian priestess wrote about war around 2300 B.C.; Sappho wrote about the Trojan War in the sixth century B.C. There are legends of warlike women such as the Amazons or histories of warrior queens who led men into battle—Zenobia, Boadicea, Joan of Arc. There are thousands of stories, poems, diaries, and accounts of war by women.

Yet war literature is still seen as almost exclusively male. The reason is one of definition: war literature is traditionally about being *in war*, more precisely about being *in combat*. Women are more likely to be victims than perpetrators of war. By limiting war literature to actual combat, men have claimed war as their subject. The claim is no longer valid, if it ever has been. The twentieth century has redefined the meaning of combat and expanded the territory of war to include women in larger numbers than ever before. When the technological advances of modern war targeted civilians, the homefront became the frontline. Women took an active part in war whether or not by choice. Modern war reaches everywhere. There is less demarcation between where war is and is not taking place and where it begins and ends.

Violence pervades our world. The unofficial war zones extend to our gun-ridden inner cities, to the desolated countries where civilians starve while their rulers buy more arms, to the busy marketplaces where terrorist bombs explode, and to the towns where deadly radioactive materials from the manufacture of weapons leak into the ground. Statistics tell part of the story. During World War I, 5 percent of the casualties were civilian. The figure rose to 75 percent in World War II. In the 1990s, 90 percent of the many millions of casualties in wars around the world were civilians, most of them women and children. According to the United Nations, women and their families fleeing conflicts make up 80 percent of the world's refugees. A May 21, 1995 *New York Times* article speaks of a "postmodern" war in which armies and peoples are indistinguishable so "everybody who gets in the way gets killed." Another way to look at the changes in warfare is to see civilization as going back to a total war of earlier times when the purpose was to wipe out the opponent's entire population.

There is another important reason why women can claim a war literature—women's opportunities as writers have expanded vastly. As women moved into occupations previously closed to them, they began to describe in writing all those areas that had traditionally been off-limits. Women covered wars for their newspapers, wrote war propaganda for their governments, published their wartime diaries, described fighting alongside men. They used their wartime experiences for their fiction and poetry, choosing the right to *imagine* war, just as men for centuries had written about war without actually experiencing it. Their determination to write about it has produced a women's war literature that can no longer be ignored or marginalized.

The selections in this anthology only suggest the richness of this literature. In selecting them, I have attempted to follow certain principles. The first was to choose pieces that give a historical and narrative picture of women's part in the wars of our century. The second was to choose good writing, the finest of fiction and poetry as well as of journalism and diary writing. I used interviews only when they were needed to fill in the historical narrative. Brief biographies emphasize the connections between each author and the war or wars of her time.

A bibliography provides suggestions for further reading in the works of women writing about war and lists some of the many critical works scholars are producing in both the fields of women's war writing and of women's roles in war. This anthology owes much to literary scholars such as Sandra Gilbert and Susan Gubar. My hope is that it will complement and illustrate their work and the work of others who are making contributions to our understanding of both human nature and the nature of war.

Many works of outstanding women writers of war literature are not included here due to their ready availability elsewhere and the limitations in size and scope of this anthology. Some kinds of women's writing are left out, particularly science fiction, where writers such as Ursula Le Guin and Joanna Russ explore the furthest dimensions of human behavior from a feminist viewpoint. The broad area of men's war literature is only mentioned here occasionally; again, the major works are accessible to the interested student and reader. The modern part of the anthology was the most difficult to compile as much of the writing is only beginning to emerge along with our historical perspective on the events.

Although it is commonly held that women are more opposed to war than men, I did not deliberately choose literature that was ideologically against war. It was my intention to reflect as many facets of women's experience and imagining of war as possible. "The glamour of war," in Vera Brittain's words, affects women and men alike. War is not yet an "equal-opportunity" employer, but it has called forth women's skills and potential, bravery and aggression, attraction and disgust, just as it has men's.

Now that war involves women as never before, we can look to them for new viewpoints and ideas. As "outsiders" to the war system, Virginia Woolf pointed out, women can bring fresh thinking to traditional explanations and justifications for war. They question whether making war is an inevitable part of human nature. They envision societies without war. Told they are naive idealists for doing so, women stubbornly maintain that their idealism is in fact common sense. Survival depends on understanding and arresting the impulse to destroy, which today—as never before in history—is capable of extinguishing humanity altogether.

There are many people to thank for the completion of this book. First, many students at Boston University read and discussed the material with me and gave every indication that they found it stimulating, informative, and often, inspiring. Second, the groups, colleagues, friends, and family I spoke to about this project generously gave every kind of help, including recommending sources I did not know. These included my colleagues in disarmament work, who continually provide new insights into war and peace issues. Third, the great libraries available to me—Hilles and Schlesinger at Radcliffe, Harvard's Widener, the Boston Athenæum, and the Cambridge Public Library—provided much help, particularly the first two where I often sought and received advice. Lastly, the members of the Southern Illinois University Press transformed a complicated, unwieldy manuscript into a completed book.

The Great War

The **twentieth century** began with a sense of optimism that wars—at least major ones—were a thing of the past. After a century that had produced so much scientific and political progress for the European powers, it was difficult to recognize the tinderbox Europe had become. The "balance of power" imposed after the end of the Franco-Prussian War in 1871 had held in spite of years of imperialistic rivalry and military buildup. It was unthinkable that an assassination in the Balkan city of Sarajevo could lead to the outbreak of a war unprecedented in scale, intensity, and casualties, which would change the lives of all of those

I

whose countries fought in it and would have repercussions around the world.

But as Barbara Tuchman wrote in *The Guns of August*, "Europe was a heap of swords piled as delicately as jackstraws; one could not be pulled out without moving the others" (34). The existing alliances between France and Russia and between Germany and the Austro-Hungarian Empire were set to take action once Germany invaded Belgium in order to attack France, a plan that the German military had been evolving since the beginning of the century. Britain was pledged to defend the Belgian neutrality they had helped establish. The assassination of the heir to the Austrian throne was simply the tinder producing the conflagration.

At the war's outset, both sides suffered from the delusion that theirs would be a swift victory. Five years of trench warfare with millions of casualties was a nightmare prospect visible as yet to only a few. Two new developments had a major part in expanding and prolonging the war: mass conscription and advances in the technology of warfare. These changes had begun in the nineteenth century during the Napoleonic wars, Britain's war in the Crimea, and the American Civil War. However, in numbers of soldiers and resulting casualties, the "Great War," as World War I came to be known, outstripped all others. In the first two weeks of August 1914, close to four million Frenchmen were mobilized and transported by train to the front. During the next four years, an estimated twenty-five thousand miles of trenches were built. Improved and new weapons such as the machine gun, the airplane, poison gas, and the tank, used against large numbers of men in close proximity, produced vast numbers of casualties.

The Battle of the Somme was the largest battle ever fought. One half million men were killed or wounded. In small strips of "No Man's Land," churned into mud and littered with bodies, spent shells, and barbed wire, a whole generation of young men struggled, despaired, went mad—some even drowned in the mud. When it finally came in the autumn of 1918, the Allied "victory" had cost more than ten million dead and more than thirty-seven million casualties. The survivors and the writers who told the story of this war would come to be known as a "lost generation."

Changes for Women

Olive Schreiner witnessed a war at the beginning of the century between the British settlers and the Dutch settlers, known as Boers, in South

Africa. Brought up in South Africa as the child of German missionaries and educated in England, Schreiner wrote as a newspaper correspondent during the Boer War. In 1911, Schreiner published what for many women became a textbook for feminism, *Woman and Labour*. Now that women, she said, were "to take all labor for our province" (172), they would have to take part in war and once there would bring to it a different point of view—words that were to be proved in the century of war ahead.

During the Great War's early months, however, women celebrated their new opportunities much as poet Rupert Brooke described young men going off eagerly to the adventure of war. Radclyffe Hall's banned novel, *The Well of Loneliness*, described how all women but especially lesbian women had come out of their holes and corners to contribute their skills and abilities. Nina Macdonald's cheerful "Sing a Song of War-time" was published in a book called *War-Time Nursery Rhymes*. Macdonald uses the viewpoint of a young boy, mystified by his new surroundings in which "Mummie" now does the housework, girls drive vans, and "[a]ll the world is topsy-turvy." The technology and scale of modern war created vast needs for armaments and made more complex demands on women's labor than Macdonald's poem implied. One young writer who had begun making her mark as a journalist saw wider implications for women in their new war-making roles. Under the pen name of Rebecca West, Cicily Fairfield in a series of newspaper articles "Hands That War" described the women munition workers, living in barracks in isolated areas, facing great dangers, working twelve-hour days, and proving that "industry has at last recognized that women have brains as well as hands." Although the young women in their white dresses and caps might look as if they were involved in a domestic process like baking, they were actually handling deadly materials that could kill or maim them and that dyed their hair and skin yellow from chemical exposure.

Thousands of well-to-do young women volunteered for service before official army groups for women had been established. The patriotic families of these privileged and protected young women paid their daughters' expenses, proudly sending them off with little idea of the situations they were going into. Vera Brittain's books trace the development of a sheltered, middle-class British woman born at the end of the Victorian era through both world wars. In *Testament of Youth*, she describes how in 1914 she left "provincial young ladyhood" behind forever. As a Voluntary Aid Detachment (V.A.D.) nurse, Brittain found herself walking the poorest streets of London unchaperoned. As she wrote in *Testament*, she had never in her life seen a nude man, but "[s]hort of actually going to bed with them, there was hardly an intimate service that I did not perform for one or another in the course of four years" (165).

In the diary upon which *Testament of Youth* was partly based, Brittain reveals the innocence of the war's early stages, writing to her fiancé Roland Leighton of dreaming that "he should come home wounded not too seriously, & that I should have a little practice in nursing first, & be able to look after him & thoroughly spoil him." Her diary includes long passages from his letters and conveys the intensity with which she and thousands of other women tried to share the war experiences of the men they knew. Roland's death in 1915 made her even more determined to nurse at the front.

Women at the Front

British women got to the front in World War I with difficulty, often financing their own ambulances and medical supplies. There was no official army corps for women until 1917. The public was uneasy about women in uniform. They were criticized for "aping men" and accusations of immorality and lesbianism were common. Women who managed to get to France had to overcome not only physical difficulties and red tape but prejudice against their being there at all. Women doctors had to form their own medical units.

This prejudice did not extend to accounts of the front by women—there were eager audiences at home for firsthand information and an official sanction for propaganda that could help the war effort. Books such as Louise Mack's *A Woman's Experiences in the Great War* used expressions like "The Cult of the Brute" to describe the Germans and told of piles of torn women's clothing, corroborating the atrocity stories of German mass rape of Belgian women.

Edith Wharton, already a celebrated American author, had moved to France permanently in 1912. Believing that the defeat of France would mean the end of civilization, she plunged into war work with characteristic American pragmatism and was later decorated by the French for her monumental contributions. In her book *Fighting France: From Dunkerque to Belport*, a collection of her articles for *Scribner's Magazine* on touring the front, Wharton had only admiration for French fighting methods and indomitable spirit. She went on to write several stories and two novels about the war, both dedicated to Ronald Simmons, a young friend whose death affected her greatly.

As the war went on and women came closer to its actual conditions, their writing became more graphic. The results were often more than the public or the censors had bargained for. Many of these outspoken and revealing accounts were either withdrawn or not published until long after the war's end in 1918. Other survivors of the front, male and female, could not face their experiences to write about them until many years later.

American women Ellen La Motte and Mary Borden came as nurses in the early part of the war. Both wrote books based on their experiences. Both recognized and emphasized the horror of healing men in order for them "to be torn to pieces again on the firing line." Novelist Mary Borden conveys in "Conspiracy" a dispassionate, almost surreal sense of the absurdity and horror in a hospital close to the front. Another story "Blind" ends with Borden showing symptoms that would not yet have been recognized as shell shock—the same disorder afflicting thousands of men at the front and causing widespread desertion and hospitalization.

La Motte's book *The Backwash of War: The Human Wreckage of the Battlefield as Witnessed by an American Hospital Nurse*, written in 1916, was withdrawn in Great Britain and not republished until 1934. In the chapter, "Women and Wives," La Motte examines the paradox of official French policy towards women: "[A]lways there are plenty of women. . . . wives are forbidden, because lowering to the morale, but women are winked at, because they cheer and refresh the troops." Her analysis includes another paradox, the belief that the enemy overpowers women with force, whereas on the French side, the young women entice the soldiers.

Colette, already a well-known French writer, smuggled herself to Verdun to be with her husband. In her account for the newspapers, she found wives as well as mistresses in hiding, having returned to "an Oriental way of life"—indicating that the French were more lenient about wives than La Motte had observed. La Motte was also observing enlisted men; Colette's husband, an aristocrat and an officer, had special privileges. The operation of the class system in war—in fact, the absolute necessity of it in war on this scale—is another common topic for the women writing about war.

Not So Quiet . . . : Stepdaughters of War is a fictional re-creation written by popular British writer Helen Zenna Smith in 1930. She was asked by a publisher for a parody of Erich Maria Remarque's classic *All Quiet on the Western Front*. Basing her book on an actual nurse's diary, Smith produced instead a scathing contrast between the horrors of the front and the complacency of the homefront. Smith's particular targets were the mothers in England who compete in sacrificing their children to the war effort. Her heroine is too traumatized by her experiences to recover. She becomes a prostitute in the book's sequel and commits suicide in Smith's final book in the trilogy.

Borden, La Motte, and Smith had ventured into a "forbidden zone" for women of the time. They wrote about bodies and their hitherto unmentionable functions, about mutilation and appalling suffering, about lice and lack of sanitation, about cleaning the shit and vomit out of ambulances, about being sexually attacked by maddened wounded men. They learned to swear and speak in the language they heard from the men they nursed. To write about all this meant using new language and forms. Their writing is episodic and jagged, sardonic and bitter. In attempting to convey the extraordinary nature of mass warfare, they anticipated the changes that would come in postwar literature eventually to be labeled "modernism." Women writers could claim not only a place in the lost generation but in creating its new literature.

America Comes In

As the war dragged on, American supporters of France were impatient with their native country for staying out of the conflict. There were many reasons for the United States to remain neutral in World War I, some to be repeated in World War II. The United States had strong ties with Germany as well as with the Allies. Woodrow Wilson had been reelected president in 1916 with the slogan, "He kept us out of war." The decision to join the Allies was strongly influenced by German submarine warfare, which as well as revoking a promise not to sink ships with Americans on board, threatened Britain's ability to import necessary supplies. By 1917, fighting on the Western Front had slowed down, and a fresh infusion of manpower and munitions was desperately needed.

Dorothy Canfield Fisher's story, "A Honeymoon . . . Vive L'Amerique" shows impatience with the Americans for taking so long. Her book *Home Fires in France*, published in 1918, is dedicated to the American general John Pershing. Each sketch is based on Fisher's own relief experience—she and her husband returned to France where they had previously lived to do war work. She describes the generosity of Americans, contrasting their pragmatism and optimism with the self-serving and cynical exploitation of relief work by some of the aristocratic Parisians.

Amy Lowell's poem "In the Stadium" describes the reviewing of a Harvard University regiment by French marshal Joseph Joffre just weeks after the United States entered the war. Because her brother was the president of Harvard, Lowell was able to shake Joffre's hand at a reception following this event. By 1917, there was little left of the patriotic sentiments of the early war years. Instead of heroic language, Lowell uses the image of cannon fodder: "Boys flung into a breach."

When American troops finally arrived in 1918, the exhausted Allies greeted them as somewhat of a miracle. Vera Brittain, by this time nursing at the front, described her reaction in *Testament of Youth*: "I pressed forward with the others to watch the United States physically entering the War, so god-like, so magnificent, so splendidly unimpaired in comparison to the tired, nerve-wracked men of the British army. So these were our deliverers at last, marching up the road to Camiers in the spring sunshine." With the realization that "we were not, after all, defeated," she broke into tears (420–21).

Willa Cather romanticized the experience of the American troops in her novel *One of Ours*. Claude, the central character in the book, was an amalgam of Cather's nephew and a friend's son. The young American hero finds release from his culturally barren life at home through his exposure to France and his war experiences. His death in combat is not seen as tragic but as a kind of fulfillment. Male war writers, including Ernest Hemingway, cited the book as proof that women could not write about war. Cather's glorification of the war, however, does not extend to the book's conclusion where she develops the lost generation theme, writing that "thousands who unlike Claude, returned, killed themselves later."

In her late twenties, Bostonian Mary Lee served with the American Expeditionary Forces in France. She was able to get to the front by helping the Y.M.C.A. set up canteens for the troops. She titled her book *The Farce*, but it was unpublishable until she changed the title to *It's a Great War!* In her preface, she states that her episodic writing style in the book was necessary because "[w]ar moves in jerks." Daringly, she went on to say, "A book about war may not, perhaps, be written by a man. A man who goes to war . . . sees only one small corner of the army. . . . Furthermore emotion blurs the picture."

Elizabeth Shepley Sergeant, a journalist as well as a friend and biographer of Willa Cather, touring the front near the war's end, was severely injured when a companion picked up an unexploded grenade. Her account, out-of-print today, is written with the kind of immediacy few women at the front could achieve. In her book about Cather, Sergeant writes that Cather's war writing is too bloodless to be convincing to a veteran. Sergeant as well as Lee believed that all romance had to be removed from war writing before it could effectively prevent other wars.

Gertrude Stein's account of World War I in *The Autobiography of Alice B. Toklas* carries the reader into the armistice. For expatriates Stein and her companion, Toklas, the war provided excitement and action once they decided "to get into the war" by driving for the American Fund for the French Wounded. Although Stein would write about war again and again, often with penetrating objectivity and characteristic originality, and would live through World War II in occupied France, she describes this war as a pleasant experience, especially after her countrymen arrived: "We did enjoy life with these doughboys. . . . [T]he war was so much better than just going to America. Here you were with America in a kind of way that if you only went to America you could not possibly be."

The United States, arriving so late on the scene and suffering the loss of one hundred thousand compared to Europe's millions, was still to have its scars from the war. It was also to lose many of its young artists and intellectuals to the lure of Europe. Some who took part in the war stayed on to become expatriates, often congregating in Paris to recuperate from their war experiences and join the forces creating modernism. Stein observed in *The Autobiography of Alice B. Toklas*: "Paris was crowded. As Clive Bell remarked, they say that an awful lot of people were killed in the war but it seems to me that an extraordinary large number of grown men and women have suddenly been born."

Mourning and Memory

The armistice brought only short-lived rejoicing—the costs had been far too great. The men who returned, if not physically impaired, were often psychically damaged. According to Ernest Hemingway, Gertrude Stein had heard the term "lost generation" first from a garage owner addressing an inept mechanic who was a veteran. Stein explained it further with the idea that the young men who went to war had skipped the civilizing period of their lives and could never make up for it.

Many women also faced the struggle of finding a place in a postwar world. Vera Brittain in a poem called "The Lament of the Demobilized" reflected on the bitterness of her return to college where the younger students preferred to ignore the returning scarred "veterans" such as herself. Brittain tells of lying weeping on the cold floor of her Oxford room, lamenting that she hadn't died in the war with the others. "I'm nothing but a piece of wartime wreckage, living on ingloriously in a world that doesn't want me!" (*Testament* 490). Melodramatic youthful despair, Brittain says in writing about this period later. The depth of her pain was revealed by the delusion that her face was changing in some sinister way. She wrestled alone with this delusion and with dreams, hallucinations, and insomnia, unaware that these were normal symptoms for war survivors.

Memorializing their dead became a major task for women. The diary of German artist Käthe Kollwitz records her change from believing that it was right to send her son to war to the realization that she had been drastically wrong. She struggles with her loss of faith in the war—is it a breach of faith with her son? Her memorial took years to complete. It evolved into two massive figures—a grieving father and mother—very different from the conventional heroic soldier model of previous wars.

Charlotte Mew's poem "The Cenotaph" begins as a conventional elegy, comparing women's grief to the wound of "an inward sword," continues with the construction of the monument to Britain's unknown soldier in London, and concludes, jarringly, with the crass buying and selling in the marketplace, where the dead are mocked by "every busy whore's and huckster's face."

Katherine Mansfield's story "The Fly" explores the lives of two fathers who have lost their sons and live with their grief very differently. The class theme is strong in the story. On a deeper level, when one father torments a fly, Mansfield probes the causes of war with images of the sadism with which the strong torment those weaker than themselves. Mansfield's own grief over the death of her brother in France fueled her work. She wrote in her journal on October 29, 1915: "Dearest heart, I know you are there, and I live with you, and I will write for you" (37).

The loss of a brother continues as a strong theme in women's writing after World War I. American poet Louise Bogan did not publish the poem "To My Brother Killed: Haumont Wood: October, 1918" until 1935, yet it reverberates with the pain of loss as well as the irony that peace alone does not last. In 1939, at the outset of World War II, Bogan described herself, "I am still a violent pacifist and refuse to be railroaded into any side-taking that might lead to the air being let into people by means of bullet-holes" (183).

In 1973, American writer Toni Morrison, in her book *Sula*, describes Shadrack, a veteran of World War I, whose shell shock relegates him to a life on the fringes of the black community from which he emerges only for his "National Suicide Day." Morrison, in the powerful imagery she uses to re-create historical events, shows how the trauma of battle repeats itself throughout Shadrack's life and eventually enables him to lead the residents of his town, like military recruits in World War I, to their destruction.

In *The Great War and Modern Memory*, Paul Fussell writes that the years from 1914 to 1918 opened a chasm between traditional nineteenth-century values and the modern world and were responsible for many new ways of thinking and writing about ourselves. Women writers continue to revisit the topic of World War I. For example, in the last decade of this century, a British woman Pat Barker has written a prizewinning trilogy, mingling historical fact with fiction about the mental disorders encountered by the men who fought and the struggles of the doctors who tried to restore their sanity in order to send them back to the insanity of the trenches.

Changes for Women

Nina Macdonald

"Sing a Song of War-time"

Sing a song of War-time,
Soldiers marching by,
Crowds of people standing,
Waving them 'Good-bye'.
When the crowds are over,
Home we go to tea,
Bread and margarine to eat,
War economy!

If I ask for cake, or
Jam of any sort,
Nurse says, 'What! in War-time?
Archie, cert'nly not!'
Life's not very funny
Now, for little boys,
Haven't any money,
Can't buy any toys.

Mummie does the house-work,
Can't get any maid,
Gone to make munitions,
'Cause they're better paid,
Nurse is always busy,
Never time to play,
Sewing shirts for soldiers,
Nearly ev'ry day.

Ev'ry body's doing
Something for the War,

Girls are doing things
They've never done before,
Go as 'bus conductors,
Drive a car or van,
All the world is topsy-turvy
Since the War began.

Rebecca West

"The Cordite Makers"

The world was polished to brightness by an east wind when I visited the cordite factory, and shone with hard colours like a German toy-landscape. The marshes were very green and the scattered waters very blue, and little white clouds roamed one by one across the sky like grazing sheep on a meadow. On the hills around stood elms, and grey churches and red farms and yellow ricks, painted bright by the sharp sunshine. And very distinct on the marshes there lay the village which is always full of people, and yet is the home of nothing except death.

In the glare it showed that like so many institutions of the war it has the disordered and fantastic quality of a dream. It consists of a number of huts, some like the government-built cottages for Irish labourers, and some like the open-air shelters in a sanatorium, scattered over five hundred acres; they are connected by raised wooden gangways and interspersed with green mounds and rush ponds. It is of such vital importance to the State that it is ringed with barbed-wire entanglements and patrolled by sentries, and its products must have sent tens of thousands of our enemies to their death. And it is inhabited chiefly by pretty young girls clad in a Red-Riding-Hood fancy dress of khaki and scarlet.

Every morning at six, when the night mist still hangs over the marshes, 250 of these girls are fetched by a light railway from their barracks on a hill two miles away. When I visited the works they had already been at work for nine hours, and would work for three more. This twelve-hour shift is longer than one would wish, but it is not possible to introduce three shifts, since the girls would find an eight-hour day too light and would complain of being debarred from the opportunity of making more money; and it is not so bad as it sounds, for in these airy and isolated huts there is neither the orchestra of rattling machines nor the sense of a confined area crowded with tired people which make the ordinary factory such a fatiguing place. Indeed, these girls, working in teams of six or seven in those clean and tidy rooms, look as if they were practising a neat domestic craft rather than a deadly domestic process.

When one is made to put on rubber over-shoes before entering a hut it might be the precaution of a pernickety housewife concerned about her floors, although actually it is to prevent the grit on one's outdoor shoes igniting a stray scrap of cordite and sending oneself and the hut up to the skies in a column of flame. And there is something distinctly domestic in the character of almost every process. The girls who stand round the great drums in the hut with walls and floor awash look like millers in their caps and dresses of white waterproof, and the bags containing a white substance that lie in the dry anteroom might be sacks of flour. But, in fact, they are filling the drum with gun-cotton to be dried by hot air. And the next hut, where girls stand round great vats in which steel hands mix the gun-cotton with mineral jelly, might be part of a steam-bakery. The brown cordite paste itself looks as if it might turn into very pleasant honey-cakes; an inviting appearance that has brought gastritis to more than one unwise worker.

But how deceptive this semblance of normal life is; what extraordinary work this is for women and how extraordinarily they are doing it, is made manifest in a certain row of huts where the cordite is being pressed through wire mesh. This, in all the world, must be the place where war and grace are closest linked. Without, a strip of garden runs beside the huts, gay with shrubs and formal with a sundial. Within there is a group of girls that composes into so beautiful a picture that one remembers that the most glorious painting in the world, Velasquez's 'The Weavers', shows women working just like this.

One girl stands high on a platform against the wall, filling the cordite paste into one of the two great iron presses, and when she has finished with that she swings round the other one on a swivel with a fine free gesture. The other girls stand round the table laying out the golden cords in graduated sizes from the thickness of rope to the thinness of macaroni, the clear khaki and scarlet of their dresses shining back from the wet floor in a perpetually changing pattern as they move quickly about their work. They look very young in their pretty, childish dresses, and one thinks them good children for working so diligently. And it occurs to one as something incredible that they are now doing the last three hours of a twelve-hour shift.

If one asks the manager whether this zeal can possibly be normal, whether it is not perhaps the result of his presence, one is confronted by the awful phenomenon, beside which a waterspout or a volcano in eruption would be a little thing, of a manager talking about his employees with reverence. It seems that the girls work all day with a fury which mounts to a climax in the last three hours before the other 250 girls step into their places for the twelve-hour night shift. In these hours spies are sent out to walk along the verandah to see how the teams in the other huts are getting on, and their reports set the girls on to an orgy of competitive industry. Here again it was said that for attention, enthusiasm and discipline, there could not be better workmen than these girls.

There is matter connected with these huts, too, that showed the khaki and scarlet hoods to be no fancy dress, but a military uniform. They are a sign, for they have been dipped in a solution that makes them fireproof, that the girls are ready to face an emergency, which had arisen in those huts only a few days ago. There had been one of those incalculable happenings of which high explosives are so liable, an inflammatory mixture of air with acetone, and the cordite was ignited. Two huts were instantly gutted, and the girls had to walk out through the flame. In spite of the uniform one girl lost a hand. These, of course, are the everyday dangers of the high-explosives factory. There is very little to be feared from our enemies by land, and it is the sentries' grief and despair that their total bag for the eighteen months of their patrol of the marshes consists of one cow.

Surely, never before in modern history can women have lived a life so completely parallel to that of the regular Army. The girls who take up this work sacrifice almost as much as men who enlist; for although they make on an average 30s a week they are working much harder than most of them, particularly the large number who were formerly domestic servants, would ever have dreamed of working in peacetime. And, although their colony of wooden huts has been well planned by their employers, and is pleasantly administered by the Young Women's Christian Association, it is, so far as severance of home-ties goes, barrack life. For although they are allowed to go home for Sunday, travelling is difficult from this remote village, and the girls are so tired that most of them spend the day in bed.

And there are two things about the cordite village which the State ought never to forget, and which ought to be impressed upon the public mind by the bestowal of military rank upon the girls. First of all there is the cold fact that they face more danger every day than any soldier on home defence has seen since the beginning of the war. And secondly, there is the fact—and one wishes it could be expressed in terms of the saving of English and the losing of German life—that it is because of this army of cheerful and disciplined workers that this cordite factory has been able to increase its output since the beginning of the war by something over 1,500 per cent. It was all very well for the Army to demand high explosives, and for Mr Lloyd George to transmit the demand to industry; in the last resort the matter lay in the hands of the girls in the khaki and scarlet hoods, and the State owes them a very great debt for the way in which they have handled it.

Vera Brittain

from *Chronicle of Youth: The War Diary, 1913–1917*

Sunday June 27th

Behold, a new experience beginneth!

I got up at 6.30 & went to the Devonshire Hospital. The Devonshire is a convalescent hospital, chiefly for rheumatism resulting from wounds. I ran round the Men's Day-Room, where meals for the soldiers are served, putting out forks & spoons which seem to be permanently greasy. After that I took trays to patients still in bed. Another nurse & I have three wards to look after, numbers 5, 6, & 7. There were three men in bed in 7, all dears. Two of them were about thirty, & both very anxious to talk & tell me how they got here. Neither of them could walk. One had been 3 months in France in hospital, 12 weeks at Sheffield & 19 in Buxton! The third man was younger than the other two, dark & good-looking. He was very quiet and read, or pretended to read, a magazine while I was talking to the other two. He speaks in a perfectly refined voice & when I afterwards cleared up the table by his bed, he apologised for making such a mess. I rather suspect he is a gentleman ranker. There were three men in Ward 5 and four in Ward 6. These latter were singing "Killarney" in harmony. One in Ward 5 was pretty ill, though very cheerful, & could not get up; I straightened his bed for him; I didn't have to make the other beds until they were up. This man asked me if I had come on here from another hospital, which I thought one of the nicest compliments I had ever been paid! It is very nice to be addressed as "Nurse" and "Sister". After breakfasts & beds I had to dust the wards, wash the doctors' tables, and put hot water in the jugs. One man told me that it hadn't had such a dusting for weeks! All this means a considerable amount of running about, as the Hospital is a huge place. I managed to find out where were the kitchen, the sink, & the rubbish baskets, which are the things chiefly used in my work. The military nurses are a quite young & very kind, and showed me everything. At 10.30 one of them took me round to give me instructions in how to hand out the milk to those that have it—a job I have to do every day. Afterwards I collected the mugs, put them back in the day-room & put one or two things ready for dinner. This was all very strenuous, & after it I had nothing particular to do until dinner-time.

I talked to a Scotch soldier they called "Jock", who had been there ever since Christmas, when he was sent back from the front after a month with frost-bitten feet. This man told me he had frequently stood up to his waist in water in mid-winter, and hadn't had any hot meals either. He also told me how many young officers & men had been shot soon after going out through over-carelessness about putting their heads above the parapet of the trench. The men are keen to have a look at the battlefield, put up their heads to see,—and it is all over with them. He told me how they had lost one of their officers in this way—a Capt. MacGregor, who was a splendid officer & greatly loved by all his men. The first day they went in the trenches he exhorted his men all the time to keep their heads below, but was not at all careful of himself; he said it was only his men that mattered. He was a big man & used to walk upright in his trench, so that his head was visible above the parapet. The first day shells fell all around him but nothing touched him. But the second day through not stooping down he was shot through the head by a rifle 10 minutes after they went into the trenches.

I hear dozens of war stories and if I wished could hear hundreds. The men like to talk about their experiences, and a new person to tell their stories to is quite enough to start any of them off. I had the dinner to see to, and to take to patients still in bed—three upstairs this time—and then was off duty for the rest of the day. I am only going in the mornings to begin with, but when they get a little busier & I am a little more experienced I shall go in the evenings as well. Oh! I love the British Tommy! I shall get so fond of these men, I know. And when I look after any one of them, it is like nursing Roland by proxy. Oh! if only one of them could be the Beloved One! . . .

Sunday August 1st
I was back at the Hospital this morning. There was a good deal of work to do. Smith is very ill now & is thought to be dying so cannot be left. I had to

leave my work & sit with him for about an hour this morning. Had anyone told me a month ago that I should sit by a dying man, lift him when he choked and constantly turn him over, I should have been terrified at the idea. Now I do it—not with equanimity, for I cannot think with equanimity of anyone's dying—but with calm.

Tuesday August 3rd

Roland is—alas for me!—back in the trenches. "I have been back with the Battalion a day now. My little experience with Corps Headquarters was most interesting, though short-lived." They went back into the trenches 3 days from when the letter was written—to-day; "which was chiefly why I and the 100 men I had with me were recalled. Also two of the officers in my Company are away—one with a badly sprained ankle, and the other, I am afraid, dying of appendicitis in a Military Hospital a few miles away." He is now acting junior Captain. Edward thinks he has a chance of promotion. He continues "While I was at Corps Headquarters I didn't have any real Staff work to do, or much chance of showing that Roland Leighton has any more ability than the average subaltern. I think they were very pleased with me, though, as the A.D.M.S. asked the General specially whether I could not be kept there permanently. The General said that was impossible in the circumstances, but that if he got together a permanent Headquarters Company, as he intended to do soon, he would offer me the command of it." Meanwhile he has learnt a good deal and enjoyed himself. He got a glimpse of civilisation one afternoon by motoring into Amiens, which was "filled with French officers & very gay & unwarlike".

Wednesday August 4th

The anniversary of our declaration of War on Germany. There is nothing to be said about this New Year of War, for it is so obvious that a year ago no one expected a second year of it that disquisitions on the subject take the form of mere truisms. There is more to be done than there is to be said—the renewal of our determination & our vows in a cause which now is much more obviously that of justice and freedom than it was a year ago. Whatever the papers may say, the majority of us have passed beyond our blatant loud-voiced "patriotism", our want of realisation, our irresponsibility, our inappropriate indifference, and are quiet & resolute, weary but still tenacious, confident of the issue and determined that come what may, it *shall* be.

It was an appropriate day, perhaps, for Edward's last with us. He is typical, in some ways, of England's best spirit at the present moment; confident & tranquil, ready for death if it must be, anxious to possess a thorough knowledge of the part demanded of him and not over-troubled about the rest of events which he cannot affect. He never worries and is never sentimental; never even emotional.

I had an unsatisfactory sort of letter from the Red Cross, talking vaguely of delays and numerous interviews. British authorities & their Red Tape are distinctly depressing. Strange that they should plead for volunteers and then make it as unpleasant as possible for you when you have volunteered.

Being the anniversary of the war, there were special intercession services and prayers for the renewal of vows. There was a service at 7.0 and both Mother & Daddy were anxious that Edward & I should go, though we should both have preferred to stop away. Neither the Church of England nor one's relations allow themselves to think for a moment that one can renew one's vows much better in a private place, in resolutions not put into elegant clerical language by other people. God—if there be a God—is much nearer to one on the night-enshrouded moorlands than in a crowded & stuffy church. The only part of the service I liked was Cowper's hymn "God moves in a mysterious way", which I am always very fond of.

Edward & I walked up the Manchester Road right as far as the turning down to the Goyt Valley. The night wind blew fresh in our faces, and all around us lay the hills and moorlands, dark and silent. In the distance the lights from the town gleamed faintly & now & again a dim glow shone out from the window of some solitary cottage on the hillside. We talked for a long time & very seriously—much of it was about Roland & much of course about the war. Edward expressed again, as he did that evening in the garden at Oxford, the half-haunting instinct that he may not return. He says it is not as if he were a full-fledged & well-known composer; he cannot see that his life at present is much use to anyone; he is not even sure that it is much good to himself. We walked back the last part of the way almost in silence. There was so much to think—so little to be said. Afterwards he & Mother sat up talking in his room till a quarter to 12.0.

When I said good-night to Roland's photograph I realised that I owed him an apology. This afternoon I showed it to Miss Bervon & she exclaimed with great enthusiasm "*What* a nice straight face." I was seized with a sudden embarrassment & said hastily & quite irrelevantly "Yes, he *is* very plain, isn't he!" My dear love! Even if he has hair like a brush & a mouth too resolute for the smallest degree of beauty, no one could be plain with such dark well-defined eyebrows & deep intelligent eyes. His photograph reminds me so much of that first parting—the worst. For to lose Edward, though he seems to take many of my pleasant recollections with him—does not, cannot, mean the same to me as it meant to lose Roland. What does happen is that the remembrance of that morning's agony, all too intense before, is now intensified. My future, my work, and above all Roland, are all—for the time being at least—gone from me.

Thursday August 5th

I said goodbye to Miss Heath Jones & Miss Bervon before going to the Hospital; they are departing even before Edward. I said one goodbye to him at the bathroom door; he seemed cheerful enough but his eyes looked very sad. But I managed to get 10 minutes' respite from the Hospital a little later to see him off by the 9.50. We all assembled there on the station, Edward & I, soldier & nurse, & Mother & Daddy. Fortunately we had not long to wait. We were all calm & cheerful and talked of nothing in particular. I looked long & carefully at Edward as he stood there, tall & sunburnt, the typical soldier; I was committing his image to my mind. I wish I had done the same with Roland, but I felt too half-crazed the morning he went away to have presence of mind for any such thing. As the train went out I stood & waved to him, with a sick sense that it was perhaps for the last time in these our short years. So we have seen him off—to France, the Dardanelles, the Persian Gulf? What matter which. In all these stricken countries there are thousands of British graves, and there is so little reason to hope that what one loves best may not make one more. Fortunately the station had not the desolate look it wore when Roland departed. There was no icy stillness, no snowy roofs, no pitiless gleaming rails, to make matters worse. Edward just went, that was all. And I said "Au Revoir," but he said "Goodbye."

There was no time for grief. I went back to the Hospital straight away. All day long the house—as much as I saw of it—was very depressed. Mother was quiet & quite sensible but Daddy too mournful for words, constantly saying that all his interest in life is gone & we may as well put him in the churchyard, etc. etc. I was sorry for him of course; for I know what it means, even to a less selfish person than he, to see the light of one's eyes depart. But I wonder if it ever strikes him that I too may any moment lose my heart's desire, that I have in fact stood to lose him all these months, and that the hour of darkness, if it comes, will be all the harder to bear because it has been so long delayed.

I received a letter from him just before I went back to the Hospital this evening. "Dear Child—I have always liked this name for you, though I ought not to call you 'child' ought I?—thank you so much for Rupert Brooke. It came this morning, and I have just read it straight through. It makes me feel as if I want to sit down and write things myself instead of doing what I have to do here. I used to talk of the Beauty of War; but it is only War in the abstract that is beautiful. Modern warfare is merely a trade, and it is only a matter of taste whether one is a soldier or a greengrocer, as far as I can see. Sometimes by dint of an opportunity a single man may rise from [the] sordidness to a deed of beauty: that is all." They were going into the trenches the next day & were then in a village just behind the line. "Much troubled by flies but otherwise nothing to report, as the newspapers say." The officer Roland mentioned in his last letter died of appendicitis last Friday. Roland went to the funeral on Sunday. "Such a waste of life! It is a pity he did not die like a soldier when he had lived as one." He goes on "Please don't do too much work at the Hospital, will you? You seem to, dear, by your letters." He adds a p.s. asking for socks if Mother is making any, and says he is "still trying to get leave but with no result." I feel inclined to say with the Psalmist "Lord, how long?"

Women at the Front

Edith Wharton

from *Fighting France: From Dunkerque to Belport*

The first sight of Châlons is extraordinarily exhilarating. The old town lying so pleasantly between canal and river is the Head-quarters of an army—not of a corps or of a division, but of a whole army—and the network of grey provincial streets about the Romanesque towers of Notre Dame rustles with the movement of war. The square before the principal hotel—the incomparably named "Haute Mère-Dieu"—is as vivid a sight as any scene of modern war can be. Rows of grey motor lorries and omnibuses do not lend themselves to as happy groupings as a detachment of cavalry, and spitting and spurting motor-cycles and "torpedo" racers are no substitute for the glitter of helmets and the curvetting of chargers; but once the eye has adapted itself to the ugly lines and the neutral tints of the new warfare, the scene in that crowded clattering square becomes positively brilliant. It is a vision of one of the central functions of a great war, in all its concentrated energy, without the saddening suggestions of what, on the distant periphery, that energy is daily and hourly resulting in. Yet even here such suggestions are never long out of sight; for one cannot pass through Châlons without meeting, on their way from the station, a long line of "éclopés"—the unwounded but battered, shattered, frost-bitten, deafened and half-paralyzed wreckage of the awful struggle. These poor wretches, in their thousands, are daily shipped back from the front to rest and be restored; and it is a grim sight to watch them limping by, and to meet the dazed stare of eyes that have seen what one dare not picture.

If one could think away the "éclopés" in the streets and the wounded in the hospitals, Châlons would be an invigorating spectacle. When we drove up to the hotel even the grey motors and the sober uniforms seemed to sparkle under the cold sky. The continual coming and going of alert and busy messengers, the riding up of officers (for some still ride!), the arrival of much-decorated military personages in luxurious motors, the hurrying to and fro of orderlies, the perpetual depleting and refilling of the long rows of grey vans across the square, the movements of Red Cross ambulances and the passing of detachments for the front, all these are sights that the pacific stranger could forever gape at. And in the hotel, what a clatter of swords, what a piling up of fur coats and haversacks, what a grouping of bronzed energetic heads about the packed tables in the restaurant! It is not easy for civilians to get to Châlons, and almost every table is occupied by officers and soldiers—for, once off duty, there seems to be no rank dstinction in this happy democratic army, and the simple private, if he chooses to treat himself to the excellent fare of the Haute Mère-Dieu, has as good a right to it as his colonel. . . .

Looking at the faces at Châlons, one sees at once in which sense the French are "une nation guerrière." It is not too much to say that war has given beauty to faces that were interesting, humorous, acute, malicious, a hundred vivid and expressive things, but last and least of all beautiful. Almost all the faces about these crowded tables—young or old, plain or handsome, distinguished or average—have the same look of quiet authority: it is as though all "nervosity," fussiness, little personal oddities, meannesses and vulgarities, had been burnt away in a great flame of self-dedication. It is a wonderful example of the rapidity with which purpose models the human countenance. More than half of these men were probably doing dull or useless or unimportant things till the first of last August; now each one of them, however small his job, is sharing in a great task, and knows it, and has been made over by knowing it.

Mary Borden

"Conspiracy" from *The Forbidden Zone*

It is all carefully arranged. Everything is arranged. It is arranged that men should be broken and that they should be mended. Just as you send your clothes to the laundry and mend them when they come back, so we send our men to the trenches and mend them when they come back again. You send your socks and your shirts again and again to the laundry, and you sew up the tears and clip the ravelled edges again and again just as many times as they will stand it. And then you throw them away. And we send our men to the war again and again, just as long as they will stand it; just until they are dead, and then we throw them into the ground.

It is all arranged. Ten kilometres from here along the road is the place where men are wounded. This is the place where they are mended. We have all the things here for mending, the tables and the needles, and the thread and the knives and the scissors, and many curious things that you never use for your clothes.

We bring our men up along the dusty road where the bushes grow on either side and the green trees. They come by in the mornings in companies, marching with strong legs, with firm steps. They carry their knapsacks easily. Their knapsacks and their guns and their greatcoats are not heavy for them. They wear their caps jauntily, tilted to one side. Their faces are ruddy and their eyes bright. They smile and call out with strong voices. They throw kisses to the girls in the fields.

We send our men up the broken road between bushes of barbed wire and they come back to us, one by one, two by two in ambulances, lying on stretchers. They lie on their backs on the stretchers and are pulled out of the ambulances as loaves of bread are pulled out of the oven. The stretchers slide out of the mouths of the ambulances with the men on them. The men cannot move. They are carried into a shed, unclean bundles, very heavy, covered with brown blankets.

We receive these bundles. We pull off a blanket. We observe that this is a man. He makes feeble whining sounds like an animal. He lies still; he smells bad; he smells like a corpse; he can only move his tongue; he tries to moisten his lips with his tongue.

This is the place where he is to be mended. We lift him on to a table. We peel off his clothes, his coat and his shirt and his trousers and his boots. We handle his clothes that are stiff with blood. We cut off his shirt with large scissors. We stare at the obscene sight of his innocent wounds. He allows us to do this. He is helpless to stop us. We wash off the dry blood round the edges of his wounds. He suffers us to do as we like with him. He says no word except that he is thirsty and we do not give him to drink.

We confer together over his body and he hears us. We discuss his different parts in terms that he does not understand, but he listens while we make calculations with his heart beats and the pumping breath of his lungs.

We conspire against his right to die. We experiment with his bones, his muscles, his sinews, his blood. We dig into the yawning mouths of his wounds. Helpless openings, they let us into the secret places of his body. We plunge deep into his body. We make discoveries within his body. To the shame of the havoc of his limbs we add the insult of our curiosity and the curse of our purpose, the purpose to remake him. We lay odds on his chances of escape, and we combat with Death, his saviour.

It is our business to do this. He knows and he allows us to do it. He finds himself in the operating room. He lays himself out. He bares himself to our knives. His mind is annihilated. He pours out his blood, unconscious. His red blood is spilled and pours over the table on to the floor while he sleeps.

After this, while he is still asleep, we carry him into another place and put him to bed. He awakes bewildered as children do, expecting, perhaps, to find himself at home with his mother leaning over him, and he moans a little and then lies still again. He is helpless, so we do for him what he cannot do for himself, and he is grateful. He accepts his helplessness. He is obedient. We feed him, and he eats. We fatten him up, and he allows himself to be fattened. Day after day he lies there and we watch him. All day and all night he is watched. Every day his wounds are uncovered and cleaned, scraped and washed and bound up again. His body does not belong to him. It belongs to us for the moment, not for long. He knows why we tend it so carefully. He knows what we are fattening and cleaning it up for; and while we handle it he smiles.

He is only one among thousands. They are all the same. They all let us do with them what we like. They all smile as if they were grateful. When we hurt them they try not to cry out, not wishing to hurt our feelings. And often they apologise for dying. They would not die and disappoint us if they could help it. Indeed, in their helplessness they do the best they can to help us get them ready to go back again.

It is only ten kilometres up the road, the place where they go to be torn again and mangled. Listen; you can hear how well it works. There is the sound of cannon and the sound of the ambulances bringing the wounded, and the sound of the tramp of strong men going along the road to fill the empty places.

Do you hear? Do you understand? It is all arranged just as it should be.

Ellen La Motte

"Women and Wives" from *The Backwash of War: The Human Wreckage of the Battlefield as Witnessed by an American Hospital Nurse*

There are many women at the Front. How do they get there, to the Zone of the Armies? On various pretexts—to see sick relatives, in such and such hospitals, or to see other relatives, brothers, uncles, cousins, other people's husbands—oh, there are many reasons which make it possible for them to come. And always there are the Belgian women, who live in the War Zone, for at present there is a little strip of Belgium left, and all the civilians have not been evacuated from the Army Zone. So there are plenty of women, first and last. Better ones for the officers, naturally, just as the officers' mess is of better quality than that of the common soldiers. But always there are plenty of women. Never wives, who mean responsibility, but just women, who only mean distraction and amusement, just as food and wine. So wives are forbidden, because lowering to the morale, but women are winked at, because they cheer and refresh the troops. After the war, it is hoped that all unmarried soldiers will marry, but doubtless they will not marry these women who have served and cheered them in the War Zone. That, again, would be depressing to the country's morale. It is rather paradoxical, but there are those who can explain it perfectly.

No, no, I don't understand. It's because everything has two sides. You would be surprised to pick up a franc, and find Liberty, Equality, and Fraternity on one side, and on the other, the image of the Sower smoothed out. A rose is a fine rose because of the manure you put at its roots. You don't get a medal for sustained nobility. You get it for the impetuous action of the moment, an action quite out of keeping with the trend of one's daily life. You speak of the young aviator who was decorated for destroying a Zeppelin single-handed, and in the next breath you add, and he killed himself, a few days later, by attempting to fly when he was drunk. So it goes. There is a dirty sediment at the bottom of most souls. War, superb as it is, is not necessarily a filtering process, by which men and nations may be purified. Well, there are many people to write you of the noble side, the heroic side, the exalted side of war. I must write you of what I have seen, the other side, the backwash. They are both true. In Spain, they bang their silver coins upon a marble slab, accepting the stamp upon both sides, and then decide whether as a whole they ring true.

Every now and then, Armand, the orderly, goes to the village to get a bath. He comes back with very clean hands and nails, and says that it has greatly solaced him, the warm water. Then later, that same evening, he gets permission to be absent from the hospital, and he goes to our village to a girl. But he is always as eager, as nervous for his wife's letter as ever. It is the same with Simon, the young surgeon. Only Simon keeps himself pretty clean at all times, as he has an orderly to bring him pitchers of hot water every morning, as many as he wants. But Simon has a girl in the village, to whom he goes every week. Only, why does he talk so incessantly about his wife, and show her pictures to me, to everyone about the place? Why should we all be bored with tales of Simon's stupid wife, when that's all she means to him? Only perhaps she means more. I told you I did not understand.

Then the *Gestionnaire*, the little fat man in khaki, who is purveyor to the hospital. Every night he commandeers an ambulance, and drives back into the country, to a village twelve miles away, to sleep with a woman. And the old doctor—he is sixty-four and has grandchildren—he goes down to our village for a little girl of fourteen. He was decorated with the Legion of Honour the other day. It seems incongruous.

Oh yes, of course these were decent girls at the start, at the beginning of the war. But you know women, how they run after men, especially when the men wear uniforms, all gilt buttons and braid. It's not the men's fault that most of the women in the War Zone are ruined. Have you ever watched the village girls when a regiment comes through, or stops for a night or two, *en repos*, on its way to the Front? Have you seen the girls make fools of themselves over the men? Well, that's why there are so many accessible for the troops. Of course the professional prostitutes from Paris aren't admitted to the War Zone, but the Belgian girls made such fools of themselves, the others weren't needed.

Across the lines, back of the German lines, in the invaded districts, it is different. The conquering armies just ruined all the women they could get hold of. Any one will tell you that. *Ces sales Bosches!* For it is inconceivable how any decent girl, even a Belgian, could give herself up voluntarily to a Hun! They used force, those brutes! That is the difference. It's all the difference in the world. No, the women over there didn't make fools of themselves over those men—how could they! No, no. Over there, in the invaded districts, the Germans forced those girls. Here, on this side, the girls cajoled the men till they gave in. Can't you see? You must be pro-German! Any way, they are all ruined and not fit for any decent man to mate with, after the war.

They are pretty dangerous, too, some of these women. No, I don't mean in that way. But they act as spies for the Germans and get a lot of information out of the men, and send it back, somehow, into the German lines. The Germans stop at nothing, nothing is too dastardly, too low, for them to attempt. There were two Belgian girls once, who lived together in a room, in a little village back of our lines. They were natives, and had always lived there, so of course they were not turned out, and when the village was shelled from time to time, they did not seem to mind and altogether they made a lot of money. They only received officers. The common soldiers were just dirt to them, and they refused to see them. Certain women get known in a place, as those who receive soldiers and those who receive officers. These girls were intelligent, too, and always asked a lot of intelligent, interested questions, and you know a man when he is excited will answer unsuspectingly any question put to him. The Germans took advantage of that. It is easy to be a spy. Just know what questions you must ask, and it is surprising how much information you can get. The thing is, to know upon what point information is wanted. These girls knew that, it seems, and so they asked a lot of intelligent questions, and as they received only officers, they got a good lot of valuable information, for as I say, when a man is excited he will answer many questions. Besides, who could have suspected at first that these two girls were spies? But they were, as they found out finally, after several months. Their rooms were one day searched, and a mass of incriminating papers were discovered. It seems the Germans had taken these girls from their families—held their families as hostages—and had sent them across into the English lines, with threats of vile reprisals upon their families if they did not produce information of value. Wasn't it beastly! Making these girls prostitutes and spies, upon pain of reprisals upon their families. The Germans knew they were so attractive that they would receive only officers. That they would receive many clients, of high rank, of much information, who would readily fall victims to their wiles. They are very vile themselves, these Germans. The curious thing is, how well they understand how to bait a trap for their enemies. In spite of having nothing in common with them, how well they understand the nature of those who are fighting in the name of Justice, of Liberty and Civilization.

Colette

"Verdun, December–January, 1915"

It's ended, that beautiful terrified journey. Here I am—and I wonder for how long?—hidden in Verdun. A fake name, borrowed identity papers were not enough to protect me, during the thirteen hours of the trip, from the new-style gendarme that the war has made shrewd, jeering, indiscreet, or from the bossy railway superintendent at the Châlons station. En route, I ran into every possible peril. There was the volunteer nurse, appointed to meet the trainloads of wounded, she who happened to know me. "Imagine, you here!" she exclaimed. Then there was the ex-journalist in uniform who inquired: "Is your husband all right? Have you come to be with him?" Besides these, there was the army medical officer who "understood what was up," and gave me winks that would have been enough to alert a track watchman . . . The least troublesome hours were those of the "black train," when we ran with all lights out between Châlons and Verdun, going slowly, slowly, as if the train were groping its way, repressing its asthma and its whistle. Long hours? Yes, perhaps, because of my impatience to arrive, but full and anxious hours, alight with the aurora borealis of an incessant cannonading, a rosy glimmer palpitating on the horizon toward the northeast.

A magnificent thunder accompanied it, continuous, sustained, which did not hurt the ear but sounded throughout one's body, in the limbs, the stomach, the head; and sometimes on the horizon a flare sprayed its floral bouquet and splintered the night.

No one slept or talked until the wintry daybreak and our arrival at Verdun. And how I envied, in my disguise, those merchants of Verdun who passed the gendarme with a "How goes it?" and a handshake.

No matter. I have arrived, and I will try to remain here, a voluntary prisoner. The nearby cannonading does not roar alone: a coke fire crackles and flames, and my accomplices—a noncommissioned officer the color of ripe wheat, his young wife brown as a chestnut, who are letting me stay in their house—and their laughter, over our coffee with condensed milk. Provided that I don't go out of doors, that I don't approach the windows—"Beware of the medical officers billeted on the other side of the street!"—all will be well. The windowpanes emit a shrill "ee-eee" when the cannonading becomes more intense and obliges us to raise our voices, and a winter sunshine warns of freezing weather to come.

I am wild to hear about everything, to shudder, and to hope. I put questions.

"What's new?"

The noncommissioned officer, who is in the Quartermaster Department, frowns and pulls at his Vercingetorix mustache.

"New? Well, I can tell you the upholsterer is a swine!"

"The . . . "

"The upholsterer, that's right. The butter the upholsterer sells is margarine!"

"Yes . . . and what else?"

"Well, there's the piano merchant. He's just received a marvelous shipment of sardines. I'm hurrying over to his store on my way to look at our horses . . . "

"Yes, yes, and what else?"

"Why," exclaims the brown-haired young woman, "there's this shameful thing of making us pay three sous for one leek! But the sub-prefect is outraged, and he's going to get a stock of things put in the sub-prefecture—rice, macaroni, potatoes—and then we'll see if the grocers will still have the nerve to . . . "

"Yes, yes, yes! But please, what about the war?"

"The war?"

Vercingetorix looks at me reflectively, his innocent blue eyes wide open. I lose patience.

"The war, in the name of God, yes! What people are saying, what people are reading, what you are doing!"

The blue eyes narrow with laughter.

"Oh yes, of course, the war! Well, it still goes on, it keeps going, it's going very well, don't worry."

I deserved that reply from a calm and courageous man. It did not take me a week to realize that here in Verdun, chock-a-block full of troops, with the railway its unique supply line, war becomes a habit, the inseparable cataclysm of life, as natural as thunder and rainstorms; but the danger, the real danger, is that one may soon not be able to eat. Food comes first, everything else takes second place: the stationer sells sausages, the sewing woman sells potatoes. The piano merchant stacks a thousand tins of sardines and mackerel on his tired pianos that he used to rent out; but butter is a luxurious rarity, a can of condensed milk a precious object, and vegetables exist only for the fortunate of this world . . .

Eat, eat, eat. Well, yes, one must eat. The freezing weather nips, the East wind makes those who spend the nights out of doors ravenous. The important thing is to keep the blood hot in our veins, although it may at any time pour out in floods, immeasurable floods. Great courage goes with a great appetite, and the stomachs of the people in Verdun are not stomachs that are shrunken by fear.

Some German prisoners passed down the rue d'Antouard. I saw them, between the blades of my Persian blinds, which are always closed. Some civilians were standing in their doorways watching them go by, with a bored look. Their faces yellowed with fatigue and dirt, the prisoners marched in a slovenly way, many of them showing only unconcern and relief from tension, as though saying, "Good! It's over with, for us!" A German soldier, puny but high-spirited, stuck his tongue out at a woman as he passed.

Between seven and eight in the morning and between two and three in the afternoon, the German planes punctually come to drop bombs. They fall just about everywhere, without causing much damage or casualties. But the bombing and the response of our fighter planes and antiaircraft guns, my, what a din it makes! All the same, the neighbor across the street mourns her garden that was ravaged yesterday and her shed that was smashed. Also, a roof of the administration building quite near here, at the foot of the fortress, now yawns open to the sky. The noncommissioned officer, Vercingetorix, swears like a pagan against those *Aviatik*, as he calls them, "that try to keep us from taking care of our horses!"

His wife sets me an example of complete imprudence and comes home today under a veritable hail of shrapnel that didn't touch her.

"Oh, what a nuisance, what a nuisance!" she exclaims. "Just imagine, I had to take shelter under the porte-cochere of the X. family, and we're not on speaking terms!"

In the evening, toward nine or ten o'clock, I risk taking a furtive walk for my health, my legs trembling in fear of encountering a patrol. Not a street light, not a sound, not a glimmer behind the closed shutters of between the crisscrossed window curtains. But sometimes a muffled cry, the fleeing of slippered little feet, a panting: I have blindly bumped into one of those veiled and cloistered wives, one of the voluntary prisoners Verdun hides, she, too, out for a breath of night air. People know about these wives and mistresses, returned to an Oriental way of life; if you name them in a low voice, it is by no means a betrayal. People mention one of the women, they say she has not crossed the threshold of her jail for seven months or seen a human face except that of the man she loves. They say she is an occasional writer, and that she is the happiest of women . . .

A rather gloomy level pathway beside the canal. But a warm sun that is melting the frost and the cloudless sky give a rosy hue to the fortress and the archbishop's palace and make the water blue. We risk this walk in broad daylight, despite all marital interdictions and the dangers of what my hostess calls "the half-past-two airplanes."

The towpath is lined at intervals with sentinels and with bare poplars, and on the moored canal boats from Belgium, flaxen-haired children play. The spongy fields steam, and the thaw has swollen the streams. A regular peal of thunder scans our steps; it is one of those days when the people of Verdun say gravely, "They're getting a pounding in the Argonne."

"Do you see those dance halls stuck right in the fields?" asks my companion. "You can't imagine what fun we had in them last summer . . . "

A sharp detonation, a muffled din which comes down from the upper air, interrupts her.

"That's one of *theirs*," she says. "The .75's are firing at it . . . Look, there's the *Aviatik!*"

While I can still hear nothing but the humming of the engine, my Verdun hostess's sharp eyes have already found on the clear blue of the sky the minuscule pigeon which grows bigger and leaves the horizon; here it is, borne by two convex wings, new, gleaming; it circles the town, rises, seems to meditate, hesitates . . . Five white bouquets blossom in a wreath around it, five pompons of immaculate smoke which mark, suspended in the windless sky, the point where our antiaircraft shells are exploding—five, then seven, and their concerted blasts reach our ears later still . . .

"Oh, here come some of ours!" my companion exclaims.

And from a nearby post rise, with the buzzing of a furious wasp, two biplanes, two others rushing up from the town. They climb the sky in spirals, show their light bellies in the sunshine, the tricolor on their tails, their flat surfaces . . . They are buzzards, male falcons, slender swallows, and at a great distance, merely flies . . .

"Another German!"

"Yes! And another, and another!"

It took only a few seconds to fill that sky, vast and empty just now, with a flight of enemy wings. How many of them will the east, black with pines and rolling hills, hurl at us? One would say that the vertiginous blue space was barely big enough to hold them; they circle, return as suddenly as a bird striking the windowpane, and our guns fill the azure with white roses . . .

"Those over there are ours! There's going to be an air battle!"

"They are enemy planes. No. At this distance I can't distinguish . . . "

We shout, for the tumult has increased, necessary to the beauty of the aerial chase. The guns of the town and of the fortress bay like a pack of hounds, deep bass some of them; the others sharp, furious barks. The magnificent pursuit is right over our heads . . .

"He's hit, he's hit! No, no . . . Oh, he's getting away . . . "

"Farther ahead, farther ahead!" my companion shouts, as if the gunners could hear her. "Can't you see that all your shells are falling short?"

We run, unconsciously following the planes, screaming, and it took the shouts of a company of fusiliers and their emphatic advice to make us seek shelter under an iron bridge. Shelter . . . But why?

We soon know the reason: a weird hailstorm has begun to pepper the canal at our feet, a hot hail that makes the water hiss. Who is hurling this boiling shrapnel at us? We had not thought of this. Excitedly watching the fighter planes, we had forgotten the sparks, the burning cinders that would fall from a battle of demigods contesting the rights to the upper airs.

Under the narrow iron bridge, we tensely wait. We hope for and imagine the finest issue of the combat: the fall, the sudden stripping off of all the curved wings, the planes spiraling down, defeated, to crash on the grassy bank . . . Nothing falls there but a bomb, and the soaked field drinks it up, covers it over without its exploding. It was one of the last projectiles, a wicked tapered seed, thrown out by the German who is vanishing in the distance. The racing of a storm cloud is less rapid than his magical flight: the white smoke of the shells still floats up there where the enemy planes are now only a dotted line, far off, at the bottom of the sky swept clean. The baying of the guns is now intermittent; the fusiliers rejoice.

Returning toward the town, we find the first traces of the aerial bombardment: the trees along the promenade have undergone a brutal pruning, and in a freshly opened hole in the ground children are looking for shrapnel, babbling and scratching like chickens after a shower . . .

(*Translated by Herma Briffault*)

Helen Zenna Smith

from *Not So Quiet . . . : Stepdaughters of War*

If the War goes on and on and on and I stay out here for the duration, I shall never be able to meet a train-load of casualties without the same ghastly nausea stealing over me as on that first never-to-be-forgotten night. Most of the drivers grow hardened after the first week. They fortify themselves with thoughts of how they are helping to alleviate the sufferings of wretched men, and find consolation in so thinking. But I cannot. I am not the type that breeds warriors. I am the type that should have stayed at home, that shrinks from blood and filth, and is completely devoid of pluck. In other words, I am a coward. . . . A rank coward. I have no guts. It takes every ounce of will-power I possess to stick to my post when I see the train rounding the bend. I choke my sickness back into my throat, and grip the wheel, and tell myself it is all a horrible nightmare . . . soon I shall awaken in my satin-covered bed on Wimbledon Common . . . what I can picture with such awful vividness doesn't really exist. . . .

I have schooled myself to stop fainting at the sight of blood. I have schooled myself not to vomit at the smell of wounds and stale blood, but view these sad bodies with professional calm I shall never be able to. I may be helping to alleviate the sufferings of wretched men, but commonsense rises up and insists that the necessity should never have arisen. I become savage at the futility. A war to end war, my mother writes. Never. In twenty years it will repeat itself. And twenty years after that. Again and again, as long as we breed women like my mother and Mrs. Evans-Mawnington. And we are breeding them. Etta Potato and The B.F.—two out of a roomful of six. Mother and Mrs. Evans-Mawnington all over again.

Oh, come with me, Mother and Mrs. Evans-Mawnington. Let me show you the exhibits straight from the battlefield. This will be something original to tell your committees, while they knit their endless miles of khaki scarves, . . . something to spout from the platform at your recruiting meetings. Come with me. Stand just there.

Here we have the convoy gliding into the station now, slowly, so slowly. In a minute it will disgorge its sorry cargo. My ambulance doors are open, waiting to receive. See, the train has stopped. Through the occasionally drawn blinds you will observe the trays slotted into the sides of the train. Look closely, Mother and Mrs. Evans-Mawnington, and you shall see what you shall see. Those trays each contain something that was once a whole man . . . the heroes who have done their bit for King and country . . . the heroes who marched blithely through the streets of London Town singing "Tipperary," while you cheered and waved your flags hysterically. They are not singing now, you will observe. Shut your ears, Mother and Mrs. Evans-Mawnington, lest their groans and heart-rending cries linger as long in your memory as in the memory of the daughter you sent out to help win the War.

See the stretcher-bearers lifting the trays one by one, slotting them deftly into my ambulance. Out of the way quickly, Mother and Mrs. Evans-Mawnington—lift your silken skirts aside . . . a man is spewing blood, the moving has upset him, finished him. . . . He will die on the way to hospital if he doesn't die before the ambulance is loaded. I know. . . . All this is old history to me. Sorry this has happened. It isn't pretty to see a hero spewing up his life's blood in public, is it? Much more romantic to see him in the picture papers being awarded the V.C., even if he is minus a limb or two. A most unfortunate occurrence!

That man strapped down? That raving, blaspheming creature screaming filthy words you don't know the meaning of . . . words your daughter
uses in everyday conversation, a habit she has contracted from vulgar contact of this kind. Oh, merely gone mad, Mother and Mrs. Evans-Mawnington. He may have seen a headless body running on and on, with blood
spurting from the trunk. The crackle of the frost-stiff dead men packing the
duck-boards watertight may have gradually undermined his reason. There
are many things the sitters tell me on our long night rides that could have
done this.

No, not shell-shock. The shell-shock cases take it more quietly as a rule,
unless they are suddenly startled. Let me find you an example. Ah, the man
they are bringing out now. The one staring straight ahead at nothing . . .
twitching, twitching, twitching, each limb working in a different direction,
like a Jumping Jack worked by a jerking string. Look at him, both of you.
Bloody awful, isn't it, Mother and Mrs. Evans-Mawnington? That's shell-
shock. If you dropped your handbag on the platform, he would start to rave
as madly as the other. What? You won't try the experiment? You can't watch
him? Why not? *Why not?* I have to, every night. Why the hell can't you do it
for once? Damn your eyes.

Forgive me, Mother and Mrs. Evans-Mawnington. That was not the kind
of language a nicely-brought-up young lady from Wimbledon Common
uses. I forget myself. We will begin again.

See the man they are fitting into the bottom slot. He is coughing badly.
No, not pneumonia. Not tuberculosis. Nothing so picturesque. Gently, gently,
stretcher-bearers . . . he is about done. He is coughing up clots of pinky-
green filth. Only his lungs, Mother and Mrs. Evans-Mawnington. He is coughing well to-night. That is gas. You've heard of gas, haven't you? It burns and
shrivels the lungs to . . . to the mess you see on the ambulance floor there.
He's about the age of Bertie, Mother. Not unlike Bertie, either, with his gentle
brown eyes and fair curly hair. Bertie would look up pleadingly like that in
between coughing up his lungs. . . . The son you have so generously given to
the War. The son you are so eager to send out to the trenches before Roy
Evans-Mawnington, in case Mrs. Evans-Mawnington scores over you at the
next recruiting meeting. . . . "I have given my only son."

Cough, cough, little fair-haired boy. Perhaps somewhere your mother is
thinking of you . . . boasting of the life she has so nobly given . . . the life
you thought was your own, but which is hers to squander as she thinks fit.
"My boy is not a slacker, thank God." Cough away, little boy, cough away.

What does it matter, providing your mother doesn't have to face the shame of her son's cowardice?

These are sitters. The man they are hoisting up beside me, and the two who sit in the ambulance. Blighty cases . . . broken arms and trench feet . . . mere trifles. The smell? Disgusting, isn't it? Sweaty socks and feet swollen to twice their size . . . purple, blue, red . . . big black blisters filled with yellow matter. Quite a colour-scheme, isn't it? Have I made you vomit? I must again ask pardon. My conversation is daily growing less refined. Spew and vomit and sweat . . . I had forgotten these words are not used in the best drawing-rooms on Wimbledon Common.

But I am wasting time. I must go in a minute. I am nearly loaded. The stretcher they are putting on one side? Oh, a most ordinary exhibit, . . . the groaning man to whom the smallest jolt is red hell . . . a mere bellyful of shrapnel. They are holding him over till the next journey. He is not as urgent as the helpless thing there, that trunk without arms and legs, the remnants of a human being, incapable even of pleading to be put out of his misery because his jaw has been half shot away. . . . No, don't meet his eyes, they are too alive. Something of their malevolence might remain with you all the rest of your days, . . . those sock-filled, committee-crowded days of yours.

Gaze on the heroes who have so nobly upheld your traditions, Mother and Mrs. Evans-Mawnington. Take a good look at them. . . . The heroes you will sentimentalise over until peace is declared, and allow to starve for ever and ever, amen, afterwards. Don't go. Spare a glance for my last stretcher, . . . that gibbering, unbelievable, unbandaged thing, a wagging lump of raw flesh on a neck, that was a face a short time ago, Mother and Mrs. Evans-Mawnington. Now it might be anything . . . a lump of liver, raw bleeding liver, that's what it resembles more than anything else, doesn't it? We can't tell its age, but the whimpering moan sounds young, somehow. Like the fretful whimpers of a sick little child . . . a tortured little child . . . puzzled whimpers. Who is he? For all you know, Mrs. Evans-Mawnington, he is your Roy. He might be anyone at all, so why not your Roy? One shapeless lump of raw liver is like another shapeless lump of raw liver. What do you say? Why don't they cover him up with bandages? How the hell do I know? I have often wondered myself, . . . but they don't. Why do you turn away? That's only liquid fire. You've heard of liquid fire? Oh, yes. I remember your letter. . . . "*I hear we've started to use liquid fire, too. That will teach those Germans. I hope we use lots and lots of it.*" Yes, you wrote that. You were glad some new fiendish torture had been invented by the chemists who are running this war. You were delighted to think some German mother's son was going to have the skin stripped from his poor face by liquid fire. . . . Just as some equally patriotic German mother rejoiced when she first heard the sons of Englishwomen were to be burnt and tortured by the very newest war gadget out of the laboratory.

Don't go, Mother and Mrs. Evans-Mawnington, . . . don't go. I am loaded, but there are over thirty ambulances not filled up. Walk down the line. Don't go, unless you want me to excuse you while you retch your insides out as I so often do. There are stretchers and stretchers you haven't seen yet. . . . Men with hopeless dying eyes who don't want to die . . . men with hopeless living eyes who don't want to live. Wait, wait, I have so much, so much to show you before you return to your committees and your recruiting meetings, before you add to your bag of recruits . . . those young recruits you enroll so proudly with your patriotic speeches, your red, white and blue rosettes, your white feathers, your insults, your lies . . . any bloody lie to secure a fresh victim.

What? You cannot stick it any longer? You are going? I didn't think you'd stay. But I've got to stay, haven't I? . . . I've got to stay. You've got me out here, and you'll keep me out here. You've got me haloed. I am one of the Splendid Young Women who are winning the War. . . .

"Loaded. Six stretchers and three sitters!"

I am away. I slow up at the station gate. The sergeant is waiting with his pencil and list.

I repeat, "Six stretchers and three sitters."

"Number Eight."

He ticks off my ambulance. I pass out of the yard.

America Comes In

Dorothy Canfield Fisher

"A Honeymoon . . . Vive L'Amerique"

I never knew many of the mere facts of their existence; where all their money came from, nor the extraordinary romance which must have lain back of them. Nor did I care to. They were too epic a pair for realism to touch. I find on thinking them over that I never quite came to believe in their actual existence; and yet, whatever value this slight sketch of them may have will be due to its literal truthfulness to fact.

My first sight of them was on a very cold day in the second year of the war when they suddenly filled with their resplendent presence the dreary room which was known as my "office." For several difficult months, against all the obstacles which made up everyday life in war-time France, I had been laboring to organize and get into shape a Braille printing establishment which would provide books for those most tragic of war-victims, the blind. Together with a crew of devoted volunteers I had tugged at the task, struggling like everybody else in France with a universal shortage of supplies, which began with able-bodied men and ran down to tacks and cheesecloth. There was also the difficulty of getting the "Authorization from the Government" before drawing your breath; but unless you have experienced this potent brake on enterprise, there is no use trying to describe it to you.

And yet, somehow, we had managed to get along, had added to our two plaque-making machines a couple of presses (very poor, both of them), had scrambled together a home-made device for wetting and drying the paper, had hunted down enough men to run the machines, had trained enough proof-readers and assembled enough voluntary editors, so that after a fashion we were really printing. The magazine, liberally bedewed with our blood and sweat, came out once a month; and although the two presses broke down with great frequency, we managed, by dint of incessant repairing, to keep at least one in shape to do tolerable work. We really had something patched-up, ungainly, but reasonably valid to show the sightseers who came

through on the weekly visiting day, when all the rest of the institution was
open to visitors.

I took my two Olympian guests for the usual idle, visiting-day couple. I
went the rounds with them, pointing out with a weary satisfaction our various makeshifts. When I found that they listened receptively, I indulged in
considerable self-pity over our difficulties, past and present. On their part
they asked a good many pointed questions about the business end of our enterprise, about the financial status of the institution, about the probability
of permanence for the venture. They came back to the "office" with me, the
goddess in sables taking the solitary chair, while her mate sat down on the
edge of my little table, stretching out before him legs clad in cloth of a fine-
ness I had forgotten could exist. Quite casually, like the diamonds and pearls
of the fairy-tales, amazing words now issued from their lips. "See here," said
he of the broadcloth overcoat, "this is no way to do business. You can't get
good work done with any such junk as those two presses! Why, I wouldn't
take them as a gift, not for old iron! And turned by hand-power! Isn't that
Europe for you? Why, for twenty-five cents a day of electric current, you
could do ten times the work you are doing now, and have women run the
presses! Go find a modern electric press that a man can look at and not think
he's Benjamin Franklin come to life again, and let us know how much it
costs."

He handed me his card as he spoke.

The goddess quitted my rickety, cane-bottomed chair and from her superb height dropped down on me, "You know, the kind that opens and shuts
its jaws like a whale; perhaps you've seen them in printing establishments at
home." She tempered her assumption of my ignorance by a smile out of the
loveliest eyes imaginable and added: "My father was a printer out West. I
used to play 'round in his shop. That's how I happen to know."

Gazing up at her fascinated, I noted how deep the little lines of kindli-
ness were at the corners of her smiling gray eyes, and how, beyond the usual
conventional coating of powder, no effort had been made to hide the fact
that the beautiful face was not in its first youth. The consequent effect of
honesty and good faith was ineffable, and had its perfect counterpart in the
extraordinary simplicity and directness of her gentle manner. She drew her
regal fur up around her long neck and her husband put his hat back on his
thick white hair. "While you're about it, you'd better get those two plaque-
making machines electrified," he remarked. "Any electrician could do it for
you. There's no sense in having your operators push down that pedal for
every letter they make. Manpower again! Europe!"

I realized that they were moving towards the door and shook myself out of my entranced silence. "But you *can't* buy a press of that kind in Paris!" I called after them, all the bitterness of my past struggles in my voice. "You can't buy anything in war-time France. There hasn't been a press or anything else manufactured in France for two years! Don't you know that all the factories are making munitions?"

Mr. Robert J. Hall—that was the name on the card—came back to me and said earnestly: " Money can't *do* everything, but I tell you that it can buy anything buyable if you've got enough of it. Now we'll give you money enough to buy that press. It's up to you to find it." From the doorway his wife smiled to mitigate his intense seriousness and said again, "It's the kind that opens and shuts its jaws, you know." The door swung shut behind them to a last call-to-arms, "Go to it!" from Mr. Hall.

Five minutes later a proof-reader coming found me still standing, staring at their card.

"What's the matter?" she asked.

I took her by the arm. "Look here," I said, "did I just show two visitors around the place?"

"Do you mean that awfully good-looking man with the white hair and the royal-princess-effect in sables and eyes like Trilby's?"

I nodded, reassured. I had not dreamed them! . . .

Then I knew of what they had reminded me. They had reminded me of America, they *were* America incarnate, one side of her, the dear, tender-hearted, uncomprehending America which did not need to understand the dark old secrets of hate and misery in order to stretch out her generous hand and ease her too happy heart by the making of many gifts. . . .

Amy Lowell

"In the Stadium"

Marshall Joffre Reviewing the Harvard Regiment, May 12, 1917
    A little old man
    Huddled up in a corner of a carriage,
    Rapidly driven in front of throngs of people
    With his hand held to a perpetual salute.

The people cheer,
But he has heard so much cheering.
On his breast is a row of decorations.
He feels his body recoil before attacks of pain.

They are all like this:
Napoleon,
Hannibal,
Great Caesar even,
But that he died out of time.
Sick old men,
Driving rapidly before a concourse of people,
Gay with decorations,
Crumpled with pain.

The drum-major lifts his silver-headed stick,
And the silver trumpets and tubas,
The great round drums,
Each with an H on them,
Crash out martial music.
Heavily rhythmed march music
For the stepping of a regiment.

Slant lines of rifles,
A twinkle of stepping,
The regiment comes.
The young regiment,
Boys in khaki
With slanted rifles.
The young bodies of boys
Bulwarked in front of us.
The white bodies of young men
Heaped like sandbags
Against the German guns.

This is war:
Boys flung into a breach
Like shovelled earth;
And old men,

Broken,
Driving rapidly before crowds of people
In a glitter of silly decorations.

Behind the boys
And the old men,
Life weeps,
And shreds her garments
To the blowing winds.

Willa Cather

from *One of Ours*

VII

On the march at last; through a brilliant August day Colonel Scott's battalion was streaming along one of the dusty, well-worn roads east of the Somme, their railway base well behind them. The way led through rolling country; fields, hills, woods, little villages shattered but still habitable, where the people came out to watch the soldiers go by.

The Americans went through every village in march step, colours flying, the band playing, "to show that the morale was high," as the officers said. Claude trudged on the outside of the column,—now at the front of his company, now at the rear,—wearing a stoical countenance, afraid of betraying his satisfaction in the men, the weather, the country.

They were bound for the big show, and on every hand were reassuring signs: long lines of gaunt, dead trees, charred and torn; big holes gashed out in fields and hillsides, already half concealed by new undergrowth; winding depressions in the earth, bodies of wrecked motor-trucks and automobiles lying along the road, and everywhere endless straggling lines of rusty barbed-wire, that seemed to have been put there by chance,—with no purpose at all.

"Begins to look like we're getting in, Lieutenant," said Sergeant Hicks, smiling behind his salute.

Claude nodded and passed forward.

"Well, we can't arrive any too soon for us, boys?" The Sergeant looked over his shoulder, and they grinned, their teeth flashing white in their red, perspiring faces. Claude didn't wonder that everybody along the route, even the babies, came out to see them; he thought they were the finest sight in the world. This was the first day they had worn their tin hats; Gerhardt had shown them how to stuff grass and leaves inside to keep their heads cool. When they fell into fours, and the band struck up as they approached a town, Bert Fuller, the boy from Pleasantville on the Platte, who had blubbered on the voyage over, was guide right, and whenever Claude passed him his face seemed to say, "You won't get anything on me in a hurry, Lieutenant!"

They made camp early in the afternoon, on a hill covered with half-burned pines. Claude took Bert and Dell Able and Oscar the Swede, and set off to make a survey and report the terrain. Behind the hill, under the burned edge of the wood, they found an abandoned farmhouse and what seemed to be a clean well. It had a solid stone curb about it, and a wooden bucket hanging by a rusty wire. When the boys splashed the bucket about, the water sent up a pure, cool breath. But they were wise boys, and knew where dead Prussians most loved to hide. Even the straw in the stable they regarded with suspicion, and thought it would be just as well not to bed anybody there.

Swinging on to the right to make their circuit, they got into mud; a low field where the drain ditches had been neglected and had overflowed. There they came upon a pitiful group of humanity, bemired. A woman, ill and wretched looking, sat on a fallen log at the end of the marsh, a baby in her lap and three children hanging about her. She was far gone in consumption; one had only to listen to her breathing and to look at her white, perspiring face to feel how weak she was. Draggled, mud to the knees, she was trying to nurse her baby, half hidden under an old black shawl. She didn't look like a tramp woman, but like one who had once been able to take proper care of herself, and she was still young. The children were tired and discouraged. One little boy wore a clumsy blue jacket, made from a French army coat. The other wore a battered American Stetson that came down over his ears. He carried, in his two arms, a pink celluloid clock. They all looked up and waited for the soldiers to do something.

Claude approached the woman, and touching the rim of his helmet, began: *"Bonjour, Madame. Qu'est que c'est?"*

She tried to speak, but went off into a spasm of coughing, only able to gasp, " 'Toinette, 'Toinette!"

'Toinette stepped quickly forward. She was about eleven, and seemed to be the captain of the party. A bold, hard little face with a long chin, straight black hair tied with rags, uneasy, crafty eyes; she looked much less gentle and more experienced than her mother. She began to explain, and she was very clever at making herself understood. She was used to talking to foreign soldiers,—spoke slowly, with emphasis and ingenious gestures.

She, too, had been reconnoitering. She had discovered the empty farm-house and was trying to get her party there for the night. How did they come here? Oh, they were refugees. They had been staying with people thirty kilo-meters from here. They were trying to get back to their own village. Her mother was very sick, *presque morte*, and she wanted to go home to die. They had heard people were still living there; an old aunt was living in their own cellar,—and so could they if they once got there. The point was, and she made it over and over, that her mother wished to die *chez elle, comprenez-vous?* They had no papers, and the French soldiers would never let them pass, but now that the Americans were here they hoped to get through; the Americans were said to be *toujours gentils.*

While she talked in her shrill, clicking voice, the baby began to howl, dissatisfied with its nourishment. The little girl shrugged. *"Il est toujours en colère,"* she muttered. The woman turned it around with difficulty—it seemed a big, heavy baby, but white and sickly—and gave it the other breast. It began sucking her noisily, rooting and sputtering as if it were famished. It was too painful, it was almost indecent, to see this exhausted woman trying to feed her baby. Claude beckoned his men away to one side, and taking the little girl by the hand drew her after them.

"Il faut que votre mère | | se reposer," he told her, with the grave caesural pause which he always made in the middle of a French sentence. She under-stood him. No distortion of her native tongue surprised or perplexed her. She was accustomed to being addressed in all persons, numbers, genders, tenses; by Germans, English, Americans. She only listened to hear whether the voice was kind, and with men in this uniform it usually was kind.

Had they anything to eat? *Vous avez quelque chose à manger?*

"Rien. Rien du tout."

Wasn't her mother *trop malade à marcher?*

She shrugged; Monsieur could see for himself.

And her father?

He was dead; *mort à la Marne, en quatorze.*

"At the Marne?" Claude repeated, glancing in perplexity at the nurs-ing baby.

Her sharp eyes followed his, and she instantly divined his doubt. "The baby?" she said quickly. "Oh, the baby is not my brother, he is a Boche."

For a moment Claude did not understand. She repeated her explanation impatiently, something disdainful and sinister in her metallic little voice. A slow blush mounted to his forehead.

He pushed her toward her mother, *"Attendez là."*

"I guess we'll have to get them over to that farmhouse," he told the men. He repeated what he had got of the child's story. When he came to her laconic statement about the baby, the looked at each other. Bert Fuller was afraid he might cry again, so he kept muttering, "By God, if we'd a-got here sooner, by God if we had!" as they ran back along the ditch.

Dell and Oscar made a chair of their crossed hands and carried the woman,—she was no great weight. Bert picked up the little boy with the pink clock; "Come along, little frog, your legs ain't long enough."

Claude walked behind, holding the screaming baby stiffly in his arms. How was it possible for a baby to have such definite personality, he asked himself, and how was it possible to dislike a baby so much? He hated it for its square, tow-thatched head and bloodless ears, and carried it with loathing . . . no wonder it cried! When it got nothing by screaming and stiffening, however, it suddenly grew quiet; regarded him with pale blue eyes, and tried to make itself comfortable against his khaki coat. It put out a grimy little fist and took hold of one of his buttons. "Kamerad, eh?" he muttered, glaring at the infant. "Cut it out!"

Before they had their own supper that night, the boys carried hot food and blankets down to their family.

VIII

Four o'clock . . . a summer dawn . . . his first morning in the trenches.

Claude had just been along the line to see that the gun teams were in position. This hour, when the light was changing, was a favourite time for attack. He had come in late last night, and had everything to learn. Mounting the fire-step, he peeped over the parapet between the sandbags, into the low, twisting mist. Just then he could see nothing but the wire entanglement, with birds hopping along the top wire, singing and chirping as they did on the wire fences at home. Clear and flute-like they sounded in the heavy air,—and they were the only sounds. A little breeze came up, slowly clearing the mist away. Streaks of green showed through the moving banks of vapour. The birds became more agitated.

That dull stretch of grey and green was No Man's Land. Those low, zig-zag mounds, like giant molehills protected by wire hurdles, were the Hun trenches; five or six lines of them. He could easily follow the communication trenches without a glass. At one point their front line could not be more than eighty yards away, at another it must be all of three hundred. Here and there thin columns of smoke began to rise; the Hun was getting breakfast; everything was comfortable and natural. Behind the enemy's position the country rose gradually for several miles, with ravines and little woods, where, according to his map, they had masked artillery. Back on the hills were ruined farmhouses and broken trees, but nowhere a living creature in sight. It was a dead, nerveless countryside, sunk in quiet and dejection. Yet everywhere the ground was full of men. Their own trenches, from the other side, must look quite as dead. Life was a secret, these days.

It was amazing how simply things could be done. His battalion had marched in quietly at midnight, and the line they came to relieve had set out as silently for the rear. It all took place in utter darkness. Just as B Company slid down an incline into the shallow rear trenches, the country was lit for a moment by two star shells, there was a rattling of machine guns, German Maxims,—a sporadic crackle that was not followed up. Filing along the communication trenches, they listened anxiously; artillery fire would have made it bad for the other men who were marching to the rear. But nothing happened. They had a quiet night, and this morning, here them were!

The sky flamed up saffron and silver. Claude looked at his watch, but he could not bear to go just yet. How long it took a Wheeler to get round to anything! Four years on the way; now that he was here, he would enjoy the scenery a bit, he guessed. He wished his mother could know how he felt this morning. But perhaps she did know. At any rate, she would not have him anywhere else. Five years ago, when he was sitting on the steps of the Denver State House and knew their nothing unexpected could ever happen to him . . . suppose he could have seen, in a flash, where he would be today? He cast a long look at the reddening, lengthening landscape, and dropped down on the duckboard.

Claude made his way back to the dugout into which he and Gerhardt had thrown their effects last night. The former occupants had left it clean. There were two bunks nailed against the side walls,—wooden frames with wire netting over them, covered with dry sandbags. Between the two bunks was a soap-box table, with a candle stuck in a green bottle, an alcohol stove, a *bain-marie*, and two tin cups. On the wall were coloured pictures from *Jugend*, taken out of some Hun trench.

He found Gerhardt still asleep on his bed, and shook him until he sat up. "How long have you been out, Claude? Didn't you sleep?"

"A little. I wasn't very tired. I suppose we could heat shaving water on this stove; they've left us half a bottle of alcohol. It's quite a comfortable little hole, isn't it?"

"It will doubtless serve its purpose," David remarked dryly. "So sensitive to any criticism of this war! Why, it's not your affair; you've only just arrived."

"I know," Claude replied meekly, as he began to fold his blankets. "But it's likely the only one I'll ever be in, so I may as well take an interest."

Mary Lee

from *It's a Great War!*

Two Y.M.C.A. men, two Red Cross men, an Engineer Captain, two Medics, talking about the merits of different gas masks. For half an hour, the train jolted onward. Then it stopped and stood two hours, quite still. Anne gazed out at a stubble field, a low hill. Her head ached fiercely. Joan . . . Joan . . . Getting late, later . . . Would they be furious in Neufchâteau that she had taken two weeks to come from Paris? No, two days . . . Two days a long time . . . Still, this was war . . . Nobody ever hurried . . .

Pitch dark. The train stopped. Still raining. No lights on the train, and no lights at the station. The Red Cross men in the compartment thought it was Neufchâteau, this place of muddy darkness. The Y. men thought it wasn't. There was no way of telling. Anne got out. She bumped into people as she lugged her bags along the platform, through the darkness. An old, old man in a dark smock appeared from somewhere. " C'est Neufchâteau?"

"Oui, Madame." He grabbed her bags. "Hôtel Agriculture?" he queried.

"Oui." She stumbled after him through the rain, the darkness. What sort of place would the Hôtel Agriculture be? With every step, her feet slipped. A door opened off a sidewalk into a dingy room, filled with smoke, lit by two candles. A high counter opposite the door, behind it, shelves of bottles. A desk, with an old Frenchman, peering at you over glasses. A flight of stairs that rambled up toward darkness. "Voilà l'Hôtel, Madame!" The porter thumped Anne's bags down.

"Miss Wentworth?" American voice,—here in this foreign barroom. A stoutish man in a Y. uniform came forward, his overseas cap well to the back of his head. "My name's Tompkins, L. C. Tompkins, of Great Bend, Iowa. What part of the States are you from?" Anne told him, Massachusetts. What could it possibly matter where you came from? "Pleased to meet you." Mr. Tompkins held his hand out. He felt at ease,—he and the lady had been introduced now . . . He had come, he explained, to greet her, and to tell her that Mrs. Phillips, the Regional Director, was off on an inspection. Anne was to wait in Neufchâteau till she came back. There was a room engaged for her upstairs, and the Y. ran a mess down the street that she would find real cosy. Mr. Tompkins hoped she'd be comfortable in their little town . . . Not quite like God's Country, but still, not a bad little place if you didn't mind mud . . . Mr. Tompkins, with another handclasp, bade her good night.

Russian officers sat at tables in the hotel dining room, drinking champagne. They walked about the lobby, and up and down the stairs in high, black boots. Anne watched them in the dining room, while she waited. Hungry . . . After an hour, the serving woman brought her a stewed rabbit, fried potatoes, salade. She sipped red wine. French food,—good . . .

She stood in the doorway of the hotel after supper. Could not bear to mount that dingy stairway . . . Trucks rattled past, their engines snorting, great wheels splashing mud across the narrow sidewalk. Mud, littering the house walls, flattening, drooling downward. In the dark drizzle an American soldier stood in rubber coat and tin helmet, blowing a whistle, gesturing to the trucks to come or stop. A soldier crossed the street and strolled past Anne.

"Could you come to the station and carry my trunk for me?" Anne said.

"You bet your life I could," said the soldier.

The corridor of the Hôtel Agriculture had an evil smell, an eerie darkness. The smell met Anne at the landing as she followed the concierge up the stairway. In the old Frenchman's hand the candle flickered. A row of blue doors, closed, opposite each other. Outside each door, a pair of Russian boots,—huge, black, with their tops flopping over. Beside each pair of boots, perched under the shadowing tops, a pair of small, French slippers . . . One door with no shoes. Before this door the concierge set Anne's bags down. He pushed the door. In the small, boxlike room, the American soldier dumped

Anne's trunk. He looked round. "Some apartment, this, I'll tell the world!" He laughed.

"It's a great war!" Anne said . . .

The footsteps of the soldier and the concierge died out. She was alone. Between the blue doors, the Russian boots, the slippers,—that atmosphere of maleness and femaleness . . . Nobody, within two hundred miles, who knew her. The door had no lock. Anne pulled and shoved the washstand out across it. She undressed, put the light out. She stood a minute in the open window. Rain, dripping on the helmet of the American M.P. standing down there. The soldier waves his arms, blew a shrill whistle. Trucks snorted past, splashing mud onto the walls of houses . . .

Elizabeth Shepley Sergeant

from *Shadow-Shapes: The Journal of a Wounded Woman*

October 22

Last night the ward was like a sombre tunnel, full of smoke and noxious gas; monstrous moving shadows; painful reverberation. Feet, feet, trampling, trampling; *brancardiers*, shuffling into the tent with new burdens. Shall I ever forget how their feet are sucked into the glutinous mud of the Marne? It is as if the mud were insatiable. And it gives out, in the dark and silence, the muted sound of all those other stretcher-bearing feet which it has sucked and strained at for four years. Mont-Notre-Dame was an important French hospital centre until the Germans took it last spring. On the recovered ground a French hospital has been planted again. And yet again come the *brancardiers* bearing still, horizontal shapes on their shoulders, shapes once vivid, earth-loving; now writhen, agonized, indifferent. War is a doom, trampling, shuffling itself out to eternity.

And the orderly on duty last night was a doddering old fellow who let the men get completely out of hand. It is no kindness, as I have discovered. The least serious cases make the worst row. The "thigh" began it:

"*Ô là, là, là, là, Ô là, là, là, là*"—each "*Ô*" a note higher in the scale and the "*là's*" running down in Tetrazzini's manner.

"*C'est-il-mal-heur-eux, c'est-il-mal-heur-eux,*" responds the "arm" in the next bed, who has no intention of being outdone.

"*Damnée guerre, damnée guerre,*" echoes the "shoulder blade."

This had been going on perhaps fifteen minutes when the little *poilu* opposite me tore off his bandages. Patience is a terrible virtue. Would not wars end if ten thousand wounded men tore off their bandages and bled to death? But the process is hideous. The *vieux,* badly scared, called Mercier, and with much stifled gasping and cursing they together bound him up again in the flicker of a lantern.

Can it be that only forty or fifty miles from here people are discussing, over partridge and *fraises des bois,* whether it would be better for Foch to accept an armistice or to push the Germans to a complete *débâcle?* Better give a few months more, and several thousands more men, say some. I wish they could spend a night in my cot. Can it be that in Paris I, too, believed in the end of the war? The very evening before my accident, the evening of the day when the French army entered Lille, I came out of the Castiglione, after dinner, into light. *Light* in Paris at eleven o'clock at night. *Light* after nearly four years of war-darkness! Those great torches, flaring brazenly from the Tuileries terrace, on brazen enemy guns strewn over the place de la Concorde, conveyed, as they were intended to do, a sort of shout of triumph. The enemy had been driven so far, so far, that not the boldest or fleetest of his bombers could any longer threaten the heart of France.

Yet here the fear of air raids is not conjured. I shall not soon forget the whirring pulse that throbbed and burrowed into our tent tunnel in the small hours of last night. Ominous, discomposing. Airplanes, squadron after squadron, passing just overhead. Boche or our own? The complete defencelessness I felt so long as the uncertainty lasted made me aware that what I had hitherto taken for moral courage during raids was purely physical; a pair of good legs and a convenient mediæval cellar had sustained me. I know something about the psychology of the bomber, too. Great to drop off your load on a group of tents; to get a direct hit, a tongue of flame. (Lord, it was a hospital!)

After all, I am just as bad as the men at night but for New England pride. My soul also escapes from what Jules Romains would call the *unanimisme* of the ward; from the bonds of a common fate which enjoin a decent patience. I become an impotent, aching creature, full of unpleasant holes, lost in a corner of devastated France infinitely remote from every one I care for. The hospital unit had moved up from Château-Thierry the night before I got here. No telephone connection with Paris yet. So I cannot get cables through to my family in America; or to the N.R. I can't even telegraph my brother-in-law, Ernest, at Dijon; or Colonel Lambert at the Red Cross; or Rick, who has just lost his brother, on top of losing almost his entire squadron in the Argonne, and is due in Paris on leave. He wired me the night before my accident to cable his mother; and there should be an answer by now—and I of no use.

I ask for tea. The orderly comes running. (*"Ça change, une femme,"* thinks he. And I—"I can't see his dirty hands in the dark.") But tea is no sedative. I hug my stone jar of hot water tight but I can't escape from memory. The memory that my work has come to a fortuitous end just as the war approaches its final crisis. The memory of the accident itself. These three nights, which have dragged like as many centuries, I have relived it, step by step, image by image: a series of sharp, visual images strung together by blindly logical circumstance.

Four American women, with a Frenchwoman in nurse's uniform, their guide, are descending from the train at Épernay, where they are met by a French officer. Plump, pink, smiling, the officer. They have come for an afternoon's drive to Rheims and the American battle-fields of the Marne, and will return to Paris *via* Château-Thierry in the evening.

Ravaged fields, shapeless villages. . . . Soon the Lieutenant has stopped the motor by a steep hillside. The battle-field of Mont-Bligny, very important in the defence of Rheims. He warns us that it has not been "cleaned up"; that we must touch nothing unless we are sure of its nature.

The ladies stream up and across the field, littered indeed with all sorts of obscene rubbish. Some one finds a German prayer-book. Some one else an Italian helmet. There may be a skull in it, warns the Lieutenant; but hangs a French one on his own arm for me. Mademoiselle has a queer-looking object—a series of perpendicular tubes set in a half-circle, with a white string hanging down at either end. The inside of a German gas-mask, she says. We all walk across the hilltop as far as the holes dug in the ground by the forward French sentries; we look toward the German lines beyond—then turn back along the crest of the hill, where it drops off sheer to a wide valley. The Lieutenant, Mademoiselle, and I are ahead, the others some fifteen yards behind. Suddenly the officer notes what Mademoiselle is carrying:

"Put that on the ground, please," he says curtly. "I am not sure what it is."

A stunning report, a blinding flash, and I am precipitated down the bank, hearing, it seems, as I go the Lieutenant's shriek of horror:

"My arm, my arm has been carried away!"

I lift my head at once: two women cowering with pale faces, then running toward the road; the third standing quiet by a stark, swollen figure—the Frenchwoman, stretched on her back, with her blue veils tossed about her. Great gashes of red in the blue.

"*Macabre* of the movies" . . . and aloud I hear a voice, which is mine, add: "She is dead."

"Yes. . . . Terrible."

I seem oddly unable to get up. Ringing in my ears. Faintness. The effect of the explosion. Very tiresome, not to be able to help. I crawl farther down the hill to get away from blood. But something warm is running down my own face. Blood! I sit up and take out of the handbag still on my arm a pocket-mirror. Half a dozen small wounds in my left check. Unimportant. But my eyes fall casually on my feet, extended before me. Blood! Thick and purplish, oozing slowly out of jagged holes in my heavy English shoes and gaiters. I seem to be wounded. Queer, because no pain. I call to one of the women. She makes a meteoric appearance, tells me I am splashed with blood from the dead; is gone again. I must, I think, lie down. The chauffeurs seem to be above me on the hill now, carrying the officer away. A long interval. They are bending over me.

"Can you walk?"

"I'll try."

It doesn't work. So they make a chair with their arms. One of them is grumbling that the other women aren't on hand.

"*Les blessés sont plus intéressants que les morts*—the wounded are more interesting than the dead," he remarks.

From my "chair" I note more objects, innumerable objects similar to the one that exploded, straggling like octopi in different parts of the field. The soldiers grin when, in a voice of warning, I point them out. Hand-grenades, they say. Now we have reached the first limousine. The officer is propped on the right half of the back seat, his bloody sleeve (not empty yet) hanging at his side. I am lifted in beside him, my shoes removed, my feet placed on the folding seat. Those nice, expensive brown wool stockings from "Old England" ruined. . . .

The chauffeurs refuse to wait for the other ladies. Must find hospital at once. Unpleasant sensation of severing all connections with the friendly world. Inhuman country. Badly rutted roads. The officer, quite conscious, desperately worried:

"I did tell them not to touch anything, didn't I, Mademoiselle? They'll break me for this." Repeated again and again. Also the reply, "It wasn't your fault, Monsieur."

A bleak barrack at last. An amazed "*major*," who sticks his head into the bloody car. But can do nothing for us. Gas hospital, this. Surgeons eight kilometres farther on. I feel pain at last and the Lieutenant is suffering. But we talk a little—about his wife, and his profession of teacher. Will I write to his wife to-night for him? Say he is not so badly hurt. . . .

Dusk already. Two more dreary barracks in a plain, lean and grey. Another French doctor, black-bearded and dour. Very displeased to see both of us, especially the woman. Two stretchers. The Lieutenant disappears in one direction while I am carried into the *triage* and dumped on the ground. To be tagged, I suppose, like the wounded I have seen in the attacks of the last year. At least twenty Frenchmen lounging in this barn-like place. Orderlies, stretcher-bearers, wounded soldiers, all pleasantly thrilled.

"We must cut off your clothes, Madame."

"*Bien, monsieur.*"

I can be dry too. But if there were the least kindness in his grim eyes, I should tell him how desolated I feel to be giving so much trouble in a place where—I know it as well as he—women are superfluous.

Compound fracture of both ankles. Flesh wounds from *éclats*. A little soldier writes out a *fiche* in a deliberate hand while I am being bandaged, and given ante-tetanus serum. The *fiche* goes in a brown envelope, pinned on my breast as I lie on the stretcher.

"Is it serious, Monsieur?"

"The left foot, yes, very."

"Can I not make connections with the rest of my party, so as to send a message to Paris?"

No, the chauffeurs had gone already. I am to be sent to a hospital near Fismes. And the stretcher proceeds to the door. Stygian darkness now. As the men slide me into the lower regions of the ambulance I look up and see, peering down from the top layer, the very white, rolling eyeballs of two very black Senegalian negroes.

"You thought you'd be alone?" remarks the dry surgical voice. "No . . . *Bon voyage, madame.*"

The ambulance door seems hermetically closed. How the engine groans on the hills. . . . How heavily the black men breathe above me. . . . How my foot thumps. . . . How the hammering on the wheels pounds in my head when we break down.

Another lighted *triage*. I am lying on another mud floor, surrounded again by men, men. Perhaps I am the only woman in the world. . . . But the atmosphere is more friendly. An orderly approaches:

"You have three compatriots here."

"American soldiers?"

"American nurses."

Were ever such blessed words? And the tall, sure, white-veiled woman who comes in to take my hand, and not reproach me for my sex, seems to divine just how I feel. *Croix de Guerre*, with palm—Mayo graduate—can this be the nurse who lived so long in a cellar at Soissons, nursing American soldiers? I put her in a Red Cross article months ago! A presence to inspire instant confidence.

"Only a bed in a *poilu* tent," she apologizes. "Impossible to make a *woman* comfortable."

The bed is grateful. Long, long wait. Finally a surgeon with a woman assistant materialize beside me. Surgeon with red face and shabby uniform, and, as bandages unroll, a troubled look. He says immediate operation is necessary.

Miss Bullard confides me to an orderly, Mercier. She cannot see me again to-night. Must prepare two hundred new arrivals, *blessés* of yesterday's attack, for operation. Mercier seems kind. To be brought out of ether by an *ex-coiffeur* is normal, after all this. When the stretcher-bearers come he helps them lift me; wraps blankets about my bloody and exiguous clothing. He says he ought not to leave his ward, but he comes along beside the stretcher, snubbing the *brancardiers*, who are lower in the hospital hierarchy than *infirmiers*, as I have already discovered. The movement of the stretcher on these human shoulders is soothing, though. And the rain that falls on my face from the black night. Too bad to leave it for the lighted X-ray room, so narrow and stuffy, and full of perspiring men. They can't even find the *éclats*. I point out where they must be. Long wait on the floor. At last the summons to the operating-room.

The surgeon is ready. In a white blouse, with a large black pipe in his mouth. He removes it to caution the men who are lifting me on to the table:

"*Voyons, voyons!* Don't you see it is a *woman?*"

A true Gaul. Unable not to point the ruthless fact.

I turn my eyes to the green-painted ceiling. It is spotted with black, black like the surgeon's pipe. Flies. The assistant ties my hands to the table. (In peace-time, I reflect, they wait till one is unconscious.) The surgeon is bending over my wounds now, shaking his head, and his next phrase has no double meaning, and his voice no irony:

"All because a foolish woman wanted a little souvenir of this great, great war. . . . "

I am getting ether in large quantities. Sensation of vibration—of waves beating, and through it voices very clear:

"Who is she?"

"A journalist." . . .

Gertrude Stein

from *The Autobiography of Alice B. Toklas*

Time went on, we were very busy and then came the armistice. We were the first to bring the news to many small villages. The french soldiers in the hospitals were relieved rather than glad. They seemed not to feel that it was going to be such a lasting peace. I remember one of them saying to Gertrude Stein when she said to him, well here is peace, at least for twenty years, he said.

The next morning we had a telegram from Mrs. Lathrop. Come at once want you to go with the french armies to Alsace. We did not stop on the way. We made it in a day. Very shortly after we left for Alsace.

We left for Alsace and on the road had our first and only accident. The roads were frightful, mud, ruts, snow, slush, and covered with the french armies going into Alsace. As we passed, two horses dragging an army kitchen kicked out of line and hit our ford, the mud-guard came off and the toolchest, and worst of all the triangle of the steering gear was badly bent. The army picked up our tools and our mud-guard but there was nothing to do about the bent triangle. We went on, the car wandering all over the muddy road, up hill and down hill, and Gertrude Stein sticking to the wheel. Finally after about forty kilometres, we saw on the road some american ambulance men. Where can we get our car fixed. Just a little farther, they said. We went a little farther and there found an american ambulance outfit. They had no extra mud-guard but they could give us a new triangle. I told our troubles to the sergeant, he grunted and said a word in an undertone to a mechanic. Then turning to us he said gruffly, run-her-in. Then the mechanic took off his tunic and threw it over the radiator. As Gertrude Stein said when any american did that the car was his.

We had never realised before what mud-guards were for but by the time we arrived in Nancy we knew. The french military repair shop fitted us out with a new mud-guard and tool-chest and we went on our way.

Soon we came to the battle-fields and the lines of trenches of both sides. To any one who did not see it as it was then it is impossible to imagine it. It was not terrifying it was strange. We were used to ruined houses and even ruined towns but this was different. It was a landscape. And it belonged to no country.

I remember hearing a french nurse once say and the only thing she did say of the front was, c'est un paysage passionant, an absorbing landscape. And that was what it was as we saw it. It was strange. Camouflage, huts, everything was there. It was wet and dark and there were a few people, one did not know whether they were chinamen or europeans. Our fanbelt had stopped working. A staff car stopped and fixed it with a hairpin, we still wore hairpins.

Another thing that interested us enormously was how different the camouflage of the french looked from the camouflage of the germans, and then once we came across some very very neat camouflage and it was american. The idea was the same but as after all it was different nationalities who did it the difference was inevitable. The colour schemes were different, the designs were different, the way of placing them was different, it made plain the whole theory of art and its inevitability.

Finally we came to Strasbourg and then went on to Mulhouse. Here we stayed until well into May.

Our business in Alsace was not hospitals but refugees. The inhabitants were returning to their ruined homes all over the devastated country and it was the aim of the A.F.F.W. to give a pair of blankets, underclothing and children's and babies' woollen stockings and babies' booties to every family. There was a legend that the quantity of babies' booties sent to us came from the gifts sent to Mrs. Wilson who was supposed at that time to be about to produce a little Wilson. There were a great many babies' booties but not too many for Alsace.

Our headquarters was the assembly-room of one of the big school-buildings in Mulhouse. The german school teachers had disappeared and french school teachers who happened to be in the army had been put in temporarily to teach. The head of our school was in despair, not about the docility of his pupils nor their desire to learn french, but on account of their clothes. French children are all always neatly clothed. There is no such thing as a ragged child, even orphans farmed out in country villages are neatly dressed, just as all french women are neat, even the poor and the aged. They may not always be clean but they are always neat. From this standpoint the parti-coloured rags of even the comparatively prosperous alsatian children were deplorable and the french schoolmasters suffered. We did our best to help him out with black children's aprons but these did not go far, beside we had to keep them for the refugees.

We came to know Alsace and the alsatians very well, all kinds of them. They were astonished at the simplicity with which the french army and french soldiers took care of themselves. They had not been accustomed to that in the german army. On the other hand the french soldiers were rather mistrustful of the alsatians who were too anxious to be french and yet were not french. They are not frank, the french soldiers said. And it is quite true. The french whatever else they may be are frank. They are very polite, they are very adroit but sooner or later they always tell you the truth. The alsatians are not adroit, they are not polite and they do not inevitably tell you the truth. Perhaps with renewed contact with the french they will learn these things.

We distributed. We went into all the devastated villages. We usually asked the priest to help us with the distribution. One priest who gave us a great deal of good advice and with whom we became very friendly had only one large room left in his house. Without any screens or partitions he had made himself three rooms, the first third had his parlour furniture, the second third his dining room furniture and the last third his bedroom furniture. When we lunched with him and we lunched well and his alsatian wines were very good, he received us in his parlour, he then excused himself and withdrew into his bedroom to wash his hands, and then he invited us very formally to come into the dining room, it was like an old-fashioned stage setting.

We distributed, we drove around in the snow we talked to everybody and everybody talked to us and by the end of May it was all over and we decided to leave.

We went home by way of Metz, Verdun and Mildred Aldrich.

We once more returned to a changed Paris. We were restless. Gertrude Stein began to work very hard, it was at this time that she wrote her Accents in Alsace and other political plays, the last plays in Geography and Plays. We were still in the shadow of war work and we went on doing some of it, visiting hospitals and seeing the soldiers left in them, now pretty well neglected by everybody. We had spent a great deal of our money during the war and we were economising, servants were difficult to get if not impossible, prices were high. We settled down for the moment with a femme de ménage for only a few hours a day. I used to say Gertrude Stein was the chauffeur and I was the cook. We used to go over early in the morning to the public markets and get in our provisions. It was a confused world.

Mourning and Memory

Käthe Kollwitz

from *The Diary and Letters of Kaethe Kollwitz*

August 27, 1914

In the heroic stiffness of these times of war, when our feelings are screwed to an unnatural pitch, it is like a touch of heavenly music, like sweet, lamenting murmurs of peace, to read that French soldiers spare and actually help wounded Germans, that in the franc-tireur villages German soldiers write on the walls of houses such notices as: Be considerate! An old woman lives here.—These people were kind to me.—Old people only.—Woman in childbed.—And so on.

A piece by Gabriele Reuter in the *Tag* on the tasks of women today. She spoke of the joy of sacrificing—a phrase that struck me hard. Where do all the women who have watched so carefully over the lives of their beloved ones get the heroism to send them to face the cannon? I am afraid that this soaring of the spirit will be followed by the blackest despair and dejection. The task is to bear it not only during these few weeks, but for a long time—in dreary November as well, and also when spring comes again, in March, the month of young men who wanted to live and are dead. That will be much harder.

Those who now have only small children, like Lise her Maria, seem to me so fortunate. For us, whose sons are going, the vital thread is snapped.

September 30, 1914

Cold, cloudy autumnal weather. The grave mood that comes over one when one knows: there is war, and one cannot hold on to any illusions any more. Nothing is real but the frightfulness of this state, which we almost grow used to. In such times it seems so stupid that the boys must go to war. The whole thing is so ghastly and insane. Occasionally there comes the foolish thought: how can they possibly take part in such madness? And at once the cold shower: they *must, must!* All is leveled by death; down with all the youth! Then one is ready to despair.

Only one state of mind makes it at all bearable: to receive the sacrifice into one's will. But how can one maintain such a state?

[Peter Kollwitz was killed on October 22, 1914.]

December 1, 1914
Conceived the plan for a memorial for Peter tonight, but abandoned it again because it seemed to me impossible of execution. In the morning I suddenly thought of having Reike ask the city to give me a place for the memorial. There would have to be a collection taken for it. It must stand on the heights of Schildhorn, looking out over the Havel. To be finished and dedicated on a glorious summer day. Schoolchildren of the community singing, "On the way to pray." The monument would have Peter's form, lying stretched out, the father at the head, the mother at the feet. It would be to commemorate the sacrifice of all the young volunteers.

It is a wonderful goal, and no one has more right than I to make this memorial.

December 9, 1914
My boy! On your memorial I want to have your figure on top, *above* the parents. You will lie outstretched, holding out your hands in answer to the call for sacrifice: "Here I am." Your eyes—perhaps—open wide, so that you see the blue sky above you, and the clouds and birds. Your mouth smiling. And at your breast the pink I gave you.

February 15, 1915
In the studio I looked at my former sketches. Saw that I have gone along by roundabout ways—which were perhaps necessary—and yet am making progress. I do not want to die, even if Hans and Karl should die. I do not want to go until I have faithfully made the most of my talent and cultivated the seed that was placed in me until the last small twig has grown. This does not contradict the fact that I would have died—smilingly—for Peter, and for Hans too, were the choice offered me. Oh how gladly, how gladly. Peter was seed for the planting which should not have been ground. He was the sowing. I am the bearer and cultivator of a grain of seed-corn. What Hans will

become, the future will show. But since I am to be the cultivator, I want to serve faithfully. Since recognizing that, I am almost serene and much firmer in spirit. It is not only that I am permitted to finish my work—I am obliged to finish it. This seems to me to be the meaning of all the gabble about culture. Culture arises only when the individual fulfils his cycle of obligations. If everyone recognizes and fulfils his cycle of obligations, genuineness emerges. The culture of a whole nation can in the final analysis be built upon nothing else but this.

September 1916

My work seems so hopeless that I have decided to stop for the time being. My inward feeling is one of emptiness. How shall I find joy outside of the work? Talking to people means nothing at all. Nothing and no one can help me. I see Peter far, far in the distance. Naturally I will not give it up—possibly I cannot—but I shall make a pause. Now I have no joy in it. All day yesterday I took care of a host of things. But what for?

October 11, 1916

Everything remains as obscure as ever for me. Why is that? It's not only our youth who go willingly and joyfully into the war; it's the same in all nations. People who would be friends under other conditions now hurl themselves at one another as enemies. Are the young really without judgment? Do they always rush into it as soon as they are called? Without looking closer? Do they rush into war because they want to, because it is in their blood so that they accept without examination whatever reasons for fighting are given to them? Do the young want war? Would they be old before their time if they no longer wanted it?

This frightful insanity—the youth of Europe hurling themselves at one another.

When I think I am convinced of the insanity of the war, I ask myself again by what law man ought to live. Certainly not in order to attain the greatest possible happiness. It will always be true that life must be subordinated to the service of an ideal. But in this case, where has that principle led us? Peter, Erich, Richard, all have subordinated their lives to the idea of patriotism. The English, Russian and French young men have done the same. The consequence has been this terrible killing, and the impoverishment of Europe. Then shall we say that the youth in all these countries have been cheated?

Has their capacity for sacrifice been exploited in order to bring on the war? Where are the guilty? Are there any? Or is everyone cheated? Has it been a case of mass madness? And when and how will the awakening take place?

I shall never fully understand it all. But it is clear that our boys, our Peter, went into the war two years ago with pure hearts, and that they were ready to die for Germany. They died—almost all of them. Died in Germany and among Germany's enemies—by the millions.

When the minister blessed the volunteers, he spoke of the Roman youth who leaped into the abyss and so closed it. That was one boy. Each of these boys felt that he must act like that one. But what came of it was something very different. The abyss has not closed. It has swallowed up millions, and it still gapes wide. And Europe, all Europe, is still like Rome, sacrificing its finest and most precious treasure—but the sacrifice has no effect.

Is it a breach of faith with you, Peter, if I can now see only madness in the war? Peter, you died believing. Was that also true of Erich, Walter, Meier, Gottfried, Richard Noll? Or had they come to their senses and were they nevertheless forced to leap into the abyss? Was force involved? Or did they want to? Were they forced?

I think of Richard's poem:

Then let me now be snatched away
And keep me here no more.
For I have had before today
More than my fill of gore.

Charlotte Mew

"The Cenotaph"

September 1919
Not yet will those measureless fields be green again
Where only yesterday the wild sweet blood of wonderful youth
    was shed;
There is a grave whose earth must hold too long, too deep a stain,
Though for ever over it we may speak as proudly as we may
    tread.

But here, where the watchers by lonely hearths from the thrust of
    an inward sword have more slowly bled,
We shall build the Cenotaph: Victory, winged, with Peace,
    winged too, at the column's head.
And over the stairway, at the foot—oh! here, leave desolate,
    passionate hands to spread
Violets, roses, and laurel, with the small, sweet, twinkling
    country things
Speaking so wistfully of other Springs,
From the little gardens of little places where son or sweetheart
    was born and bred.
In splendid sleep, with a thousand brothers
             To lovers—to mothers
             Here, too, lies he:
Under the purple, the green, the red,
It is all young life: it must break some women's hearts to see
Such a brave, gay coverlet to such a bed!
Only, when all is done and said,
God is not mocked and neither are the dead.
For this will stand in our Market-place—
             Who'll sell, who'll buy
             (Will you or I
Lie each to each with the better grace)?
While looking into every busy whore's and huckster's face
As they drive their bargains, is the Face
Of God: and some young, piteous, murdered face.

Katherine Mansfield

"The Fly"

"Y'are very snug in here," piped old Mr. Woodifield, and he peered out of the great, green leather armchair by his friend the boss's desk as a baby peers out of its pram. His talk was over; it was time for him to be off. But he did not want to go. Since he had retired, since his . . . stroke, the wife and the girls kept him boxed up in the house every day of the week except Tuesday. On Tuesday he was dressed up and brushed and allowed to cut back to the City for the day. Though what he did there the wife and girls couldn't imagine. Made a nuisance of himself to his friends, they supposed. . . . Well, perhaps so. All the same, we cling to our last pleasures as the tree clings to its last leaves. So there sat old Woodifield, smoking a cigar and staring almost greedily at the boss, who rolled in his office chair, stout, rosy, five years older than he, and still going strong, still at the helm. It did one good to see him.

Wistfully, admiringly, the old voice added, "It's snug in here, upon my word!"

"Yes, it's comfortable enough," agreed the boss, and he flipped the *Financial Times* with a paper-knife. As a matter of fact he was proud of his room; he liked to have it admired, especially by old Woodifield. It gave him a feeling of deep, solid satisfaction to be planted there in the midst of it in full view of that frail old figure in the muffler.

"I've had it done up lately," he explained, as he had explained for the past—how many?—weeks. "New carpet," and he pointed to the bright red carpet with a pattern of large white rings. "New furniture," and he nodded towards the massive bookcase and the table with legs like twisted treacle. "Electric heating!" He waved almost exultantly towards the five transparent, pearly sausages glowing so softly in the tilted copper pan.

But he did not draw old Woodifield's attention to the photograph over the table of a grave-looking boy in uniform standing in one of those spectral photographers' parks with photographers' storm-clouds behind him. It was not new. It had been there for over six years.

"There was something I wanted to tell you," said old Woodifield, and his eyes grew dim remembering. "Now what was it? I had it in my mind when I started out this morning." His hands began to tremble, and patches of red showed above his beard.

Poor old chap, he's on his last pins, thought the boss. And, feeling kindly, he winked at the old man, and said jokingly, "I tell you what. I've got a little drop of something here that'll do you good before you go out into the cold again. It's beautiful stuff. It wouldn't hurt a child." He took a key off his watch-chain, unlocked a cupboard below his desk, and drew forth a dark, squat bottle. "That's the medicine," said he. "And the man from whom I got it told me on the strict Q. T. it came from the cellars at Windsor Cassel."

Old Woodifield's mouth fell open at the sight. He couldn't have looked more surprised if the boss had produced a rabbit.

"It's whisky, ain't it?" he piped, feebly.

The boss turned the bottle and lovingly showed him the label. Whisky it was.

"D'you know," said he, peering up at the boss wonderingly, "they won't let me touch it at home." And he looked as though he was going to cry.

"Ah, that's where we know a bit more than the ladies," cried the boss, swooping across for two tumblers that stood on the table with the water-bottle, and pouring a generous finger into each. "Drink it down. It'll do you good. And don't put any water with it. It's sacrilege to tamper with stuff like this. Ah!" He tossed off his, pulled out his handkerchief, hastily wiped his moustaches, and cocked an eye at old Woodifield, who was rolling his in his chaps.

The old man swallowed, was silent a moment, and then said faintly, "It's nutty!"

But it warmed him; it crept into his chill old brain—he remembered.

"That was it," he said, heaving himself out of his chair. "I thought you'd like to know. The girls were in Belgium last week having a look at poor Reggie's grave, and they happened to come across your boy's. They're quite near each other, it seems."

Old Woodifield paused, but the boss made no reply. Only a quiver in his eyelids showed that he heard.

"The girls were delighted with the way the place is kept," piped the old voice. "Beautifully looked after. Couldn't be better if they were at home. You've not been across, have yer?"

"No, no!" For various reasons the boss had not been across.

"There's miles of it," quavered old Woodifield, "and it's all as neat as a garden. Flowers growing on all the graves. Nice broad paths." It was plain from his voice how much he liked a nice broad path.

The pause came again. Then the old man brightened wonderfully.

"D'you know what the hotel made the girls pay for a pot of jam?" he piped. "Ten francs! Robbery, I call it. It was a little pot, so Gertrude says, no bigger than a half-crown. And she hadn't taken more than a spoonful when they charged her ten francs. Gertrude brought the pot away with her to teach 'em a lesson. Quite right, too; it's trading on our feelings. They think because we're over there having a look around we're ready to pay anything. That's what it is." And he turned towards the door.

"Quite right, quite right!" cried the boss, though what was quite right he hadn't the least idea. He came round by his desk, followed the shuffling footsteps to the door, and saw the old fellow out. Woodifield was gone.

For a long moment the boss stayed, staring at nothing, while the grey-haired office messenger, watching him, dodged in and out of his cubbyhole like a dog that expects to be taken for a run. Then: "I'll see nobody for half an hour, Macey," said the boss. "Understand? Nobody at all."

"Very good, sir."

The door shut, the firm heavy steps recrossed the bright carpet, the fat body plumped down in the spring chair, and leaning forward, the boss covered his face with his hands. He wanted, he intended, he had arranged to weep. . . .

It had been a terrible shock to him when old Woodifield sprang that remark upon him about the boy's grave. It was exactly as though the earth had opened and he had seen the boy lying there with Woodifield's girls staring down at him. For it was strange. Although over six years had passed away, the boss never thought of the boy except as lying unchanged, unblemished in his uniform, asleep for ever. "My son!" groaned the boss. But no tears came yet. In the past, in the first months and even years after the boy's death, he had only to say those words to be overcome by such grief that nothing short of a violent fit of weeping could relieve him. Time, he had declared then, he had told everybody, could make no difference. Other men perhaps might recover, might live their loss down, but not he. How was it possible? His boy was an only son. Ever since his birth the boss had worked at building up this business for him; it had no other meaning if it was not for the boy. Life itself had come to have no other meaning. How on earth could he have slaved, denied himself, kept going all those years without the promise for ever before him of the boy's stepping into his shoes and carrying on where he left off?

And that promise had been so near being fulfilled. The boy had been in the office learning the ropes for a year before the war. Every morning they had started off together; they had come back by the same train. And what congratulations he had received as the boy's father! No wonder; he had taken to it marvellously. As to his popularity with the staff, every man jack of them down to old Macey couldn't make enough of the boy. And he wasn't in the lease spoilt. No, he was just his bright, natural self, with the right word for everybody, with that boyish look and his habit of saying, "Simply splendid!"

But all that was over and done with as though it never had been. The day had come when Macey had handed him the telegram that brought the whole place crashing about his head. "Deeply regret to inform you . . . " And he had left the office a broken man, with his life in ruins.

Six years ago, six years . . . How quickly time passed! It might have happened yesterday. The boss took his hands from his face; he was puzzled. Something seemed to be wrong with him. He wasn't feeling as he wanted to feel. He decided to get up and have a look at the boy's photograph. But it wasn't a favorite photograph of his; the expression was unnatural. It was cold, even stern-looking. The boy had never looked like that.

At that moment the boss noticed that a fly had fallen into his broad ink-pot, and was trying feebly but desperately to clamber out again. Help! help! said those struggling legs. But the sides of the inkpot were wet and slippery; it fell back again and began to swim. The boss took up a pen, picked the fly out of the ink, and shook it on to a piece of blotting-paper. For a fraction of a second it lay still on the dark patch that oozed round it. Then the front legs waved, took hold, and, pulling its small sodden body up it began the immense task of cleaning the ink from its wings. Over and under, over and under, went a leg along a wing, as the stone goes over and under the scythe. Then there was a pause, while the fly, seeming to stand on the tips of its toes, tried to expand first one wing and then the other. It succeeded at last, and, sitting down, it began, like a minute cat, to clean its face. Now one could imagine that the little front legs rubbed against each other lightly, joyfully. The horrible danger was over; it had escaped; it was ready for life again.

But just then the boss had an idea. He plunged his pen back into the ink, leaned his thick wrist on the blotting paper, and as the fly tried its wings down came a great heavy blot. What would it make of that? What indeed! The little beggar seemed absolutely cowed, stunned, and afraid to move because of what would happen next. But then, as if painfully, it dragged itself forward. The front legs waved, caught hold, and, more slowly this time, the task began from the beginning.

He's a plucky little devil, thought the boss, and he felt a real admiration for the fly's courage. That was the way to tackle things; that was the right spirit. Never say die; it was only a question of . . . But the fly had again finished its laborious task, and the boss had just time to refill his pen, to shake fair and square on the new-cleaned body yet another dark drop. What about it this time? A painful moment of suspense followed. But behold, the front legs were again waving; the boss felt a rush of relief. He leaned over the fly and said to it tenderly, "You artful little b . . . " And he actually had the brilliant notion of breathing on it to help the drying process. All the same, there was something timid and weak about its efforts now, and the boss decided that this time should be the last, as he dipped the pen into the inkpot.

It was. The last blot on the soaked blotting-paper, and the draggled fly lay in it and did not stir. The back legs were stuck to the body; the front legs were not to be seen.

"Come on," said the boss. "Look sharp!" And he stirred it with his pen— in vain. Nothing happened or was likely to happen. The fly was dead.

The boss lifted the corpse on the end of the paper-knife and flung it into the waste-paper basket. But such a grinding feeling of wretchedness seized him that he felt positively frightened. He started forward and pressed the bell for Macey.

"Bring me some fresh blotting-paper," he said, sternly, "and look sharp about it." And while the old dog padded away he fell to wondering what it was he had been thinking about before. What was it? It was . . . He took out his handkerchief and passed it inside his collar. For the life of him he could not remember.

Louise Bogan

"To My Brother Killed: Haumont Wood: October, 1918"

O you so long dead,
You masked and obscure,
I can tell you, all things endure:
The wine and the bread;

The marble quarried for the arch;
The iron become steel;
The spoke broken from the wheel;
The sweat of the long march;

The hay-stacks cut through like loaves
And the hundred flowers from the seed;
All things indeed
Though struck by the hooves

Of disaster, of time due,
Of fell loss and gain,

All things remain,
I can tell you, this is true.

Though burned down to stone
Though lost from the eye,
I can tell you, and not lie,—
Save of peace alone.

Toni Morrison

"1919" from *Sula*

Except for World War II, nothing ever interfered with the celebration of National Suicide Day. It had taken place every January third since 1920, although Shadrack, its founder, was for many years the only celebrant. Blasted and permanently astonished by the events of 1917, he had returned to Medallion handsome but ravaged, and even the most fastidious people in the town sometimes caught themselves dreaming of what he must have been like a few years back before he went off to war. A young man of hardly twenty, his head full of nothing and his mouth recalling the taste of lipstick, Shadrack had found himself in December, 1917, running with his comrades across a field in France. It was his first encounter with the enemy and he didn't know whether his company was running toward them or away. For several days they had been marching, keeping close to a stream that was frozen at its edges. At one point they crossed it, and no sooner had he stepped foot on the other side than the day was adangle with shouts and explosions. Shellfire was all around him, and though he knew that this was something called *it*, he could not muster up the proper feeling—the feeling that would accommodate *it*. He expected to be terrified or exhilarated—to feel *something* very strong. In fact, he felt only the bite of a nail in his boot, which pierced the ball of his foot whenever he came down on it. The day was cold enough to make his breath visible, and he wondered for a moment at the purity and whiteness of his own breath among the dirty, gray explosions surrounding him. He ran, bayonet fixed, deep in the great sweep of men flying across this field. Wincing at the pain in his foot, he turned his head a little to the right and saw the face of a soldier near him fly off. Before he could register shock, the rest of the soldier's head disappeared under the inverted soup bowl of his helmet. But stubbornly, taking no direction from the brain, the body of the headless soldier ran on, with energy and grace, ignoring altogether the drip and slide of brain tissue down its back.

When Shadrack opened his eyes he was propped up in a small bed. Before him on a tray was a large tin plate divided into three triangles. In one triangle was rice, in another meat, and in the third stewed tomatoes. A small round depression help a cup of whitish liquid. Shadrack stared at the soft colors that filled these triangles: the lumpy whiteness of rice, the quivering blood tomatoes, the grayish-brown meat. All their repugnance was contained in the near balance of the triangles—a balance that soothed him, transferred some of its equilibrium to him. Thus reassured that the white, the red and the brown would stay where they were—would not explode or burst forth from their restricted zones—he suddenly felt hungry and looked around for his hands. His glance was cautious at first, for he had to be very careful—anything could be anywhere. Then he noticed two lumps beneath the beige blanket on either side of his hips. With extreme care he lifted one arm and was relieved to find his hand attached to his wrist. He tried the other and found it also. Slowly he directed one hand toward the cup and, just as he was about to spread his fingers, they began to grow in higgledy-piggledy fashion like Jack's beanstalk all over the tray and the bed. With a shriek he closed his eyes and thrust his huge growing hands under the covers. Once out of sight they seemed to shrink back to their normal size. But the yell had brought a male nurse.

"Private? We're not going to have any trouble today, are we? Are we, Private?"

Shadrack looked up at a balding man dressed in a green-cotton jacket and trousers. His hair was parted low on the right side so that some twenty or thirty yellow hairs could discreetly cover the nakedness of his head.

"Come on. Pick up that spoon. Pick it up, Private. Nobody is going to feed you forever."

Sweat slid from Shadrack's armpits down his sides. He could not bear to see his hands grow again and he was frightened of the voice in the apple-green suit.

"Pick it up, I said. There's no point to this . . . " The nurse reached under the cover for Shadrack's wrist to pull out the monstrous hand. Shadrack jerked it back and overturned the tray. In panic he raised himself to his knees and tried to fling off and away his terrible fingers, but succeeded only in knocking the nurse into the next bed.

When they bound Shadrack into a straitjacket, he was both relieved and grateful, for his hands were at last hidden and confined to whatever size they had attained.

Laced and silent in his small bed, he tried to tie the loose cords in his mind. He wanted desperately to see his own face and connect it with the word "private"—the word the nurse (and the others who helped bind him) had called him. "Private" he thought was something secret, and he wondered why they looked at him and called him a secret. Still, if his hands behaved as they had done, what might he expect from his face? The fear and longing were too much for him, so he began to think of other things. That is, he let his mind slip into whatever cave mouths of memory it chose.

He saw a window that looked out on a river which he knew was full of fish. Someone was speaking softly just outside the door . . .

Shadrack's earlier violence had coincided with a memorandum from the hospital executive staff in reference to the distribution of patients in high risk areas. There was clearly a demand for space. The priority or the violence earned Shadrack his release, $217 in cash, a full suit of clothes and copies of very official-looking papers.

When he stepped out of the hospital door the grounds overwhelmed him: the cropped shrubbery, the edged lawns, the undeviating walks. Shadrack looked at the cement stretches: each one leading clearheadedly to some presumably desirable destination. There were no fences, no warnings, no obstacles at all between concrete and green grass, so one could easily ignore the tidy sweep of stone and cut out in another direction—a direction of one's own.

Shadrack stood at the foot of the hospital steps watching the heads of trees tossing ruefully but harmlessly, since their trunks were rooted too deeply in the earth to threaten him. Only the walks made him uneasy. He shifted his weight, wondering how he could get to the gate without stepping on the concrete. While plotting his course—where he would have to leap, where to skirt a clump of bushes—a loud guffaw startled him. Two men were going up the steps. Then he noticed that there were many people about, and that he was just now seeing them, or else they had just materialized. They were thin slips, like paper dolls floating down the walks. Some were seated in chairs with wheels, propelled by other paper figures from behind. All seemed to be smoking, and their arms and legs curved in the breeze. A

good high wind would pull them up and away and they would land perhaps
among the tops of the trees.

Shadrack took the plunge. Four steps and he was on the grass heading
for the gate. He kept his head down to avoid seeing the paper people swerv-
ing and bending here and there, and he lost his way. When he looked up, he
was standing by a low red building separated form the main building by a
covered walkway. From somewhere came a sweetish smell which reminded
him of something painful. He looked around for the gate and saw that he
had gone directly away from it in his complicated journey over the grass.
Just to the left of the low building was a graveled driveway that appeared to
lead outside the grounds. He trotted quickly to it and left, at last, a haven of
more than a year, only eight days of which he fully recollected.

Once on the road, he headed west. The long stay in the hospital had left
him weak—too weak to walk steadily on the gravel shoulders of the road.
He shuffled, grew dizzy, stopped for breath, started again, stumbling and
sweating but refusing to wipe his temples, still afraid to look at his hands.
Passengers in dark, square cars shuttered their eyes at what they took to be
a drunken man.

The sun was already directly over his head when he came to a town. A
few blocks of shaded streets and he was already at its heart—a pretty, quietly regulated downtown.

Exhausted, his feet clotted with pain, he sat down at the curbside to take
off his shoes. He closed his eyes to avoid seeing his hands and fumbled with
the laces of the heavy high-topped shoes. The nurse had tied them into a
double knot, the way one does for children, and Shadrack, long unaccustomed to the manipulation of intricate things, could not get them loose.
Uncoordinated, his fingernails tore away at the knots. He fought a rising
hysteria that was not merely anxiety to free his aching feet; his very life depended on the release of the knots. Suddenly without raising his eyelids, he
began to cry. Twenty-two years old, weak, hot, frightened, not daring to ac-
knowledge the fact that he didn't even know who or what he was . . . with
no past, no language, no tribe, no source, no address book, no comb, no pencil, no clock, no pocket handkerchief, no rug, no bed, no can opener, no
faded postcard, no soap, no key, no tobacco pouch, no soiled underwear and
nothing nothing nothing to do . . . he was sure of one thing only: the unchecked monstrosity of his hands. He cried soundlessly at the curbside of a
small Midwestern town wondering where the window was, and the river,
and the soft voices just outside the door . . .

Through his tears he saw the fingers joining the laces, tentatively at first, then rapidly. The four fingers of each hand fused into the fabric, knotted themselves and zigzagged in and out of the tiny eyeholes.

By the time the police drove up, Shadrack was suffering from a blinding headache, which was not abated by the comfort he felt when the policemen pulled his hands away from what he thought was a permanent entanglement with his shoelaces. They took him to jail, booked him for vagrancy and intoxication, and locked him in a cell. Lying on a cot, Shadrack could only stare helplessly at the wall, so paralyzing was the pain in his head. He lay in this agony for a long while and then realized he was staring at the painted-over letters of a command to fuck himself. He studied the phrase as the pain in his head subsided.

Like moonlight stealing under a window shade an idea insinuated itself: his earlier desire to see his own face. He looked for a mirror; there was none. Finally, keeping his hands carefully behind his back he made his way to the toilet bowl and peeped in. The water was unevenly lit by the sun so he could make nothing out. Returning to his cot he took the blanket and covered his head, rendering the water dark enough to see his reflection. There in the toilet water he saw a grave black face. A black so definite, so unequivocal, it astonished him. He had been harboring a skittish apprehension that he was not real—that he didn't exist at all. But when the blackness greeted him with its indisputable presence, he wanted nothing more. In his joy he took the risk of letting one edge of the blanket drop and glanced at his hands. They were still. Courteously still.

Shadrack rose and returned to the cot, where he fell into the first sleep of his new life. A sleep deeper than the hospital drugs; deeper than the pits of plums, steadier than the condor's wing; more tranquil than the curve of eggs.

The sheriff looked through the bars at the young man with the matted hair. He had read through his prisoner's papers and hailed a farmer. When Shadrack awoke, the sheriff handed him back his papers and escorted him to the back of a wagon. Shadrack got in and in less than three hours he was back in Medallion, for he had been only twenty-two miles from his window, his river, and his soft voices just outside the door.

In the back of the wagon, supported by sacks of squash and hills of pumpkins, Shadrack began a struggle that was to last for twelve days, a struggle to order and focus experience. It had to do with making a place for fear as a way of controlling it. He knew the smell of death and was terrified of it, for he could not anticipate it. It was not death or dying that frightened him, but the unexpectedness of both. In sorting it all out, he hit on the notion that if one day a year were devoted to it, everybody could get it out of the way and the rest of the year would be safe and free. In this manner he instituted National Suicide Day.

On the third day of the new year, he walked through the Bottom down Carpenter's Road with a cowbell and a hangman's rope calling the people together. Telling them that this was their only chance to kill themselves or each other.

At first the people in the town were frightened; they knew Shadrack was crazy but that did not mean that he didn't have any sense or, even more important, that he had no power. His eyes were so wild, his hair so long and matted, his voice was so full of authority and thunder that he caused panic on the first, or Charter, National Suicide Day in 1920. The next one, in 1921, was less frightening but still worrisome. The people had seen him a year now in between. He lived in a shack on the riverbank that had once belonged to his grandfather long time dead. On Tuesday and Friday he sold the fish he had caught that morning, the rest of the week he was drunk, loud, obscene, funny and outrageous. But he never touched anybody, never fought, never caressed. Once the people understood the boundaries and nature of his madness, they could fit him, so to speak, into the scheme of things.

Then, on subsequent National Suicide Days, the grown people looked out from behind curtains as he rang his bell; a few stragglers increased their speed, and little children screamed and ran. The tetter heads tried goading him (although he was only four or five years older than they) but not for long, for his curses were stingingly personal.

As time went along, the people took less notice of these January thirds, rather they thought they did, thought they had no attitudes or feelings one way or another about Shadrack's annual solitary parade. In face they had simply stopped remarking on the holiday because they had absorbed it into their thoughts, into their language, into their lives.

Someone said to a friend, "You sure was a long time delivering that baby. How long was you in labor?"

And the friend answered, "'Bout three days. The pains started on Suicide Day and kept up till the following Sunday. Was borned on Sunday. All my boys is Sunday boys."

Some lover said to his bride-to-be, "Let's do it after New Years, 'stead of before. I get paid New Year's Eve."

And his sweetheart answered, "OK, but make sure it ain't on Suicide Day. I ain't 'bout to be listening to no cowbells whilst the weddin's going on."

Somebody's grandmother and her hens always started a laying of double yolks right after Sucide Day.

Then Reverend Deal took it up, saying the same folks who had sense enough to avoid Shadrack's call were the ones who insisted on drinking themselves to death or womanizing themselves to death. "May's well go on with Shad and save the Lamb the trouble of redemption."

Easily, quietly, Suicide Day became a part of the fabric of life up in the Bottom of Medallion, Ohio.

Between the Wars

The **"war to end wars"** left few illusions that it would do so. A generation of young men of Great Britain, France, and Germany had been effectively destroyed. Thousands of disabled, damaged survivors came back to a dazed, deprived civilian population. A peace aimed at destroying the losers led to years of starvation and bitterness on the war-ravaged continent. While the politicians of the victorious countries tried to justify the war as having served a purpose, their citizens tried to rebuild their lives. For the defeated, it was more a question of trying to survive.

The years between 1918 and 1939 contained other upheavals, including the continuing breakup of colonialism and a worldwide financial collapse. In Europe, particularly in the defeated countries, years of hunger were followed by catastrophic inflation. This prepared the ground for fascism and its strong men, Benito Mussolini in Italy in 1922, Adolf Hitler in Germany in 1933. A few years of relative economic recovery ended when the 1929 financial crash in the United States contributed to a worldwide depression. Communist revolutions, beginning as early as 1917 in Russia and the 1930s in China, had produced totalitarian leaders, Vladimir Lenin and Joseph Stalin in Russia, Sun Yat-sen and Mao Tse-tung in China. By the early 1930s, major expansionist wars had broken out, such as the Italian invasion of Ethiopia and the Japanese invasion of China. A few years later, a civil war in Spain began, which many saw as a preliminary to World War II.

At the end of World War I, giving women the vote could no longer be postponed. In Great Britain, women received it soon after the Armistice, although suffrage was limited to women thirty and over because it was feared the vote of younger women would overwhelm the votes of the depleted population of young males. In the United States, female suffrage was granted in 1920.

Women had won other gains from their years of war work. Many educated women continued to work outside the home, unwilling to relinquish their new independence and incomes. Poorer women had, of course, always worked, but socialism and unions offered hope of increasing women's opportunities for staying in the work force and for earning better wages.

These gains were only partial. Critics Sandra Gilbert and Susan Gubar have written about the resentment men felt towards women for surviving and even bettering themselves during the war years. The backlash was soon made visible. Vera Brittain's friend and colleague, journalist, novelist, and poet, Winifred Holtby, wrote in 1924 of the almost complete reversal of women's roles in industry from wartime: "The old, deeply-rooted feeling that women ought not to be in industry at all, combined with the perfectly justifiable, but indiscriminately applied, sense of gratitude to the ex-soldier; together they formed an effective smoke-screen behind which many men gained places which, in open competition, they could not hold against the women" (qtd. in Berry and Bishop 53).

Changes for women went on, however, including new freedoms of dress, movement, and sexual behavior; advances in contraception; and even some gains in openness for lesbian women. In the years after World War I, women took on new roles, including those of the "flapper" in the Jazz Age popularized by F. Scott and Zelda Fitzgerald. Women were part of every movement in these troubled but innovative years. As artists they joined the new bohemians, helping to create modernism in its many aspects. As thinkers, they shared the fascination with the socialist experiment being carried out in Russia and supported radical reforms. The "new woman" of the 1920s and 1930s would have only a short life span but she would leave a legacy to be returned to later in this century.

Trying to Prevent the Next War

The time between the wars was to become for some women a time to transform the bitter lessons of World War I into a better plan for humanity. "It's my job, now, to find out all about it, and try to prevent it, in so far as one person can, from happening to other people in the days to come," Vera Brittain wrote in *Testament of Youth* (471), explaining why she studied history and how she recovered her purpose in life after finishing Oxford by traveling around England, giving speeches to promote the League of Nations.

American pacifist Jane Addams had continued to work during the war, for what she called "that most unpopular of all causes—peace in time of war" (241). The meeting of Allied and non-Allied women in The Hague in 1915, organized by Addams and other women leaders, was groundbreaking. Women from opposing sides found more to join than to separate them. The women spelled out concrete methods by which the war could be terminated, and when these were not acted on, laid out most of the principles that American president Woodrow Wilson would adopt later in his Fourteen Points.

In *Peace and Bread in Time of War*, Addams describes her return to Europe after the war to meet with the same women. The meeting could not take place in Paris as planned because German women were not allowed there. Addams, like Vera Brittain, traveled through the war zones searching for her nephew's grave (Brittain, her brother's and fiancé's). Both wrote about the near starvation of the children and the bitterness they saw, which they believed would inevitably lead to another war unless the League of Nations could prevent it.

Addams spent much of the remainder of her life working through the organization Women's International League for Peace and Freedom (WILPF), which she helped found, to establish effective structures to outlaw war. The U.S. Congress, dominated by isolationists, voted against joining the League of Nations, thereby dooming it to failure. Addams and her colleagues were

accused of being "red" and hounded for what were considered revolutionary ideas. Emily Balch, Addams's colleague and, like her, a Nobel Peace Prize
recipient, lost her job at Wellesley College for her ideas. Balch wrote, "Never
had the goals towards which the women at The Hague set out in 1915 and
Zurich in 1919—the goals of peace and freedom—seemed more distant or
been more threatened than in the decade between 1929–1939" (qtd. in
Randall 315).

Addams's British colleague in WILPF Emmeline Pethick-Lawrence,
writing her autobiography in the late 1930s, described the failure of peace
efforts and the subsequent rise of Nazism. Her book *My Part in a Changing
World* covers many of the ensuing women's peace congresses and shows the
strength of the movement for peace in Germany. She was more hopeful
about the movement towards equality for women and wrote of how closely
allied the suffrage movement in England was to peace efforts.

In 1934, Edna St. Vincent Millay wrote "Apostrophe to Man," a poem of
unmitigated pessimism and scorn. Her line "Put death on the market" echoed the anger after World War I at the so-called "war profiteers" who had
supplied shoddy materials to armies at vast profit. Millay's disgust with the
false patriotism used to promote war reflected her desire for radical reform
along with many of the intellectuals and artists in America, especially in
her Greenwich Village political and cultural circles. Their ideas for social
change would result in their strong support for the Republican side in the
coming war in Spain.

Women in Spain

The Spanish Civil War began in 1936, officially ending for many the uneasy years of peace "between the wars." Leftists and intellectuals opposed
General Francisco Franco's attempted takeover of Spain's first democrati-
cally elected republic, especially after Hitler and Mussolini brought in forces
to support Franco. Soon afterwards, the Soviet Union sent forces to support
the Republican side. Initially, the war in Spain had seemed to be a clear-cut
case of a legitimately elected government being attacked by a repressive oli-
garchy backed by Europe's two fascist countries, Italy and Germany. Even
more importantly, it seemed to be the place where fascism could be stopped.
Europeans and Americans went to Spain to fight or at least to observe and
publicize a cause that they saw as the last stand against the rising tide of
fascism in Europe.

The Spanish Civil War was a proving ground for the coming World War

II in other ways: the military strategies and technologies beginning to be developed in World War I had greatly advanced during the intervening years of rearmament, especially those of air warfare. The targeting of civilian populations by air power changed the meaning of frontlines. The world's attention was caught when the small undefended Spanish town of Guernica was bombed, an event commemorated in Picasso's famous painting of the same name.

Well-known writers such as Lillian Hellman came from the United States to make radio broadcasts for the purpose of gaining American support for the Republicans. In her memoir *An Unfinished Woman*, Hellman described meeting Martha Gellhorn with Hemingway in Madrid where Gellhorn got her start as one of the century's most powerful writers about war. Gellhorn's personal history stands for many. Gellhorn described in the introduction to "The War of Spain" how seeing Nazi behavior firsthand in Germany in 1934 had transformed her pacifism into antifascism and had convinced her that the Nazis must be stopped. She went to Spain in 1937, beginning a career of covering wars that continued for over fifty years. With a letter from *Collier's*, she had her first article accepted. The second put her on the masthead and "[o]nce on the masthead, I was evidently a war correspondent" ("The War in Spain" 14). "High Explosives for Everyone" describes war in the streets of Madrid with bombs and mortars raining down as citizens go about their daily business of queuing for food and water.

Frances Davis covered the opposing side in Spain. Her memoir, *My Shadow in the Sun*, tells of how she began newspaper work at age fourteen and was determined to be a foreign correspondent. Told by an editor, "There is very little chance for a woman in the foreign field," she persisted and with advice from Dorothy Thompson, paid for her trip to Paris by signing up small papers for a "mail column." From Paris she could get to Spain. She carried the stories of established reporters across the lines until her own stories were accepted and she was hired by the *London Daily Mail* as the "only woman correspondent with the anti-Red armies."

Dorothy Parker, already a successful American writer and humorist, claimed to have come to Spain "without my axe to grind" and with many unanswered questions. Her short story, "Soldiers of the Republic" uses poignant detail to convey her admiration for the soldiers who endure the miseries of modern warfare along with the additional continual worry about their families, no longer safe in a war where there is no "behind the lines." Atrocities are suggested and indeed have been documented as carried out by both sides.

In Edna St. Vincent Millay's "Say That We Saw Spain Die," the war is compared to a bullfight, "the game gone vulgar, the rules abused." Millay sees the bull as alone and unarmed, an emblem of a proud people overwhelmed by forces beyond its control. Many came back from Spain with the bitter knowlege that what had seemed to them a clear case of right and wrong, had instead become a struggle between the forces of communism and fascism with Spain, an ideological victim, as the booty.

Women Against Fascism

Women did not have to go to Spain to fight fascism. A growing number of them, perceiving it as a force inimical to any freedom of expression for women, recognized it much closer to home—in the patriarchal politics of their countries or even in their homes. It was clear to women observing the rise of fascism that separating men's and women's worlds was essential to the policies of dictators. Hitler and Mussolini redefined roles for men and women, demanding new sacrifices and public service. Mussolini accused women of being a major source of unemployment. Under Hitler, women were removed from the professions and the labor force. With abortion already a criminal offense, women were now rewarded for the number of children they bore, especially sons. In Italy, women with fourteen to nineteen children could meet Mussolini and be given a special award. In Germany, Mother's Day became a national holiday. At the same time, under Hitler's eugenic policies, sterilization was forced on "undesirable" women.

Writers and artists were particularly sensitive to the rise of fascism, which inevitably produced censorship if not outright suppression of their works and even danger to their lives. Women writers felt more threatened, particularly if they were homosexual. Janet Flanner, an American expatriate, covered Paris for the *New Yorker* throughout these years. She wrote about the Spanish refugees flooding into France; documented the growing restrictions on artists; and showed how the Left Bank communities, particularly those of lesbian women, were breaking up as Hitler's menace grew.

Anti-Semitism was an essential component of German fascism. Manifestations of it began as early as the Nazi Party's rise to power in the early 1930s. After Hitler's election in 1933, overt persecution began. Sinister forces were developing that would produce the Holocaust. A Jewish poet in Germany, Gertrud Kolmar, wrote sometime in the mid-1930s of the coming cataclysm. Yet Jews in Germany were more assimilated than anywhere else in Europe. Only a prophetic voice such as Kolmar's could have imagined the horrors ahead. Using the Jews' past history of persecution, she warns of what is to come.

A major delineator of the nature of fascism was Virginia Woolf, never more clearly than in her long essay *Three Guineas*, little understood and heartily criticized at the time of its publication in 1938. British politicians were slow to shake off their admiration for Hitler's economic successes and see the true nature of his ambitions and the lengths he would go in order to carry them out. Woolf had begun her essay as a sequel to *A Room of One's Own*. When her favorite nephew, Julian Bell, was killed in the Spanish Civil War, she began an imaginary dialogue with him on how to end war. The "three guineas" apply to three requests to contribute to institutions that presumably could prevent war: education, the professions, and a "society for the protection of culture and individual liberty." Woolf's response is a long, dense diatribe on the exclusion of women from these institutions and their resulting freedom to challenge the existing order and to set up their own "Outsiders' Society," which should refuse to take part in the war culture.

A more political opposition to fascism was that of Dorothy Thompson, for a time one of the world's best-known journalists. Her column "Let the Record Speak" was read by millions of Americans. Thompson had access to the highest sources of information; in 1931 she had interviewed Hitler. By the end of the war in Spain, Thompson was consumed by her convictions that fascism could not be appeased and that each failure to prevent Hitler's seizing of territory meant a step closer to war.

These "Cassandras" along with other women writers did their best to avert the coming catastrophe. Kolmar would perish in a Nazi death camp; Woolf would take her own life towards the end of World War II; millions more would be consumed in a war that would effectively wipe out the boundaries between battleground and homefront. Dorothy Thompson's ironic cry "Women and children first!" would prove true.

Trying to Prevent the Next War

Jane Addams

from *Peace and Bread in Time of War*

We had, of course, seen something of the widespread European starvation before we went into Germany; our first view in Europe of starved children was in the city of Lille in Northern France, where the school children were being examined for tuberculosis. We had already been told that forty per cent of the children of school age in Lille had open tuberculosis and that the remaining sixty per cent were practically all suspects. As we entered the door of a large school room, we saw at the other end of the room a row of little boys, from six to ten years of age, passing slowly in front of the examining physician. The children were stripped to the waist and our first impression was of a line of moving skeletons; their little shoulder blades stuck straight out, the vertebrae were all perfectly distinct as were their ribs, and their bony arms hung limply at their sides. To add to the gruesome effect not a sound was to be heard, for the French physician had lost his voice as a result of shell shock during the first bombardment of Lille. He therefore whispered his instructions to the children as he applied his stethoscope and the children, thinking it was some sort of game, all whispered back to him. It was incredibly pathetic and unreal and we could but accept the doctor's grave statement that only by a system of careful superfeeding, could any of these boys grow into normal men. We had also seen starved children in Switzerland: six hundred Viennese children arriving in Zurich to be guests in private households. As they stood upon the station platforms without any of the bustle and chatter naturally associated with a large number of children, we had again that painful impression of listlessness as of a mortal illness; we saw the winged shoulder blades standing out through their meagre clothing, the little thin legs which scarcity supported the emaciated bodies. The committee of Swiss women was offering them cakes and chocolates, telling them of the children at home who were waiting for them, but there was little response because there was no vitality with which to make it.

We were reminded of these children week after week as we visited Berlin, or Frankfort am Main, or the cities of Saxony and the villages throughout the Erzgebirge in which the children had been starved throughout the long period of the war and of the armistice. Perhaps an experience in Leipzig was typical when we visited a public playground in which several hundred children were having a noonday meal consisting for each of a pint of "war soup," composed of war meal stirred into a pint of hot water. The war meal was, as always, made with a foundation of rye or wheat flour to which had been added ground vegetables or sawdust in order to increase its bulk. The children would have nothing more to eat until supper, for which many of the mothers had saved the entire daily ration of bread because, as they sometimes told us, they hoped thus to avert the hardest thing they had to bear; hearing the children whimper and moan for hours after they were put to bed because they were too hungry to go to sleep.

These Leipzig children were quite as listless as all the others we had seen; when the playground director announced prizes for the best gardens, they were utterly indifferent; only when he said he hoped by day after to-morrow to give them milk in their soup did they break out into the most ridiculous, feeble little cheer ever heard. The city physician, who was with us, challenged the playground director as to his ability to obtain the milk, to which the director replied that he was not sure that he could, but that there was a prospect for it, and that the children must have something to hope for, that that was the prerogative of the young. With this uncertain hope we left them to visit day nurseries, child welfare stations, schools and orphanages where the midday meal was practically the same war soup. We were told by probation officers and charity workers of starved children who stole the family furniture and clothing, books and kitchen utensils in order to sell them for food, who pulled unripe potatoes and turnips from the fields for miles surrounding the cities, to keep themselves alive.

Our experiences in the midst of widespread misery, did not differ from those of thousands of other Americans who were bent upon succor and relief and our vivid and compelling impressions of widespread starvation were confirmed by the highest authorities. Mr. Hoover had recently declared that, owing to diminished food production in Europe, approximately 100,000,000 Europeans were then dependent upon imported food. Sir George Paish, the British economist, repeated the statement when he said that 100,000,000 persons in Europe were facing starvation. All this was made much worse by the rapid decline in the value of European money in the markets of the world.

One turned instinctively to the newly created League of Nations. Could it have considered this multitude of starving children as its concrete problem, feeding them might have been the quickest way to restore the divided European nations to human and kindly relationship. Was all this devastation the result of hypernationalism and might not the very recognition of a human obligation irrespective of national boundaries form the natural beginning of better international relationships?

Emmeline Pethick-Lawrence

from *My Part in a Changing World*

After the 1918 election there arose many international problems. The hunger blockade against Germany was still in force; Mr. Nevinson and other journalists in Germany sent home pitiful accounts of the starvation of women and particularly of infants. The Women's International League announced a protest meeting in Trafalgar Square in April 1919 and a big banner was erected on the plinth for all to see the explicit nature of our demand: *Lift the Hunger Blockade!* I was the Chairman. One of the most bellicose of the daily newspapers had launched in advance, an attack on the meeting and had represented it as an insult to the army and had called upon soldiers to come and break it up. I saw at a glance that the army had taken the hint. It was well represented. Fortunately I was very closely in touch with the psychology of the British soldier. It sometimes seemed to me as if soldiers, who had fought at the front, alone had resisted the contagion of hatred that possessed the majority of the civilian population. I addressed what I had to say mainly to them. We carried our resolution with the enthusiasm of the crowd. But they were not satisfied. "What are you going to do with the resolution?" they shouted. "What do you want me to do with it?" I asked. "Take it to Downing Street!" cried several voices. "I will take it to Downing Street if the army will come with me," I said. "Yes, we will come," they responded. "Then form up in procession, four abreast," I said, "and I will lead you." Mrs. Ayrton Gould marched with me, and Madeleine Doty was on my other side. It was a Sunday afternoon. No attempt was made to stop us as we marched quietly, with the banner which announced our purpose, to Downing Street. Mrs. Ayrton Gould and I left the procession and walked alone to the door of No. 10. Here we rang the bell and asked to see the Prime Minister. We were given an appointment for an interview later in the same week. I feel sure that the courtesy shown on this occasion was due to the presence of our bodyguard, waiting at the end of the street. In 1919 the Army could do no wrong.

In May 1919, I met again those women from whom I had taken farewell four years earlier at The Hague. In 1915 we had promised each other that we would gather together at the same time as the Powers that would at the conclusion of the war meet to formulate the terms of peace. Our second International Congress took place from May 12th to 17th in Zurich while the fate of Europe was being decided at the Peace Conference in Paris. It was perhaps the most moving experience of my life. In the faces of many I saw traces of the misery and starvation they had suffered during the war and were still suffering, and yet there was amongst all a splendid spirit of friendship, courage and hope. It is only in circumstances such as these that the reserve that in normal intercourse puts a barrier between us is swept away. It may be that the warmer temperaments of southern climates prevailed and made us feel how close we were to each other. Jane Addams presided over all our deliberations, and her spirit seemed to brood upon us. Those who had looked tragedy in the face, those who came from the devastated areas of Belgium and France, and from starving Germany, seemed to catch a glimpse of new light as she quietly told us that President Wilson had declared that our resolutions at The Hague were "the best formulations" for peace that he had seen. In response to an urgent cable which was sent to him pleading for the immediate lifting of the blockade, he sent an encouraging message, he thought that "means might be found"! Those were the early days of the Paris Conference while he still had hope.

But alas! while we waited in Zurich the terms of the Treaty of Versailles were published. We were shocked and distressed beyond limit. Mrs. Philip Snowden—now Viscountess Snowden—came to the Congress after a sleepless night of misery and in a most eloquent speech called upon the Congress to pass a resolution of grave censure and protest against conditions which obviously made reconciliation between the nations of Europe impossible. I seconded her resolution. Could those men in Paris have realized the spirit that was in the women at Zurich, surely they would have seen that only by reconciliation could peace be made secure in the world. One moment stands out from the rest. Jeanne Melin—one of the delegates—arrived late from the devastated area of Carignan and in a speech, eloquent as only a French speech can be, described what she had witnessed. As she appealed to "les forces de demain", Lida Gustava Heymann sprang to her feet holding out both her hands to the speaker. As these two women—German and French—

stood on the platform in fervent handclasp, the audience rose, and I for one found difficulty in restraining tears.

On that day and at that moment all who were present dedicated themselves spontaneously, yet specifically and dramatically, to the promotion of world-peace. It is eighteen years and more ago. Some who made that vow are now in exile and some have died, but all who are living are still true to their pledge. Yet to-day the world in general is in a state of mental warfare. War on the physical plane is already doing its devastating work in many countries. Why this frustration? I, for one, believed then, and believe now, that until the nations who dictated the Versailles peace have atoned for the wrongs they inflicted upon the defeated peoples, a nemesis will rest upon the world. When I remember the greed-inspired lie that was given currency in 1918—the lie that the whole guilt of the war rested upon one nation who, for this reason, should be forced to pay the whole cost of it—a fantastic impossibility—it seems to me that the Spirit of Truth must be vindicated by confession and repentance before we can have peace. But to get back to the story.

At this second Congress, twenty national societies adopted a constitution for the Women's International League for Peace and Freedom (the full name that was chosen on this occasion) and decided to remove its headquarters from The Hague to Geneva, the seat of the League of Nations. We appointed a deputation, headed by Jane Addams, to carry the findings of the Zurich Congress to the Peace Conference in Paris. From that time forward the Congress has met every other year either in one of the capital cities of Europe or in Washington.

From Zurich I went on with Yella Hertzka, the President of the Austrian League, to Salzburg and Vienna, where we spoke together at meetings for promoting reconciliation. At Salzburg I received a cordial welcome from the Mayor because I was the first English visitor that his town had received since the war. He presented us with three loaves of bread, a precious gift which we carried with us on our journeyings for several days, for owing to the hunger rations rigidly enforced upon the whole country, it was the only bread that we saw for a week. In the hotels where we stayed no food was served until the principal meal at midday, only coffee "ersatz" which was a substitute for the real article.

In the years immediately following the war the Women's International League of Germany arranged from time to time a number of public meetings in large German towns and invited me with other speakers to join them in their effort to promote a spirit of reconciliation. After these meetings new members of the League were enrolled. On two occasions Marcelle Capy from

Paris was with me and I experienced with vivid appreciation the power of the spoken word. Large audiences were held spell-bound as, with dramatic eloquence, she spoke of the anguish that war brought to women, of the suffering it wrought on disinherited children and of the madness which destroyed the young virile men of the nations. Night after night I listened to her, always wrapt in the same wonder and admiration. What it cost her to pour out her passion in this way I realized one night, when she was offered a bouquet of roses. She made a gesture of horror, "Je n'ai pas envie de roses," she said, and burst into tears.

During the years following immediately upon the conclusion of peace I was often in Germany and Austria visiting my friends as well as taking part in their united campaigns. I was overwhelmed with admiration for the spirited courage in which all those with whom I came in contact faced their difficulties and tribulations. I was impressed anew with the great qualities of the Germanic people, and often asked myself: Would any other nations have met calamity with such quiet endurance and strength?

In 1919 and subsequently I enjoyed the hospitality of my friend Yella Hertzka, who was the director of a horticultural college in Vienna, and one of the most original and constructive minds in the Women's International League. Her husband was a music publisher—a man of utmost gentleness and charm—well known in London and in other centres of Europe. In Vienna, when there was no bread to be had, special gala performances were given in the Opera House, and all the artistes gave their service free. People flocked there to forget their hunger in enjoyment of art and beauty. "A bread famine," Yella told me, "is never announced in the papers, but when we see the announcement that many operas are to be performed free to all, then we know there will be food shortage." Dr. and Mrs. Scheu-Riesz, of Vienna, were dear friends of ours also; Fred and I spent many delightful times with them: but that was in more normal circumstances some years later.

Amongst the many brave people that I have known, there stand out in special vividness in my mind two very gallant German women, Dr. Anita Augsburg and Lida Gustava Heymann, with whom I have shared ideas and work since 1907 when they invited me to speak in Frankfurt. These two women, who were living together then, as they are now, in completely harmonious friendship and unity of purpose, are powerful personalities, utterly single-minded and devoted as workers for women's freedom, and, since 1914, for world peace. Both are passionate and fearless champions for social justice. Before the war they possessed considerable property and have always been great lovers of nature and of beauty. They had a farm estate, but no animal reared upon it was killed. Horses and cattle and even chickens and ducks were regarded as individuals to be respected and loved for their qualities. Thus before the war, they lived with each other a wonderfully fulfilled yet selfless life. During the years of war they, like the mass of the German people, were deprived of all but the barest necessities of life: at the Congress at Zurich in 1919 they bore upon their bodies the marks of the privation and sorrow they had endured. Their courage and energy were not lessened, however. They threw themselves into the work for reconciliation and peace and took up the task of educating the women of Germany for the new opportunities of civic service which were thrown open to them in the revolution that followed the end of the war.

But with the rise of the Nazi regime to supreme power they became marked people, and had they not gone into exile their life no doubt would have been forfeited. The home that they had got together again since the end of the war was seized, and everything in it was confiscated, together with all revenues due to them from their family property. For many years now they have been wandering without a passport, without nationality, cut off from recognition by their own country. Yet they have continued to work incessantly for the assistance of refugees more unfortunate than themselves, and for the furtherance of their ideals, and have played an important part in all the business of the Women's International League. Moreover, though one member of this dual partnership is over eighty, they maintain their gay courage and their joy in life, and are good company always. They have kept their colours flying in all the winds of life and they are still flying bravely now. They are an outstanding example of the staunch and heroic character of many women of their race that I have been proud to call my friends.

In the summer of 1924 I was invited to represent my country and to speak at a great international demonstration for peace in the German Reichstag. The meeting took place on a Sunday and was packed to the roof. It opened with Beethoven's Funeral March. Amongst others on the tribune were Herr Loebe, the President of the Reichstag, Dr. Fridtjof Nansen from Norway, Senator La Fontaine from Belgium, one of the French senators and myself. I shall never forget the passion for peace that was expressed in those speeches and the depth of response they evoked in that great gathering. There followed a peace conference. I was amongst the delegates chosen by the conference to be received by the German President, Herr Ebert. Dr. Nansen, who was in this delegation, towered above us in stature, and yet was the most simple and child-like of all. Like everybody else I fell under the spell of his great sincerity and charm. He was like a hero from one of the great Scandinavian sagas—a giant in height and strength, a fearless champion of the weak and helpless, with a manner of great consideration and courtesy to all, and particularly to women. I heard him speak later in the Assembly of the League of Nations. He was the one man who could dominate the Assembly and could move it to *act*. He undertook—it will be remembered—the repatriation of war exiles and prisoners after the war.

If my hopes and dreams connected with various peace crusades in my own and other countries have not yet been realized, the same cannot be said of the woman suffrage issue, which has brought results beyond all expectation. It would be outside the scope of this story to touch upon the many laws that have been placed upon the Statute Book to change the status of women and to enlarge their liberties. Many books have been written on this subject, and if anyone is eager to know more about it, they could not do better than to get hold of *Our Freedom and its Results*, by five women. Not only women but the entire human family have reaped the fruits of women's emancipation. Amongst the many changes for the better that have taken place, none is more significant than the new attitude of the Government towards questions of public health, illustrated by the sensational fall in the infantile death-rate. Much remains to be done before women enjoy a fair deal in the industrial and professional world. Women's interests are not yet adequately represented in Parliament; women's societies, however, are not resting upon their past achievements but are following up their victory with characteristic persistence. Amongst the suffrage organizations that never swerved from their purpose of winning complete equality for women I place first and foremost the Women's Freedom League. Even during the war the committee quietly carried on its work and held a watching brief for women lest their interests should be lost sight of in the preoccupation of the country with the interests of the army. When, in 1918, the Act was passed which enfranchised six millions of women, the W.F.L. hardly paused to celebrate the victory, so intent were they in their pursuit of complete equality.

Edna St. Vincent Millay

"Apostrophe to Man"

(on reflecting that the world is ready to go to war again)

Detestable race, continue to expunge yourself, die out.
Breed faster, crowd, encroach, sing hymns, build bombing airplanes;
Make speeches, unveil statues, issue bonds, parade;

Convert again into explosives the bewildered ammonia and the
    distracted cellulose;
Convert again into putrescent matter drawing flies
The hopeful bodies of the young; exhort,
Pray, pull long faces, be earnest, be all but overcome, be photographed;
Confer, perfect your formulae, commercialize
Bacteria harmful to human tissue,
Put death on the market;
Breed, crowd, encroach, expand, expunge yourself, die out,
Homo called *sapiens*.

Women in Spain

Martha Gellhorn

"High Explosives for Everyone"

July 1937

At first the shells went over: you could hear the thud as they left the Fascists' guns, a sort of groaning cough; then you heard them fluttering toward you. As they came closer the sound went faster and straighter and sharper and then, very fast, you heard the great booming noise when they hit.

But now, for I don't know how long—because time didn't mean much—they had been hitting on the street in front of the hotel, and on the corner, and to the left in the side street. When the shells hit that close, it was a different sound. The shells whistled toward you—it was as if they whirled at you—faster than you could imagine speed, and, spinning that way, they whined: the whine rose higher and quicker and was a close scream—and then they hit and it was like granite thunder. There wasn't anything to do, or anywhere to go: you could only wait. But waiting alone in a room that got dustier and dustier as the powdered cobblestones of the street floated into it was pretty bad.

I went downstairs into the lobby, practising on the way how to breathe. You couldn't help breathing strangely, just taking the air into your throat and not being able to inhale it.

It seemed a little crazy to be living in a hotel, like a hotel in Des Moines or New Orleans, with a lobby and wicker chairs in the lounge, and signs on the door of your room telling you that they would press your clothes immediately and that meals served privately cost ten per cent more, and meantime it was like a trench when they lay down an artillery barrage. The whole place trembled to the explosion of the shells.

The concierge was in the lobby and he said, apologetically, "I regret this, Mademoiselle. It is not pleasant. I can guarantee you that the bombing in November was worse. However, it is regrettable."

I said yes, indeed, it was not very nice, was it? He said that perhaps I had better take a room in the back of the house, which might be safer. On the other hand, the rooms were not so agreeable; there was less air. I said of course there wouldn't be so much air. Then we stood in the lobby and listened.

You could only wait. All over Madrid, for fifteen days now, people had been waiting. You waited for the shelling to start, and for it to end, and for it to start again. It came from three directions, at any time, without warning and without purpose. Looking out the door, I saw people standing in door-ways all around the square, just standing there patiently, and then suddenly a shell landed, and there was a fountain of granite cobblestones flying up into the air, and the silver lyddite smoke floated off softly.

A little Spaniard with a lavender shirt, a ready-made bow tie and bright brown eyes was standing in the door watching this with interest. There was also no reason for the shells to stay out of the hotel. They could land inside that door as well as anywhere else. Another shell hit, halfway across the street, and a window broke gently and airily, making a lovely tinkling musical sound.

I was watching the people in the other doorways, as best I could, watching those immensely quiet, stretched faces. You had a feeling you had been waiting here forever, and yesterday you felt the same way. The little Spaniard said to me, "You don't like it?"

"No."

"Nothing," he said. "It is nothing. It will pass. In any case, you can only die once."

"Yes," I said, but without enthusiasm.

We stood there a moment, and there was silence. Before this the shells had been falling one a minute.

"Well," he said, "I think that is all. I have work to do. I am a serious man. I cannot spend my time waiting for shells. *Salud*," he said, and walked out calmly into the street, and calmly crossed it.

Seeing him, some other men decided the shelling was finished too, and presently people were crossing that square, which now was pock-marked with great round holes, and littered with broken cobblestones and glass. An old woman with a market basket on her arm hurried down a side street. And two boys came around the corner, arm in arm, singing.

I went back to my room, and again suddenly there came that whistle-whine-scream-roar and the noise was in your throat and you couldn't feel or hear or think and the building shook and seemed to settle. Outside in the hall, the maids were calling to one another, like birds, in high excited voices. The concierge ran upstairs looking concerned and shaking his head. On the floor above, we went into a room in which the lyddite smoke still hung mist-ily. There was nothing left in that room, the furniture was kindling wood, the walls were stripped and in places torn open, a great hole led into the next room and the bed was twisted iron and stood upright and silly against the wall.

"Oh, my," the concierge said miserably.

"Look, Conchita," one of the maids said to the other; "look at the hole there is in 219 too."

"Oh," one of the youngest maids said, "imagine, it has also spoiled the bathroom in 218."

The journalist who lived in that room had left for London the day before.

"Well," the concierge said, "there is nothing to do. It is very regrettable."

The maids went back to work. An aviator came down from the fifth floor. He said it was disgusting; he had two days leave and this sort of thing went on. Moreover, he said, a shell fragment had hit his room and broken all his toilet articles. It was inconsiderate; it wasn't right. He would now go out and have a beer. He waited at the door for a shell to land, and ran across the square, reaching the café across the street just before the next shell. You couldn't wait forever; you couldn't be careful all day.

Later, you could see people around Madrid examining the new shell holes with curiosity and wonder. Otherwise they went on with the routine of their lives, as if they had been interrupted by a heavy rainstorm but nothing more. In a café which was hit in the morning, where three men were killed sitting at a table reading their morning papers and drinking coffee, the clients came back in the afternoon. You went to Chicote's bar at the end of the day, walking up the street which was No Man's Land, where you could hear the shells whistling even when there was silence, and the bar was crowded as always. On the way you had passed a dead horse and a very dead mule, chopped with shell fragments, and you had passed crisscrossing trails of human blood on the pavement.

You would be walking down a street, hearing only the city noises of streetcars and automobiles and people calling to one another, and suddenly, crushing it all out, would be the huge stony deep booming of a falling shell, at the corner. There was no place to run, because how did you know that the next shell would not be behind you, or ahead, or to the left or right? And going indoors was fairly silly too, considering what shells can do to a house.

So perhaps you went into a store because that was what you had intended doing before all this started. Inside a shoe shop, five women are trying on shoes. Two girls are buying summery sandals, sitting by the front window of the shop. After the third explosion, the salesman says politely: "I think we had better move farther back into the shop. The window might break and cut you."

Women are standing in line, as they do all over Madrid, quiet women, dressed usually in black, with market baskets on their arms, waiting to buy food. A shell falls across the square. They turn their heads to look, and move a little closer to the house, but no one leaves her place in line.

After all, they have been waiting there for three hours and the children expect food at home.

In the Plaza Major, the shoeblacks stand around the edges of the square, with their little boxes of creams and brushes, and passers-by stop and have their shoes polished as they read a paper or gossip together. When the shells fall too heavily, the shoeblacks pick up their boxes and retreat a little way into a side street.

So now the square is empty, though people are leaning close against the houses around it, and the shells are falling so fast that there is almost no time between them to hear them coming, only the steady roaring as they land on the granite cobblestones.

Then for a moment it stops. An old woman, with a shawl over her shoulders, holding a terrified thin little boy by the hand, runs out into the square. You know what she is thinking: she is thinking she must get the child home, you are always safer in your own place, with the things you know. Somehow you do not believe you can get killed when you are sitting in your own parlor, you never think that. She is in the middle of the square when the next one comes.

A small piece of twisted steel, hot and very sharp, sprays off from the shell; it takes the little boy in the throat. The old woman stands there, holding the hand of the dead child, looking at him stupidly, not saying anything, and men run out toward her to carry the child. At their left, at the side of the square, is a huge brilliant sign which says: Get out of Madrid.

No one lived here any more because there was nothing left to live in, and besides the trenches were only two blocks away, and there was another front, in the Casa de Campo, down to the left. Stray bullets droned over these streets, and a stray is just as dangerous as any other kind of bullet if it hits you. You walked past the street barricades, past the ruined houses and the only sound you heard was a machine gun hammering in University City, and a bird.

It was a little like walking in the country, over gutted country roads, and the street barricades made it all seem very strange, and the houses were like scenery in a war movie; it seemed impossible that houses could really be like that.

We were going to visit a janitor who lived in this section; he and his family. They were the only people here, except the soldiers who guarded the barricades. His name was Pedro.

Pedro lived in a fine apartment house; he had been the janitor and caretaker for eight years. In November a bomb fell on the roof; Pedro and his family had been in their tiny basement apartment when the bomb hit, and they were all safe. They saw no reason to move. They were used to living there, and in time of war a basement is more desirable than in time of peace.

They showed us their building with pride. We went into a marble hall, past an elevator, through a mahogany front door, and were in a room that was all dust and broken plaster. Looking up, for eight stories, you could see the insides of all the apartments in that building. The bomb had fallen squarely, and now only the outside walls remained. There was a very fine bathroom on the seventh floor, and the tub was hanging into space by its pipes. A cabinet with china in it stood on the fourth floor, and all the china was in neat unbroken piles. The concierge's two little daughters played in this destruction as children play in an empty lot, or in caves they have found beside a river.

We sat in their underground apartment, with the lights burning, and talked. They said yes, of course, it was difficult to get food, but then it was difficult for everyone and they had never really been hungry. Yes, the bombing had been very bad, but they had just waited in the basement and finally it had stopped. The only trouble, they said, was that the children couldn't go to school because the school had been bombed, and it was impossible to let the children go all the way across Madrid to another school, because bullets whined up past the street barricades at the end of their block and they couldn't risk having the children hurt.

Juanita remarked that she didn't like school anyhow very much, she wanted to be an artist and it was better to sit at home and paint. She had been copying a picture—with crayons on wrapping paper—of a very elegant Spanish gentleman whose portrait hung on the wag of a ruined first-floor apartment in their building.

Mrs. Pedro said it was wonderful now, women could have careers in Spain, did I know about that? That was since the Republic. "We are very in favor of the Republic," she said. "I think Maria may be able to get training as a doctor. Isn't it fine? Can women be doctors in North America?"

I always got a shock from the Palace Hotel, because it had a concierge's desk and a sign saying "Coiffeur on the First Floor," and another sign saying how beautiful Majorca was and they had a hotel to recommend there. The Palace Hotel had its old furniture, but it smelled of ether and was crowded with bandaged men. It is the first military hospital of Madrid now. I went around to the operating room, which used to be the reading room.

There were bloody stretchers piled in the hall, but it was quiet this afternoon. The Empire bookcases, where they used to keep dull reading for the hotel guests, were now used for bandages and hypodermic needles and surgical instruments, and there were brilliant lights in the cut-glass chandeliers to make operating easier. The nurse on duty told me about the men on the sixth floor and I went up to see them.

The room was full of sun. There were four men. One of them was sitting with his leg up on a chair; it was in plaster. He had on a red blouse and was sitting in profile. Beside him, a man with a beret was working quietly, drawing his portrait in pastels. The two other men were in bed. One of them I tried not to look at. The other one was quiet and pale and looked tired. Once or twice he smiled, but did not speak. He had a bad chest wound.

The man in the red blouse was a Hungarian; his knee had been smashed by a piece of shell. He was handsome and very polite and refused politely to talk about his wound because it was of no importance. He was alive, he was very lucky, the doctors were fine and his knee would probably get well. At any rate, he would be able to limp. He wanted to talk about his friend who was making his portrait. "Jaime," he said, "is a fine artist. Look how well he works. He always wanted to be an artist but he never had so much time before."

Jaime smiled and went on; he was working very close to the paper, stopping now and again and peering at the man in the red blouse. His eyes looked a little strange, filmed over and dim. I said it was a fine portrait, a great likeness, and he thanked me. A little later someone called him and he left and then the man in the red blouse said, "He was wounded in the head; he covers it with the beret. His eyes are not very good; they are very bad, really. He does not see much. We ask him to paint pictures of us to keep him busy and make him think he still sees well. Jaime never complains about it."

I said, softly, "What happened to that boy over there."

"He's an aviator."

He was blond and young, with a round face. There was nothing left except the eyes. He had been shot down in his plane and burned, but he had been wearing goggles and that saved his sight. His face and hands were a hard brown thick scab, and his hands were enormous; there were no lips, only the scab. The worst was that his pain was so great he couldn't sleep.

Then a soldier I knew, a Pole, came in, and said, "Listen, Dominie in room 507 has some mimosa. A whole big branch of it. Do you want to come up and see it? He says it grows all around where he lives in Marseille. I never saw any flowers like that before."

Every once in a while the actors would stop talking and wait; shells were exploding down the street in the Plaza Major and to the right of the Gran Via and when they hit too close you couldn't hear the lines of the play, so they waited. It was a benefit performance on Sunday morning; it was to make money for the hospitals.

An amateur had written the play and amateurs directed, costumed and acted it; it couldn't have been more amateur. The audience was delighted; it was a dramatic play, all about the moral and psychological crisis of a young man who decided not to enter the priesthood. The audience thought it was terribly funny and laughed with great good will at the emotional places.

The hero came out, after the curtain rang down, and said he was sorry he'd forgotten his lines that way but he hadn't had time to memorize them. He'd been in the trenches near Garabitas until just a few hours ago (everyone knew an attack had been going on there for two days), and so he couldn't memorize things.

The audience applauded and shouted that it was quite all right; they didn't care anyhow. Then he said he had written a poem up there in the trenches and he would like to recite it. He did. It rolled and tossed and was full of enormous big words and remarkable rhymes and his gestures were excellent and when he was through the audience cheered him and he looked very happy. He was a nice boy, if not a brilliant poet, and they knew he had been in a bad piece of trench, and they liked plays and theaters, even bad plays and even theaters just down the street from where the shells were landing.

Every night, lying in bed, you can hear the machine guns in University City, just ten blocks away. Every once in a while you can hear the dull, heavy explosion of a trench mortar. When the shells wake you, you think first that it is thunder. If they are not too close, you do not really wake.

You know that in November there were black Junker planes flying over and dropping bombs, that all winter long there was no fuel and the days were cold and the nights were colder, you know that food is scarce, and that all these people have sons and husbands and sweethearts at the front somewhere. And now they are living in a city where you take your chances and hope your chances are good. You have seen no panic, no hysteria, you have heard no hate talk. You know they have the kind of faith which makes courage and a fine future. You have no right to be disturbed. There are no lights anywhere and the city itself is quiet. The sensible thing is to go back to sleep.

Frances Davis

from *My Shadow in the Sun*

In the morning the cars are lined up in the cobbled square, the chauffeurs walking up and down a little nervously or talking in groups.

There is a scurrying about, in and out of the hotel, the porter and the chauffeurs bringing out the typewriters and paper bags filled with rolls and meat and fruit.

The Spaniards stand and watch the reporters. The reporters come out of the hotel, seek out their chauffeurs, checking arrangements with them. It is cold and damp and the street is filled with fog. We wear scarves and sweaters, wrapped up against the cold fog.

One by one the cars fill and Rosales goes up and down the line of cars, checking on the passes of those who are allowed to go.

Knickerbocker, restless, gets in and out of his fast roadster, consulting with Rosales. "Come on, come on, can't you speed it up!"

The long line of cars starts off, leaving the Spaniards watching on the sidewalk. We go around the corner and follow the lead car through the streets that leave the town, each car keeping its allotted place.

The lead car has stopped. Each following car stops, pulling up on the road's edge. Rosales gets out of the lead car and walks down the line, halting at each car, giving his command to each chauffeur.

"Five hundred yards now," he says, rapping the fender of our car with his stick to emphasize the precision of his words. "You're under military orders from here on. Y'understand? No crowding. No breaking line. Y'understand? Five hundred yards."

"What do we do if a plane comes over?" Ed asks, sticking his head out the window after him. The line gets into motion again and moves on slowly.

We are entering the foothills of the Guadarramas. We are to climb until we reach the ridge that splits the Spains. There we will look down into the guns of the other Spaniards.

There begin to be signs along the road: the body of a horse, its belly bloated; a truck overturned in a ditch; a long, elegant Rolls, peppered with bullet holes, deserted in a half skid; a single figure slumped against the white-washed wall of a house; three old ladies lying in a row, their skirts neatly arranged over their stiff legs.

In the woods of the foothills scattered fires smoke. Fitfully, the sun breaks through a cloud and pours down upon the bronzed plain. There is going to be a storm. Above the mountains the clouds are black and thick.

The bodies of the beasts, long dead in the fields, smell. The vultures, disturbed by our coming, rise and circle and settle again when we are past.

The cars ahead of us appear and disappear winding deeper into the mountains.

Knick's roadster swings around the curve and into view, impatiently keeping its allotted place behind the lead car.

"There's Knickerbocker," I say, watching the fast, neat car.

"This," says the Major, "is a damned stupid business. A caravan to the front! Stupid. We'll have the whole damned Red aviation thinking we're the whole damned G.H.Q. Damned lucky for us it's clouding over. Damned stupid. Y'understand?"

We all laughed a little at his mimicry of Rosales.

Three of the cars have broken line, turned about and are coming back along the road we've come.

"Clutch trouble," laughs the Major. "Half these drivers get clutch trouble every time they smell the front!"

"From the Alte Leon pass," reads John, "Madrid is visible on a clear day."

The thunder shower is over. We sit upon the wet ground behind the guns like campers behind their fire.

I have my hands ready for my ears.

Knick and the Major stand below us, under the hill's crest, glasses to their eyes. Every time the guns fire they fix their glasses upon the village in the ravine, noting the position of the hit.

I stay behind the guns. I can stand the noise better if I am prepared for it. I stay where I can watch the men pack the gun, slam true the shell and step back.

When they step back I put my hands tight over my ears.

The gun draws in its breath, slips back, and then lurches itself forward.

Between the firing I keep my head drawn into my shoulders like a turtle. When you stand up you draw rifle fire. The bullets sound like bees. When you stand up you bend your knees and crunch your head between your shoulders.

It makes me feel better to see the men do this.

They laugh at me, looking down. "Listen," they say, "if we were your height we wouldn't have to bend. You're only half our height, anyhow!"

A soldier lent me his poncho during the rain. Now I give it back to him, the two of us standing nodding, smiling at one another. The soldier looks at the sky and grins at me. "*Aviones,*" he says, conversationally.

Perhaps my eyes have gone wide. "He means," says John, "now that the storm is past the planes will probably come over to search out this battery! We're doing some damage." John waves a freckled hand at the village below.

On the slope below the crest a cow grazes. I watch the cow, grateful for its bucolic presence.

The cow disappears in a spout of smoke.

The Major comes back up the crest to the gunnery captain. "Getting our range, eh?" he says in English, and as it always is with the Major, the gunnery captain nods, understanding him.

After that there are two puffs of smoke to watch. Ours in the valley. Theirs, climbing, climbing up the mountainside. And I cannot put my hands to my ears for the explosions because I cannot gauge them.

Knick comes up from the slope. "We'd better be getting out of this," he says, and goes off down the path.

Pray God that the Major will think so too.

We trot in single file down the path that recrosses the road to our cars, our heads hunched in and our knees bent. The bullets make a little whistling, splitting the air above our heads. Now and again a twig snaps off, drops.

When we reach the road we have to break cover and run for it.

There is a half-burned, half-demolished house, with no wall to its upper story and the bedroom exposed, like an open-faced doll's house. Christ in Gethsemane still hangs, crooked, upon the back wall. The bed is unmade. A brass bed of shining frame.

This is headquarters. The commanding officer has a face pitted as though by smallpox. He got a face full of shrapnel, and healing, the wounds left pits.

He is standing on the step of the house, one knee resting on an upper step to make a table for a map. In one hand he holds a heel of bread, out of which he takes great bites. With the other he is pointing out to Knick the positions on the map.

There is an instant when both of them lift their heads from the map. Their jaws fall lax. They listen. And then the picture dissolves. Everyone is fleeing from there.

The planes have come.

The soldiers run, the officers run, the newspapermen run. Delmar's coat-tails flap on his fat rear as he hurdles a rock. Rosales' voice rises in English, "Break it up there! You're making targets. Get under cover! Break it up, y'understand?"

There is a furious popping of rifles. Behind the rocks and the tree stumps the soldiers crouch, potting at the planes. The bullets ping in every direction.

There is a flat-topped rock. I am possessed to get on the other side of it, and I clamber and skid down its flat surface. And then I am on my feet again, running, having barely touched the earth.

I have to get out of there! If I had touched that thing it would have burst. Oh, God, how close I came to touching— Under the rock a dead man lies. He has been burnt and his black skin is stretched tight across his putrified fat and muscle and insides. His arms reach up.

His arms stretch up to embrace my fall, skidding down the rock. The fingers are pulled wide apart. The black burnt skin is tight on the upstretched arms.

He grins. He grins from ear to ear.

Upon one thigh a strip of flesh, unburnt, is green.

The black leather flesh encases the ribs. On the chest it is tight. On the ribs it is wrinkled. The stomach has fallen in and the leather flesh wrinkles, falling in after it; and if I touched it, if I barely grazed that leather flesh, it would break and crumble and the gas of the putrid insides would rise and engulf me.

Once I find myself with John. We sit together like two people at a picnic, sitting quietly upon the ground.

John is concerned that I will catch cold upon the damp ground and wants to take off his coat so I may sit upon his coat.

Once I find myself with Ed. We run together hand in hand between the onslaughts of the planes. Between each wave of planes we all get up and run for the cars, scrambling, scattering, falling when the planes are over us again. Getting up, scrambling, running again when the wave has passed over. Each time nearer the cars.

There is once when Ed and I lie in a shell hole, flat on our backs, hand in hand. I have a bit of pine twig with which I cover my face.

There is once when we wedge into the V of a rock. Ed thrusts me into the V. It is a great slab of a rock, and if a bomb lands, not even on it, but near by, the rock may tip and tilt and lie flat upon us. . . .

There is not quite room in the V to shelter both Ed and me. His side is out. His arm is out. I struggle to get tighter into the V so that Ed can get his arm in. On the rock's surface the bullets of the soldiers sniping at the planes ping. . . .

I crush my fingers holding to Ed's hand. Here it comes! Here it comes! I squeeze my eyes tight closed as their muscles will close them. I hold my breath. I crush Ed's hand. Here we go! Here we go together! . . .

As each group makes its car, they tumble in, slam the doors, yank the car out of its parking place and shoot off down the road.

Knick's car rounds the curve ahead of us. We are all traveling like mad.

I can see Knick's roadster shooting down the straightaway.

The tires squeal as Antoine hits the curve.

John Elliott says, "There they are again, over to the left, Major!"

The Major swivels his head abruptly to the left. We all look to the left and search the sky. Except Antoine. Antoine never takes his eyes off the ribbon of road.

"Run for it!" shouts the Major. I hear the motors of the planes. "*Allez-y, Antoine!*" Antoine finishes with the curve and levels out on the straightaway, licking up the road.

"We can't make it, Major! We can't make it!" Ed is on the edge of his seat, his hand on the door handle.

In another instant the planes will be above us.

Now we scream in chorus, *"Arrêtez, Antoine! Arrêtez!"*

The car, pinned in flight by the brakes, swerves in a semicircle. Ed already has the door open and is running with the still skidding car, running in the embrace of the open door, to keep his balance.

There is a stone wall. There is a field.

I lie on my face in the field. "Open, O earth, open and hide me!" And then I cry nothing, and think nothing, and feel nothing, suspended in the scream of the diving planes.

The road has been marked and remarked, marked and remarked with the spatters of the machine-gun bullets. Two bombs fell close, tearing great wounds. But the car is untouched. Antoine, his hand shaking, is smoothing the fenders.

We get back in.

"That should be all for the day," says the Major, settling himself, putting his beret back on. "We should be through with that for the day, you know. Sun's setting."

Knick made the village before the planes came. When we pull up in the square he is sitting on the running board of his car, typing.

Over the village walls the gray sky is lit with red. The light changes, gently.

One by one the cars of the caravan draw up in the square. Here and there typewriters click.

The people who have been in their cellars all day come out and stand around the cars, watching. Children stare at the men poking at the typewriters. Everyone is taking deep purchases upon the cooling air, breathing it in to relax his blood. A soldier finds me a bottle of hot pop. The soldiers make a circle round me and we pass it one to the other. They laugh at my scratched and bleeding legs, the dirt and twigs in my hair, my torn skirt.

It is glorious, being alive.

Sharply a bullet ricochets against the stones of the square. Somebody's typewriter clatters to the cobbles. Car doors slam. Fighting for the doorway of the nearest house, someone, heavier than I, pushes me and I fall against the wall of the house, am up, and through the doorway into the blackness of the house.

From the square, stillness.

There in the dark house only the sound of many people, waiting, breathing.

Nothing happens. Outside, the square lies in quiet twilight.

In the dark house somebody says something. Somebody else answers. A murmur of talk springs up like a breeze.

And then a voice speaks out loud, in impatience. A soldier moves out of the dark into the light of the doorway. For an instant he stands there, black and heavy against the last of the day's light, and then he plunges into the square.

Across the square, heavy boots pound the cobbles. Across the square voices call, one to another. Loud laughter rings.

What was it? What was it?

The people again fill the square, crowding about the soldiers, pushing to get in nearer the crowd's center, asking their neighbors, as they elbow and stand upon tiptoe to see: What was it, what was it?

"*Nada.*"

A soldier shot a sheep.

Dorothy Parker

"Soldiers of the Republic"

That Sunday afternoon we sat with the Swedish girl in the big café in Valencia. We had vermouth in thick goblets, each with a cube of honey-combed gray ice in it. The waiter was so proud of that ice he could hardly bear to leave the glasses on the table, and thus part from it forever. He went to his duty—all over the room they were clapping their hands and hissing to draw his attention—but he looked back over his shoulder.

It was dark outside, the quick, new dark that leaps down without dusk on the day; but, because there were no lights in the streets, it seemed as set and as old as midnight. So you wondered that all the babies were still up. There were babies everywhere in the café, babies serious without solemnity and interested in a tolerant way in their surroundings.

At the table next ours, there was a notably small one; maybe six months old. Its father, a little man in a big uniform that dragged his shoulders down, held it carefully on his knee. It was doing nothing whatever, yet he and his thin young wife, whose belly was already big again under her sleazy dress, sat watching it in a sort of ecstasy of admiration, while their coffee cooled in front of them. The baby was in Sunday white; its dress was patched so delicately that you would have thought the fabric whole had not the patches varied in their shades of whiteness. In its hair was a bow of new blue ribbon, tied with absolute balance of loops and ends. The ribbon was of no use; there was not enough hair to require restraint. The bow was sheerly an adornment, a calculated bit of dash.

"Oh, for God's sake, stop that!" I said to myself. "All right, so it's got a piece of blue ribbon on its hair. All right, so its mother went without eating so it could look pretty when its father came home on leave. All right, so it's her business, and none of yours. All right, so what have you got to cry about?"

The big, dim room was crowded and lively. That morning there had been a bombing from the air, the more horrible for broad daylight. But nobody in the café sat tense and strained, nobody desperately forced forgetfulness. They drank coffee or bottled lemonade, in the pleasant, earned ease of Sunday afternoon, chatting of small, gay matters, all talking at once, all hearing and answering.

There were many soldiers in the room, in what appeared to be the uniforms of twenty different armies until you saw that the variety lay in the differing ways the cloth had worn or faded. Only a few of them had been wounded; here and there you saw one stepping gingerly, leaning on a crutch or two canes, but so far on toward recovery that his face had color. There were many men, too, in civilian clothes—some of them soldiers home on leave, some of them governmental workers, some of them anybody's guess. There were plump, comfortable wives, active with paper fans, and old women as quiet as their grandchildren. There were many pretty girls and some beauties, for whom you did not remark, "There's a charming Spanish type," but said, "What a beautiful girl!" The women's clothes were not new, and their material was too humble ever to have warranted skillful cutting.

"It's funny," I said to the Swedish girl, "how when nobody in a place is best-dressed, you don't notice that everybody isn't."

"Please?" the Swedish girl said.

No one, save an occasional soldier, wore a hat. When we had first come to Valencia, I lived in a state of puzzled pain as to why everybody on the streets laughed at me. It was not because "West End Avenue" was writ across my face as if left there by a customs officer's chalked scrawl. They like Americans in Valencia, where they have seen good ones—the doctors who left their practices and came to help, the calm young nurses, the men of the International Brigade. But when I walked forth, men and women courteously laid their hands across their splitting faces and little children, too innocent for dissembling, doubled with glee and pointed and cried, "*Olé!*" Then, pretty late, I made my discovery, and left my hat off; and there was laughter no longer. It was not one of those comic hats, either; it was just a hat.

The café filled to overflow, and I left our table to speak to a friend across the room. When I came back to the table, six soldiers were sitting there. They were crowded in, and I scraped past them to my chair. They looked tired and dusty and little, the way that the newly dead look little, and the first things you saw about them were the tendons in their necks. I felt like a prize sow.

They were all in conversation with the Swedish girl. She has Spanish, French, German, anything in Scandinavian, Italian, and English. When she has a moment for regret, she sighs that her Dutch is so rusty she can no longer speak it, only read it, and the same is true of her Rumanian.

They had told her, she told us, that they were at the end of forty-eight hours' leave from the trenches, and, for their holiday, they had all pooled their money for cigarettes, and something had gone wrong, and the cigarettes had never come through to them. I had a pack of American cigarettes—in Spain rubies are as nothing to them—and I brought it out, and by nods and smiles and a sort of breast stroke, made it understood that I was offering it to those six men yearning for tobacco. When they saw what I meant, each one of them rose and shook my hand. Darling of me to share my cigarettes with the men on their way back to the trenches. Little Lady Bountiful. The prize sow.

Each one lit his cigarette with a contrivance of yellow rope that stank when afire and was also used, the Swedish girl translated, for igniting grenades. Each one received what he had ordered, a glass of coffee, and each one murmured appreciatively over the tiny cornucopia of coarse sugar that accompanied it. Then they talked.

They talked through the Swedish girl, but they did to us that thing we all do when we speak our own language to one who has no knowledge of it. They looked us square in the face, and spoke slowly, and pronounced their words with elaborate movements of their lips. Then, as their stories came, they poured them at us so vehemently, so emphatically that they were sure we must understand. They were so convinced we would understand that we were ashamed for not understanding.

But the Swedish girl told us. They were all farmers and farmers' sons, from a district so poor that you try not to remember there is that kind of poverty. Their village was next that one where the old men and the sick men and the women and children had gone, on a holiday, to the bullring; and the planes had come over and dropped bombs on the bullring, and the old men and the sick men and the women and the children were more than two hundred.

They had all, the six of them, been in the war for over a year, and most of that time they had been in the trenches. Four of them were married. One had one child, two had three children, one had five. They had not had word from their families since they had left for the front. There had been no communication; two of them had learned to write from men fighting next them in the trench, but they had not dared to write home. They belonged to a union, and union men, of course, are put to death if taken. The village where their families lived had been captured, and if your wife gets a letter from a union man, who knows but they'll shoot her for the connection?

They told about how they had not heard from their families for more than a year. They did not tell it gallantly or whimsically or stoically. They told it as if—Well, look. You have been in the trenches, fighting, for a year. You have heard nothing of your wife and your children. They do not know if you are dead or alive or blinded. You do not know where they are, or if they are. You must talk to somebody. That is the way they told about it.

One of them, some six months before, had heard of his wife and his three children—they had such beautiful eyes, he said—from a brother-in-law in France. They were all alive then, he was told, and had a bowl of beans a day. But his wife had not complained of the food, he heard. What had troubled her was that she had no thread to mend the children's ragged clothes. So that troubled him, too.

"She has no thread," he kept telling us. "My wife has no thread to mend with. No thread."

We sat there, and listened to what the Swedish girl told us they were saying. Suddenly one of them looked at the clock, and then there was excitement. They jumped up, as a man, and there were calls for the waiter and rapid talk with him, and each of them shook the hand of each of us. We went through more swimming motions to explain to them that they were to take the rest of the cigarettes—fourteen cigarettes for six soldiers to take to war—and then they shook our hands again. Then all of us said "*Salud!*" as many times as could be for six of them and three of us, and then they filed out of the café, the six of them, tired and dusty and little, as men of a mighty horde are little.

Only the Swedish girl talked, after they had gone. The Swedish girl has been in Spain since the start of the war. She has nursed splintered men, and she has carried stretchers into the trenches and, heavier laden, back to the hospital. She has seen and heard too much to be knocked into silence.

Presently it was time to go, and the Swedish girl raised her hands above her head and clapped them twice together to summon the waiter. He came, but he only shook his head and his hand, and moved away.

The soldiers had paid for our drinks.

Edna St. Vincent Millay

"Say That We Saw Spain Die"

Say that we saw Spain die. O splendid bull, how well
    you fought!
Lost from the first.
            . . . the tossed, the replaced, the
    watchful *torero* with gesture elegant and spry,

Before the dark, the tiring but the unglazed eye
　　deploying the bright cape,
Which hid for once not air, but the enemy indeed, the
　　authentic shape,
A thousand of him, interminably into the ring
　　released . . . the turning beast at length between
　　converging colours caught.

Save for the weapons of its skull, a bull
Unarmed, considering, weighing, charging
Almost a world, itself without ally.

Say that we saw the shoulders more than the mind
　　confused, so profusely
Bleeding from so many more than the accustomed
　　barbs, the game gone vulgar, the rules abused.

Say that we saw Spain die from loss of blood, a rustic
　　reason, in a reinforced
And proud punctilious land, no *espada*—
A hundred men unhorsed,
A hundred horses gored, and the afternoon aging, and
　　the crowd growing restless (all, all so much later
　　than planned),
And the big head heavy, sliding forward in the sand,
　　and the tongue dry with sand,—no *espada*
Toward that hot neck, for the delicate and final thrust,
　　having dared thrust forth his hand.

Women Against Fascism

Gertrud Kolmar

"We Jews"

The night alone can hear. I love you, I love you, oh my
    people,
In my embrace I want to hold you warm and close
Just as a wife would hold her husband on the scaffold steps,
Or like a mother who cannot allow her son to die alone.

And when your throat is gagged, your bleeding cry
    suppressed,
When brutal shackles bind your trembling arms,
Oh let me be the voice that echoes down the shaft of all
    eternity,
The hand stretched high to touch God's towering heaven.

For the Greeks have struck white gods like sparks from
    mountain crags,
And Rome threw brazen shields across the earth,
Mongolian hordes whirled forth from deep in Asia,
And the emperors in Aachen gazed enchanted to the South.

And Germany and France hold high their books and
    shining swords,
And England wanders silver paths on ocean-going ships,
And Russia grew to giant shadows with a flame upon its
    hearth,
And we, we have proceeded through the gallows and the
    rack.

This bursting of our hearts, this sweat of death, this gaze
    without a tear,

And the eternal windblown sigh of martyrs at the stake,
The withered claw, the weary fist with veins like vipers
Raised against the murderers from ropes and funeral pyres
    of ages,

The gray beard singed in hellfires, torn by devils-grip,
The mutilated ear, the wounded brow and fleeing eye:
Oh all of you! Now, when the bitter hour strikes I will arise
And stand like a triumphal arch above your cavalcade of
    anguish!

I will not kiss the arm that wields the weighty scepter,
Nor the brazen knee, the earthen feet of demigods in
    desperate hours;
If only I could raise my voice to be a blazing torch
Amidst the darkened desert of the world, and thunder:
    JUSTICE! JUSTICE! JUSTICE!

And yet my ankles are in chains; I drag a ringing prison as
    I go.
My lips are sealed in glowing wax.
My soul is like a swallow fluttering helpless in its cage.
And I can feel the fist that drags my weeping head toward
    the hill of ashes.

Virginia Woolf

from *Three Guineas*

Now that we have tried to see how we can help you to prevent war by attempting to define what is meant by protecting culture and intellectual liberty let us consider your next and inevitable request: that we should subscribe to the funds of your society. For you, too, are an honorary treasurer, and like the other honorary treasurers in need of money. Since you, too, are asking for money it might be possible to ask you, also, to define your aims, and to bargain and to impose terms as with the other honorary treasurers.

What then are the aims of your society? To prevent war, of course. And by what means? Broadly speaking, by protecting the rights of the individual; by opposing dictatorship; by ensuring the democratic ideals of equal opportunity for all. Those are the chief means by which as you say, "the lasting peace of the world can be assured." Then, Sir, there is no need to bargain or to haggle. If those are your aims, and if, as it is impossible to doubt, you mean to do all in your power to achieve them, the guinea is yours—would that it were a million! The guinea is yours; and the guinea is a free gift, given freely.

But the word "free" is used so often, and has come, like used words, to mean so little, that it may be well to explain exactly, even pedantically, what the word "free" means in this context. It means here that no right or privilege is asked in return. The giver is not asking you to admit her to the priesthood of the Church of England; or to the Stock Exchange; or to the Diplomatic Service. The giver has no wish to be "English" on the same terms that you yourself are "English." The giver does not claim in return for the gift admission to any profession; any honour, title, or medal; any professorship or lectureship; any seat upon any society, committee or board. The gift is free from all such conditions because the one right of paramount importance to all human beings is already won. You cannot take away her right to earn a living. Now then for the first time in English history an educated man's daughter can give her brother one guinea of her own making at his request for the purpose specified above without asking for anything in return. It is a free gift, given without fear, without flattery, and without conditions. That, Sir, is so momentous an occasion in the history of civilization that some celebration seems called for. But let us have done with the old ceremonies—the Lord Mayor, with turtles and sheriffs in attendance, tapping nine times with his mace upon a stone while the Archbishop of Canterbury in full canonicals invokes a blessing. Let us invent a new ceremony for this new occasion. What more fitting than to destroy an old word, a vicious and corrupt word that has done much harm in its day and is now obsolete? The word "feminist" is the word indicated. That word, according to the dictionary, means "one who champions the rights of women." Since the only right, the right to earn a living, has been won, the word no longer has a meaning. And a word without a meaning is a dead word, a corrupt word. Let us therefore celebrate this occasion by cremating the corpse. Let us write that word in large black letters on a sheet of foolscap; then solemnly apply a match to the paper. Look, how it burns! What a light dances over the world! Now let us bray the ashes in a mortar with a goose-feather pen, and declare in unison singing together that anyone who uses that word in future is a ring-the-bell-and-run-away-man, a mischief maker, a groper among old bones, the proof of whose defilement is written in a smudge of dirty water upon his face. The smoke has died down; the word is destroyed. Observe, Sir, what has happened as the result of our celebration. The word "feminist" is destroyed; the air is cleared; and in that clearer air what do we see? Men and women working together for the same cause. The cloud has lifted from the past too. What were they working for in the nineteenth century—those queer dead women in their poke bonnets and shawls? The very same cause for which we are working now. "Our claim was no claim of women's rights only;"—it is Josephine Butler who speaks—"it was larger and deeper; it was a claim for the rights of all—all men and women—to the respect in their persons of the great principles of Justice and Equality and Liberty." The words are the same as yours; the claim is the same as yours. The daughters of educated men who were called, to their resentment, "feminists" were in fact the advance guard of your own movement. They were fighting the same enemy that you are fighting and for the same reasons. They were fighting the tyranny of the patriarchal state as you are fighting the tyranny of the Fascist state. Thus we are merely carrying on the same fight that our mothers and grandmothers fought; their words prove it; your words prove it. But now with your letter before us we have your assurance that you are fighting with us, not against us. That fact is so inspiring that another celebration seems called for. What could be more fitting than to write more dead words, more corrupt words, upon more sheets of paper and burn them—the words, Tyrant, Dictator, for example? But, alas, those words are not yet obsolete. We can still shake out eggs from newspapers; still smell a peculiar and unmistakable odour in the region of Whitehall and Westminster. And abroad the monster has come more openly to the surface. There is no mistaking him there. He has widened his scope. He is interfering now with your liberty; he is dictating how you shall live; he is making distinctions not merely between the sexes, but between the races. You are feeling in your own persons what your mothers felt when they were shut out, when they were shut up, because they were women. Now you are being shut out, you are being shut up, because you are Jews, because you are democrats, because of race, because of religion. It is not a photograph that you look upon any longer; there you go, trapesing along in the procession yourselves. And that makes a difference. The whole iniquity of dictatorship, whether in Oxford or Cambridge, in Whitehall or Downing Street, against Jews or against women, in England, or in Germany, in Italy or in Spain is now apparent to you. But now we are fighting together. The daughters and sons of educated men are fighting side by side. That fact is so inspiring, even if no celebration is yet possible, that if this one guinea could be multiplied a million times all those guineas should be at your service without any other conditions than those that you have imposed upon yourself. Take this one guinea then and use it to assert "the rights of all—all men and women—to the respect in their persons of the great principles of Justice and Equality and Liberty." Put this penny candle in the window of your new society, and may we live to see the day when in the blaze of our common freedom the words tyrant and dictator shall be burnt to ashes, because the words tyrant and dictator shall be obsolete.

That request then for a guinea answered, and the cheque signed, only one further request of yours remains to be considered—it is that we should fill up a form and become members of your society. On the face of it that seems a simple request, easily granted. For what can be simpler than to join the society to which this guinea has just been contributed? On the face of it, how easy, how simple; but in the depths, how difficult, how complicated. . . . What possible doubts, what possible hesitations can those dots stand for? What reason or what emotion can make us hesitate to become members of a society whose aims we approve, to whose funds we have contributed? It may be neither reason nor emotion, but something more profound and fundamental than either. It may be difference. Different we are, as facts have proved, both in sex and in education. And it is from that difference, as we have already said, that our help can come, if help we can, to protect liberty, to prevent war. But if we sign this form which implies a promise to become active members of your society, it would seem that we must lose that difference and therefore sacrifice that help. To explain why this is so is not easy, even though the gift of a guinea has made it possible (so we have boasted) to speak freely without fear or flattery. Let us then keep the for unsigned on the table before us while we discuss, so far as we are able, the reasons and the emotions which make us hesitate to sign it. For those reasons and emotions have their origin deep in the darkness of ancestral memory; they have grown together in some confusion; it is very difficult to untwist them in the light.

To begin with an elementary distinction: a society is a conglomeration of people joined together for certain aims; while you, who write in your own person with your own hand are single. You the individual are a man whom we have reason to respect; a man of the brotherhood, to which, as biography proves, many brothers have belonged. Thus Anne Clough, describing her brother, says: "Arthur is my best friend and adviser. . . . Arthur is the

comfort and joy of my life; it is for him, and from him, that I am incited to
seek after all that is lovely and of good report." To which William
Wordsworth, speaking of his sister but answering the other as if one nightingale called to another in the forests of the past, replies:

> The Blessing of my later years
> Was with me when a Boy:
> She gave me eyes, she gave me ears;
> And humble cares, and delicate fears;
> A heart, the fountain of sweet tears;
>   And love, and thought, and joy.

Such was, such perhaps still is, the relationship of many brothers and
sisters in private, as individuals. They respect each other and help each other
and have aims in common. Why then, if such can be their private relationship, as biography and poetry prove, should their public relationship, as law
and history prove, be so very different? And here, since you are a lawyer,
with a lawyer's memory, it is not necessary to remind you of certain decrees
of English law from its first records to the year 1919 by way of proving that
the public, the society relationship of brother and sister has been very different from the private. The very word "society" sets tolling in memory the dismal bells of a harsh music: shall not, shall not, shall not. You shall not learn;
you shall not earn; you shall not own; you shall not—such was the society
relationship of brother to sister for many centuries. And though it is possible, and to the optimistic credible, that in time a new society may ring a car-
illon of splendid harmony, and your letter heralds it, that day is far distant.
Inevitably we ask ourselves, is there not something in the conglomeration of
people into societies that releases what is most selfish and violent, least rational and humane in the individuals themselves? Inevitably we look upon
society, so kind to you, so harsh to us, as an ill-fitting form that distorts the
truth; deforms the mind; fetters the will. Inevitably we look upon societies as
conspiracies that sink the private brother, whom many of us have reason to
respect, and inflate in his stead a monstrous male, loud of voice, hard of fist,
childishly intent upon scoring the floor of the earth with chalk marks,
within whose mystic boundaries human beings are penned, rigidly, sepa-
rately, artificially; where, daubed red and gold, decorated like a savage with
feathers he goes through mystic rites and enjoys the dubious pleasures of
power and dominion while we, "his" women, are locked in the private house
without share in the many societies of which his society is composed. For

such reasons compact as they are of many memories and emotions—for who shall analyse the complexity of a mind that holds so deep a reservoir of time past within it?—it seems both wrong for us rationally and impossible for us emotionally to fill up your form and join your society. For by so doing we should merge our identity in yours; follow and repeat and score still deeper the old worn ruts in which society, like a gramophone whose needle has stuck, is grinding out with intolerable unanimity "Three hundred millions spent upon arms." We should not give effect to a view which our own experience of "society" should have helped us to envisage. Thus, Sir, while we respect you as a private person and prove it by giving you a guinea to spend as you choose, we believe that we can help you most effectively by refusing to join your society; by working for our common ends—justice and equality and liberty for all men and women—outside your society, not within.

But this, you will say, if it means anything, can only mean that you, the daughters of educated men, who have promised us your positive help, refuse to join our society in order that you may make another of your own. And what sort of society do you propose to found outside ours, but in co-operation with it, so that we may both work together for our common ends? That is a question which you have every right to ask, and which we must try to answer in order to justify our refusal to sign the form you send. Let us then draw rapidly in outline the kind of society which the daughters of educated men found and join outside your society but in co-operation with its ends. In the first place, this new society, you will be relieved to learn, would have no honorary treasurer, for it would need no funds. It would have no office, no committee, no secretary; it would call no meetings; it would hold no conferences. If name it must have, it could be called the Outsiders' Society. That is not a resonant name, but it has the advantage that it squares with facts—the facts of history, of law, of biography; even, it may be, with the still hidden facts of our still unknown psychology. It would consist of educated men's daughters working in their own class—how indeed can they work in any other?—and by their own methods for liberty, equality and peace. Their first duty, to which they would bind themselves not by oath, for oaths and ceremonies have no part in a society which must be anonymous and elastic before everything, would be not to fight with arms. This is easy for them to observe, for in fact, as the papers inform us, "the Army Council have no intention of opening recruiting for any women's corps." The country ensures it. Next they would refuse in the event of war to make munitions or nurse the wounded. Since in the last war both these activities were mainly discharged by the daughters of working men, the pressure upon them here too would be slight, though probably disagreeable. On the other hand the next duty to which they would pledge themselves is one of considerable difficulty, and calls not only for courage and initiative, but for the special knowledge of the educated man's daughter. It is, briefly, not to incite their brothers to fight, or to dissuade them, but to maintain an attitude of complete indifference. But the attitude expressed by the word "indifference" is so complex and of such importance that it needs even here further definition. Indifference in the first place must be given a firm footing upon fact. As it is a fact that she cannot understand what instinct compels him, what glory, what interest, what manly satisfaction fighting provides for him—"without war there would be no outlet for the manly qualities which fighting develops"—as fighting thus is a sex characteristic which she cannot share, the counterpart some claim of the material instinct which he cannot share, so is it an instinct which she cannot judge. The outsider therefore must leave him free to deal with this instinct by himself, because liberty of opinion must be respected, especially when it is based upon an instinct which is as foreign to her as centuries of tradition and education can make it. This is a fundamental and instinctive distinction upon which indifference may be based. But the outsider will make it her duty not merely to base her indifference upon instinct, but upon reason. When he says, as history proves that he has said, and may say again, "I am fighting to protect our country" and thus seeks to rouse her patriotic emotion, she will ask herself, "What does 'our country' mean to me an outsider?" To decide this she will analyse the meaning of patriotism in her own case. She will inform herself of the position of her sex and her class in the past. She will inform herself of the amount of land, wealth and property in the possession of her own sex and class in the present—how much of "England" in fact belongs to her. From the same sources she will inform herself of the legal protection which the law has given her in the past and now gives her. And if he adds that he is fighting to protect her body, she will reflect upon the degree of physical protection that she now enjoys when the words "Air Raid Precaution" are written on blank walls. And if he says that he is fighting to protect England from foreign rule, she will reflect that for her there are no "foreigners," since by law she becomes a foreigner if she marries a foreigner. And she will do her best to make this a fact, not by forced fraternity, but by human sympathy. All these facts will convince her reason (to put it in a nutshell) that her sex and class has very little to thank England for in the past; not much to thank England for in the present; while the security of her person in the future is highly dubious. But probably she will have imbibed, even from the governess, some romantic notion that Englishmen, those fathers and grandfathers whom she sees marching in the picture of history, are "superior" to the men of other countries. This she will consider it her duty to check by comparing French historians with English; German with French; the testimony of the ruled—the Indians or the Irish, say—with the claims made by their rulers. Still some "patriotic" emotion, some ingrained belief in the intellectual superiority of her own country over other countries may remain. Then she will compare English painting with French painting; English music with German music; English literature with Greek literature, for translations abound. When all these comparisons have been faithfully made by the use of reason, the outsider will find herself in possession of very good reasons for her indifference. She will find that she has no good reason to ask her brother to fight on her behalf to protect "our" country. " 'Our country,' " she will say, "throughout the greater part of its history has treated me as a slave; it has denied me education or any share in its possessions. 'Our' country still ceases to be mine if I marry a foreigner. 'Our' country denies me the means of protecting myself, forces me to pay others a very large sum annually to protect me, and is so little able, even so, to protect me that Air Raid precautions are written on the wall. Therefore if you insist upon fighting to protect me, or 'our' country, let it be understood, soberly and rationally between us, that you are fighting to gratify a sex instinct which I cannot share; to procure benefits which I have not shared and probably will not share; but not to gratify my instincts, or to protect myself or my country. For," the outsider will say, "in fact, as a woman, I have no country. As a woman I want no country. As a woman my country is the whole world." And if, when reason has said its say, still some obstinate emotion remains, some love of England dropped into a child's ears by the cawing of rooks in an elm tree, by the splash of waves on a beach, or by English voices murmuring nursery rhymes, this drop of pure, if irrational, emotion she will make serve her to give to England first what she desires of peace and freedom for the whole world.

Such then will be the nature of her "indifference" and from this indifference certain actions must follow. She will bind herself to take no share in patriotic demonstrations; to assent to no form of national self-praise; to make no part of any claque or audience that encourages war; to absent herself from military displays, tournaments, tattoos, prize-givings and all such ceremonies as encourage the desire to impose "our" civilization or "our" dominion upon other people. The psychology of private life, moreover, warrants the belief that this use of indifference by the daughters of educated men would help materially to prevent war. For psychology would seem to show that it is far harder for human beings to take action when other people are indifferent and allow them complete freedom of action, than when their actions are made the centre of excited emotion. The small boy struts and trumpets outside the window: implore him to stop; he goes on; say nothing; he stops. That the daughters of educated men then should give their brothers neither the white feather of cowardice nor the red feather of courage, but no feather at all; that they should shut the bright eyes that rain influence, or let those eyes look elsewhere when war is discussed—that is the duty to which outsiders will train themselves in peace before the threat of death inevitably makes reason powerless.

Such then are some of the methods by which the society, the anonymous and secret Society of Outsiders would help you, Sir, to prevent war and to ensure freedom.

Dorothy Thompson

from *Let the Record Speak*

I SEE BY THE PAPERS

New York Times   *October 7, 1938*
Prime Minister Chamberlain in a speech to the House of Commons on October 6, 1938 (after Munich):
'. . . To accuse us of having by that advice betrayed Czechoslovakia is simply preposterous. All we did was to save her from annihilation, to give her a chance of a new life as a new state which, even although it involved the loss of territory and fortifications, perhaps she may be able to enjoy in the future and develop a national existence in a neutrality and security comparable to that which we see in Switzerland today.'

Cassandra Speaking

We are, at least, no longer susceptible to shocks over what is happening in central Europe. We feel pain and sorrow. But we do not share the perennial and amazing surprise of Mr. Chamberlain.

On February 18, 1938—that is more than a year ago now, and before the entrance of Hitler into Austria—I wrote:

'Write it down. On Saturday, February 12, 1938, Germany won the world war, and dictated in Berchtesgaden a peace treaty to make the Treaty of Versailles look like one of the great humane documents of the ages.

'Write is down. On Saturday, February 12, 1938, militarism, paganism and despotism started on the march across all of Europe east of the Rhine.

'Write it down that the world revolution began in earnest—and perhaps the world war.

'Why does Germany want Austria? For raw materials? It has none of consequence. To add to German prosperity? It inherits a poor country with serious problems. But strategically, it is the key to the whole of central Europe. Czechoslovakia is now surrounded. The wheat fields of Hungary and the oil fields of Rumania are now open. *Not one of them will be able to stand the pressure of German domination. . . .*

'It is horror walking. Not that "Germany" joins with Austria. We are not talking of "Germany." We see a new Crusade, under a pagan totem, worshiping "blood" and "soil," preaching the holiness of the sword, glorifying conquest, despising the Slavs, whom it conceives to be its historic "mission" to rule; subjecting all of life to a collectivist, militarized state. Persecuting men and women of Jewish blood, however diluted it may be. Moving, now, into the historic stronghold of Catholic Christianity, into an area of mixed races and mixed nationalities, which a thousand years of Austro-Hungarian Empire could only rule tolerably with tolerance.'

On September 21, I wrote an 'Obituary for Europe' and on October 1, following the Pact of Munich, I wrote 'Peace—And the Crisis Begins!' which was severely criticized in some quarters for its failure to rejoice over the peace. I said:

'What happened on Friday is called " Peace." Actually it is an international Fascist *coup d'état*.

'The "Four-Power Accord" is not even a diplomatic document. It is certainly not a normal treaty. It is such a fantastic piece of paper that it is difficult to describe except as a hurriedly concocted armistice made in advance of a war to permit the occupation by German troops of a territory which by sheer threat and demonstration of force they have conquered by "agreement." . . .

'*There is not the most elementary consideration of justice. . . .*

'The pressure of the Nazis in contiguous territories occupied by German troops, their immense and cunningly organized propaganda, their house-by-house and name-by-name political organizations; the ever-present threat that if the territories go German the political minorities will be exterminated, will assure the outcome of these plebiscites. *One might just as well cede them to Germany in the first place.* . . .

'Even on the basis of what by internal evidence would seem to be a rigged report [the Runciman Report], Germany is guilty of provoking what was nearly an all-European war. And the punishment for this guilt is that she received everything that she was going to fight the war over.

'*This "everything" is more than the Sudeten territories. It is more than a free hand in the east. It is the domination of Europe.* . . .

'In this whole affair, described as an attempt to keep peace, the democratic process has been completely suspended. In both Britain and France the facts have been suppressed by the exercise of government pressure on the controlled radio and on the newspapers. The people of England and France are confronted with a *fait accompli* without even being able to gain in advance possession of the facts on which it is based! . . .

'*Not only is Czechoslovakia dismembered—what is left is destroyed as a democratic republic. It will be utterly impossible for the new state to exist under the conditions created.*' . . .

On October 17, in 'The Case of Cardinal Innitzer,' the prophecy of Heine was recalled:

'It is the greatest merit of Christianity to have assuaged the joy of the German in brutal bellicosity, but . . . when, one day, the Cross of Christ is broken, the savagery of the old warriors, the wild berserker wrath, will break forth anew in all the barbaric fury of which our Nordic poets tell in song and saga. Even today the talisman of Christianity has begun to rot, and the day will come when its power will piteously collapse. Then will the old stone gods arise from the accumulated rubbish of the past. . . . When that day comes . . . take good care, Frenchmen, and do not interfere with those affairs which we are settling among ourselves. Take care neither to fan the fire nor to quench it. . . . Do not laugh at my advice . . . the advice of a dreamer. . . . German thunder is admittedly German: it is not very agile . . . but it will come one day, and . . . you will hear an explosion such as has never yet occurred in the history of the world.

'The hour will come, when, like spectators in an amphitheater, the nations will crowd around Germany to watch the great tourney.'

Chamberlain umbrellas are being advertised to wear in one's coat lapel this spring. I am not wearing this symbol. I recall what happens to umbrellas when carried in cyclones. They blow inside out and have been known to bear their carriers into the whirlwind.

I SEE BY THE PAPERS

New York Times   *March 16, 1939*

Hitler follows his troops into Prague; Czechs jeer the Nazis; New régime set up—
Czech area seized—Fists shaken at soldiers—people weep, hurl snowballs at
tanks—secret police begin hunt—curfew set.

The New Heroism

In reading the accounts of the triumphal entry of the German Army in
Prague, I noticed that one correspondent recorded that when the German
tanks were met by snowballs hurled by Czech citizens 'the soldiers red-
dened.' He added that they preserved their discipline, however, in an exem-
plary manner.

I keep wondering why the German soldiers flushed. Was it repressed anger at the failure of the 'protected' to fall upon their knees in gratitude to the
'protectors'? Was it, perhaps, annoyance that the spick-and-span tanks of a
conquering army that has never encountered a shot should be smeared by
the snowballs of the infidels? Or was it, perhaps, something else that caused
a blush to mount to the cheeks of the invaders? Did the soldiers of the German Army remember, perhaps, another army that stood at Ypres? Did thy
recall the troops that stood in the swamps at Tannenberg? Did they remember the fame of an army whose dead lie buried in rows on rows, mute re-
minders of a struggle in which Germany once, for four years, kept half the
world at bay?

The United States stood opposite Germany in that war. But when it was
over no honest person could fail to pay tribute to the heroism of German
soldiers.

But this New Heroism? What is this new sort of warrior who attacks
only when he has first undermined his opponent by treachery, confused him
by propaganda, seduced him by lies and false promises, disintegrated him
from within and disarmed him?

What manner of man is the New Hero who enters with a great apparel
of banners, armed and helmeted, accompanied by bombing planes, tanks,
machine guns, only when it is certain that he is perfectly safe and likely to
encounter only weeping women, terrified Jews and disarmed men from between whose clenched teeth come the strains of a national anthem sung
into the air to be drowned in bugles and drums?

Who is this new Superman who burns asylums over the heads of or-
phaned babies, lays brands to churches and synagogues and drives the
homeless and the destitute before his bayonets?

Let it be written down to the credit of the German Army—a German soldier blushed.

The Czechs, the reporters said, covered their faces with their hands as the German troops passed by. Was it to hide the sight of their 'conquerors'? Or was it something else that impelled the gesture? Was it the counterpart of the German soldier's blush? The face of democracy is hidden in its hands lest the world see upon it the stricken look of cowardice, the bitter look of self-disdain.

What way out of this self-disdain? Obviously, the New Heroism. For there are, amongst the Czechs, those weaker and more helpless even than they! The racial and political minorities! Therefore, turn upon them and demonstrate in the face of the German soldiers that the manly instinct is not yet dead even in the democratic heart. Thus, they hurl over the frontiers not, of course, the invading hosts but the most defenseless of their own citizenry, flinging them out of the careening sleigh to appease the howling wolves.

None escapes the New Heroism! Did not Mr. Chamberlain send Lord Runciman to scold the Czechoslovak warmongers? The British Empire demonstrated that it could use all its vast power to assist in the subjugation of that dangerous republic of fifteen million souls. Afterward the conquering hero, returning from his dangerous plane ride, had flowers strewn in his path. Thus, today, are heroes made.

Mother, you didn't raise your boy to be a soldier? That was your great mistake. You want to preserve his life? You want him to be safe, do you not? Then, by all means, bring him up to be his country's warrior, so that he may safely invade against snowballs.

Do not encourage him to remain a civilian! Above all, do not encourage him to be in any sense a non-conformist. Asleep in his bed, he may be bombed from the air! Brave in his opinions, he may be sent wandering throughout the world! Encumbered with a religion or the wrong grandmother, he may rot in a concentration camp.

But in a uniform, helmeted and armed, accompanied by a tank, or aloft in a tri-motored bombing plane, he is safe to massacre babies—we do not forget Guernica—or to take a city where his only annoyance may be the song in the snowy streets of a soon-to-be-forgotten air.

Train him, if he is a believer in democracy, to retreat in close formation crowned with laurel leaves and under umbrellas.

And if he chooses the more heroic role, to march forward over bodies prostrated before he moves.

Teach him that this is the new peace and the new chivalry of heroes of the great white Gentile race.

Busily, busily our own new conquerors are being trained. Trained by a million nasty little leaflets about the menace in our midst.

The menace is not unemployment, skulduggery, political buffoonery, racketeering in high places and low, windy platitudes to meet solid problems, greedy hands in the public purse, pressure groups of the right and pressure groups of the middle and pressure groups of the left all nicely manipulated by public-relations counsels to seek their own ends at the cost of everybody else.

The menace is not our ignorance, and fear, and disunity. Not at all.

The menace is not the agents of the new barbarism, craftily using the instruments of the legal state and the privileges of civil liberties to prepare the way for a reign of permanent violence.

The menace is some five million of our citizens who happen to have the wrong ancestors. Let us turn upon them, make life miserable for them, create a vast miasmic apprehension about them, ruin their economic existences, read them out of the professions in order that the rest of us—one hundred and twenty-odd millions—may live the life of heroes in order and security. 'They' are to blame. Not, by any calculation, we, too. Just 'they.'

It was for this, mother, that you told your little boy stories of the Father of his country who could not tell a lie. It was for this that you taught him about Valley Forge and Appomattox. It was for this that you recounted to him the story of Saint George and the Dragon, of Don John of Austria against the Turks, of Wilhelm Tell, of the Miller and Frederick the Great, of King Arthur and his Round Table. It was for this that you read him the words of John of Gaunt in 'Richard II' and the words of Brutus in 'Julius Caesar.' It was for this that we wrote the heroic words on the Plymouth Rock monument; it was for this that we battled with the wilderness:

That your child might slip out in the dark to stick a nasty poster on the clothing shop of some American villager whose father came from Poland and who has done no man harm. That with a keen, appraising eye he may heroically observe which boy in his class is the most nervous and frightened and then attack him with manly vigor.

Oh, happy, and heroic breed of men! The twentieth century salutes you. For this the world has been struggling up out of the mire for thousands and thousands of years! For this, man got up from all fours to walk, most acrobatically upright, that his head might be higher than his feet.

Sometimes, of course, in curious atavism, a rapidly disappearing physiological phenomenon, a vestige of a previous plodding race, manifests itself. The soldier blushes. But do not be alarmed. Today's blush will pass in tomorrow's plunder. Today's qualm in tomorrow's pogrom. Up and at them, heroes! Women and children first!

World War Again

H itler's invasion of Poland ob-

ligated Britain and France to declare war in September 1939. Months of in-

activity—"phony war"—followed before Germany continued its march to

take over Europe. Britain's support for France was cut short when the French

capitulated in June 1940. The rest of Europe was quickly overrun by the

German fast-moving "blitzkrieg" style of warfare. Britain endured the Ger-

man air raids and threat of invasion alone until Hitler made the mistake of

opening another front against the Soviet Union in 1941. Also in December

1941, the United States responded to the Japanese attack on Pearl Harbor by declaring war on Japan. Four days later, Hitler declared war on the United States. Because Japan was in the Axis treaty with Germany and Italy, the United States had now joined the Allies in the campaign to retake Europe and achieve the unconditional surrender of Italy and Germany as well as the defeat of Japan in the Pacific.

Described by war historian John Keegan as the "largest single event in human history," World War II exceeded all previous wars in "scale, intensity, extensiveness, and material and human cost" (*Second* 11). The war was fought by the biggest armies the world had ever seen. No one believed the war would be easily won, although initially the hope was that it would be fast-moving due to all the new war-making capacities. Instead, the war lasted for six years, becoming a war of attrition in which all sides carried out destruction on a scale never seen before.

Not only were the technological advances in warfare enormous, there was a return to pre-eighteenth-century forms of warfare such as the wholesale slaughter of civilian populations. For the first time in recent centuries, civilian deaths surpassed military losses. Mass extermination took new forms. While it soon became clear that trench warfare, the cause of millions of casualties in World War I, had been outmoded by faster, mechanized forms of fighting, these new methods led to other forms of mass killing. Wiping out the enemy's means of production and destroying civilian morale became a major strategy. Air warfare, embryonic in World War I, now became the means of leveling cities in a few hours of intensive "strategic" bombing. Intensive raids created a new phenomenon—the firestorm. Allied bombers destroyed the historic city of Dresden in one night during the last months of the war, immolating at least thirty-five thousand civilians. The populations of cities and towns were forced to be refugees or to live like troglodytes in the basements of ruined buildings. In six months of U.S. bombing, 60 percent of the major Japanese cities were destroyed; hundreds of thousands were dead. Finally, in order to ensure Japan's surrender and forestall the planned American invasion of Japan, the United States dropped its new, secret weapon, the atomic bomb, on the cities of Hiroshima and Nagasaki. Tens of thousands died in seconds; thousands died more slowly of a new, man-made illness caused by radiation.

Mass extermination came in other forms: British and Dutch prisoners starved to death by the Japanese; thousands of Polish soldiers executed by the Russians; the systematic extermination of whole populations by the Germans. Genocide, carried out during World War I by the Turks on the Armenians, returned on an even larger scale with what Nazi officials termed "the final solution." Using a sophisticated technology that could gas thousands and burn their bodies in an efficient factory assembly-line system, Hitler attempted to wipe out not only Europe's Jews but its gypsies and homosexuals.

Hitler's ruthless annexation of territory—his avowed purpose, bringing first Europe and then the rest of the world under his control—made this world war easier for his opponents to justify than the first. There was less pacifism or opposition than in the earlier war. At the same time, there were far fewer illusions at the war's outset than in 1914. The memories and war literature of World War I had done their part to convince the public of the grimness of modern war. Those who had lived through World War I saw the approach of another one as catastrophic. Virginia Woolf wondered in her diary on Monday, August 28, 1939, if the next bulletin would end peace and "everything for the next 50 years."

The size and scope of this war, along with the many changes for women brought about by World War I, meant that women's participation was far greater. In Great Britain, for example, the number of women in war work and in the armed forces doubled from the previous war. Starting in 1941, women were called up. Mollie Panter-Downes described for her American audience in the *New Yorker* how the process took place. By 1942, all women over eighteen and under sixty had been conscripted for essential work, nursing, or the armed services. "There has been a busy press campaign to assure the young women that the yellow complexion munitions workers acquired in the last war handling TNT are by no means unavoidable in this one, since science has developed a protective cream" (Panter-Downes 139). Tens of thousands of women went to work in defense plants in the United States putting up with low wages and inadequate care for their children to join the ranks of "Rosie the Riveter."

Women had far more active roles in this war than in World War I. Although not classified as combatants, women in England and the United States served in war areas, flew planes, "manned" antiaircraft guns, were dropped behind enemy lines as spies. Thousands of Russian women actually served in combat—as pilots they were given substandard planes. Russian women also traveled with their armies. Martha Gellhorn, getting her first view of the Russian army, wrote that "Russian women can go to war with their men, and it seems a reasonable idea" ("The Russians" 177).

This was to be a war where propaganda and public relations took on new importance. Changes in communications and the growth of mass media meant that thousands would be employed in convincing populations of the rightness of their cause and the nobility of sacrificing to it. "Morale" became an obsession. Generals had their public relations staff, and writers hired by their governments performed under heavy restrictions on what they could say. Elizabeth Bowen, like many British writers, worked for the War Ministry. Her accounts of the bombing of London and the preparations for the expected invasion by Germany stress the pluck and resourcefulness of the public; blood and death are noticeably absent.

Dorothy Thompson joined a group of eminent American commentators making regular broadcasts to Germany. Addressing her listeners as "Hans," she told of how the Hitler regime made war against its own people and urged the Germans to ask for peace. She exposed practices that were probably kept from Hitler's subjects, such as the camps in Poland where young soldiers were mated to Polish girls to produce "racially improved" offspring.

Colette made radio broadcasts from Paris until the German occupation. Describing to an American audience how the women in Paris had decorated their obligatory gas mask cases to reflect their personal tastes, she went on to say "that their double solitude—the departure of their husbands and the evacuation of their children—has found these women armed with a dazzling courage" (428). American Janet Flanner, using the name Genet, kept up her letter from Paris to the *New Yorker* throughout the entire occupation. Gertrude Stein made a triumphant radio address to the American people when the war in Europe ended. In *Wars I Have Seen*, she described how difficult it was to be cut off from her native land for the war years.

With changes in transportation, women visited the far-flung fronts in World War II in ways that were never possible before. The wives of leaders were expected to raise the morale of the men. One of these was Eleanor Roosevelt, the wife of America's president. In 1943, on a tour of seventeen Pacific islands, New Zealand, and Australia, she saw an estimated four hundred thousand men in camps and hospitals. Observers reported on the time she took, her unflagging interest in each soldier's situation, and her exhaustion on returning to the United States, which didn't stop her from a radio broadcast expressing her admiration for the men, ending characteristically with instructions for tolerance.

Another relatively new aspect of this war was the use of entertainers, many of whom were women. British singer and comedian Joyce Grenfell was one of these, writing about her experiences in *The Time of My Life: Entertaining the Troops, Her Wartime Journals*. She spoke of the difficulties: "This hospital business demands a hell of a lot. One must be on one's toes, unselfed—and how . . . it is always worth giving everything one's got because there are always some it reaches and that justifies the effort" (22). A month later she wrote: "Oh God, the sights I've seen today. We haven't touched the war till today. Bed after bed filled with mutilated men, heads, faces, bodies. It's the most inhuman, ghastly, bloody, hellish thing in the world. I couldn't think or work or even feel in the end" (65).

Although women acting as spies were known in World War I, "Mata Hari" being a famous example, the resistance activities of women, still largely undocumented, greatly increased in World War II. In France, Holland, Denmark, and the other occupied countries, with many of the men transported to Germany for forced labor, women carried out sabotage and other guerrilla actions, risking and often enduring torture, imprisonment, and execution. Women were often sent on the most dangerous missions because they would be less suspect than men.

War Around the World

For some, World War II had started years earlier. The Japanese invaded China in 1931, appropriating Manchuria and continuing the war there until they surrendered to the United States in 1945. Chinese author Ding Ling described the effects of this invasion. The grandmother who is the heroine of the story "New Faith," having undergone horrors that are only beginning to be guessed at in Europe, overcomes their effects by becoming a political leader in the Communist Party, giving speeches to larger and larger crowds and urging them to join the fight against the Japanese.

The Russian poet Anna Akhmatova, already being persecuted by Stalin's regime, wrote in 1941 about the beginning of the siege of Leningrad, a two-year ordeal, which she lived through. Over two hundred thousand of the city's citizens died of cold and starvation before the Germans finally retreated. Akhmatova's poem personalizes the effects of long-range shells coming "casually . . . to murder my child."

By 1942, with threats of Hitler's invasion of England over, the war was still not going well in many parts of the world. Vera Brittain wrote in her journal:

> What a New Year's Day! More countries at war than ever before in the world's history. Hong Kong gone, Sarawak going. Penang gone; war surging into Malaysia; Rangoon and Singapore bombed. Manila burning and the Americans fighting a hopelessly out numbered battle in the Philippines. But in Russia the Nazis are still retreating—and in Libya. A year ago this country faced the Axis alone; now we have the United States, Russia and China as allies. By next year, what? (*Wartime Chronicle* 117)

Olivia Manning had the chance to see the war in far-flung places, moving ahead of it through the Balkans and the Middle East, working as an interpreter. She observed the defeats and successes of the Allied armies and wrote about them in her Balkan and Levant trilogies. Weaving the lives of her assorted characters into a large canvas of war, she follows some of them into combat—in this selection from *The Danger Tree*, Simon Boulderstone, a young British officer, encounters a painful experience of loss in the African desert.

The narrator of Elizabeth Bowen's story "Oh, Madam . . ." epitomizes the grit and endurance of ordinary London citizens. In this case, the housekeeper is showing the owner through her bomb-damaged house, unaware of the irony in the fact that the wealthy owner missed the bombing while the servant risked her life to save her employer's house. In a postscript to *The Demon Lover*, the collected edition that contained this story, Bowen said she had not described the actions of war. Instead, "[t]hese are . . . studies of climate, war-climate, and of the strange growths it raised. I see war (or should I say feel war) more as a territory than as a page of history." Her description could stand for much of women's war writing.

Women's War Diaries

Many women's diaries had come out of World War I; there were many more from World War II, often kept under extraordinary circumstances. Possibly the most famous is the diary of a thirteen-year-old Jewish girl in hiding in Amsterdam, restored to her father after the war and her death from typhus in the Bergen-Belsen concentration camp. Anne Frank wanted to be a writer and had begun to fictionalize her account in "Tales from the Secret Annex." The drama of the Frank family's situation, the unfolding of Anne's personality in this most moving of coming-of-age stories, the emotions generated in the reader by the knowledge that this gifted girl will not survive, combine to produce a classic that has been read by generations, performed in play and film versions, and has personified the tragedies of millions caught up and destroyed in the Holocaust.

Memoirs, diaries, and letters recorded the days of the London Blitz. Londoners who stayed, plunged into war work with a certain amount of zest: it was better to be doing something than waiting passively for the bombs to fall. Novelist and poet Rose Macaulay, who had recorded her experiences in World War I, wrote to her sister about one of her nights at an ambulance station: "I attended an incident in Camden Town—two fallen houses, a great pile of ruins, with all the inhabitants buried deep. . . . I drove to hospital another mother, who had left two small children under the ruins. I told her they would be out soon—but they never were, they were killed" (*Letters* 114). Like so many, Macaulay lost the possessions of her lifetime when her own flat was destroyed.

Winifred Ellerman (Bryher) found war in London more tedious than frightening, especially after helping smuggle German Jews into Switzerland. This passage from her book, *The Days of Mars: A Memoir, 1940–1946*, celebrates the role art played in the years of the Blitz. The event at which Bryher's companion, the American poet Hilda Doolittle (H.D.), read her poem represented an oasis of civilization during the privations of the war—privations that were made worse according to Bryher by the British bureaucracy. Poets Osbert and Edith Sitwell organized the reading, which included T. S. Eliot and John Masefield with the queen and the two princesses in attendance.

H.D. had lived in London during World War I and had anticipated the coming of the next war in her analysis with Freud. With the bombing of London, she glimpsed the apocalypse and found herself strong enough to endure. The poem she wrote for the reading, "Ancient Wisdom Speaks," uses timeless religious imagery to "remember these" who in the midst of "earthquake . . . did not forget beauty."

Mary Lee Settle left the United States for London in the fall of 1942 to join the Women's Auxiliary Air Force (WAAF). In Washington that summer she had seen the British film *Mrs. Miniver*, based on Jan Struther's popular book, and attended a reception for the Russian woman sniper who "was said to have killed five hundred Germans." The atmosphere of war was too strong for her to wait until the United States had its own services for women. Settle tells in her memoir *All the Brave Promises* how the uneducated, unhealthy working-class girls she was with were transformed with decent living conditions and strenuous training until "they had begun to fill out and glow." War was affecting the class system in ways that would profoundly change the future for women as well as men.

Japanese military successes in the Pacific war caused terrible hardships for British and American women who were made prisoners with their families, often separated from their husbands who were living and dying under even worse conditions. American Elizabeth Vaughan was one of these. Caught in the Philippines with her two small children when the Japanese invaded, she began her diary as a record for her husband who had been captured in Bataan. He was to die, a victim of the notorious Bataan Death March, although she did not learn this until after these passages were written.

Iris Origo, an Anglo-American married to an Italian aristocrat, kept a diary through the tumultuous period in which Italy was undergoing both the Allied invasion and the civil war between the fascists supporting Hitler and the partisans trying to restore a free Italy. For a time, Origo hid the diary among her children's picture books; later, when things got worse, she buried it in the garden with her jewelry. Responsible for the fifty tenant families of their Tuscan estate, La Foce, as well as for their own children and twenty-three refugee children, Origo describes the march she and her husband led when the fighting forced them to temporarily evacuate.

Diaries add important historical knowledge to what was happening in Germany during the war years when tight censorship kept Germany cut off from the outside world. Fey von Hassell began to write in 1945 to keep from thinking about her two infant sons, who had been abducted as punishment for her father's part in the plot against Hitler under Hitler's "root and branch" policy of destroying the entire family of anyone accused of treason. The diary becomes not only the story of her survival in a series of concentration camps but of how the two small boys were finally located in an orphanage. When von Hassell rewrote her diary for publication in her seventies, she remarked how the events seemed to have occurred "only yesterday." Wartime memories survive almost intact over long stretches of time. Frau von Moltke, being interviewed almost fifty years after her husband's execution for allegedly taking part in the plot against Hitler, told the interviewer: "When you talk with me . . . you understand that one lives a whole lifetime from such an experience" (qtd. in Owings 265). Marie Vassiltchikov, a young White Russian princess, found herself working for one of the leaders of the conspiracy against Hitler, Adam von Trott. Information had to be disguised or suppressed—Vassiltchikov kept notes in an invented shorthand on scraps of paper, hidden in various official files. Not published until 1985, her *Berlin Diaries, 1940–1945* is an extraordinary record of the last days of the Nazi regime while Allied bombs were destroying the city.

Also close to the conspiracy was Christabel Bielenberg, an English woman who became a German citizen in 1934 when she married a German lawyer. She did not write her memoir until 1968, reconstructing from diary notes an account of her years in Germany from 1932 to 1945. The account was originally intended to explain the history of the failed assassination attempt for her own children and some of the children whose parents had been executed. This excerpt gives an insider's view of the German Reich in its final stages and shows a woman's success in not only protecting her children but helping her husband escape.

The Unthinkable

The experience of the German death camps produced a new genre of literature, still being written today. Inmates kept diaries even under the most horrendous of conditions. Survivors wrote their stories in memoirs, poems, and fiction. Contemporary writers such as Cynthia Ozick have used their literary skills to effectively imagine the Holocaust using the techniques of magic realism.

Women's camp experiences differed somewhat from men's. Jewish women of childbearing age were especially targeted for annihilation, and there are indications that more women died than men. Women were separated from the men on arrival, often sexually abused, and endured devastating violations of privacy such as the shaving by guards of all body hair prior to the tattooing of camp numbers on their arms. Some Holocaust scholars have suggested that women actually coped better than men, forming "families" even as their own were destroyed or separated from them—sharing food and celebrating holidays.

Etty Hillesum wrote her famous letters from Westerbork concentration camp, the last stop in Holland for more than one hundred thousand Dutch Jews who were sent on to Auschwitz for extermination. An intellectual who was employed by the Jewish Council, Hillesum could have avoided Westerbork, but she wanted to care for her aged parents as long as possible. A little more than two months after this letter, she threw a card addressed to a friend out of the window of the train that was taking her with her parents and brother to their deaths at Auschwitz.

Polish writer and journalist Sara Nomberg-Przytyk survived Auschwitz. Her story "Friendly Meetings" suggests the human capacity for finding humor even in horrific situations. Much of the literature of World War II contained black comedy, a way that writers such as Kurt Vonnegut and Joseph Heller could suggest the war's absurdities. About this incident Nomberg-Przytyk writes, however, that even in "a grotesque land" some things cannot be gotten used to.

Charlotte Delbo, a French woman, came to Auschwitz because of her part in the Resistance—she too survived but spent much of the remainder of her life trying to express the meaning of her experiences. She used the term "unthinkable" (*l'inconcevable*) and also "[e]xplain the inexplicable" for what she was attempting. Forty years afterwards, the memory of Auschwitz had not changed like normal memories, Delbo wrote, it remained intact, existing alongside everything she did.

Italian writer Elsa Morante tells in *History: A Novel* of the desperate attempts of a mother with Jewish ancestry to protect her young son when the Italian government agrees to carry out Hitler's orders and round up the Jews in Rome. Raising her son, the result of her rape by a German soldier, has become the mother's sole reason for surviving. In her intermingling of history and fiction, Morante was another writer trying to suggest the almost surreal quality of the situation in Italy towards the end of the war.

An American form of "camp" literature came out of the internment of thousands of Japanese-Americans in California. Today, the policy is recognized as unfortunate and unnecessary, and those victims who are still alive are receiving some form of compensation from the U.S. government. Internment was a bewildering and often shattering experience for families, particularly for the children, who felt themselves to be as American as their former schoolmates and whose older male relatives fought and died at a high rate for the country that was interning them. Mitsuye Yamada, born in Japan, was in her twenties when she was moved from Seattle with her parents to an internment camp in Iowa. She began to write these poems while there. The experiences underlie much of what she works on today.

The atrocities of World War II are still emerging. In Japan, the truth about the thousands of Japanese and Korean "comfort" women, who were forced to sexually service the military, has only recently been revealed. The Nazis were not alone in carrying out medical experiments on humans as this story "Blind Chinese Soldiers" by Japanese writer Hirabayashi Taiko indicates. It points out how the miseries of life in wartime Japan made the people almost immune to the fate of others.

Survivors of the atom bombs dropped on Hiroshima and Nagasaki also produced another literature of the "unthinkable." Ordinary citizens with no writing experience, survivors such as Kikue Tada, were encouraged to tell their stories to peace groups in Japan who were determined to prevent any further use of nuclear weapons. Again, women, since many of the men were away fighting, had a greater burden in trying to establish some sort of normalcy for those who survived. Later, their burden was increased by the chances of giving birth to damaged children or living with the uncertainty of the longterm effects of exposure to radiation.

Victory, Occupation, and After

For civilians, there was even less of a clear ending for World War II than there had been for World War I. The final stage of the war was a race between the Soviet Union and the Western Allies to occupy as much territory as possible. Advancing armies leveled cities and towns, raped, looted, and created millions of refugees. Artist Käthe Kollwitz, old and frail in eastern Germany, forbidden to practice or show her work by the Nazi government, her Berlin house destroyed, and mourning her grandson Peter's death as she had his namesake's in World War I, wrote to her daughter-in-law, "In days to come people will hardly understand this age. It must have been like this after the Thirty Years' War. . . . Germany's cities have become rubble heaps and . . . every war already carries within it the war that will answer it."

For members of the Resistance such as Marguerite Duras in France, the war was not over when France was liberated; she took part in the hunting down of those guilty of collaboration with the Germans. Of her story "Albert of the Capitals" in *The War: A Memoir*, abandoned for many years, Duras said in her introduction: "The person who tortures the informer is me. . . . Me. I give you the torturer along with the rest of the texts. Learn to read them properly: they are sacred" (115).

The wife in Doris Lessing's novel *Landlocked* from the series *Children of Violence* is hoping to get her invalid husband, a wounded veteran of World War I, to the victory celebration in her Southern Rhodesian town. In her frustration, she lashes out at the only victim she has—her black servant. Lessing, whose parents met in World War I when her mother nursed her father, saw the war from a colonial perspective, before moving to England at the war's end. Much of her long career as a writer has been an exploration of the effects of twentieth century violence on individuals and their societies.

Kathryn Hulme describes the gigantic relief efforts to house and feed the thousands of refugees. Her book *The Wild Place*, based on personal experience, is a tribute to the endless resilience and stubbornness of Europe's population of displaced persons and to the heroism of those who took on the task of helping them. The relief workers Hulme describes performed miracles in administering aid to thousands in almost impossible situations. At the same time they had to fight the military red tape, which hindered their efforts in every direction.

Kay Boyle's story is one of a series she wrote about Americans occupying Germany, an experience she and her family shared. The stories explore many aspects of the uneasy relationship between conqueror and the conquered. The United States could not retreat from its world role after this war as it had after the last. For better or for worse, it was now dominating a good part of the world. The mother in "Fife's House" watches almost helplessly as the roles of winner and loser are enacted by her own child and a German boy.

Gwendolyn Brooks's sonnet series "Gay Chaps at the Bar" is dedicated to her brother and begins with an actual phrase from a soldier's letter. In the poems, the collective voices of the soldiers express the difficulties of adjustment to civilian life made worse because these black veterans, after suffering segregation and discrimination in the armed forces, now had to return to them in the United States. The final stanza of Brooks's poem suggests unending war or at least preparation for it—a prophetic note for the years ahead.

War Around the World

Ding Ling

from "New Faith"

3

The north wind, swirling the silent snow, swept mercilessly across the plains and the hills on a rampage. Excruciating, bitter cold and the ravening darkness ruled the universe of night. Walls and roofs were scarce in this land laid waste. People huddled together like dogs. And the dogs curled up in the ruins, tails between their legs, so worn down that even when they saw something move, they'd just close their eyes again.

Chen Xinhan's family had spent most of the night in a fervor of hope. Now only Jingu was still on her feet, feeding the fire, adding more water to the steaming wok. Again and again she asked, "Second Uncle, do you think Granny will come back?"

"No, no. Not on a night this cold. Even if they found her, Third Uncle wouldn't let her come now." Chen Zuohan reclined on the *kang* smoking. "Go to sleep, child."

"Not unless you do. Look how soundly Mommy's sleeping."

"Mmm. The ordeal's worn her out."

Jingu, however, ignored his sympathetic remark. She questioned him on and on about what was going on in the village. She also talked to him about her grandmother. They both hoped she wouldn't come back that night because it was so cold.

Then they thought they could hear cries and moans mingled with the howling of the wind. Jingu was frozen with terror, looking at her uncle and holding up her hand as if to say, don't move! Listen! Her uncle held his breath and listened closely, for nothing could be seen in the darkness outside. Even her father, half asleep on the *kang*, sat up. But there was nothing there. Still they waited in the dim lamplight until the sky turned as gray as a fish's belly and they were certain that their hopes would have to be postponed for another day. Soon it was just as silent inside as out.

A bleak day dawned. The endless blackness turned slowly to pale gray, and from the remote sky snowflakes came raining down thick and fast, whirling ever downward. No birds sang. No cocks crowed. Even the dogs did not bark. The snow covered the destruction, the tattered mess; frozen, the ordure, animal bones, and feathers all became invisible. The entire blood-soaked land disappeared under the frozen snow. The only things left were black words on a white wall: "Extirpate Communism! Support the Greater East Asia Co-Prosperity Sphere!" written over the scrubbed out, faded inscription "Drive Japanese Imperialism out of China!" Now the darker words were being disfigured too, by rivulets of melting snow running like snot and tears down a weeping face.

There was only one living thing moving about on the plain. Then it too collapsed. Covered with snow, had it not begun instinctively to crawl forward again, it would have been impossible to spot. Gradually this living thing moved into the village. It was human. But no one was around in the village, and so the figure fell on the roadside again. It struggled up once more to drive off a curious dog. Weakly it waved its arms, tried to straighten its bent back. Fearfully, listing, it staggered toward a familiar house. The dog no longer recognized this human being. Listless, yet unwilling to leave it, the dog tailed it. A simple desire had brought the thing to Chen Xinhan's yard, but once there it lay immobile, like a broken tile, on the ground. Two greedy yellow eyes gazed down; it was too weak to drive the dog away again, too weak even to cry out. It could only moan and close its dry and withered eyes. Another dog came through a hole in the courtyard wall and barked twice. The first dog leaped forward, barking back. The body on the ground groaned again.

"Father!" cried newly awakened Jingu. "I hear something outside!"

"Dogfight."

"I hate that disgusting noise. I'll go chase them off."

Jingu slipped off the *kang* and picked up a lump of coal. Both dogs barked menacingly at her as she stepped through the doorway. She threw the coal at them and they ran off barking.

"She can't even leave the dogs alone," grumbled her mother under the quilt.

"Second Uncle! Hey, there's something in the yard!"

The girl stepped closer as the dogs barked furiously. Jingu drove them off then kicked at the body. It opened its eyes a little and moaned. Then Jingu uttered a horrified, inhuman shriek like a bamboo rent in two.

Following a lot of frantic activity, the body, now dressed in dry cotton-padded garments, lay unconscious on the warm *kang*. Strands of wispy hair glued onto the sockets of her empty, sunken eyes. Second Sister-in-law fed her hot rice gruel. Jingu threw herself down next to her mommy's feet and wept. The baby, who didn't recognize the granny who'd always carried him around and kissed him all the time, sat in a corner of the *kang* afraid to make a sound. Chen Xinhan had already gone for a doctor. His wife was sobbing uncontrollably as she thought of her vanished daughter. She wanted her back!

"Ma, do you recognize us now?" Chen Zuohan asked repeatedly. But the old woman could not give him a satisfactory answer. She couldn't even gesture to him.

He watched her protectively, her terribly aged face, two dead, fishlike eyes inlaid in a piece of burnt wood. His hatred fanned into a great flame. "Ma." He directed each deliberate syllable toward that wooden face. "Ma! You can die in peace now. Your son will give his life to revenge you. I live on now only for Jap blood! I'll give my life for you, this village, Shanxi Province, the nation of China! I want Japanese blood so I can cleanse and fertilize our land. I want Jap blood!"

Like the intoned chant at an exorcism, his spell brought her slowly back to life. The old woman on the *kang* moved. Her lips quivered. "Japs!" she cried a moment later in mortal terror. She'd recovered consciousness. She looked speechlessly at her daughters-in-law and grandchildren, as tears streamed from her eyes; then, like a duck with its throat cut, wings flapping convulsively, neck writhing, she bent her head down and sobbed like a child.

"Granny! Granny! Granny!" The room was suffused with sorrow, to be sure. Yet new buds of warmth and hope had also begun to flower.

4

The strength of her desire to live quickly restored the old woman's health. A few days later she was sitting in the yard sunning herself, surrounded by the other women in the family. She was telling a story.

"Oh, that girl screamed and yelled, pounding her legs like the sticks on a big drum, her pale white belly writhing . . ."

"Don't, Granny, don't. I'm scared!" Jingu hid her face in her hands.

"Three Japs climbed on her at the same time." She seemed to enjoy intimidating her granddaughter. "She couldn't even scream anymore; her face turned purple . . . Unh . . . unh . . . unh . . . she moaned like a cow. Even childbirth isn't as painful as that. She looked at me, so I told her, 'Bite your tongue off. Bite! Hard!' I figured she'd be better off dead."

"Oh, Granny, Granny!" The women's faces blanched.

"She died too. But not from biting off her tongue," the old woman continued smugly. "Her naked carcass lay in a big pool of blood; more than if she'd had a baby. Her chest was all bloody too, blood running down her midriff, down her shoulders. They'd chewed off her little nipples." With demonic eyes she stared like a witch at her granddaughter's face. "Nipples no bigger than yours! Her sweet little face was all chewed up as well, like a maggoty apple. And she still kept looking at me with those big round eyes."

The old lady had changed. Didn't she love her own family anymore? Why was she always terrorizing them? When they sighed or cried, she'd become incensed and shout, "Go right ahead, cry your eyes out! Nothing but a pot of worthless piss. Just wait. The Japs will be back . . ." And if she saw their faces blaze red with anger, she'd feel quite satisfied at the fire she'd started.

At first she'd stop telling her stories when she saw her sons. She was afraid of their searching glances, and besides, the personal shame and sorrow she felt kept her from going on when they were around. She described how her other granddaughter had died. The thirteen-year-old child had served as a "comfort girl." Half dead of terror from being crushed under the heavy soldiers' bodies, she kept screaming for her mommy and grandma. She only "comforted" two soldiers before they threw her into a corner. She lived a day longer, tears visible on her ashen face. Just before the old lady was sent to the "Home of Respect for the Aged," they dragged Yingu off, still alive. Her grandmother said that they probably threw her to the dogs alive.

She'd also witnessed Tongguan's death. She described it in detail without a thought to the unbearable grief it would cause her daughter-in-law. She said Tongguan was a good child because he wouldn't obey them. He kept on even with a bayonet pointed at him; when he tried to get away, the Jap skewered him and even then he didn't cry. He died well.

She'd seen too much. In the last ten days, she'd seen more evil than she'd witnessed before in her whole life. When the neighbors came to ask about their relatives she would tell them truthfully how their parents, wives, and children had been sacrificed under the butcher's knife and how, while alive, they had suffered endless pain.

The old lady had never been much of a talker, but now, seeing the effect her stories had, she felt a lot more comfortable. She got sympathy and understanding from telling stories, and it made her realize that other people shared the hatred she felt. For that reason, she just forgot to be timid. At first she tended to stutter and hesitate, and then she'd cry. But by watching her listeners' faces, she'd learned how to phrase her tales most effectively.

She told them about her own humiliations too, about what she'd had to do at the "Home." She'd washed their clothes, stitched their little Japanese flags, endured their whippings. Whenever she reached that point, she'd pull back her sleeves and unbutton her collar to show where her scars were. She'd also had to sleep with a man. An old Chinese man had been forced to do it to her while the Japs all stood around watching. "Please don't hate me," the old man had sobbed, as his tears fell on her face.

She began touring the entire village, crowds following behind her, pointing out all the places where specific atrocities had taken place.

"You're not going to forget this now, are you?" she'd shout at them belligerently.

Soon she was doing this every day, and if there was only a handful of people out in the street, she'd burst into somebody's house and, gesticulating wildly, harangue them there. Her listeners invariably forgot what they were supposed to be doing and, caught up by her emotions, would begin talking. The whole village knew her, particularly the children, who called on her frequently.

Her sons and daughters-in-law talked the situation over. "We've got a maniac in the family!" The eldest daughter-in-law was always the first to speak up. "Why, she isn't eating, and doesn't take care of her hair. Now she just won't stay home!"

"Granny sure has changed. When she talks about Tongguan and Yingu, she doesn't shed a single tear. I really don't understand what's going on in her mind." The second daughter-in-law peeked at her husband. Lost in thought, he only frowned.

Chen Xinhan was thinking about the day before, when he'd gone over to listen to the old woman as she preached her stories in front of a crowd. When she got to the parts about what had happened to her personally, Xinhan had felt as though he were the one losing his mind. A son's blood coursed through his body, yet he didn't know whether to shout or go over and hug his mother or just run away. He shuddered violently, speechless all of a sudden, just as his mother caught sight of him and stopped telling her story to stare at him numbly. The audience turned around, but nobody laughed. He felt more misery than he'd ever experienced before. He walked over to her, put out his hand, and said, "I promise I'll get revenge!" Her face split with joy and she reached toward him as well, then suddenly shrank away. She shriveled up like a cornered animal, slipped through the crowd, and ran away. No one spoke. Heads bowed as though heavily weighted, people in the crowd moved away slowly, with dragging steps. He alone remained in the deserted street. He felt empty and, at the same time, as though he were being choked.

"The way I see it," Eldest Daughter-in-law started up again angrily, "the whole family's gone crazy. Why don't you say something to her? All this going on, and you act as if you're above it all."

"Say something? What do you want me to say? I know what she's suffering."

"So who isn't suffering?"

Chen Xinhan did not want to prolong this conversation. He did not want to quarrel with his mother just for the sake of argument. He looked at his brother.

His brother agreed with him. He asked the women if he should get a rope and tie the old lady up to keep her from going out. He said he thought that everything would be all right so long as Jingu went along to keep an eye on her and stop her from offending anybody.

5

When her third son, Chen Lihan—her youngest and best loved—got back, he stroked his mother's white hair and stammered, "I apologize, Ma. You wouldn't have fallen into Jap hands if I'd been home that day. But you can't always have things your own way once you join the army."

"And what good would you be to me if you hadn't enlisted?" She looked her son over. He was a young man of twenty or so, wearing a short jacket, a pistol strapped to his waist. The sight of him seemed to satisfy her. "It's a world of guns now, Sanguan. Just tell me, how many Japs have you killed?"

She didn't need to complain to him about how she'd suffered, because he didn't need to be told. She vastly preferred listening to stories about fighting the Japanese, feeling more comfort from that.

"Well," her son said, "since you are not afraid of hearing about such things, I'll tell you."

Chen Lihan's face lit up immediately. He stood straight and tall and launched into his story: how they'd counterattacked and occupied this village, Xiliu, killing more than twenty Japs, and then moved on to retake Dongliu Village and Li Village; how they'd breached the Jap line at Sanyang Village, had had to retreat, but now held it once again. It was impossible to remember for sure how many Japs they'd killed. They had captured a lot of war materiel, including rifles, bullets, and rations. He went on to say that among his group of men was the famous hero Zhang Dachuan, who'd gone to town on his own, with a light machine gun hidden under his jacket. There were too many Jap soldiers around, so he didn't use it there. But later, on his way out of town, he'd run into a dozen of the bastards, all just begging to die; so he'd shot the hell out of them. Chen Lihan also told about the time they'd caught a Jap soldier and how he and a bunch of the locals were carrying him between them on a pole. But this Jap was really fat. Somehow he'd gotten away from them along the way, and even with half a dozen of them trailing him, they never did get him back.

The old lady stuffed herself full of these stories and couldn't wait to find someone to retell them to. She'd gotten even more uninhibited lately because her oldest son, a member of the farmer's co-op, was off buying seed for the spring planting. Her second son had been drafted, and her third was gone four nights out of five. Besides, she wasn't the least bit afraid of her third son. So one night when she saw two big trucks parked in the courtyard, she asked Chen Lihan, "Are they our trucks?"

"Yeah, they're ours. They're our transport trucks."

"Well, I don't care what they haul, even if it's pigs or dogs. So long as they're ours, I know what I'm going to do with them. Tomorrow I'm going to Wangjia Village."

They all turned and stared at her.

"What do you mean there's no room on them, that they're for hauling food?" She cut their objections short. "I don't care, I'm going. I want to see my brother and sister-in-law."

So the next day, she and Jingu rode a grain transport truck to Wangjia Village. She found her brother and his wife and told them all about the atrocities. Again she watched the falling tears, the belligerence that listening to her stories evoked in people. Then to soothe their wounded spirits, she acted out all the exciting, hortatory stories she'd just heard from her son, adding her own flourishes and making people smile again. She used the moment to urge everyone there to join the guerrillas.

"You cowards!" she bawled, seeing them hesitate. "Afraid to die! Well, just wait 'til the Japs get here and butcher you all. I've seen them wipe out lots of powder puffs, just like you!"

Actually, many who heard her stories did join the guerrillas. Sometimes she'd lead a small group back home and hand them over to her son. "Take them," she'd say. "They all want to be like you. They all want guns."

After getting back from Wangjia, it was even harder for her to sit quietly at home, or even, for that matter, in Xiliu Village. So, taking Jingu along with her, she went to other villages. When there was no ride handy, she walked. "Why don't you talk too," she'd shout at Jingu.

Jingu was among the first to stand up for her grandma. She loved her and basked in the daily devotion she got from her. Each time Granny hustled her off on another trip, Jingu would gaze at her raptly in total understanding. Then Granny would embrace her, hugging her tightly, and heave a sigh of relief. It made Jingu feel warm inside again, but it was a happiness mixed with pain. Truth be told, Jingu was her grandmother's biggest supporter. Any time she talked privately with people, she'd use, with some embarrassment, phrases she'd picked up from her grandmother.

The love the old woman felt for her sons had also altered. Earlier, a great deal earlier, actually, she had thought of them as obedient little kittens. Later on, she'd only been concerned that they hurry up and grow into adults. She longed for the time when they'd be able to take over some of her burdens, things pressing down on her from society and in the family. Her sons grew up strong as bears and alert as eagles, but they never paid any attention to her. Her only recourse was to love them in silence, sadly, fearful of losing them. Later still, when they reached full maturity and things grew more difficult, her nature hardened. Since they obviously had no consideration for her at all, she hated them sometimes. Yet she became even more dependent upon their love, and that weakened her. Her fear of them had increased because all it took was a sign, a word, the sight of them, to dissolve her heart. But now she'd lost that fear. It no longer was crucial to her how they regarded her; their feelings were just not that important anymore. But didn't she love them now? Did she despise them? No, not a bit. She just saw them from a heightened perspective. When her sons talked to her about fighting Japs, she actually felt her love rekindle and was intensely pleased that the hardships she'd suffered rearing them had been worthwhile.

Slowly her daughters-in-law also stopped looking at her askance. Painful recollections and hopes for the future brought the women closer each day, harmonizing their relationships. When the women were alone, they always returned to the same topic of conversation. The frequent bickering that had afflicted the family before disappeared now, replaced by a new love founded on a common idea. The family found a closeness and unity it had never known before. And none of them ever realized that it was all the doing of the old lady.

6

The sons came home with unusual news. Some people wanted to talk to her. More than likely it was because of her conduct. Little Jingu held her Granny's hand tightly as her Granny reassured her.

"Don't be scared, Granddaughter. Who could treat me worse than the Japs already did? I've taken the worst a body could. If I'm not even afraid of Hell anymore, what's there to be afraid of?"

"What the hell business is it of theirs?" Eldest Daughter-in-law said angrily. "Do you mean we can't even talk? No one ever said 'Chinese are lousy; Japs are great.' Shoot! They can take it and shove it!"

But why did they want to see her? Her son couldn't say for sure. All he said was that someone had come from the Association looking for him, asking if she were his mother and what their address was, but that's all anyone knew about it. He wasn't real clear on what was going on, but he was pretty sure it was nothing to worry about.

The news made them rather uneasy. No stranger had ever come to call on her in her entire life. But she didn't lose any sleep over it that night. She really didn't care much about that sort of thing anymore.

The next day two women came over, one wearing a short jacket like the old woman's, the other, hair bobbed, in a uniform. They were both quite young. Without even a nod to conventional politeness, the old woman asked them in. They spoke first.

"Well, Mother," one of them addressed her in terms of special respect, "you may not know me, but I've known you for a long time. Twice I've heard you giving speeches."

"Speech." She didn't understand the word "speech" and just grunted glumly.

"When I heard you speak, really, I couldn't help crying. Mother, since the Japs got hold of you, you must have seen everything you talk about with your own eyes, right?"

Her expression got friendlier. She thought, "Aha! They've finally come for news." And she began talking in an unending flood of words. They listened patiently to the greater part of the story. "Oh yes, Mother, we're with you on everything," they said when they were able to get a word in edgewise. "We too hate Japs with everything we've got. We try like mad to get people to join up and avenge the Chinese people, but we simply can't speak the way you can. Join our Association, Mother. Our Association tries to tell people these things in order to strike a blow against the Japs . . . "

"Jingu." Without waiting for them to finish, the old lady called her granddaughter, "Jingu, they've come to invite us to join their 'Association.' What do you say to that?" Without waiting for Jingu's reply, she turned back to her visitors. "I don't understand all that stuff," she said. "If you want me, I'll join. I'm not afraid you're just playing tricks on me, either. Two of my three sons joined the guerrillas and the other's in the Peasant Association. So it's all right if I join an association too. I won't lose anything by it, no matter what. Only if I join, my granddaughter has to join too."

They gave Jingu an enthusiastic welcome on the spot and offered the same to the two daughters-in-law.

The Women's Association expanded its membership rapidly after the old woman joined it. She went around every day recruiting, and once the women learned she was a member herself, they all wanted in. And so the women began to do quite a lot of work. Because of this, the old lady felt happier and seemed younger physically and in spirit. One day they decided to hold a big meeting in honor of the victories won by the guerrillas during the last three months. The meeting would take place at the same time as the celebration of International Women's Day on the eighth of March, and women's groups from nearby villages were invited to participate.

On the day of the rally, the old lady led several dozen women from Xiliu Village. Some carried their children; others led them by the hand. But they had not gathered to chat about children. They talked about their work responsibilities. A large number whose feet were bound had walked all the way, only barely aware of their pain and fatigue.

Quite a few had already arrived at the meeting place. The old woman's sons had come too, and many of her acquaintances waved to her from here and there. Gradually all the attention gave her a new feeling, a kind of uneasiness. It resembled shyness but was, in fact, the pride of accomplishment. After a little while, she felt calm again.

Slowly the crowd swelled. To the old woman it looked like a wave rolling in, and she was filled with happiness. So! They've got this many people!

The meeting began. Someone was speaking from the platform. The old woman listened raptly. It seemed to her that the speaker didn't waste a word. Who, listening to this speech, would not be moved by it? How could anyone listening fall to be concerned about the nation? Then they wanted her up on the platform.

When she heard their invitation, she was seized with unspeakable shyness and embarrassment. But her courage returned at once, and tottering a little, she walked to the podium on a wave of applause. Standing on high gazing downward, all she could see was a great mass of densely packed heads stretching out as far as the distant village wall, each with a face looking up at her. She felt rather stunned and giddy: What should I say, she thought. So she began by talking about herself.

"I am an old woman who was molested by the Japanese Imperialist troops. Look, all of you . . . " And she rolled up her sleeves to show her scars. "What are you scared of?" she said, hearing a murmur of sympathy from below. "This? This is nothing . . . " Then she described the circumstances of her humiliation in plain, cold language, not trying to save her own face or hide her pain or spare their sensitivities. Her gaze roamed over their faces. They looked miserable! So she shouted, "Don't pity me! You should really pity yourselves! And protect yourselves! Today you think that I am the only one to be pitied. But, today, if you don't rise up, stand up to the Japs . . . Ha! Heaven! I really don't want to see you suffer the way I did . . . I'm old, after all. A little more suffering is nothing to me: when I die, that's that, and so what. But look at you, how young you are! You should go on living. You haven't enjoyed what life has to offer. Can you have been born just to suffer, just to get pushed around by Japs?"

"We want to live!" Hundreds of voices shouted in anguish, "We weren't put here for the Japs to degrade and humiliate!"

She took over the burden of pain from those voices. She felt overwhelmed by something. At that instant she had only one desire: to sacrifice herself for their gratification. "I love all of you the same as I love my own sons," she shouted, "I'd die for you; but the Japs would never be satisfied with just me. They want you. They want every place, everywhere. Even a million me's wouldn't be enough to save you. You've got to save yourselves. If you want to stay alive, you'd better find a way to do it . . . Before, I wasn't even willing to let my sons go out the door, much less fight. Now they're all guerrillas. They might get killed one day, but if they hadn't joined up, they would die even sooner. As long as there are those who can drive away Japs for everyone's sake, I wouldn't mind even if my own sons got killed. And if one of them dies, I'll remember him, you'll remember him, because he did it for all of us!"

Words gushed out of her like a wellspring. She couldn't think of how to stop them even when her excitement began flagging, and she couldn't stand straight any longer; her voice hoarsened, making it hard to shout. But the roar of applause went on and on. They wanted more.

At each shout the sea of heads broke into billows, like waves on the shore. Finally the old woman gathered all her remaining strength: "We must fight to the end!" An enormous roar answered her, the sound of a tidal wave crashing on the beach in a storm.

Leaning against arms that had come to prop her up, she gazed at the seething mass below. She felt an intimate awareness of something very powerful. Slowly she raised her eyes and looked above their heads to the vast open space, the endless blue sky. She saw the collapse of the old, the radiance of the new, and though tears blurred her vision, it was a radiance that sprang from her own steadfast faith.

(Translated by Jean James and Tani E. Barlow)

Anna Akhmatova

"The First Long Range Artillery Fire on Leningrad"

A multicolored crowd streaked about,
and suddenly all was totally changed.
It wasn't the usual city racket.
It came from a strange land.
True, it was akin to some random claps of thunder,
but natural thunder heralds the wetness of fresh water,
    high clouds
to quench the thirst of fields gone dry and parched,
a messenger of blessed rain,
but this was as dry as hell must be.
My distraught senses refused
to believe it, because of the insane
suddenness with which it sounded, swelled and hit,
and how casually it came
to murder my child.

(Translated by Daniela Gioseffi with Sophia Buzevska)

Olivia Manning

from *The Danger Tree*

Trench was replaced by a man called Fielding. Fielding, a little older than Simon, had a plain, pleasant face and hair bleached like Trench's hair. He and Simon, being concomitants, should have been friends but Simon was becoming wary of friendship. His instinct was to avoid any relationship that could again inflict on him the desolation of loss. The only person whose company he sought was Ridley. Ridley had known Arnold and Trench and he let Simon talk about them so, for short periods, memory could overcome their nonexistence.

Not much was happening at that time. The Column went on sorties carrying out small shelling raids, but there was no more close action. Even the main positions were quiet so it seemed the fight itself had sunk beneath the load of August heat.

Ridley still brought gossip and news, but there was not much of it. In the middle of the month, when Auchinleck lost his command, the officers asked each other why this had happened. Ridley, who had once seen the deposed general standing, very tall, up through a hole in a station wagon, spoke of him regretfully as though, like Arnold and Trench, he had gone down among the dead. 'He was a big chap, big in every way, they say. He slept on the ground, just like the rest of us. No side about him, they say. A real soldier.'

'What about the new chap?'

'Don't know. Could be a good bloke but we all felt the Auk was one of us.'

Later in the month, the Column, on patrol in a lonely region near the Depression, came upon three skeletons, two together and a third lying some distance from them. The sand here was a very dark red and the skeletons, white and clean, were conspicuous on the red ground. The nomad Arabs had stripped them of everything: not only clothing but identity discs, papers, even letters and photographs, for these things could be sold to German agents to authenticate the disguises of undercover men.

The staff car stopped and Hardy and Martin got out to look them over. Simon, following from curiosity, was startled when Martin said that the skeletons were of men recently dead. Had they lain there long the sand would have blown over them. They might have been the crew of a Boston that had come down in an unfrequented part of the desert and managed, in spite of injuries, to crawl this far before giving up. He touched the bones with his toe and said: 'The kites have picked them clean.'

Simon, shocked that flesh could be so quickly dispersed, remembered his friends, dead and buried, and stood in thought until Hardy called to him, 'Get a move on, Boulderstone.'

Simon turned to him with an expression of suffering that prompted Hardy to put a hand on the young man's shoulder and say with humorous sympathy, 'You won't bring them to life by staring at them.'

That evening there was no mention of the Middle East in the radio news. 'A dead calm, eh?' Martin said. 'Wonder how long it'll last?' When he went to fetch his whisky bottle, Hardy spoke to Simon. 'I remember you mentioning your brother, Boulderstone. I couldn't let you take leave at that time but I understood how you felt. Have you any idea where he is?'

'Yes, sir. Ridley says there's a Boulderstone with the New Zealanders, near the Ridge.'

'Right. I'll give you a few days and you can take the staff car and look him up.'

When Simon began to express his gratitude, Hardy enlarged his concession. 'I don't see why you shouldn't take a week as there's nothing doing. But check up on his position. You could waste a lot of time scouting round the different camps.'

As soon as he could get away, Simon went to tell Ridley of his good fortune but Ridley merely grumbled, 'What's he think he's doing, giving blokes leave at this time?'

'Why? Is anything about to happen?'

'Chaps down the line think so. Then there's old Rommel. He's not moving forward but he's not exactly dropping back, neither. If his reinforcements arrive, he'd be through us like a dose of salts.'

'That's not likely to happen in one week.'

'How do you know. I got a feeling it could happen any day. If it hots up, it'll hot up sudden like.'

Simon begged Ridley to keep his premonitions to himself, saying, 'This may be my only chance to see my brother,' and Ridley relented enough to admit that his 'feeling' could be 'just a twitch'. It occured to Simon that Ridley's annoyance might come from envy of Simon's luck, or perhaps simply an unwillingness to have Simon out of his sight. Whatever it was, he began to take an interest in the vacation, saying, 'If you got a week, you could nip back to Alex. Or Cairo, even. Which'd you rather—Cairo or Alex?'

Simon did not know. He was enticed by the thought of the seaside town, but he knew people in Cairo. Had he been granted leave during his first days in the desert, he would have wanted only one thing: to return to Garden City. Now, though he sometimes thought of Edwina, she had lost substance in his mind and her beauty was like the beauty of a statue. It related to a desire he had ceased to feel.

Here in the desert, either from lack of stimulus or some quality in the air, the men were not much troubled by sex. The need to survive was their chief preoccupation—and they did survive. In spite of the heat of the day, the cold of night, the flies, the mosquitoes, the sand-flies, the stench of death that came on the wind, the sand blowing into the body's interstices and gritting in everything one are, the human animal not only survived but flourished. Simon felt well and vigorous and he thought of women, if he thought of them at all, with a benign indifference. He belonged now to a world of men: a contained, self-sufficient world where life was organised from dawn till sunset. It had so complete a hold on him, he could see only one flaw in it: his friends died young.

The staff car, assigned to him for twenty-four hours, would take him first to the Ridge where he hoped to track down Hugo, then to the coast road where he could stop a military vehicle and get a lift into the Delta. His new driver and batman, a young red-haired, freckled squaddie called Hugman, had little contact with Simon. He did not expect Simon to speak to him and Simon did not wish to speak. He was wary of Hugman, as he was of Fielding, and sat in the back seat of the car, holding himself aloof. Hugman very likely thought him one of those 'spit and polish' officers that he despised, but Hugman could think what he liked. Simon was risking no more emotional attachments, no more emotional upsets. To excuse his silence, he sprawled in the corner of the car, propping his head against the side and keeping his eyes shut. They had started out early. Simon, anxious to be off before Hardy could change his mind, almost ran from Ridley who came towards him with a look of doom. 'There, what did I say, sir? The gen is that the jerries are preparing a push on Alam Halfa.'

'Christ!' Simon threw himself into the car and ordered Hugman to move with all speed. They were out of sight of the Column before he remembered he had not reported his departure to Hardy.

As the sun rose, he did not need to simulate sleep but sank into a half-doze which brought him images of the civilised world he was soon to reenter. He no longer could, nor did he need to, exclude women from his dreams. Now that he was due for a week of normal life, he could afford to indulge his senses a little. He remembered not only Edwina but the dark-haired girl who raced him up the pyramid, and even poor forgotten Anne returned to him become, with his change of circumstances, more real than Arnold. His attention reverted to Edwina. She was the supreme beauty although he had been too dazzled to know whether she was beautiful or not. Another face edged into his mind, a woman older than the others, with a dismayed expression that puzzled him. He could not immediately recall the dead boy in the Fayoum house, but when he did he dismissed both woman and boy as intruders on his reverie. Wasn't it enough that he had lost his friends?

When he opened his eyes, the Ridge was in sight. They were driving through a rear maintenance and supply area where petrol dumps, food dumps, canteen trucks, concentrations of jeeps and ambulances, a medical unit and a repair depot were all planted in sand and filmed with sand that covered the green and fawn camouflage patches. It was a skeleton town with netted wire instead of house-walls and sand tracks instead of streets. The noon sun glared overhead and men, given an hour's respite, lay with faces hidden, bivouacked in any shade they could find. Unwilling to disturb them, Simon told Hugman to drive until he found the Camp Commandant's truck. Both men were drenched with sweat and when Simon left the car, the wind plastered the wet stuff of his shirt and shorts to his limbs. It was a hot wind yet he shivered in the heat.

The Commandant, fetched from his mid-day meal in the officers' mess, had no welcome for Simon. 'How the hell did you get leave at a time like this?'

Simon, more wily than he used to be, said, 'Only a few days, sir.'

'A few days!' The Commandant blew out his checks in comment on Hardy's folly, but the folly was no business of his. He advised Simon to find the New Zealand division HQ. 'About a mile down the road. Can't miss it. You'll see the white fern leaf on a board.'

The car, driven out of the maintenance area into open desert, rocked in the rutted track, throwing up sand clouds that forced the two men to close the windows and stifle in enclosed heat.

The board appeared, the fern leaf scarcely visible beneath its coating of sand, and beyond, on either side of the track, guns and trucks, dug into pits, were protected by sand-bags and camouflage nets. Simon realised they were very near the front line.

At the Operations truck, a New Zealand major, a tall, thin, grave faced man, listened with lowered head as Simon explained that he was looking for a Captain Boulderstone. The major, jerking his head up, smiled on him. 'You think he's your brother, do you? Well, son, I think maybe he is. You're as like as two peas. But I don't know where he's got to—someone will have to look around for him. If you have a snack in the mess, we'll let you know as soon as we find him. OK?'

'OK, and thank you, sir.'

The mess was a fifteen hundred-weight truck from which an awning stretched to cover a few fold-up tables and chairs. Simon seated himself in shade that had the colour and smell of stewed tea. The truck itself served as a cook-house and Simon said to the man inside, 'Lot of flies about here.'

'Yes, they been a right plague this month. Our CO said something got to be done about them, but he didn't say what. I sprays DDT around and the damn things laugh at it.'

The flies were lethargic with the heat. Simon, having eaten his bully-beef sandwich and drunk his tea, had nothing better to do than watch them sinking down on to the plastic table-tops. He remembered what Harriet Pringle had said about the plagues coming to Egypt and staying there. The flies had been the third plague, 'a grievous swarm', and here they still were, crawling before him so slowly they seemed to be pulling themselves through treacle. The first excitement of arrival had left him and he could not understand why Hugo was so long in coming. Boredom and irritation came over him and seeing a fly swat on the truck counter, he borrowed it in order to attack the flies.

A dozen or so crawled on his table and no matter how many he killed, the numbers never grew less. When the swat hit the table, the surviving flies would lift themselves slowly and drift a little before sinking down again. He pushed the dead flies off the table and they dropped to the tarpaulin which covered the ground. When he looked down to count his bag of flies, he found they had all disappeared. He killed one more and watched to see what became of it. It had scarcely touched the floor when a procession of ants veered purposefully to it, surrounded it and, manoeuvring the large body between them, bore it away.

Simon laughed out loud. The ants did not pause to ask where the manna came from, they simply took it. The sky rained food and Simon, godlike, could send down an endless supply of it. He looked forward to telling Hugo about the flies and ants. He killed till teatime and the flies were as numerous as ever, then, all in a moment, the killing disgusted him. He had tea then, still waiting, he thought of the German youth he had killed on the hill. Away from the heat of battle, that killing, too, disgusted him, and he would have sworn, had the situation permitted, never to kill again.

The mess filled with officers but none of them was Hugo. About five o'clock a corporal came to tell him that Captain Boulderstone had gone out with a patrol to bring in wounded.

'Has there been a scrap, then?'

The corporal did not look directly at Simon as he said, 'There was a bit of a scrap at the Mreir Depression two days ago. Last night we heard shelling. Could be, sir, the patrol's holed up there.'

'You mean, he's been gone some time?'

The man gave Simon a quick, uneasy glance before letting him know that the patrol had left camp the previous morning. Hugo had, in fact, been away so long, his batman had gone out in the evening to look for him.

A sense of disaster came down on Simon and he got to his feet. 'They should be coming back soon. I'll go and meet them.'

'With respect, sir, you'd do better to stay. The wind's rising and there could be a storm brewing.'

Simon refused to wait. He wanted to move, as though by moving he could hasten Hugo's return to the camp. He had sent Hugman to the canteen and decided to let him stay there. The corporal told him that there was a gap in the mine fields where the track ran through the forward positions into no-man's-land and continued on to the enemy positions at El Mreir and Miteiriya. As Simon went to the car, the corporal followed him.

'You're not going alone, sir?'

'Yes.'

The car, its steering wheel almost too hot to handle, stood beside the Operations truck. The corporal said, 'Like me to come with you, sir? Only take a tick to get permission.'

'Thank you, no. I'll be all right.'

Even a tick was too long to wait while he had hope of meeting Hugo. The sand was lifting along the banks between the gun pits. Small sand devils were whirling across the track, breaking up, dropping and regathering with every change in the wind. The sky was growing dark and before he could reach the forward position, his view was blotted out. He had driven into the storm and there was nothing to do but pull to the side, stop and stare into the sand fog, watching for the batman's truck to come through it. Nothing came. He got out of the car and tried to walk down the track but the wind was furious, driving the searing particles of sand into his eyes and skin, forcing him back to shut himself in the car. He was trapped and would remain trapped until the storm blew itself out.

At sunset the sand-clogged air turned crimson. When the colour died, there was an immediate darkness and in darkness he would have to remain. He could see nothing. He could hear nothing but the roar of the wind. He opened the car door an inch expecting a light to switch on but the sand blew in and there was no light. He switched on the headlamps that showed him a wall of sand. Realising that no one was likely to see them, he switched them off to save the battery. Then, aware there was nothing more to be done, he subsided into blackness that was like nonexistence. The luminous hands of his watch showed that it was nearly nine o'clock. He climbed over to the back seat and put his head down and slept.

He awoke to silence and the pellucid silver of first light. He was nearer the perimeter than he realised. Before him was a flat expanse of desert where the light was rolling out like a wave across the sand. Two tanks stood in the middle distance and imagining they had stopped for a morning brew-up, he decided to cross to them and ask if they had seen anything of the patrol or the batman's truck. It was too far to walk so he went by car, following the track till he was level with the tanks, then walking across the mardam. A man was standing in one of the turrets, motionless, as though unaware of Simon's approach. Simon stopped at a few yards' distance to observe the figure, then saw it was not a man. It was a man-shaped cinder that faced him with white and perfect teeth set in a charred black skull. He could make out the eye-sockets and the triangle that had once supported a nose then, returning at a run, he swung the car round and drove back between the batteries, so stunned that for a little while his own private anxiety was forgotten.

The major was waiting for him at the Operations truck, his long grave face more grave as though to warn Simon that Hugo had been found. He had been alive, but not for long. All the major could do was try and soften the news by speaking highly of Hugo, telling Simon that Hugo had been a favourite with everyone, officers and men. His batman, Peters, was so attached to him, he was willing to risk his own life to find him. And he was alive when Peters came on him, but both legs had been shot away. The sand around him was soaked with blood. He didn't stand a chance.

'And the rest of the patrol? Couldn't they have done something?'

'All dead. Young Boulderstone just had to lie there with his life-blood running out till someone found him.'

The major sent for Peters so Simon could be told all that remained to be told. Peters was a thin youth who choked on his words. 'When I found him, he said, quite cheerfully, "Hello, Peters old chap, I knew you'd come".' Tears filled Peters' eyes and Simon felt surprise that this stranger could weep while he himself felt nothing.

Peters, regaining himself, explained that the patrol had been returning to the camp at sunset when it was attacked by German mortars. The ambulance moving against the red of the sky must have been an irresistible target. 'They knew what it was, the bastards. And they went on firing till they'd got the lot.'

Peters, having found Hugo, could not move him because movement would increase the haemorrhage. He intended to return to the camp for help but the storm blew up, so he had to spend the night with the wounded man.

'He told you what happened?'

'He did, sir. His speech was quite clear, right to the end. About two a.m., he said, "I think I'm going, Peters. Just as well. A chap's not much use with two wooden pins." I said, "You hold on, sir. They can do wonders these days with pins", and he laughed. He didn't speak again.'

'Thank you, Peters.'

Peters had brought in the body. The burial party had already set out.

There was nothing for Simon to see and he felt: Thank God for that. Knowing that his presence was an embarrassment in the camp, he held out his hand to the major and said he would be on his way. Hugman, who had been waiting for him, eyed him with furtive sympathy and muttered, 'Sorry to hear what happened, sir.'

Simon nodded, 'Rotten luck', then there was silence between them until they reached the coast road and he said, 'Don't wait, Hugman. The car's due back. You might tell Ridley what happened. He'll understand.'

A truck appeared on the road before Hugman was out of sight. The squaddie beside the driver offered Simon his seat but Simon refused and said he would ride in the rear. The back flap was let down for him. He threw his kit aboard, jumped after it, and the truck went on again.

Simon, sitting with his back to the cabin, looked out over the desert that had become as familiar to him as his childhood streets. He was reconciled to its neutral colour, its gritty wind, the endless stretches of arid stone and sand, but now a darkness hung over it all. He felt death as though he and Hugo had been one flesh and he was possessed by the certainty that if he returned here, he, too, would be killed.

'Both of us. They would lose both of us.'

He thought of his mother going into the greenhouse to read the wire, imagining perhaps that one of her sons was coming home on leave. He found a pad in his rucksack and began to write.

'Dear Mum and Dad, By the time you get this you will have heard about Hugo. I was there in the NZ camp when he didn't come in. His batman found him, legs blown off . . . ' Simon stopped, not knowing if he should tell them that, and started on another page.

'Dear Mum and Dad, By the time you get this, you'll know that Hugo is . . . ' but he could not write the word 'dead' and what else could he say?

Hugo was dead. The reality of Hugo's death came down on him and his unfeeling calm collapsed. He gulped and put his hands over his face. Tears ran through his fingers. There was no one to see him and the men in front would not hear his sobs above the engine noise. He gave himself up to grief. He wept for Hugo—but Hugo was safely out of it. He wept for his parents who must live with their sorrow, perhaps for years.

In the end, having stupefied himself with weeping, he lay on the floor of the truck and slept. He was wakened by passing traffic and, sitting up, he read what he had written and knew that neither letter would do.

There was nothing to be said. He tore the pages into fragments and threw them to the desert wind.

Elizabeth Bowen

"Oh, Madam . . ."

Oh, madam . . . Oh, *madam*, here you are!

I don't know what you'll say. Look, sit down just for a minute, madam; I dusted this chair for you. Yes, the hall's all right really; you don't see so much at first—only, our beautiful fanlight gone. No, there's nothing in here to hurt: I swept up the glass. Oh, *do* sit a minute, madam; you look quite white . . . This is a shock for you, isn't it! I was in half a mind to go out and meet you, but I didn't rightly like to leave everything. Not with the windows gone. They can see in.

Oh, *I'm* quite all right, madam. I made some tea this morning . . . Do I? Oh well, that's natural, I suppose. I'd be quite all right if I wasn't feeling so bad. Well, you know how I always was—I don't like a cup to go. And now . . . If you'll only sit still, madam, I'll go and get you something. I know you don't take tea, not in the regular way, but it really is wonderful what tea does for you . . . Sherry? I'll go and try, but I really don't know—the dining-room door won't—I'm *afraid*, madam, I'm afraid it's the ceiling in there gone . . . And as you know, Johnson's got the key to the cellar, and Johnson went off after the all clear. I said, 'You did ought to stay till madam's with us.' But he didn't seem quite himself—he *did* have a bad night, madam, and you know how men are, nervous . . . I don't know where—back to his wife's, I daresay: he didn't vouchsafe . . . The girls? Oh, *they're* quite well, I'm thankful to say. They were very good through it, really, better than Johnson. They'll be back for their things, that is, if—Well, oh *dear*, madam, wait till you see . . .

No, I'm all *right*, madam, really . . . Do I? Not more than you do, I'm sure. This *is* a home-coming for you—after that nice visit. I don't know what to say to you—your beautiful house! There usen't to be a thing wrong in it, used there, madam? I took too much pride in it, I daresay . . . I *know*, madam, the stairs—all plaster. I took the dustpan and brush to them, but as fast as you work it keeps flaking down. It's all got in my hair, under my cap. I caught a sight of myself in Johnson's mirror and I said to myself, 'Why, madam will think I've turned white in the night!' . . . Yes, there it goes; watch it. It's the shock to the house. Like snow? The thinks you think of! You *are* brave!

Oh *no*, madam. No, you get through it somehow. You'd have been wonderful . . . We'd have done what we could to make you comfortable, madam, but it would not have been fit for you—not last night. If I said once I said a dozen times, to the others, 'Well, thank goodness *madam's* not here tonight; thank goodness madam's away' . . . Yes, we all sat down in our sitting-room. It *is* a strong basement. It does rock, but not like the rest of the house . . . It was that one they dropped in the cinema that did our damage, madam. They say what went on the cinema weighed a ton. They should never have put a cinema, not in this neighbourhood. However—poor thing, it's not there now . . . No, *I* haven't, madam; I haven't been out this morning. I only just saw what I saw from the back. And I'm only glad *you* didn't—it would only distress you. I expect your taxi brought you the other way. All I know I heard from the warden. He seemed to consider we'd had quite an escape.

Well, I suppose we did, madam—that's if you come to think of it. They did seem to have quite set their hearts on us. I don't know how many went in the park. When it was not the bangs it was the hums . . . Well, I don't know, really—what *could* we do? As I say, all things come to an end. It would have sickened you, madam, to hear our glass going. Well, you've *seen* the front. No wonder you came in white. Then that ceiling down. I know *I* thought, 'Well, there does go the house!' Of course I ran up at once, but I couldn't do anything . . . The wardens were nice; they were very nice gentlemen. I don't know how they think of it all, I'm sure.

You won't take *anything*, madam? . . . You'll need your fur coat, excuse me, madam, you will. There's the draught right through the house. You don't want to catch cold, no on top of everything . . . No, it's useless; you *can't* move that dining-room door . . . But the house has been wonderful, madam, really—you really have cause to be proud of it. Yes, it's all right here in the little telephone room—that is—well, you can see for yourself . . . What is it—an ashtray, madam? . . . No, I don't wonder, really: I'm sure if I were a smoker—you have to have *something*, don't you, to fall back on? I'll bring the ashtray upstairs with us for the rest of the stumps . . . Yes, madam, I'll follow, madam. As you say, get it over . . . Oh dear, madam, you *are* upset.

You can't help that; you can't but walk in the plaster. I'll have it all off in a day or two.

Airy? Well yes, if you call it that. I'd sooner our landing window, I must say. You see, what the warden said happened, the blast passed through. Well, I don't know, I'm sure: that was what he said. You have to have names for things, I suppose.

The drawing-room? Oh, *madam* . . . Very well . . . *There!*

I don't know what to say: really . . . You know, madam, I'd rather last night again than have to show you all this. It's a piece in the Bible, isn't it, where they say not to set your heart on anything on this earth. But that's not nature, not when you care for things . . . Haven't you, madam? It's good of you to say so. I know how I'd have felt if I'd thought there ever *was* dust in here. It used to sort of sparkle, didn't it, in its way . . . As it is—why, look, madam: just this rub with my apron and the cabinet starts to come up again, doesn't it? Like a mirror—look—as though nothing had happened . . . If I could get started in here—but what am I talking about! The windows gone— it doesn't look decent, does it . . . Oh, I *know*, madam, I know: your satin cur- tains, madam! Torn and torn, like a maniac been at them. Well, he *is* a ma- niac, isn't he? . . . Yes, it did look worse—I swept up a bit in here. But I don't seem to have any head—I didn't know where to start.

That's right, madam, go on the balcony. You won't see so much different from there. To look at the part, you wouldn't hardly believe . . . Sun shining . . . Well, it may do good, I suppose. But this doesn't rightly feel like a day to me . . . All that mess there? That was one of those last night. Yes, it *sounded* near us, all right: I hadn't properly looked . . . Oh dear, madam, did that give you a turn?

No, I don't know yet, madam; I haven't heard. I didn't care to go asking out on the street. I expect I'd hear in good time, if—It doesn't do to meet trouble. No, not Kentish Town, madam, Camden Town . . . Well, I have been wondering, naturally. It did pass through my mind that my sister'd tele- phone me . . . Well, I would like to—just run up there for a minute? That is, if my sister doesn't telephone me. Just run up there for a minute this after- noon? That always has been my home . . . It's very kind of you, madam: I hope so, too . . .

Little houses aren't strong, madam. You always worry a bit. When I looked out at the back this morning at some of those little houses, where the mews used to be—(no, don't *you* look out that way, madam; you can't do anything; better look at the park)—I thought, 'Well, they're paper, aren't they.' They're not built to stand up. That was the big bomb they got, the cin- ema bomb . . . Yes, they always seemed to be nice people: the girls and I used to go through that way to shop. Very quiet; you wouldn't know they were there. I don't think this terrace has even had to complain . . . Didn't you, madam? No, I hardly suppose you did . . . Well, perhaps they were, madam. Let's hope that they were.

That's right madam, turn up your coal collar. The draught comes right through.

What with you being so good about everything, and now I take another look—well, it might be worse, mightn't it! When we just get the windows back in again—why, madam, I'll have the drawing-room fit for you in no time! I'll sheet my furniture till we're thoroughly swept, then take the electro to the upholstery. Because, look, madam, I don't think anything's *stained* . . . The clock's going: listen—would you believe that? We mustn't go crying after the curtains, must we? . . . Well, I did, first thing this morning: I couldn't *but* cry. It all seemed to come over me all at once. But now *you're* back—such a difference I feel! Hitler can't beat you and me, madam, can he? If I can just get these glaziers—they expect you to whistle. It's not good for a trade to be too much in demand, is it? It makes the working people ever so slow.

No such great hurry?—I don't understand—I—you—why, madam? *Wouldn't* you wish—?

Why no, I suppose not, madam . . . I hadn't thought.

You feel you don't really . . . Not after all this.

But you couldn't ever, not this beautiful house! You couldn't ever . . . I know many ladies *are*. I know many ladies feel it is for the best. You can't but notice all those good houses shut. But, madam, this seemed so much your home—

You must excuse me, madam. I had no right—It was the shock, a minute. I should have thought. The whole things come on so sudden . . . Why yes, madam; I've not doubt that you should. It will be nice for you down at her ladyship's. All that nice quiet country and everything. We should all wish you to be where it's safe, I'm sure . . . You mean, for the duration? . . . *I* see, madam. I am sure you'll only decide what's right. Only . . . this lovely house, madam. We've all cared for it so . . . I *am* a silly: I was upset this morning, but somehow I never saw us not starting again . . .

I suppose it might, yes. Happen another night . . .

All the same, I should like, if you didn't object, madam, to stay on here for the month and get things straight. I'd like to leave things as I found them—fancy, ten years ago! . . . That's very good of you, madam, but it's been my own satisfaction. If it has made any difference I'm only glad . . . I daresay I'm funny in ways, madam, but it's been quite my life here, really it has . . . I *should* prefer that, if it would suit you. I couldn't think of workmen round in here without me . . . I've been through so much with this place . . . In *any* event, madam, I should rather be here.

Tonight? . . . *I* see, madam, I'm sure they'll be glad to see you. I'm sure you should lose no time, not after a shock like this.

We should think of your packing, then, shouldn't we? If we went up now to your room perhaps you'd just show me what . . . Oh, yes, I see. I hadn't properly thought. Of course you would need to take everything. When it's for so long, and—Well, good clothes should be where it's safe.

The plaster's worse on the second flight, I'm afraid.

Yes . . . I was really dreading bringing you up here, madam. But now you won't want to sleep here for some time. Your luck's not hurt—look; there's not a mirror got cracked . . . It was that old blast got the little lamp . . . I can't picture you, if I may say so, madam, waking up in the mornings anywhere not here. Oh, you've travelled, I know, but you have always been back. Still, nothing goes on for ever, does it . . . Your dresses, madam—I've been over them: not a speck. There must be some merciful Providence, mustn't there?

You won't find such good-fitting cupboards, not at her ladyship's.

Yes, look at the sun out there. Autumn's always the nicest season just around here, I think.

Excuse me, madam—Madam, it's nothing, really. I—I—I—I'm really not taking on. I daresay I—got a bit of dust in my eye . . . You're too kind—you make me ashamed, really . . . Yes, I daresay it's the lack of sleep . . . The sun out there . . . If you'll excuse me, madam—I'll give my nose a good blow—that clears a things off . . . Yes, I will try, when I've just run up to my sister's. I'll try a good nap. But to tell you the truth madam, I shan't truly sleep till I've started to get things straight . . . I'm quite myself now, really. Hope I didn't upset you . . . I'll just run up to the boxroom after the trunks and cases—they'll need some brushing, I *should* think . . .

That really is what I'd rather, if you have no objection. Johnson and the girls will be round tomorrow, and as you won't be here, madam, no doubt you would like me to . . . And I couldn't leave this house empty, the whole night . . . I know, madam; I know that must come in time . . . Lonely? No; no, *I* don't feel lonely. And this never did feel to me a lonely house.

Women's War Diaries

Bryher

from *The Days of Mars: A Memoir, 1940–1946*

Poetry, the battle of the ration books, increasing gloom, these made up the year.

Whatever the news, the day had its welcome brightness whenever Osbert telephoned that he was in London and would I like to join him for a walk? He rang me up in February and asked me to meet him. We wandered at first across the park in such complete silence that I wondered if the war was going so badly that he dared not talk about it? Presently he stopped and looked round at the bare flower beds and wet grass. "How is Hilda?" he asked.

"Fair. She is working but things are not exactly gay, are they?"

"The time has come to do something to keep the arts alive. I have decided to organize a Poets' Reading. Do you think Hilda will help us?"

"I'm sure she will if you ask her. If I suggest it, she'll say no." (I was supposed to have too much enthusiasm and not enough perception.) "You'll have to talk to her yourself."

"I shall ask each poet to write something new for the occasion."

"Hilda has been working on something for weeks. She seldom shows me anything before it is printed." I had learned some sharp lessons about never interrupting her. "And she reads superbly."

"The Queen has consented to be Patroness."

"Oh, that will make the day for Hilda. She is always trying to balance her two nationalities." As I have written, it is foolish to belong to two countries because that always means a tug of war. Three are ideal, then one can stand aloof in what I maintain to be calmness of judgment.

"There is no need for Hilda to be nervous. Edith will read and at least a dozen others. Eliot has accepted and I've asked Masefield but with him there is a little trouble about ducks."

"Ducks, Osbert?"

"It seems they have to be fed at a certain time and he has to be there to

162

do it. Naturally there are very few trains. Do you happen to remember if their feeding time is before or after sunset?"

All I could recall at that moment was a fragment of a nursery rhyme about their being stuffed with sage. It had greatly disturbed me as a child when we had passed some ducklings regularly on a walk. "No, but Doris has a farm. I'll write and ask her."

"Morale is low at the moment." Osbert looked so regal when he made this pronouncement that I expected him to be in the gold lace and ample cloak of an eighteenth-century general concerned about the winter rot that had set in among his officers. "It is time for the arts to assert themselves."

"Not on our rations." I reflected gloomily about the soggy lump of bread that we had tried to toast that morning. It was otherwise inedible. "One way to keep the population quiet is to starve it." Then I felt that lifting of the spirit that comes only with recognition after days of being ignored and we spent the next hour discussing the hall, it had already been booked, the probable program and the convenience of the date.

I also had my task and my reward. Edith arrived at Lowndes a few days later to time Hilda's reading. She brought with her a poem she had just written and asked me to type her out a few copies. It was *Heart and Mind*, the poem I like most of all her work, a major lyric of the English language and one that brings back to me the courage of those wartime days whenever I read it. It speaks both of the conflict of the artist and the one from which no human being can escape although it is possibly the artist who is most sensitive to it: the struggle between human feelings and abstract truth, the final battle between perception and intellect.

My early life had trained me to be a servitor of the arts. Osbert, Edith and H.D. were in many ways too sensitive. There had to be a shield and I was tough. If I had bothered about what people thought of me when I was young I should never have survived. So, that afternoon, as I had copied out the poem, I felt it was a little chaplet thrown to me by the gods. I have never understood why the impact of greatness is supposed to be calm. It is like the sudden eruption of a volcano. It touches something beyond consciousness on the other side of the mind until there is, for a moment, a sense of suffocation.

Edith and Hilda were among the rare writers who could read their own poetry. Edith knew the precise value of every word and exactly how it should be spoken. She told me that she had trained herself by working with an actress from the Comédie Française while she had lived in Paris. "I knew how

English poetry ought to be read," she once told me, "but not at first the technique of its delivery. I felt it was wiser to learn this in a foreign language and in that way afterwards I could develop my own style."

Hilda read magnificently like the inspired muse she was, not only her own poems but those by other writers. Only she and Edith have spoken the sounds that, as I say, "echo in the inside of the ear." Edith had the technique, the control and complete mastery of her audience, Hilda the inspiration and the fire so that she was to me and many of her listeners the seer prophesying from the steps of a Greek temple above a brilliant sea. I have heard many people read during my life but none with the power that Hilda and Edith had at their peak, a sensation that the sound was right, the color of the words balanced and the listener carried into a different world that for me was as outer space.

April 14th. The Day at last arrived. It was memorable for me because for the first and I trust the only time in my life, I jumped on to a moving taxi. They were hard to find and how was I to get Hilda to the Aeolian Hall and the reading otherwise? It was too far for her to walk. She had had the eight coupons necessary for a new black dress and it had been made for her by the late Queen Mary's dressmaker, who happened to be a friend of mine; so as far as clothes went, all was correct. One male poet, told he had to appear in a stiff collar, found he had none and that his wife had used up all his coupons. Another man had totally disappeared. Still a third was reported to have rehearsed his offering to his wife for hours in bed. The slogan was in general, "Of course I'm not nervous, why should I be? It is such an opportunity to hear how one's verses sound." There had been endless telephone calls, "Tell Hilda we peck three times and die once" had been one mysterious message. I presumed it was a reference to curtsies. No singers ever displayed more temperament, the males being far more flamboyant than the females.

An organ had been draped with tapestries, chairs were arranged in a half circle on the platform, Kenneth Maggs had lent a large lectern for the occasion. I had selected some seats near the aisle so that I could move rapidly to Hilda's rescue if necessary. Robert was one side of me. Faith the other. We bowed solemnly to Ivy Compton-Burnett and Margaret Jourdain who were sitting a row or two away. Beatrice Lillie was selling programs, a group of gentlemen gathered unobtrusively by the entrance. People stopped talking. I heard Osbert say, "Shall I lead?" and the Queen entered followed by the two Princesses. I fixed my eyes in the best boarding-school tradition, "never stare," on the back of the chair in front of me and by the time I judged it correct to look up, the poets had been led to their places. They were going to enjoy themselves once their ordeal was over but for the time being most of them looked agitated or unhappy.

The Reading was to be in alphabetical order. This was a wise precaution. It was to have begun with Binyon but he had died a day or so previously, so first a poem was read in his memory. Blunden and Gordon Bottomley followed. Bottomley was a huge, cheerful man who enjoyed his declamation and took me back to the days when I had seen his name in some of the "little magazines."

Hilda was third. She looked like one of the Muses and like them, she was speaking of the eternal conflict between wisdom and the world. I had not heard the poem before but as I listened my mind went back to the days when I had first discovered *Sea Garden* and murmured lines from it constantly as I walked in winter beside the cold, gray English waves. Then, merging as pictures sometimes do in our minds, more swiftly and more full of the original emotion than any film can recall, I was myself knocking at a door in Cornwall and looking up for the first time at the Ionic face that was already so familiar from statues seen in the South. Then again, how swiftly our impressions dissolve and reappear, I was sitting beside her on the slopes above Sunion and looking down at a Greek sea that was the color of her eyes.

Now instead of sunshine or the colorful London of her youth where Hilda had first met so many of the people Osbert had gathered for the Reading, she was speaking to us of the inner wisdom without which creation is impossible, and remembering those

who when the earth-quake shook their city,
when angry blast and fire

broke open their frail door,
did not forget
beauty.

It was H.D. who expressed more than any other writer the deeply felt but perhaps not always conscious feelings of the Londoners during the war.

Eliot followed, it was only inappropriate that he should have ended with "London Bridge is falling down" because whatever else London was doing at that moment, it was a growling, enraged lion with a "no surrender" air firmly about its whiskers. Walter de la Mare then read *The Listeners* and the first half of the program ended with John Masefield.

H.D.

"Ancient Wisdom Speaks"

I

Where you are,
your cloak is blue as the robes
the priests of Tibet wear:

where you are,
you stare and stare at a mountain
and a picture of a mountain in the water:

and when the river is half frozen over,
still you stand,
snow on your sleeve and hood:

still you stand waiting,
not forgetting;
where were we now

if you had not said over and over,
as you watched the snow
slide down the runnels

and become, below on the slopes,
blossom of apple, quince and the wild-pear,
repeatedly, this prayer:

remember these (you said)
who when the earth-quake shook their city,
when angry blast and fire

broke open their frail door,
did not forget
beauty.

II

      O—what a picture of a mountain!
      in our desolation,
      four times, four seasons

      marched up from the valley,
      each with its retinue and panoply,
      each climbed the mountain slowly:

      though the mountain changed its colour
      as the seasons came and went,
      she did not alter.

III

      Her cloak is very old
      yet blue as the blue-poppy,
      blue as the flax in flower:

      and not an hour passed
      in our torment
      but she though of us:

      she did not change,
      the mountain changed from gold to violet,
      as the sun rose and set:

      she knew our fear,
      and yet she did not falter
      nor cast herself in anguish by the river:

      but she stood,
      the sun on her hair
      or the snow on her blue hood:

      winter and summer,
      summer and winter
         . . . again . . . again . . .

never forgetting
but remembering
our peculiar desolation:

I will stand here, she said to the mountain,
that even you must start awake, aware
that beauty can endure:

her cloak is very, very old
and blue. . . .

IV

O do not weep, she says,
for ages past I was
and I endure;

sand-castles and sand-cities
on the shore,
built carefully
with towers and gates,
patiently set about
with wall and moat,
have crumbled,
Nineveh, Tyre:

O do not weep, she says,
but let the fire burn out;
for having dared the flame,
endured the pyre,
your ashes,
sainted ones,
your chastened hearts,
your empty frames,
your very bones
still serve
to praise my name.

Mary Lee Settle

from *All the Brave Promises*

I can still recall, as hearing it again, the click of that washed, bare door clos-
ing. I was committed to, caught in among, a shy tangle of very young-faced,
very small girls standing against the walls, cowed by the waiting and the silence, shrinking a little from each other, just as I was shrinking away, isolated from them. Some of them were as dirty as the girl I had seen between
the MP's. There, with the women in uniform at the recruiting station we
were a flotsam of intruders swept together by an order from a sergeant who
walked in with that busy, slightly impatient, woman-on-the-job walk I was
to know so well.

Manipulated by the sergeant, we stood in tattered, uneasy rows, twenty
or so of us. An RAF officer came in. Through the embarrassment I could
hear him, vaguely, explaining the oath of allegiance. Somewhere, out of a
hundred and fifty years of revolution, a stop came to my American mind. I
could join their forces, fight with them, try to do my duty, but I could not,
would not, say the oath of allegiance to the King of England. It seemed important to cling to this in that minute, as the impersonal mutter of voices
grew around me.

There must have been a bus to take us through London. That is gone
from my memory. I stand again, as I stood then, in that snaggled row of
women on a long blank platform of Paddington station, under the vast
skeleton of its once-glass vault, now either bare to the sky or patched with
black.

We were ushered onto the train. With the feeling of safety a railway
journey always engenders in the British, a feeling of being able to escape
commitment at the end, the girls in the carriage began to talk, or rather, to
explain themselves to each other. They had something of the air of the
woman traveling by public coach in a Dickens story who keeps explaining
that her 'postillion' will surely come to meet her, and their whole initial pride
seemed to be in the fact that they wanted it to be understood that they were
'volunteers'—this meaning, as I found out later, that they had joined up before the date of their call-up, so all of them in the carriage except the girl
beside me must have been seventeen years old, and all except her were from
the East End of London. Seeking to stand apart, she explained to me, or to
whoever would listen, that she was from the suburbs—I have forgotten
which one—and that she looked after her 'mum,' who was far from well,

and that she was ever so worried about her, leaving her alone like that. It was the first glimpse of the stratification, almost Chinese in its complication and formality, which covered everything from a hairdo to a state of health to sugar in tea and by which each Englishman holds himself apart, himself his castle, from his fellows.

Unlike the East Enders, who wore their hair in high, hard unkempt wartime pompadours, her hair was marcelled in tight ridges close to her head, self-consciously 'Genteel.' She kept touching it, pleased, and explained that she had been to the hairdresser's that morning and had had a 'perm.' In contrast to her tight, thin little body, holding itself up to its place by not even taking a deep breath, the other girls in the carriage, six of them, sprawled, easy in their East End solidarity, growing more and more pleased at the train ride.

I had no idea where we were going, north, south, east or west. No one had told me. I was afraid to open my American mouth and ask, partly since I suspected they would not understand me. Except for the girl with the 'perm,' whose voice was as careful as her body and who still spoke with a strong tinge of what I thought of as cockney, I could understand very little— a word here and there, as of a language not well known and spoken too fast—of what the East Enders were saying.

They sounded like six small Eliza Doolittles, sitting in rows, not giving a goddamn if they never learned to speak like 'ladies'—far too proud to care. What I heard was something like 'Coo wa a sayo—a flippin tunup.' This, with a comfortable smile, was followed by an answer, 'We aynt inem fer the lolly, sa bleeding seyo. Weyo we're bleedin forut naow,' with a look of complacent agreement all round.

It was only when I caught the word 'Reading' and saw the girl by the window opposite lean forward to see us come toward the town that I realized we were going west. The brackish, red-brick rows of houses began to slide by the windows as we slowed down. Here was something to understand: Reading—a literary pilgrimage. I leaned forward, too, studied the dull-looking town and spoke, hardly realizing it.

'Where's the jail?'

There was a dead silence. I watched the legs of the girl opposite, with the same gray surface of no sun and no scrubbing as all the others, feeling that I had shouted.

She said, 'There,' proudly and pointed to, I think, a slightly higher red roof jutting above the rest.

'Know someone there?' That incredible cockney came across to me, interested.

'No. Only about someone.'

'Me bruver's in there,' she said and leaned back, comfortable against the seat.

The train pulled out of Reading station.

'Wot was he 'ad up for, the fellow you know about?' she asked. I could almost see her toes wiggling with pleasure at someone to talk about to bridge the gap of strangeness.

But I'm afraid Oscar Wilde had to let us down.

'I don't know,' I lied.

It was the deep early twilight of a rain-sodden evening when we got to the depot. I saw, in sunken, damp meadows under the heavy sky, a huddle of sterile-looking buildings, an imposed, square wartime design. We, in our civilian clothes, outsiders, without identity in such a new world, drew closer together as we shuffled along to a huge Nissen hut; other small groups of women were shuffling with us, silent with nervousness at the unknown, so when we got inside the hut, there must have been three hundred of us, jostled together, lost.

The light inside was naked, stripped. So was a woman's voice, bawling from the end of the hut for us to take off our clothes and line up. That impersonal command, taking away even the identity of clothes, was too shocking to leave time for humiliation. Stripped down, puny under the light, I looked around me and tears gathered behind my eyelids. I had never known before how food and habit developed a human body, how rare physical beauty was. All these very young products of the dole, then the war, of white bread, 'marg' and strong tea, of a hard, city life already had the shrunken upper body, the heavy-set thighs, white and doughy, of mature women. No adolescent bodies rose lightly in that room—even the taken-for-granted litheness of the young girl was a luxury there. My own body, four years older, hard from sport and protein and sun, was as different from their hardness of survival as if I had been of a different species.

We lined up for an FFI—a Free From Infection. Each copying the one before, we lifted our arms to an unspoken order as we neared the medical orderlies. My head was jerked forward, my hair parted, pulled, my shaven underarms, my pubic hair inspected closely and completely, yet without any sense of human contact. I was ordered to get dressed.

Half of the women had been isolated into a group. I heard a sob from the other queue. It was the girl from the train with her new 'perm,' calling out to anyone who would notice, 'I must 'ave leaned me 'ead back on the train. Those carriages are filthy.'

When I was dressed and waiting, I asked a WAAF what was the matter with the others, who had been quickly herded into a farther room, out of sight. She laughed. 'Most of them have nits—a few crabs,' she told me. 'They'll get a proper 'air cut and wash—good scrub down.' I could see the new careful 'perm' under the impatient medical scissors, the towering 1942 cockney headdresses piled on the bare floor.

'Half of them?' I said.

'This is a bloody clean lot compared to some.' She forgot me and walked on down the bench, hurrying women back into their clothes.

Like lines of ants, a few joining a few more, combining gradually into a mainstream of movement, we grew into a mass, moving in the night mud, which sucked against our shoes, into long, long queues. Issue bedding, heavy, harsh brown blankets that smelled of dry hay, knives, forks, spoons, cups were heaped into our arms, while a WAAF stumped up and down the queue, yelling, 'Any ST's? Any ST's?' and waving above her head a sanitary napkin from the bundle she carried. As she walked, stopping from time to time before some girl stumbling from need out of the privacy of a lifetime, her answer whispered in her shyness, the WAAF performed for us like one of those quick-talking 'buskers' who entertain theater queues in London. I heard, for the first time, a new language even more unintelligible than that of the cockneys. It was the language of the Royal Air Force. The WAAF informed us at the top of her lungs that she was 'browned' off, 'brassed' off, that she'd ' 'ad it'—that it had rained for a 'fucking' week. This word, which I first heard used so casually by her, was the adjective of simplicity—the meaningless habitual definer. In real anger or passion it was hardly used, so that it had completely lost meaning. It was simply there, sprinkled in the conversation, as mild an expletive as spit.

The corners of the huge barnlike cookhouse disappeared beyond the dim, tin-shaded lights which made the ceiling recede into darkness, cavern-like. The mud from our shoes stayed wet on the concrete floor, and the wooden tables had a cold sweat to the touch. Too late for 'tea,' we ate the Air Force 'supper'—sweet cocoa, slabs of bread and 'marg.' The drawn blackout curtains sagged, aged, greeny black, neglected and unnoticed after three years. Still clinging to a fast receding privilege of a private life, tired, cold, over-shunted, we sagged at the tables, hardly looking at each other, quiet.

I glanced up once to see that at the end of the board, on the other side, a girl sat, looking as if she were spot-lit by her own color. She was yellow, a sort of inhuman, chemical shade of yellow which had dyed her skin and her hair, which had fallen over her forehead from the rain and had made her look like a reconstruction of early man. Even her eyeballs, as she too stole a glance around her at the others, were yellow. As she moved, her broad shoulders and thick arms swelled against a dark, threadbare coat which could not have kept out the cold, much less the rain. I was repulsed by her looks and was afraid—and sorry, in a minute of shame, that my old camel's hair, chosen so carefully, must have seemed a point of luxury as glaring in the dimness as that strange yellow skin.

Trying to go to sleep the first night on three hard, square, straw-stuffed 'biscuits' that made a mattress on the iron cot, one of the thirty set in two rows down the sides of the Nissen hut, I seemed to hear sounds until nearly morning—a hard, deep cough went on and on, somebody crying, quietly at first, then releasing the sobs of a child as whoever it was drifted nearer to sleep. The cold was the new, wet-fingered cold of England, which nothing could stop; it seemed to soak through the walls, up from the damp concrete floor, untouched by the small round iron stoves at either end of the hut in which wartime coke burned sullenly, giving neither light nor heat, only a sulfury smell. Not even the heavy, weighted blankets, my pajamas and my skin stopped the cold. It permeated to my bones and made me shake as if I had a fever. I wanted to cry like the unknown girl in the darkness, but knew it was no use. The warmth of Madame Prunier's seemed a lifetime instead of an afternoon away.

Before dawn, the Tannoy growled as if it were clearing its metal throat and a clipped, cool English voice roared through the hut.

'Ladies and gentlemen, it is 0600 hours.'

For three days we seemed to be on a long march, ragged, tentative, jostling at first, gradually taking some kind of shape and ease, a melding, as we got used to walking together, being 'oriented,' tested and clothed in new stiff Air-Force-blue uniforms.

On the first day, while we were photographed like photographs in a jail, for our identity cards, we were given all-important serial numbers, at first on a clipboard pushed against our chins for the picture, then gradually tattooed on our brains. Old telephone numbers are gone, and addresses where I centered my life, but my serial number—2146391—and my rank—Aircraft Woman 2nd Class—are a part of identity, a scar that I will never lose. That identity, seeping through any former role, took over as the uniform began to set to my body, and the commands, the irresponsibility of being told every hour of the day what to do, became habit. Individual thought, another luxury, had to be buffed off. But that would be gradual, dangerous and unnoticed.

Over the crowd, waiting for the photographer, I saw the yellow girl again, a face standing out from the crowd by its color, dumb with patience.

The officers' war that I remembered receded so far from daily experience that when it was noticed at all, it seemed to intrude, blindly, interrupting the day. In the expedient blindness, the judicious lie so inculcated as a weapon of war in which the stupid and the vicious could hide as at no other time, the good officer stood out—direct as light.

On the day we were issued uniforms, we were marched past a high barbed-wire enclosure. Beyond it, WAAFs walked two by two around and around an exercise yard cemented hard by feet. I saw none of them look up, even curiously, to make contact as we went past, not even when the corporal yelled, 'Look out there. If you don't look lively, that's what will happen to you. You'll find yourself on the other side of that fence in detention.' The girls inside walked on, in another world, without contact, their uniforms the dull, lighter gray cast of blue that was the color of the uniform when it was old and worn down.

I could not forget them. On leave, months later, I sat in evening clothes at a table at a Mayfair party in one of those deceptive intervals we like to remember as 'the war,' feeling comfortable in the softness of the voices and of civilian clothes, the telltale mark of the WAAF collar button, a constant pink spot on my throat, hidden by a necklace. I tried to tell the man beside me about it—about the women behind the wire. The woman opposite me interrupted in that voice of command I knew so well.

She said, 'There are no WAAF detention barracks.'

At first I didn't recognize the 'policy' in her statement and answered, 'But this is what I saw.'

'There are no WAAF detention barracks,' she said again and turned her head, the argument over. I saw then, above the low-cut evening dress, the pink mark of a WAAF collar button on her throat. She was a squadron officer at the Air Ministry. They probably called that dead, barbed-wire enclosure a kinder, more expedient, official name.

We were in uniform: a WAAF cap with a black shining peak, a light-blue cotton shirt with a separate glossy hard collar, a black tie, a belted Air-Force-blue tunic, an Air-Force-blue skirt at the regulation ten inches from the ground, thick cotton Air-Force-blue stockings, heavy black shoes and, under it all, issue Air-Force-blue rayon bloomers to our knees, a white cotton undershirt, a 'corset cover—WAAF for the use of,' to quote King's Regulations on the issue brassiere. Over it all, we wore the heavy, well-designed Air-Force-blue greatcoat.

We were no longer undefined flotsam at the depot. Late into the night we polished the dull, new buttons and the brass insignia on our caps, so that they would begin to get the sheen of wear and time so envied in the older brass of the corporal. Spit and polish, every old wives' tale, or old soldiers', for polishing brass was used. What began to work was the incessant movement of rags over the insignia on our buttons, the hypnotic movement of our knuckles back and forth over the cleaning racks, the pleating of our caps so they would not stand up like chef's caps but lie flat, the bending and kneading of the thick, hard shoes, in which I felt, those first few days, as if I were being asked to walk across England with my feet in stone.

Then, in the language of the Air Force—whose motto, *'Per Ardua ad Astra,'* reached from the sky and the swooping Spitfires to the arduousness of my sore feet—we were formed into 'flights' to be posted to initial training units. This time, dragging still-white canvas kitbags and in our new WAAF greatcoats, we formed a unit on the platform and in the train.

I swayed along the platform, weighted down by the clothes and the loaded kitbag. Whatever attempts I made to become part of it all were still only conscious. My stomach, which had quietly refused the fat-soaked food that smelled of garbage, the glutinous masses of porridge, the thick, stewed tea, had gone into a revolt of its own and allowed me to hold down no food for nearly a week. And sleep itself is our safe state of anarchy. My body, when it touched sleep, would thrash against the hard blankets and the 'biscuits,' throwing the center one half out toward the floor, casting off the blankets wrapped around them to anchor them and letting in the cold, which would keep me just under wakefulness for the rest of the night, just under the decision to get up and touch the icy floor with my feet and remake my bed. So, without much food or sleep for a week, I felt light-headed and floating in fatigue; I tried and failed to lift the kitbag to throw it into the carriage.

Someone grabbed my kitbag and I grabbed back, instinctively, without looking.

' 'Ere, come on,' the comfortable, rough voice beside me had the impatience of a busy mother. The kitbag was wrested from me and tossed onto the train. It was the yellow-skinned girl. She jumped up after it, and I followed.

Divisions were made, quickly at first, divisions of survival, of coming together for safety. I had hardly spoken a word to anyone during the week, and no one had to me. I found no friend to fall in beside and walk along with to the cookhouse, no one to complain with. I thought it was me; I had not yet learned that the xenophobia of the English is deep—not so much a phobia as an instinctive withdrawal before the stranger, usually broken down in wartime. But in these circumstances of too much strangeness, it was harsh and strong with self-protection. Among the others, especially after the flight had been formed, it was easy to move along into protective groups—a street, a district, gestures, voices, all were like hooks to hang together with. The East Enders were the majority, and they formed a solid phalanx. I envied their security, a kind of enjoyment I could hear from them across the hut, at the cookhouse tables, in the ablutions. But I had no hooks out that they could trust. I was all stranger, and quite literally, in language, they could not understand me, nor I them.

So when the drift within the flight began, I had thought I was not drifting with it, but I was, as much as the others. The tendrils, the communications of the 'odd man out,' by the time we got into the carriage, had formed a protective group of its own and had swept me along with it. Its first sign was the rather timid and formal exposure of first names—a sign of privacy in a whole life where one was known only by one's last name—usually yelled out.

Viv, from Liverpool, was 'named for me mum. We're from Liverpool. We're Protestants.' She told us this with the shy definition the English have within their labyrinthine class system, which stated social gulfs and prides of self I could not yet read. She had been a worker in a munitions factory until she was let go because the fumes had begun to poison her. The poison, which had dyed her skin yellow, had already, in a week, begun to fade out of her eyes. Her arms, which had been able to throw my kitbag onto the train so lightly, were, from heavy work in the factory, as developed as a man's. What had been a frightening quality in her hard, ugly face, grew into a sort of kindly, doggy ugliness as she became familiar in the uniform and as the yellow faded. She moved like a steamroller, carrying within her the timidity of a not-quite-domesticated animal.

At first I thought that the rarity of the two sitting beside Viv was because of their beauty, certainly a rarity among women en masse. The first, Tina, had that fine profile of face and body that Americans identify with English aristocrats and which is so seldom seen. Already her ill-cut WAAF uniform fitted her like hunting clothes. I had noticed her first because she was as tall as I was, so that our eyes met, without recognition, over the heads of the others as we were crowded in and out of the buildings of the depot. Now she flung down her cap with one arrogant gesture of her long hand and tossed her head, loosening her short, lank, shining blond hair. That was the first level of impression of her—at once the second level intruded and both destroyed and explained it. Her eyes were dead, bitter and flat, as if when she was a child she had exposed her elegant face to the pity of people who had no pity and would never do it again. Her mouth was not cruel—that was too positive—but closed, finely formed and bitter. When she told us her name, she said, 'Clementina Beaumont Scruggs-hyphen-Smith,' as if it were a joke.

The second said, 'I'm Penny,' as if that were a joke too, but another kind. She was a vicar's daughter from Devonshire with the only true-lavender eyes I have ever seen, a perfect pink-and-white soft skin, a small, pretty pink mouth like a Romney, delicate hands and feet, a halo of blond curls. In uniform, she was already reasserting herself as a woman, wearing the androgynous clothing as a joke. She wore her cap as if it were her lover's. Every physical thing about her was a nose-thumb at the Air-Force-blue conformity. Her eyes worked even on the color, making it charming. She had been in the land army. Out of that rose-petal mouth, from the time she sat down in the carriage until we were posted to different stations after initial training, there came, quite joyfully and with perfect friendliness, a stream of language so foul it was a constant education. It came from rebellion against some vicarage I would never see, from the stable and the pig pen, like the creature in the fairy tale who poured out frogs when she spoke. She had the cot beside me for six weeks. Every morning, when the Tannoy ceased to really wake me, I would hear from dreams to reality a sort of educating blasphemous, obscene paean into wakefulness and would open my eyes to see that Penny's small feet, with their pink-shell toenails, had hit the damp, freezing concrete floor.

We were assigned to our hut. We had already learned to race for position, near the ablutions, near the stove, in a protective corner which was to take on an identity, jealously guarded, of home for a while. Viv raced ahead of us, flung her kitbag on one bed, her cap on another, her greatcoat on a third and her own bottom on a fourth. She stared with such fierce protectiveness that no one dared to take the fifth cot. Gradually the rest of the hut filled with clankings and groans, voices were raised as they had never been at the depot as we stowed our kits and began to retrieve the few precious personal belongings we could have with us—a few photographs, a 'torch,' makeup (rare, guarded fiendishly and almost impossible to replace), knitted scarves and gloves of Air-Force-blue wool some had brought with them.

Then, through all the noise, grumbling and whickering as she pulled her kitbag along the floor, came the fifth of us, ignoring Viv's stare as she dropped her gear in a pile, flung the biscuits flat on the cot, collapsed on them and whimpered, 'Dear heavenly holy merciful *God*.' At her shoulders were already carefully sewn flashes reading 'Eire.' This was Paddy, carrying, turtlelike, so there could be no mistaking her, the impossible Irish music-hall name of Siobin O'Sullivan. When she had recovered from moving, she began (toward us, the cockneys on the other side of her ignoring her as if she didn't exist), in a comfortable bourgeois educated Dublin voice that poured over us like soft water, a sorrowful story of volunteering for the English Forces because she had had a bloody fight with her husband, and that it was already the worst bloody mistake of her bloody life and that she ached and suffered in bones she hadn't known existed before in a bloody beautiful home she'd never survive to see again. By the time she paused for breath, which she seemed to have seldom to do, all of us but Viv were helpless with laughter. Paddy was one of those natural comics who transmute any disaster to comedy simply by putting it through their brains and mouths—always sadly, always with a complaint, already condemned not to be taken seriously. It was a good thing for true perspective on disaster that Paddy was not the first survivor ashore from the sinking of the *Titanic*.

RAF Hereford, the initial training unit, lay imposed on Herefordshire meadows of that incredibly bright green even in the late fall, of West Country grazing land, deep with mud, and dank. In the far distance, when the mint rose at midday, we could see the Malvern Hills. I wondered if it were accident or design to set us so low in the stripping down of the depot that when we had formed companies and had begun to learn drill our pride resurged, no longer so personal, but a growing corps pride. Marching with the others, the loss of self and the gain of communal pleasure came without realization. Arms flung out straight, in a proud, precise group stride, we marched down the roads between the low hutments to the parade ground, while the men attached to the station stopped along the side and whistled 'Bollocks, and the same to you,' which I found out much later was called 'Colonel Bogey,' or an equally familiar British march with the whispered other ranks words, 'Ain't it a pity she's only one titty to feed the baby with.'

Tina and I, being the tallest, led the company; she kept up, so low I could hardly hear it, a running sore of talk, simple and terrible, a sort of unredeemed comment on her life. Her mother had died when she was small and she had been brought up in poverty and with perverted pride by a father who had been wounded in the First World War, one of those ex-officers who can never find a place in peacetime and who fester with bitterness toward their country and their fate. His only pride had been in being a member of Mosley's Fascist party. He sounded typical of those dangerous, pretentious members, fallen there by circumstance, of the paranoid cliff-hangers just above the morass of Britain's lower middle classes, clinging to their hatreds, their self-appointed hyphens and, always, to some vague and tenuous connection with a bishop, a general or a minor peer. Ironically, all the pretension of her father had been parodied in Tina's looks and in the way, even though she hated any duty toward what she called 'they' (those who 'had all the advantages'), she stepped out on parade with a physical pride that matched her looks, looking as though she were marching to burn the Reichstag.

Just behind us marched Viv, doggedly listening, watching both of us as if we were some sort of exotic animals she could not try to understand, only watch and, as it happened later, watch over. Sometimes, when we fell onto our cots at the end of the day, Tina complaining, Penny swearing delicately, like the sound of little bells, Paddy groaning and reaching for the inevitable 'fag,' Viv would join in the talk with stories dredged up to match what we were saying.

Like Eliza Doolittle, Viv had once, she told us with pride, ridden in a taxi. We prepared to make those kindly noises people make to interrupting children who want to join in but have not quite caught the drift of the conversation, when she went on, proudly, that her husband had beaten her up, stolen her radio and gone off to take ship. The police drove her in a taxi 'all the way to the docks' to arrest him. 'I got back me wireless, too,' she finished, taking all these facts of life for granted. Viv was proud of being married, even though she hadn't seen her husband for two years and didn't know whether he was alive or dead. I think she took my look of shock at her story as the pleased surprise she expected for having ridden in a taxi, for she ended her story with, 'I did then. All the way to the docks.'

After the story, we had no more to say. I fell to that incessant polishing of shoes and buttons that in the Forces acts like a kind of Yoga hypnosis, replacing thought or despair or future. Paddy turned away from Viv, embarrassed, and began the long feminine ritual she went through every night, putting her short wiry hair in a thousand little pins, covering it with an old-fashioned pink boudoir cap, covering her face with a white herbal cream, dressing herself in a quilted robe and handknitted bed socks with wool roses. There was something so incongruous and sad about her going to bed that even Paddy didn't seem comic, only typical of those clinging to tender and private habits in the midst of all that impersonal exposure.

I still had the illusion, common to artists at moments of registering concentration and to the isolated in cities, that I was observing all that was going on around me without being noticed, except by my own few comrades in despair, complaint and constant discomfort. They had made a whole new world for me. Walking along in the pitch dark two hours before daylight, with the double-daylight saving time of the short days so far north, I was no longer alone. I could hear Paddy fall in beside me, murmuring, instead of 'It's fucking cold' like most of the others. 'Aye, the bloody mist is rising and falling over the hills and valleys of this bloody benighted country.'

In the cookhouse the smell of sleep, sweat and damp wool mingled with the sick-animal smell of the food, the sweet medicinal smell of the long-boiled tea. By the third morning I could see several of the cockney girls look up when we came in, disinterested. I took no notice of being singled out.

Perhaps we were noticed first because we were enough different to be remembered from the others. Perhaps it was because the intelligence tests taken at the depot had frightened most of the others into being more inarticulate than what I would find out later was their high degree of natural quickness, their surviving intelligence. Tina, Penny and I, who had seen such tests before, made a better showing. That morning we were singled out for interviews for Officers' Training School. To the rest, as we left the orientation lecture, we were only noticed for the difference, criminal if left unexplained, of being set apart.

At any rate, from that minute my isolation was gone, replaced by an active withdrawal, a turning away, as if strangeness were a communicable disease. Tina, detesting them and herself, and Penny, dancing with her obscene twittering through it all, already used to dealing with a life like the WAAF in the land army, could give as good as they got, could flick back remarks in the ablutions, fighting for the cold water in a common language. Paddy had the grace of making them laugh, lugubrious in her self-protection. To me, the talk was still as alien as Urdu. I was struck dumb by it and replaced talk with the retreat of the liberal snob into 'they're not knowing any better' and with the decision that I would have to go 75 per cent of the way toward them because of 'my advantages.' I did this with a puppy-dog smile whenever one or two of them jostled into me, flinging me out of the way of the water tap or of what I was learning to call the 'loo.'

I had noticed the other habits of privacy, but, of course, I had not noticed my own. The reek of unwashed bodies with their underwear kept on for a week was sickening. They in turn saw me night after night strip down to what was to them the obscenity of complete nakedness before I put on my harsh, striped WAAF pajamas. I took to going, before the call 'Ladies and gentlemen, it is 0600 hours,' out into the rain, which never seemed absent in the early morning, to the showers, where there was hot water only from six to six-thirty, and taking a hot shower. In the cookhouse I refused the soggy porridge with an upturning of my nose I could not control. I received no letters and, because of having no money, never went with the rest to drink the watery beer in the NAAFI, which was the recreation center of the RAF station, but sat in the evening in the station library reading the thumbed, torn wartime paperbacks.

I volunteered, having had no training to call out of my past but the Girl Scouts and a camp in Virginia where jollity and helpfulness, admired and envied in older 'honor girls,' had been inculcated in me like a virus and a wholly American education that the early bird got the worm. I had yet to learn the first rule, command, dogma of being an other rank in the Forces, or, I'm sure, of being in any authoritarian or conformist state: Never volunteer, never stand out. I learned it quickly. Even the sergeant who asked for 'a volunteer' grinned when I stood up.

'Take the ST's out of the ablutions and burn them,' she ordered loudly. There was a wave of snickering from the others. I could feel my face burning. The early bird had gotten not the worm, but half a ton of used sanitary napkins. I turned to leave the lecture room. 'No, not now,' the sergeant ordered, 'in your off time.' I found out later that this was usually one of the WAAF 'jankers'—the RAF term for punishment fatigues.

When I went into the first ablution, the sanitary-towel bin was empty. All down the lines of ablutions behind the huts I could find nothing but empty bins. Then I looked up onto the hill in the distance. A lone figure stood in front of a bonfire, the air above it dancing with invisible flames. I ran up. It was Viv. She watched me climb the hill and shut me up with a short 'Will you ever keep your gob stopped? This is never for the likes of you—can't even eat the food . . . ' She received my heartfelt thanks with such fierceness that I trudged off down the hill again, leaving her standing in the mist.

Finally we were paid—ten shillings—and given time off. The bus going into Hereford was overflowing with WAAFs, singing loudly, as military as only women could be, self-conscious in their new role, freed for the first afternoon since joining up. They, in their new military role in public, called out the Forces' insult to civilians out of the bus windows, 'Ah, you dirty civvy, get some in!' the 'some' being time in the service, of which they had had about three weeks. I went alone. It was my first chance to see an English town, and I wanted to wander through it instead of going with the others to the 'flicks.'

It was already afternoon. In half an hour I had broken my newly incul- cated military stride and was wandering around the small and delicate elev- enth-century Hereford cathedral, gawking at the mixture of nineteenth- century Reconstruction and Early English, not able to tell them apart. As I walked along the high street of Hereford later I saw a shop with military dress; in the window were piles of flashes: Eire, Canada, NZ, Australia and two, amazingly, reading 'USA.' I bought them with too much of my ten bob, some writing paper and a bag of 'sweets.' It was already late afternoon, and I wandered into a pub to watch the RAF men, or boys rather, from the sta- tion play darts. I sat quietly, drinking a small, warm beer. Several of them came and sat down at the table, polite, disinterested, more involved in the dart game. The swinging doors of the saloon bar opened, and two WAAFs I recognized from the hut looked in. One of them was a pinched-faced girl with one of those pointed English noses which looks like it has a questing life of its own. She was almost emaciated. I had wondered how she stood the constant drill without fainting. I smiled and half waved. They let the doors swing together again. I thought they hadn't seen me.

It was time to go back to the station, and I still had two shillings six pence for the next week. The hut was empty. I got out my 'housewife' and sewed my USA flashes on my uniform shoulders, wandered away to late tea and on to the library to write letters, having at last time enough to think through what had happened and sift it down to a letter setting a lying tone of amusement to a world that could not have the least idea of what it was like there in the empty Nissen hut, with the blackout curtains already pulled and my Air-Force-blue sleeve moving over the onionskin airmail form. The letters were finished. I was relaxed and at peace from the afternoon's letting- go. It was nine o'clock. The rain had started again. I picked my way alone through the wetness, protecting the letters and my new-bought sweets un- der my groundsheet, avoiding the deep puddles that days of rain had made soft with hidden mud. Through the blackout I counted the vague outlines of the huts until I came to my own. When I started up the six steps to the door, counting them carefully in the dark to keep from stumbling, I saw that it was open. The flick of the blackout curtain let out a pencil of light that lit my face and disappeared again. It was dead quiet.

I pushed open the curtain. Something fell against me like a dead weight, too quickly to frighten me or, fortunately, for me to tense my muscles. I felt myself grabbed by my arms and legs and flung out in an arc into the empty air like a sack of grain. I landed on my back in a large puddle in the soft mud. My letters flew out of sight; my sweets were gone. There was a roar of noise. In the door above me stood a mass of WAAFs, yelling. One, the leader, the little pinched-faced girl, kept calling over the others, 'That'll teach the fuckin' toffy-nose.'

Something broke, and it wasn't a bone. It was the massed fury against the ignominy of all the brave promises, all the decision, ending up flat on my back in the rain with my cap rolled away in the dark, my few treasures lost and a bunch of drunken foreign conscripts yelling at me. Out of me rumbled a fury all the way from Morgan's raiders and a language I didn't know I knew. I just lay there on the ground and swore until there was a dead silence. Then, knocking the others into each other, down the steps came Viv and Tina, clearing them out.

'If it gets me twenty-eight days CC I'll murder you,' Viv was yelling. They picked me up. The letters had sunk in the mud; the sweets were gone. Fury was melting toward tears.

'Don't let the buggers see you cry,' Tina said and jerked at my arm.

We walked into the barracks. The usually clean, dead-looking hut was a bacchanal. Drunken girls danced on the cots, for once unafraid of Viv or the kind little round corporal who had appeared in her door and was trying to make herself heard.

The pinched-faced girl was jumping up and down on her cot. When she saw me she screamed, 'You think we're a dirty lot, with your baths and your bare body. Oo wants to look at it? A ten-bob tart's wot you are. We seen you getting trade in the pub! She's a ten-bob tart from up west.'

I supposed she'd set my price at ten bob because that was the largest sum we could think of on our first pay day, my job as prostitution because, to their minds, there could be no other reason for my mystery and my home as 'up west,' the West End of London, because that was as far away, as glamorous, as 'toffy-nosed,' as a seventeen-year-old East Ender could imagine. I didn't know then that ten bob was the top price in 1942.

Viv pulled me into the corporal's room and slammed the door against the noise. I stood pouring mud onto the corporal's floor while they helped my groundsheet over my streaming mud-soaked hair. My forehead had been cut—how I don't know. Mud, tears and blood splattered my face. I kept say-

ing, 'What have I done? I don't know what I've done,' as if in that few minutes they could answer the questions of all strangers, all who drew attack in
the world, from wounded chickens to Jews.

Tina took off my greatcoat and the corporal saw the USA flashes on my
shoulders. 'Well, I'll be buggered,' was all she said.

Later, we marched through the barracks to the ablutions. The noise was
over, the long room calm, dark except for the red glow from the stoves, where
we had already learned to make the coke glow with liberal doses of Brasso.
We went into the ablutions, with the one dim blackout bulb burning, to
wash my hair in the cold water and clean my face.

In bed, waiting to sleep, the women in the room were awake but dead
quiet. I knew they were listening. So did Viv and Penny, who had missed the
fight, to her own fury. From her bed I heard a last mutter, 'Bugger the lot of
them.'

I said, 'Ten bob, for God's sake!'

Out of the darkness on the other side came Viv's voice, admiring and
sad, 'That's a lot, isn't it? I was a waitress in a house once. But they didn't
get that. I couldn't be nothing but a waitress. Not good-looking enough. But
I got smashing tips.'

Elizabeth Vaughan

from *The Ordeal of Elizabeth Vaughan: A Wartime Diary of the Philippines*

Aboard the Naga 1943
2:30 P.M., March 2, 1943, Tuesday. Like lightning from a dark cloud came the
order to leave for Manila in one hour. "The boat is waiting at the pier and
trucks on which you will load what belongings you can pack in the time allowed are at the camp gate." There was pandemonium in camp. The order to
break camp was not entirely unexpected, but the short time for preparation
left us breathless.

Fifteen Philippine Constabulary came to camp at 2:30 with Japanese officers and eight empty trucks. Constabulary went into rooms saying casually
that they had come to supervise packing and loading of trucks.

What rushing about pulling down mosquito nets, folding cots, throwing clothes and foodstuffs into knapsacks. Packing washcloths, tin cups, food-stuffs, and change of clothing in bag to carry in hand. Boxes nailed tightly were ripped open crudely before being loaded on trucks and all boxes containing canned goods—especially milk—were set aside and "forgotten" to be loaded when the trucks pulled out.

Rode to the pier standing and bundled together tightly. Truck drivers seemed concerned only with getting driving done in shortest possible time. At the pier soap, rice, and odd pieces of clothing lay scattered about. The clothing had been spilled from boxes opened by the Japanese for inspection and incompletely and insecurely repacked before being put aboard ship. When the last truckload of internees arrived at the littered pier, it was dusk. We were told to form two columns for a final Bacolod roll call before we departed. A drizzling rain had set in and mothers did their best to keep babies and children covered as we carried out the contradictory orders of the Japanese—first to arrange ourselves by nationality groups, then by sixes [sexes?], then to segregate those with children from those without children—in whatever manner the Japanese demanded, for they seemed of different opinions themselves as to how they wished us to be counted and recounted. Before roll call was completed darkness had set in and we had to tread the steep and slippery gangplank by the light of a kerosene lantern which showed us nothing of the black interior of the boat on which we were to travel.

We soon found to our distress that the slipperiness of the gangplank was due not entirely to the rain, as we had thought, but that the boat was covered with the greasy, dirty overflow from a cargo of crude oil, loaded in leaking barrels on the boat shortly before us and which was to accompany us to Manila. From our unsteady and treacherous walking of the gangplank into the boat until our exit in Manila, crude oil and passengers mixed freely. The hand rail of the deck which we clutched to steady us as we climbed aboard left our hands gummy and slimy. As we felt our way along oily hand rails leading to second deck which was to house us, Japanese soldiers, bare-footed and clad only in a G-string, watched us by a lamp which had been lighted as we filed past the deck space where they were sleeping. The soldiers were to sleep on one half of the deck, the women and children on the other. The men of our group were to sleep on the hatches on the main deck.

We filed aboard—three American Indians, one Negro, two nuns in their most inappropriate flowing robes, and the Dutch, British, and American priests who had long before abandoned ecclesiastical attire, and the run-of-the-mill internees.

"What do we sleep on?" asked someone. "On the bare floor," we were told. "But it's filthy with oil tracked by everyone walking over it," we protested. We got no response and began to take mental measurement of individuals and space to see if everyone could stretch out on the floor. We found, when this was tried, that we would have to try to relax on the hard floor in relays, half of the women to stretch out the first half of the night and the remaining women to have the use of the floor space the last half of the night. The children were to be allowed to lie down all night, though none of them slept well the first night due to the hardness of the floor, the crowded condition, and the excitement caused by moving and being aboard ship.

The men sat on top of the miscellaneous surplus baggage which cluttered the lower deck after the hatch assigned to our use had been filled. Men, like the women, found sitting more comfortable than lying on the unaccustomed hardness of the floor, which seemed to rub the very flesh from thigh joints when one stayed in a single prone position for more than a few minutes. The natural fleshiness of the hips made a sitting position more tolerable.

Wednesday, March 3, 1943. At dawn we pulled our still bodies from the filthy floor to stand on cramped legs while we planned breakfast for the children, crying and irritable from lack of sleep.

One of our women ventured out and squatted precariously over one of the holes on the rear of the deck. One of the Japanese soldiers quietly took the same position over the hole next to her. She left in haste and confusion. A council of women aboard was held. We decided to use the children's potties brought aboard ship, though there is no spot of privacy for the users. A bucket tied to the end of a rope thrown over the side of the ship for water will be used for cleaning the potties.

Our disappointments were two: we were still tied up at the Bacolod pier and were told we should probably be here for several days, and the Japanese had made no plans for feeding us—we were to provide and cook our own food. Someone opened a can of coffee and with hot water obtained from the Filipino cook for the Japanese aboard ship made a weak hot drink for each adult person. In the middle of the morning, when the Japanese had finished their own breakfast and the kitchen was empty, three mothers slipped into the dirty hole which served as the kitchen to prepare oatmeal for children who were by now crying with hunger.

Since the unexplained and unexpected delay in sailing would cause a drain on our personal food supplies, Mr. Pope ordered an immediate checkup on food brought aboard. Each person was supposed to have brought aboard his "emergency rations" given out some months before when the first rumor concerning our transfer to Manila caused a flurry in Bacolod for these "emergency rations." A food inventory of canned goods brought aboard ship by internees revealed the following: Many internees failed to bring "emergency rations" aboard with them in the rush of packing; other internees had already consumed a large part of rations during the night; many cases of canned goods from the Bacolod Camp bodega had been opened and looted by our own men during the night. Seeing cases pilfered by our own men, the Japanese pulled cans also from cases ripped on the sides sufficient for a hand to enter to draw out a can. One Japanese soldier showed other soldier large size tin of Crisco which was his loot. Later, Japanese soldier ate this happily with a spoon from the tin.

Daylight offered us our first real glimpse of the ship to transport us to Manila—the Naga, the name printed in dull letters on the grey side of the ship. The Japanese had not removed nor changed the name of the boat, a small inter-island lumber ship of 372,000 tons net built in Hong Kong in 1929 for the Manila Railroad Co. (for inter-island use in the P.I.). The Naga has fifteen tiny staterooms on the lower deck and ten on the upper, in addition to captain's quarters on the bridge. She carries a crew of twenty-three Filipinos. There are no toilet facilities nor provisions for bathing. No one understood the first night but now many of us plan to arrive in Manila in the clothes, already ruined by oil, in which we boarded the Naga. Most of us have too few clothes to ruin more than one outfit on this dirty boat.

A look around disclosed a small open platform built off the stern, extending out over the rudders. In the floor of the platform were three round holes. These were toilets for men, women, and children. (Due to size of holes and danger of children falling through, no mother would let her child venture out.)

Thursday, March 4, 1943. Still at the pier! First birthday of Douglas White, whose mother died a year ago today when he was born.

Friday, March 5, 1943. Permitted to walk on pier today and stretch our legs. We discovered joyfully that oil drums on the pier had collected an inch of rain water on tops. I took out a washcloth and laundry soap, disrobed filthy Beth and Clay for the first bath since coming aboard Naga. I scraped off much oil with my fingernails to the discomfort of the children, for soap and water alone failed to remove the heavy grease. Put their same clothes back on, stiff with dirt and oil, for these must last the trip, after which they will be burned in Manila.

The Japanese are openly perplexed at the sudden boldness of American women prisoners. We are no longer the humble internees of yore. Prisoners and soldiers are constantly bumping into each other due to conditions. No prisoner says, "Excuse me," but looks straight ahead into the slant eyes before him with an air which has in some instances brought an apology (in Japanese) from an astounded soldier.

As we have become more dirty, men have become more brazen. We are already so uncomfortable we have little to lose on the filthy, stifling boat. Our cockiness conceals a fear for the uncertainties as we wait at the pier for we know not what nor for how long.

A dark, narrow, slimy passageway leads to the kitchen. We stand in this to eat, after which we hold our plate for a minute under cold, soapless water which hardens grease rather than removes it. We wipe our plates and spoons with odd pieces of paper and scraps of cloth which we toss overboard and which float on the water around us.

Sunday, March 7, 1943. Today we left the pier, to which we madly rushed on Tuesday. A sigh of relief broke from every lip as we left the stinking, steaming pier. Our delay, we learned, was due to failure of our escort to arrive to accompany us to Manila. Two lightly armed motor launches had come to our side during the night. The snow-white flags on which the Nippon sun rose, above the masts of launches, was the first clean sight before our eyes in many days. On the Naga there flies a smoke-blackened insignia of the Japanese empire and also the black and white lightning flash of the Japanese army—a zig-zag perpendicular from corner to corner of a white square. This military flag adorned our "escorts" also.

Additional soldiers came aboard the Naga before we sailed. They were assigned to the captain's bridge, from which they urinated and defecated over the side of the ship, to the disgust of us below, as wind blew the matter on crowded prisoners who could not withdraw far from railing for lack of space.

We discovered that in addition to soldiers, taken on at last minute, we had also added a cargo of six large, lusty, live pigs, domiciled in a pen constructed under the steps from our deck to a lower one. In an undrained small enclosure the pigs wallowed in their own filth as well as the soured remnants of food waste tossed to them. We passed up and down these steps for our food. Having worn our own clothes for five days and nights without bathing or without a change we didn't want to protest too much about the pigs.

Pillow cases, grass bags of all sizes and shapes, overflowed with dirty towels, overripe fruit and a change of clothes to have handy in Manila. Baby diapers, freshly washed in the clear, pure water of the open sea, flutter from ropes strung across the deck at head level. Diapers washed in salt water without soap have given no baby a rash.

The sea wind is a wondrous relief for the days at the pier when we sat drenched in our own perspiration, limp and listless. Our sailing today at dawn eased tension of nerves, and the spirits of all were raised.

Monday, March 8, 1943. Stayed up late last night sitting on steps listening to discussion by two of our group as to whether parallel lines meet at infinity. Took off shoes and stepped over sleeping forms in darkness—we have been in blackout since we left Bacolod—to find room to lie down. I lay on my side, knees under my chin, and slept.

Tuesday, March 9, 1943. The Japanese soldiers aboard are putting their personal belongings in boxes in preparation for going ashore.

At 5:30 P.M. we sighted Corregidor. We were looking for this fortress by the sea. At the sight of Corregidor we saw our first real evidence of the struggle for the capital of the Philippines. From the sea protruded the funnels and masts of sunken craft—sharp and gaunt like the arms of stiffened dead protruding from a watery grave. On Corregidor beach lay the dry and bleached remains of barges and boats, large and small. Great holes gaped on the slopes of Corregidor (the Captain) where explosives had blasted the earth. The sight was both awesome and depressing.

Iris Origo

from *War in Val d'Orcia*

June 22nd [1944]
The day begins badly. During the first lull in the firing a tragic procession begins to struggle down to our cellar: those of our farmers who, until then, have preferred to take shelter in the woods. All night they have been under fire, and their drawn, terrified faces bear witness to what they have been through. They thankfully take refuge in the cellar and the vat-room—old men, women and children—about sixty more people to shelter and feed. An

old grandmother from a neighbouring farm is among them; half paralysed, with a weak heart, she has been dragged along by her son and daughter, and now collapses, utterly exhausted. The babies whimper from cold and hunger. The older children go and whisper to ours, frightening them with the tales that I have tried to spare them until now. We go up to the kitchen (since fortunately the lull still continues) and produce hot barley-coffee and bread-and-milk, the keeper having succeeded in finding and milking the cows. The farmers' account of their nights in the woods is not such as to encourage us to try to get through to the Allied lines with the children, a plan which again, this morning, we had considered. Sporadic firing goes on all through the morning.

This glimpse of a tiny segment of the front increases my conviction of the wastefulness of this kind of warfare, the disproportion between the human suffering involved and the military results achieved. In the last five days I have seen Radicofani and Contignano destroyed, the countryside and farms studded with shell holes, girls raped, and human beings and cattle killed. Otherwise the events of the last week have had little enough effect upon either side: it is the civilians who have suffered.

Later

The above reflections were written during a lull in the shelling, in the kitchen, while boiling some milk for the children. But, in the midst of them, a louder burst of shell-fire than any we had experienced brought me down to the cellar, where we turned on the gramophone and started songs with the children, and waited. 'Now,' we felt, 'it really is beginning.' It had already been evident for some hours that shells of larger calibre were now being used, and both Antonio and I (though fortunately no one else) realized that the cellar was by no means proof against them. After a while, in another slight lull, the door opened, and a German sergeant came in: space would at once be required, he said, in the cellar (already filled to overflowing) for some German troops. A few minutes later an officer appeared: 'You must get out,' he said, 'and get the children away. You can't keep them here. And we need the cellar.' (That same morning we had again asked this officer what we should do with the children, and he had said emphatically, 'Stay on!') 'If you get out at once,' he added, 'you may be able to get out of range during this lull.' There followed a few minutes of considerable confusion. Antonio and I were besieged by a crowd of terrified people, asking when and where they should go, what they should take with them, what they should leave behind, and so on. We could only answer: 'At once. To Montepulciano or Chianciano, wherever you have friends. Take only what you can carry with you—the clothes on your back, and some food.' The babies were howling, and, with Donata in my arms, I couldn't help Schwester much, but we managed to pack a basket with the babies' food, and the pram with some of their clothes and nappies. I took a tiny case, which we had in the cellar, containing a change of underclothes for Antonio and me, a pair of shoes, some soap and eau de cologne and face powder, my clock and Giorgio's photographs; and that is all that we now possess. Each of the children carried his own coat and jersey. The grown-ups each carried a baby, or a sack of bread. And so, in a long, straggling line, with the children clutching at our skirts, half walking, half running, we started off down the Chianciano road.

I did not think, then, that we should get all the children through safely. We had been warned to stick to the middle of the road, to avoid mines, and to keep spread out, so as not to attract the attention of Allied planes. German soldiers, working at mine-laying, looked up in astonishment as we passed. '*Du lieber Gott!* What are those children still doing here?' Some corpses lay, uncovered, by the roadside. A German Red Cross lorry came tearing up the hill, nearly running over us. And all the time the shells were falling, some nearer, some farther off, and the planes flew overhead. The children were very good, the older ones carrying whatever they could, the smaller ones stumbling along as fast as their small legs could carry them. Donata shouted with glee on Antonio's shoulder. No one cried except the tiny babies, but now and again there was a wail: 'I can't go so fast!' and someone would pick up that child for a few hundred yards. The sun was blazing overhead, the hill very steep, and none of us had had any food since early breakfast. But every stumbling, weary step was taking us farther away from the cellar, and from what was still to come.

When we got to the top of the hill before Chianciano we divided into two parties. Those who had friends in Chianciano went on there, the rest of us, sixty in all (of whom four were babies in arms, and twenty-eight others children) started across country towards Montepulciano. The road itself was, we knew, under continual shell-fire, but we hoped to be able to cut across to the Villa Bianca cross-roads. The first part went well, and when at last we had a ridge between us and La Foce, we called a first halt. The children fell exhausted and thankful on the ground, only to rise again hastily, having sat down on an ant-hill. They made, indeed, much more fuss about the ants than about the shells.

The shelling seemed farther off, the mined path was behind us, and a peasant brought us glasses of water. Until then, time had been no moment in which to stop and think, but now we began to realize, with dismay, all that we had left behind. The people in the vat-room—had they been warned? No one knew, and we looked at each other in horror. Then at last Assunta remembered: 'Yes, she had seen the fattore go in to warn them.' But what they could do next it was difficult to imagine, for the old grandmother who was with them was unable to walk, and there were also several children. Probably they would merely hide in terror in a ditch. One could only pray that none of them would be killed.

And then there was Giorgio's body. We had hoped to bury him the night before, so that at least we could show his grave to his family when we are able to trace them, but the firing on the road to the cemetery prevented us from getting there. So we had had to leave him in that little room, unburied.

And then the dogs—they, too, had been forgotten. We fed them up to yesterday, but in the hurry of leaving we did not remember to go up to the kennels (five hundred yards away, and under shell fire) to fetch them. And poor Gambolino, the poodle, is terribly gun-shy. Even if he is not killed he will go almost mad with fear. It does not bear thinking of.

After a brief rest (too brief, but as long as we dared) we went on again—Antonio and the keeper, Porciani, taking the longer and more dangerous road, on which the pram could be pushed, and the rest of us scrambling along a rough track up and down steep gulleys. The children were getting very tired, but struggled manfully on, and we lifted them over the steepest places. Twice planes came hovering over us, and we all crouched down in a ditch. Then when we came out into the open cornland, beyond Pianoia, came the worst part of the journey. The shelling had begun again, and on the Montepulciano road, a few hundred yards below us, shells were bursting with a terrific din. The children were afraid to go on, but on we must. Some more planes came over, and we lay down for cover in the tall corn. I remember thinking at that moment, with Benedetta lying beside me and two other children clutching at my skirts: 'This can't be real—this isn't really happening.'

At last we reached a farm on the road, occupied by a German Red Cross unit, and there again we got some water and a short rest. But the officer came out and, hearing that it was a *Kinderheim*, gave us disconcerting advice: take refuge at once in the Capuchin convent on the hill, he said, and don't push on to Montepulciano. 'What is happening at La Foce to-day, will happen there to-morrow.' For a minute we hesitated, but the convent, we knew, had no food and no sort of shelter, so we decided to risk it and push on. From this point onward, the Germans said, the road was safe, and so we took it, a long, straggling, foot-sore procession. Half an hour after we had passed, that very stretch of the road was shelled.

After four hours we got to San Biagio, at the foot of the Montepulciano hill, and there sat down in a ditch for a breather before the last pull. We were very tired now, and a dreadful thought came over us: 'What if the Braccis should have left?' 'What if we find no shelter here?' But as we sat there, a little group of Montepulciano citizens appeared, then yet another: they had seen us from the ramparts, and were coming down to meet us with open arms. Never was there a more touching welcome. Many of them were partisans; others were refugees themselves from the south whom we had helped; yet others old friends among the Montepulciano workmen. They shouldered the children and our packages, and in a triumphant procession, cheered by so much kindness, we climbed up the village street, Antonio at the head, with Donata on his shoulder. Bracci and his wife Margherita came out to meet us, the children were at once settled on cushions on the terrace, and the Montepulcianesi vied with each other in offering accommodation. Antonio and I acted as billeting officers. Three went to one house, four to another, and the Braccis nobly took in not only our whole family, but all the refugee children as well. The Braccis' mattresses and blankets, which had been walled up, were pulled out again and laid on the ground, the children (after a meal of bread and cheese) put to bed, and at last we were able to wash and rest. Only one child was the worse for the terrible experience: Rino, who had a touch of the sun and suddenly fainted. Benedetta (sharing a bed with me) woke up, when I came to bed, to say: 'We've left the bangs behind at last, haven't we?' and then fell into a twelve hours' sleep.

We have left behind everything that we possess, but never in my life have I felt so rich and so thankful as looking down on all the children as they lay asleep. Whatever may happen to-morrow, to-night they are safe and sound!

July 1st
And now we have come home. This morning Ulick sent a staff car to fetch us, and Schwester Marie and I, with the two babies and Benedetta, triumphantly drive back over the road which we had taken—so much less agreeably—ten days ago in the opposite direction. (The other children are to follow in a few days.) Plenty of shell and bomb-holes on the road and in the fields, and as we got nearer home we looked out anxiously for damages. At

the Castelluccio there are some large shell-holes; the clinic, too, has been badly hit. Then, as we drive up to La Foce, chaos meet our eyes. The house is still standing, with only one shell-hole in the garden façade, another on the fattoria, and several in the roof. The latter have been caused by the explosion of a mine, the Germans' parting gift, bursting on the road to Chianciano, not thirty yards from the house. An enormous crater marks the spot, but has not blocked the road, since the Allies merely made a diversion into the field beside it.

In the garden, which has also got several shell-holes and trenches for machine-guns, they have stripped the pots off the lemons and azaleas, leaving the plants to die. The ground is strewn with my private letters and photographs, mattresses and furniture-stuffing. The inside of the house, however, is far worse. The Germans have stolen everything that took their fancy, blankets, clothes, shoes and toys, as well, of course, as anything valuable or eatable, and have deliberately destroyed much of sentimental or personal value. Every drawer of my writing-desk has been ransacked, and stained or torn-up photographs, torn out of their frames, strew the floors. In the dining-room the table is stiff laid, and there are traces of a drunken repast; empty wine-bottles and smashed glasses lie beside a number of my summer hats (which presumably have been tried on), together with boot-trees, toys, overturned furniture and W.C. paper. In the library, where the leather has been ripped off the arm-chairs and some books have been stolen, more empty bottles lie in the fireplace. The lavatory is filled to the brim with filth, and decaying meat, lying on every table, adds to the foul smell. There are innumerable flies. In our bedroom, too, it is the same, and only the nurseries, which the maids have been cleaning ever since they arrived (five hours before us) are habitable. Some of the toys have been stolen or deliberately broken, but curiously enough, the English Kate Greenaway alphabet is still upon the wall, and the children's beds are untouched. So we put the children to bed for their afternoon nap, and then go on investigating the damage. There is no water in the house, and also, of course, no light.

Antonio is away, having had to go down to Chianciano to take up his work as mayor, and cope with the spearhead A.M.G. officials, but in the farm courtyard, in a wilderness of refuse, gravel and waste paper, a few men are standing about gloomily. They come forward to greet me—and later the fattore, too, appears, and with tears in his eyes takes both my hands in his. He and his family are all safe, but have had a very bad time. And he gives us tragic news. Gigi—our beloved gardener, with his crooked mouth and limp, with his passion for flowers, and his short temper and wry smile—Gigi has been killed by a shell in the ditch in which he had taken shelter. It was not even possible, owing to the mines that are strewn in the woods, to bring his body back to the graveyard for burial, and his son has buried him in the woods where he fell. One of the peasants of our home-farm, Giocondo, has also been killed by shells, and two children from another farm, and the Capoccia of Chiarentana, Doro; all these, too, are buried in the fields where they fell. And all the survivors are profoundly downhearted. At least ten of the farmhouses they say (later on we learn that it is fifteen) have been destroyed, and those that have not been shelled, have been looted. A third of the cattle and sheep and pigs have gone (either stolen, or killed by shells); all the chickens and turkeys, and many of the farm instruments.

I go back into the farm, and there, crouching under a sofa, I see a black shadow. I whistle, and, half incredulously, he crawls out, then leaps upon me in wild delight, and from that minute never leaves my side. It is Gambolino, the poodle, miraculously safe, but pitifully thin, and so nervy that the slightest noise sends him trembling under the nearest bed. But our other dog, Alba, the pointer, was not so lucky. The fattore tells us that he found her inside the fountain with a wound in her side—dead.

In the lower part of the property, where the French coloured troops of the Fifth Army have passed, the Goums have completed what the Germans have begun. They regard loot and rape as the just reward for battle, and have indulged freely in both. Not only girls and young women, but even an old woman of eighty has been raped. Such has been the Val d'Orcia's first introduction to Allied rule—so long, and so eagerly awaited!

July 5th

But now, at once, we must begin again. On the first day Antonio set the men to reaping. There has been an accident in one field already: a mine has blown up an ox-cart, killing the oxen and smashing the driver's legs; there will no doubt be others. But the harvest will be saved.

We cannot hope that the Allies, who have already enough to do in clearing the main roads for the troops, will be able to help us with mine-detectors. But the resourceful postmaster of Chianciano, who says he has some knowledge of explosives, has volunteered to attempt the job, so we will try to clear at least those mines and bombs that are lying on the surface. The Germans have been very lavish: in the mine just outside the garden door, alone, they laid three quintals of dynamite.

We have now been round the most-damaged farms. Of those on the Castelluccio ridge, two—San Bernardino and Poggio-meriggi—are totally destroyed; in the others, one or two rooms still have a roof, no more. In all of them the looting has been thorough: either the Germans or the Goums have taken all that was not destroyed by shells or fire. In one farm thirteen people are sleeping in two beds, and the neighbour's family, nine persons more, are camping downstairs in the stable. At Lucciolabella eleven people are sleeping on the floor. All the farms have lost their cooking utensils, their linen, most of their blankets, and their dearly-prized furniture (*la camera in nocino degli sposi*), bought one piece at a time, year by year, and all their clothes, except those on their backs. The houses at Chiarentana—a medieval group of houses around a stone courtyard, which have seen other wars, other invasions—are almost equally bad. Here, in addition to the destruction caused by shells, the inhabitants have suffered the looting of the room in which they had walled up their most valuable possessions; the Germans discovered, by tapping, that the wall was hollow. One young woman, who is expecting a baby, has seen its whole layette deliberately burned before her eyes. Since they have no furniture left, and the roof lies open to the sky, their few remaining possessions are being devoured by mice. In all these farms there is no doubt as to what must be done first: we must get a roof on to at least two or three rooms before the winter. The furnaces which make the tiles and bricks are not working now for lack of lignite, and transport is an almost insuperable problem. But I expect that we shall manage somehow. Glass for windows, however, will be practically impossible.

Almost the most immediate necessity is to get cooking-pots and pans, and these I have been lucky enough to find in Montepulciano. (The shops had buried them during the German occupation.) No less thin fifty farms have to be provided for! Next, before the winter, will come clothes, especially for the small children. We will do what we can with the wool of the sheep that have not been taken, and perhaps later on there may be help from the Red Cross. After that, the imagination boggles: where, at a time like this, shall we find linen, blankets, or shoes?

There is cause for anxiety, too, about the general health. The place is still strewn with unburied corpses, both of men and of cattle. At San Bernardino there is still an unburied man in the stable, and six or seven other German corpses on the hill were only burned yesterday. And the flies swarm everywhere, bringing infection with them. In every farm there are severe cases of gastro-enteritis and we fear something worse—paratyphoid or what here is called *colerina*. When I drove into Montepulciano yesterday I heard that there is an epidemic there, too, and that eleven out of the twenty children in the Foundling Hospital have died. So we have brought our little refugees home as quickly as possible—singing all the way—in a great lorry provided by the British Army. For the sick I have bought some milk ferments, the only remedy available. At the hospital there is a lack of all medicines and medical supplies; they have even come to an end of their anaesthetics.

In Chianciano, too, where Antonio is working all day, the problems are numerous: lack of Diesel oil for the threshing, of light, of water, of sugar and salt and soap, of all medicines or hospital supplies, of any transport. The refugees from southern Italy clamour unceasingly to be sent home, but the A.M.G. refuses permits, as we are still in the battle area, and the roads must be kept clear. I have formed a women's committee, have issued an appeal for old clothes of any sort, and hope to set up a little workroom to prepare babies' layettes, etc. But at the moment, with very little stuff or thread, there is not much that we can do.

Nevertheless, for the future I am hopeful. The whirlwind his passed, and now, whatever destruction it may have left, we can begin to build again. And it is here that the deepest qualities of the Italian people will have a chance to show themselves. To speak of the patience and endurance, the industry and resourcefulness of the Italian workman has become almost a commonplace. But, like other commonplaces, it is true, and sometimes, in times of crisis, these qualities reach a degree that is almost heroic. Time and suffering have engraved them in the lines of the peasant-women's faces—a sorrow too deep for complaint, a patience that has something sculptural, eternal. Resigned and laborious, they and their men-folk turn back from the fresh graves and the wreckage of their homes to their accustomed daily toil. It is they who will bring the land to life again.

The Fascist and German menaces are receding. The day will come when at last the boys will return to their ploughs, and the dusty clay-hills of the Val d'Orcia will again 'blossom like the rose'. Destruction and death have visited us, but now—there is hope in the air.

Christabel Bielenberg

from *The Past Is Myself*

The Plot of July 20th
(Autumn 1944)
I wandered slowly up the valley, past the Church and the Schoolhouse and the schoolteacher Lorenz's vegetable patch. The day was cloudless and wonderfully warm. One of those early autumn days in the Black Forest which

were worth waiting for through weeks of rain and storm. The hills were clear and near and the trees on their summit a deep purplish black; the only autumn splash of colour a sudden flame of mountain ash or wild cherry. I had an old tin tied round my waist with the coloured rope which Frau Muckle used to tie down the corn cocks. I had told her that I was going mushrooming. I had entered so deeply into the peasant routine that this subterfuge came to me quite naturally and I would have had a guilty conscience about just taking a walk.

I turned up a farm track, which wound uphill away from the road, past piles of neatly stacked logs, across a field, hot and steaming in the morning sun, and I moved into the coolness and silence of the dark woods. Through the trees ahead, like patches of *Pfifferlinge*, pools of brilliant yellow, sparkled at me in the half light, and the thought of Frau Muckle's satisfaction if I brought back a free supper made me automatically start to fill my tin. I reached a sunlit clearing and I was glad to sit down—sit down in the warm sun leaning against a fallen tree trunk, breathing in the smell of heather and pine-needles, with the hum of bees around me.

For the last few weeks I had gone through the motions of living, no more. Since that morning, or was it afternoon in July, when the 'Kopp-wife' had come bursting out of her cottage, scarlet in the face, first with the news as usual, shouting 'turn on the wireless, turn on the wireless, they've thrown a bomb at that Hitler', and I had stood next to the water trough transfixed, kettle in hand—'yes, yes—go on'—I was trying not to shout, 'What happened?—Have they succeeded?'

I don't know, but it's all being said on the wireless.' Frau Kopp at least had succeeded as never before. I ran through the kitchen to the parlour and she was panting hard on my heels. With my heart bumping I waited for the elderly contraption to heat up and to put me out of my agony. Goebbels was speaking—not Goebbels, it did not matter, the same suave smooth voice—that was enough as soon as I heard the voice, I knew that it had failed. The wireless said that an attempted coup had been made on the life of the Leader by some generals, whose names I had heard of but did not know; only the name Stauffenberg tolled a bell, a very near bell. Yet even then I could hardly have dared hope that the action was an isolated one, and that those I knew and those I loved were not involved; for without quite realizing what I was doing I pushed blindly through the little crowd of awed faces which had gathered in the kitchen, and made for Kern's shop. Half an hour before I had posted a letter to Adam—I retrieved it—and I was not a moment too soon, for the incoming post had just arrived, and with it a letter from Peter, addressed to Tante Ulla. I tore it open—nearly tore it in half indeed, since my hands were shaking. 'Dear Ulla, I know from Chris that you always take over the children when she is not there, and now I want to thank you for this and to beg you to continue to play substitute mother to our little family. Above all I think it wise to separate up the possessions that we have collected during the years, and to house them with trustworthy peasants. Great changes may be coming in the near future and everything at the moment is slightly unclear. Please look after my family.' The letter was unsigned and I had looked at the date and the postmark, July 14th, posed in Graudenz, and for a moment it was as if my heart had stopped beating and I was held rigid, almost paralysed, in some cold, inflexible vice.

What was it that Hitler said later that night on the wireless, as he rasped hoarsely about Providence having saved him to carry on his task? I could not remember. I had only listened in the faint ridiculous hope that Goebbels' earlier announcement might prove to be untrue. From that moment I had gone about my daily chores as if in a dream, and the sun had risen and the sun had set, as step by fateful step, heralded by sparse announcements over the wireless or in the newspapers, the menace had moved in closer, and the full portent of those happenings gradually beat down upon me.

Some days after that Radio announcement, a week perhaps, they published a first list of 'conspirators'. They were all Army officers and Peter Yorck's and von Haeften's names were amongst those given. No news from Peter. Nicky's birthday—no news. An unsigned postcard on August 8th, from Berlin—'Adam was arrested on July 25th. I can't imagine why. Love and blessings to you all.' Afterwards—nothing—and four long weeks had passed. I had sent off three letters begging Peter to write, as the air-raids on Berlin were mounting in ferocity. I had sent a telegram asking for money. I had written to Herr Seiler, Peter's boss—no answer. It was as if there was an echoless void, out beyond the rounded horizon of our hills. Now two days ago they published the names of the main civilian 'conspirators', those who were to have taken over the government when Hitler was dead. Adam's name was amongst the eight—they are to be hanged. Yes, that's what they said—they are to be hanged. I have learned that, just as in physical pain a stage can be reached where the body can stand no more, and becomes unconscious, so too there is a limit to mental suffering beyond which you can feel no more; a sort of numbness takes over which is merciful.

'Failed'—'failure', wherever I went I could not escape those words and the dreadful meaning behind them. I had read somewhere of some lady in France who had lost a beloved husband and who had not been able to escape the word *seule*. She'd had it embroidered into the coverings and curtainings, woven into the carpets: *seule*—alone, failure—failed: I could not escape it either, even in the silence of the forest.

How had it failed? Why had it failed? Could it be that God, as the German saying goes, is always on the side of the strongest battalions? I sheered away from the thought, but with Adam perhaps already dead and Peter possibly too, and Hitler, the personification of evil, with all his hordes and evildoers about him allowed to live, it was hard to keep faith.

There was no comfort anywhere. The newspaper headlines: 'I will continue with my work since Providence has guarded me.' The telegrams of congratulation—nauseating smirch, 'I cannot sleep at nights, my Leader, when I think how near the traitor's hand—' The English wireless—Churchill's ponderous satisfaction at 'Germans killing Germans'; or that jaunty crew from *Soldatensender Eins*, usually good for a laugh, but now like macabre boy scouts gleefully hammering nails into coffins by implicating everyone they could think of in what they called 'the Peace Plot'; or having to stand by and listen when Dr R., a pompous ass whose children were living with Frau Kopp, returned for the weekend from Strasbourg and announced that he had talked with many responsible people there, and all had agreed it would have been a tragedy for Germany if Hitler had died on July 20th.

Why, oh why, had it failed? How *could* it have failed? I supposed there must be some reason why, some reason beyond my comprehension but I could not think, there was nothing to think about; except I supposed that I would have to learn to think again, to adjust, to talk, perhaps even to laugh and somehow to go on living, in a world which no longer held any meaning.

The sun had moved westwards and long shadows dimmed the glow of heather in my little clearing. The autumn afternoon had turned cold. I shivered a bit and picking up my tin of mushrooms, made my way back to the *Adler*. The faint tinkle of cowbells from the cow-sheds as I passed told me that it must be getting late and that it would not be long before the long-legged hill cattle would be let out into the fields. The children must be out of school, lunch must be over long ago.

Nicky was sitting in his corner doing his homework as I opened the door of the *Nebenstube*; his book was propped up by his satchel in front of him. 'Didn't you want any lunch, Mum? We had blueberries and milk and pancakes.' 'No thank you, darling.' I turned to put my mushroom tin on the spinet and saw the letter; letters were a rarity those days. A small square white envelope; Frau Dr Peter Bielenberg, Gasthaus zum Adler, Rohrbach im Schwarzwald. Berlin postmark, August 25th, 1944. I did not recognize the handwriting. I sat on the sofa and slit open the envelope and its contents came almost as an anti-climax, the reiteration of an oft-told tale, read a thousand times in bed at night, on waking in the morning—for the last three weeks I had known it had to come. The handwriting was Mabel Horbottle's. 'Dear Chris, I do not like having to give you this news. Peter was arrested in Graudenz on August 6th. We only heard about it yesterday. We naturally feel certain that he will soon be out again and send you our love and we will let you know as soon as we have further news.'

Nicky's pen scratched along over the rough paper of his copy book, the old wooden clock on the wall ticked off the seconds, some cows passed the window on their way to pasture and the little herd's whip cracked smartly over their backs; a low keening moan beside me made me start. Funny thing, I thought I had been alone with my letter. I had not noticed that Tante Ulla had come into the room and was leaning over my shoulder. 'Oh no, Chris, oh no,' she sobbed, 'first my Albrecht and now Peter, oh no, oh my God no.' I came to life suddenly and glanced at Nicky whose pen had stopped scratching and who was looking at us both with a startled stare, his eyes in his brown face suddenly very brilliantly blue. 'Let's go upstairs, Ulla,' I heard myself muttering, as her sobbing threatened to turn to hysteria, 'let's go upstairs, come—' and I found myself leading her gently up the narrow staircase which led to the bedroom above. 'Look lie down my dear, it's not that bad really.' I fumbled through the bottles on my dressing table, trying to find some pill which might help to quieten her—an aspirin, any darn thing. Then I sat on my bed holding her hand, glad to hold her hand, until her sobs subsided and she lay there staring blankly at the ceiling.

Back in the sitting room, at first, I could not see my son. His head was buried in his arms and his satchel hid his face. As I crossed the room he lifted his head and I realized that I was no longer looking at a child. His face had gone small, very small, almost wizened, and he was struggling with hard, dry, convulsive sobs which shook him, as if with ague. 'Is Daddy dead?' he whispered as I stood next to his table with my hand resting gently on his bony little shoulder. 'No, he's not dead,' I said, 'he's in prison.' He jerked away suddenly and stood up next to me, his head shoulder high to mine. 'In prison? Daddy in prison—but why?' I hesitated for a moment, realizing that the lie I told now was the one I had to stick to. 'Well,' I said rather hesitantly, 'Daddy has an enemy up in Graudenz, an enemy who was out to do him down. He had made all sorts of false accusations against Daddy and has managed to get him into prison.' 'Yes, but what about the police? Daddy's done nothing wrong, so why didn't the police stop Daddy's enemy getting him into prison?' I was not making a very good job of it. A flicker of doubt was dawning behind Nicky's direct, enquiring, somehow adult look. 'The police, yes, the police. Well, as soon as they find out that the accusations are false, they will, of course, let him out.' With a tact born perhaps of his new adulthood, Nicky averted his gaze, gave a short sigh and turned away. He stood with his back to me looking out of the window. He did not believe my tale and every line of his straight little back told me so. 'Anyway, that's my story, Nick, and I'm sticking to it,' I said as lightly as I could, trying perhaps to make some approach to that lonely little figure at the window. He did not move, but without turning round he burst out suddenly in clear German with no trace of Baden dialect, 'When this war is over I don't want to stay in Germany. I want to go back to England. I want to be English. Mummy, do you hear? I want to be English. In England the police don't let you go to prison for things you haven't done. In England'—his voice was deserting him again—'in England things are different.'

I, too, was very near the end of my tether and I could think of nothing better to do than to go and stand beside him at the window. Soon I felt a wet, rather inky little hand push its way into mine and we stood together, a truly forlorn pair, gazing out at the green slopes and wooded hills on the far side of the valley. A faint yodel and, 'You'd better go fetch your whip, Nick, Martina will be waiting with the cows.' He clambered through the window and dropped to the grass outside and he rounded the corner of the house without turning back or saying a word.

When I went to tuck the boys in that night it was obvious that John had heard the news. His eyes sparkled at me over the bulging eiderdown. 'I have just heard that Daddy is in prison,' he said. 'Yes.' 'And he has an enemy who has got him put in prison.' 'Yes, that's right.' 'Oh golly, I am just longing to see what happens to Daddy's enemy when Daddy gets out of prison, aren't you Mummy? There'll be the whale of a scrap. Bang, bang, de dong, de dong— Daddy will make mincemeat of him.' He wriggled in anticipation and punched his eiderdown so smartly that Christopher, who was watching the scene intently through the bars of his cot, simply exploded with laughter.

Later, I was alone in the parlour—alone, except for Frau Muckle, who was sleeping behind the stove. The little nightlight burned in 'God's corner' and the old inn was sleeping too, silent except for the sound of trickling water from the trough outside the window and the flowers in the window boxes tapping gently on the panes, as they were stirred by the wind which came sighing up the valley. Boom, boom, boom—Boom: the English time signal on the wireless; I listened to the ten o'clock news and it was then that

I knew what I must do. Boom, boom, boom—Boom, I had not much time to spare, for allowing for every kind of misinformation, there was no doubt whatsoever that the Allies were really on the move. Their tanks were sweeping ahead—Brussels, Antwerp, Verdun. The Rhine might hold them up for a little while, but for an army that had crossed the Channel, it could not be for long. They must know—trust Churchill—yes, they must know because even I knew that they had to reach Berlin before the Russians. What they could not know was that the prisons were full of men, condemned or awaiting trial. Men who would be needed after the war was over, and whose only hope of survival depended on the speed of their advancing tanks. How I wished that I could signal the news to some reconnaissance plane as it hummed over us, aloof and remote—'There is nothing, just nothing barring your way. There's hardly a Nazi to be seen these days. Most of the voluntary offerings for the last Winter-help clothing collection consisted of brown uniforms. The rats are leaving the sinking ship and your enemies have been reduced to old men and schoolboys. Keep it up, just please keep it up, but before over-running us all, allow me a fortnight, three weeks perhaps, just to get to Berlin and back again to the children—'

For it seemed that the letter, in spite of its dread contents, had succeeded in rousing me to action; it had been perhaps the harrowing uncertainty which had taken all the spirit out of me. Peter, after all, was still alive. Adam, too, for all I knew, and Carl, and Helmuth and the others—but Peter must be got away from Graudenz somehow. The Graudenz Gestapo, those hideous masks seen through a haze of smoke, if he were left in their charge he might be liquidated without trial. I knew that I must go to Munich to see Herr Seiler and then on to Berlin. Perhaps with the war's end just around the corner, the fact that I was English might help rather than hinder. Travelling I had heard was safer nowadays, since the Allies were using all their aeroplanes in France. I was suddenly alive with half formulated plans, and I knew that I had no time at all to spare, but must leave on the morrow for Munich and Berlin. . . .

Berlin greeted me with a bang, or rather a series of very loud bangs. After a seemingly endless journey of two days and two long nights, the train stopped in Potsdam. It grated to a halt in complete silence, and seemed determined never to move again. We passengers did not look very elegant in the bright morning sunshine, slumped as we were about the carriage as if we had been drugged. The man opposite me, who had been staring blindly out of the window, suddenly tapped me on the knee.

'*Gnädige Frau*,' he mumbled, 'didn't I hear you say yesterday that you lived in Dahlem and that you were in some hurry? Well, if you get out here and take the *S. Bahn* to Zehlendorf, you're no way from Dahlem. You could get a bus or something—even walk. We may be stuck here for hours.'

It took me no time to decide. I was suddenly wide awake and, pushing my way down the corridor, I jumped to the platform and came back to our window. My neighbour handed me down my rucksack and I made for the entrance to the Underground. Hardly had I reached the staircase, however, before I regretted my sudden decision, for the train I had left jerked to life, and without warning steamed off down the tracks towards Berlin. Oh well, I had not long to wait for the *S. Bahn*, I thought, and it would not be more than an hour or so before I reached Falkenried; but I had not reckoned with the Americans. As we stopped and started again on the way to Zehlendorf, the passing platforms looked more and more deserted.

'Looks like there's going to be a raid,' said the man opposite me, looking at his watch and glancing at the sky. 'Twelve o'clock, punctual as usual.' He went on reading his paper.

In Zehlendorf, the guard on the platform was using the platform tele-phone. 'How long? Two minutes? Thank you; how many by the way? Fifteen hundred? Aha, thank you.' He hung up and ran from carriage to carriage— '*Alle aussteigen, bitte, Alle aussteigen* (everyone out please). Air-raid warning imminent.'

I was a little ahead of the crowd, but I had hardly got to the bottom of the stairs before the sirens started wailing and howling about me. Although I knew Zehlendorf well, I could not recognize a single landmark. Since I had been there last, every house, every street had changed its face. Boarded win-dows, heaps of rubble, walls blown in, blown out, blown away, like open-fronted dolls' houses they disclosed sudden intimate glimpses of furnishings and decorations within.

I sprinted off at right angles in what I thought was the direction of Dahlem, trying to put as much ground as possible between me and the rail-way track; my footsteps echoed along the silent and deserted streets. I ran until I could hear a dull booming in the distance; the outer ring of anti-air-craft guns, how well I remembered that sound. A louder rumbling, the sec-ond ring, and then, above the guns, the high even purposeful humming which I knew so well from Rohrbach—the 'heavies'; only this time, God help me I was in the target area. The humming became a remorseless roar. An arrow, marked Public Air-raid Shelter, pointed down a side street and I made for what looked like a narrow concrete-sided trench which had been dug out of someone's backyard and covered with a tin roof. At the top of a flight of rough steps I stopped to unhitch my rucksack which was too bulky to get through its narrow entrance. A long drawn out and piercing whistle, a tremendous explosion and a gust of sudden wind from behind—and from that moment I had no idea how I descended the stairs and landed across the lap of a small personage who was trying to keep her balance on a narrow bench inside by pressing her hands and feet against the wall opposite. '*Allmächtiger Gott, Oh Heiland*,' she was moaning, 'and Schnucki is all alone in the flat.' 'I'm sorry, oh God, I'm sorry,' I said, as I tried to get to my feet. Sorry for Schnucki, sorry for having nearly flattened her, sorry indeed that I had come to Berlin. The whole concrete dug-out was rocking about like a dinghy in a stormy sea, and what with the pandemonium of whines and crashes outside, and a certain deafness after the first explosion, I could not hear what my companion was saying. Suddenly, 'Eight', she said loudly and firmly, 'peace now until the next wave comes over.' Sure enough our refuge quietened itself and she removed her feet from the wall opposite. 'Eight? What's eight got to do with it?' I wondered if she had found some magic formula. 'Eight bombs in each bomb cradle,' she announced with professional exactitude, 'and we were obviously in direct line.'

In the dusty half-light I could see that my rucksack was blocking the entrance to our shelter. I retrieved it quickly and came back to sit next to her on her bench against the wall. 'How long do you think this will go on for?' I looked at her with some respect. She was not at all young and was wearing an odd assortment of rather well-cut clothes, topped by the inevitable severe black pork-pie hat with broad green ribbon—*chapeau de rigueur* for the Bavarian gentry, and much to their resigned resentment, *chapeau d'adoption* by Prussians of the same ilk. She looked, in fact, rather like a waxwork figure of Queen Victoria which hadn't been dusted for months. 'Not long,' she said precisely, 'an hour, perhaps two. An American carpet raid. They send over high-flying pathfinder planes which drop lights, they are more easily seen at night. Christmas trees we call them. They drop them at each corner of a large square—one, two, three, four'—she drew a square in the dust on the floor with the toe of her shabby button boot. 'Then, my dear, over come the heavy bombers and drop everything they have into the square. Friendly, isn't it?' Whilst we were talking, the thumping and thudding seemed to have retreated a little, but now the humming roar seemed to be advancing on us again. My companion cocked her ears. 'Yes, here they come again—one, two—' the fifth explosion was so near that the walls about us shivered as if they were about to fall to bits. Suddenly we were in each other's arms, Queen Victoria and I. This was the end—there would be no 'six' for us. Clutching each other as if we were drowning we bent our heads under the hurricane of sound. 'Oh God,' I prayed, 'look after Peter, look after the children, look after—' Six—the trench was still rocking and a cloud of gritty dust had come belching down the stairway. Coughing and spluttering with our heads pressed into each other's shoulders, we heard the thudding retreat once more. We were alive. I was suddenly crying—tears turning the dust to mud on my hands and face. My companion was crying too; I was glad, for she became more human that way. Dreadful, I thought rather hysterically, if she had merely sat there and repeated those famous words of her royal proto-type. 'We are not amused.' But no—'That's the nearest I have ever had,' she said between coughs and sobs, 'the very nearest.' Then, suddenly pulling herself together she adjusted her hat and added, 'An extremely expensive method of trying to kill us, isn't it?'

The rest of the raid was almost an anti-climax. Sometimes it seemed to flow nearer, sometimes further away. The narrow entrance glowed red and yellow and red again as the fires took a hold, but our refuge stayed firmly put. My companion passed the time until the All Clear sounded, cleaning and dusting out the contents of her handbag; an old lady's handbag, filled with odds and ends of junk and memories. She was shaking out a little fur tippet which had fallen to the floor, when she suddenly remembered 'Schnucki'. It was all I could do to persuade her not to leave the trench there and then. 'Who is Schnucki?' 'No, he is not a person, he is my dog; I will never go shop-ping without him again.' She managed to root out and dust a faded brown photograph of a dachshund sitting at the top of a broad flight of stone steps, leading to an elegant brass-studded doorway. 'Your home?' 'Yes, my home; at least, my home that was. East Prussia, the Russians will be there soon, I suppose. My children thought I should not wait for the Russians. Pure non-sense—it only goes to show that one should never listen to one's children.'

She did not want to communicate further, she was anxious to be off and I had got used to asking no unnecessary questions.

After the final All Clear, when the danger of time bombs was also past, we stood for a moment with our heads above ground, surveying the scene around us, from the blazing sky-line to what must have been a bus depot nearby. It had become an incongruous heap of twisted metal, and the buses had been tossed around like abandoned toys. We shook hands and parted at the top of the shelter steps, and I watched her pick her way through the smoking rubble and around the giant bomb craters. The wind, the unnatu-ral air-raid wind blustered about her, and she had need to hold fast to her tippet and also her pork-pie hat; but she had great dignity that dusty little *grande dame*, and I found myself rather hoping sincerely that Schnucki had survived to take part in further shopping expeditions.

I walked to the Falkenried and, as our garden door was open, I passed around the house and looked into the french window of the sitting-room. Mabel was doing some ironing and jumped as she heard my voice. For a moment she hardly seemed to recognize me, then—'Chris, my dear Chris.' She put down her iron and still looking at me in a shocked almost embarrassed sort of way, she added 'Come in, come in and sit down; I did not know when to expect you—come.' She took me by the arm and led me to the sofa; she was treating me like an elderly imbecile. 'Come, let me make you some tea.' She went to the radiator, and removed a bit of paper which was covered in tea leaves. As she went to the door she turned and gave me a scared sort of smile.

I went to the bathroom to wash my hands when I looked in the mirror a stranger looked back at me—a white-haired stranger with huge black-rimmed eyes and powdered lips. For a moment I, too, was aghast, and lurid tales of people going white-haired overnight flashed across my mind. I looked more closely and then grabbed the hand-shower and watched with some relief as the dust and dirt trickled down the wastepipe.

Back in the sitting room Mabel was waiting for me with two cups of hot water faintly tinged with yellow. 'I'm sorry, my dear, but the leaves have been used twice before,' she said without looking up. Then as I sat down beside her she glanced at me shyly, and suddenly burst out laughing. 'Gracious, Chris, I am sorry,' she said, 'but you gave me such a fright. I just didn't recognize you. Wherever have you been?'

I told her of the little *entr' acte* in Zehlendorf, and she said thoughtfully that she imagined that that part of Berlin had got the worst of it. She herself had not gone to the shelter but had managed to do all her ironing, having taken advantage of the boost in electric current when the factories closed down for the raid. As we sipped our tea and I watched her worn face, it occurred to me how incongruous it was that we two Englishwomen should be sitting there bomb dodging, and passing the time of day. She even had an English passport, but a German mother, I believed, and had, therefore, somehow evaded being interned. I did not know her very well, but we spoke the same language and so it was not long before I was asking her what she knew of the circumstances of Peter's arrest. She told me first that she did not know much more than I did. He had arrived in Berlin on July 28th and had stayed for several days. Neither she nor Arnold had seen much of him, nor had he spoken much with either of them. He had seemed continuously on the go; he had been arrested immediately on his return to Graudenz.

As her rather barren little story came to an end, she seemed to hesitate and then she quickly put her hand over mine and added, 'It's no use, Chris, I can't hold it back. Two days before he left he seemed to have a high temperature; he was shivering and sweating and I took a hot drink to his room. I don't know if he was delirious or what, but he suddenly burst out to me that he had had some teleprint message from von Trott on July 15th, asking him when he would be in Berlin and that he had teleprinted back that he would be here on the 28th. As you know, there is now a *Führerbefehl* that at least one director must be on the factory premises day and night—the death penalty for all directors if there should be a slip-up. His co-director was away and he was sleeping in the office, so that he could not leave earlier than the 28th; and then he arrived too late to see von Trott before his arrest. He said he was not going to allow Trott to remain in custody. He had found out the exact time of day that Trott was being transported from Oranienburg, I think he said, to the Prinz Albrechtstrasse for interrogation; and that he was going back to Graudenz to collect a machine gun from the factory arsenal and he and another friend were going to shoot von Trott out. He would have the factory car with him and intended taking Trott to the Tucheler Heide, some huge wooded moorland area near Graudenz which is still in the hands of Polish partisans. It all sounded a bit crazy to me, Chris, but these are crazy times. He asked me to tell you if he failed, and he told me he knew that you would understand.'

Her voice was pitched so low that I could hardly hear what she was saying. 'I haven't told Arnold of this,' she went on, 'and you can rest assured that Arnold is doing his utmost for Peter. But I'm haunted at nights wondering whether he was arrested before or after he got those machine guns, or whether he told anyone who was not reliable about his plan.'

The telephone ringing on my writing table made us both jump. I plugged it into the wall and lifted the receiver. An unusual whirring sound greeted me and, seeing my slightly puzzled look, Mabel grabbed a piece of paper. 'TAPPED,' she wrote on it in big letters and pushed it under my nose. 'Oh, hallo—' it was Arnold. 'Is that you Chris?' His voice sounded brisk and businesslike. 'I must say, I'm glad to hear you've arrived, you took some other train of course. You didn't? But that's impossible, the only train from Mu-

nich was bombed and strafed all the way from Schmargendorf to the Pots-
damer Bahnhof. Three or four hundred casualties. You were on that train?
You what? You got out in Potsdam and came by the *S. Bahn?* My God—
well—I'll be home soon. Goodbye.'

Whilst I was talking, I had been idly turning over the papers on my
desk. One particular envelope propped up against the inkstand caught my
eye; a square green business envelope, the telephone bill or receipt—perhaps, but it was not the typewritten address I was looking at. On the bottom
right-hand corner of the envelope was our name written in ink, and the
handwriting was Adam's. I put back the receiver and opened the envelope.
It had not been stuck down, and inside the bill was a thin slip of paper. 'Love
to you both, A.' It was as if I was gripped by a sudden violent pain. I had to
stand very still. I think that was the first time I realized irrevocably that
Adam was no longer living. I asked Mabel if she knew how the envelope had
reached my desk. She did not know. I asked her whether the house had been
searched and she said it had not. I asked no more. It seemed that the age of
miracles, little miracles at least, had not completely passed.

Arnold arrived about an hour later and the genuine warmth of his
greeting made me glad that he was Peter's friend. 'My dear Chris, you
shouldn't have come, of course, but now you have, it's jolly good to see you.'
He spoke excellent English. 'We have a whole heap to talk about. I am extremely optimistic; but wait 'til I've washed my hands and we'll get down to
it. Mabel, what about those tea leaves?' I had forgotten to disconnect the
telephone; he tugged it out of the wall and added—'It's been tapped since
Peter's arrest, so we have to be a bit careful.' He came back to the sitting
room, brushed and spruce, and sat down in front of what was now a cup of
hot water. I looked at his tough, handsome face and realized that he had
changed a good deal since I had seen him last, some two years back. He was
thin and fit-looking, but his face had that transparent pallor, particularly
about the eyes, which everyone seemed to have who had to live in this belea-
guered and bombarded city.

'The age of miracles has not passed,' he said, as if reading my thoughts.
I thought for a moment that he must be referring to Adam's note, but his
face had gone taut. 'To think that you should have left that train in Potsdam;
actually I went down to meet it thinking that you might be on it. I spent the
raid in the Underground and came up just as they were taking away the
casualties. Rows and rows of stretchers on the platform. Men, women and
children, and some people still clutching bunches of flowers hurrying from

stretcher to stretcher.' He shook himself. 'I'm sorry Chris, I know we're going to be accused of all sorts of horrors after this war, but for the life of me I can't see where the hell the difference comes in.'

The cup of hot water had gone luke warm; even Arnold couldn't cope with it. He took a sip and pushed the cup away. 'Well, my dear, let's get down to our Piet'—he used the Hamburg vernacular—'for the moment I think he is just as well off where he is. He's away from air-raids and he's away from the centre of things so to speak. Before the Courts get round to examining his case'—he paused—'Chris, I am going to be perfectly honest with you. I do not agree with what happened on July 20th. I think I once told Peter that to try and get rid of this régime would be as foolhardy as to grab hold of a live wire with wet gloves. Anyway I am absolutely certain that Peter had nothing to do with it.' Perhaps it was the quick glance at the telephone, and the way he raised his voice which made me think he could have left out the 'perfectly honest with you' part. For the time being at least one thing was certain, Arnold and I were not going to be able to be perfectly honest with each other. 'I utterly agree with you; we need not even discuss it,' I said firmly, 'but I must disagree on one point and it is for this reason I have come to Berlin. Peter must be got away from Graudenz as soon as possible.'

I went on to describe what I knew of his relationship with the local Gestapo there and at the thought of the brutal face, 'Peter's private headache' seen through the smoky haze of that hotel restaurant, my voice gave way. 'He hasn't a chance up there, not a chance. He will be murdered, if he hasn't already been murdered, before he even comes up for trial.'

'Come, come, things are not as bad as that,' Arnold said as he jumped to his feet, and it was all I could do to stop myself replying 'You know damn well they are.' But from the way he was pacing the room, I knew that my words had gone home. Suddenly he swung round and stood in front of me, equally suddenly he was speaking German.

'Listen Chris,' he said earnestly, 'you know me and you know what I feel about Peter. He is my friend. I've known him since we were students together and I'm living in his house. You know, too, some of the arguments we've had together, Piet and I. We did not agree but it has made no difference to our friendship. It was my opinion at the time, it still is, that this régime was the last card we had to play here in Germany, and that if we did not back it with everything we had, this country would go communist and a communist Germany would have meant that Peter and I, and you as well for that matter, could look forward to a nice long stay in Siberia, if we even got that far. Believe me, I know the communists. In England, in spite of the miserable conditions I met with in the north, Marxism seemed to me never to get beyond being something of a mental exercise; the lecturers and the talkers, however brilliant, destructively brilliant I might say, could never have succeeded in giving birth to one single communist member of Parliament—well, one perhaps. It was very different here.'

I knew it had been different, and I knew too that Arnold, as a student during the dying months of the Weimar Republic and the early days of National Socialism, had been in the thick of it, in fact in 1933 he had organized a students' march to protest against the arbitrary dismissals of Jewish professors from Hamburg University. As a boy he had belonged to the Nationalist *Jung-Stahlhelm* and had lived in a left-wing district amongst those others—the Red Front, the Social Democratic Reichs Banner, and finally the Nazis—who had felt passionately enough about their various creeds to fight pitched battles in the streets, until Hitler had succeeded in swallowing the lot; rewarding them for their extinction by giving work to the workless, an Army to the militant, and a host of scapegoats on which to focus their manifold resentments—not to forget concentration camps for those who did not approve of his methods. How was it though that Hitler had succeeded with some of the more intelligent ones, with those who still possessed personal integrity, unless he had provided something more, something which had made them long for his leadership to succeed, in spite of the ever more obvious viciousness of his régime? Would it have been that sense of national identity which he could conjure up with such mastery? That awareness of belonging somewhere, which in England just came naturally, but which I believed amongst Germans to be a rare, almost unique phenomenon? Never mind, I gave up. I was suddenly very tired. I knew that Arnold was on my side and as for the rest that was for him to puzzle out.

'Listen,' I said, 'it's no use you and I arguing about the rights and wrongs. I have just been nearly killed by my so-called American cousins, and I'm in a thorough muddle myself. It's just that instinct tells me that Graudenz is not the place where Peter should be. If it is possible to get him transferred to Berlin, I think we shall have to risk the fact that some of our friends were mixed up in that plot of July 20th.' Without looking up or seeming to listen Arnold said suddenly: 'von Trott came here twice after the 20th, in fact he was here the evening before his arrest.'

'He was—and?' I may have sounded too eager.

'Oh, nothing really. We chatted together for quite a time actually. He hoped to see Peter, I guess.' A slight pause, then he added with a sigh, 'A splendid fellow, I would say. He showed no undue concern, just walked

around the room looking at things, then wandered out into the garden and
left as he had come.'

Arnold was staring thoughtfully at his tea cup, and for a moment it almost seemed that we were no longer alone in the room. 'You'll have to write
a book, Chris—Life amongst the Huns, what about that? I don't regret for
one moment that I did not leave my country—we have to solve this *ourselves*,
before the Allies have to do it for us—I know there are people out there who
speak the same language.'

"Walked about the room, looking at things." I knew how it had been;
past the sofa, up to the bookcase, hesitating at the telephone, leaning against
the mantelpiece with eyes half closed and a sudden young, very personal
smile; asking, probing, suggesting, listening attentively, and unconsciously
weaving his spell. Determined, in spite of every rebuff and at great risk, that
the threads which bound friend to friend, like-minded to like-minded, should
hold fast and survive the storm. With Hitler's armies stretching from the Bay
of Biscay to the Crimea, purposefully considering a Europe not dominated
by one man, but united in mutual respect. As the concentration camps filled,
confident in the intrinsic saneness of his people, and the rôle they could play
holding the delicate balance between East and West, in a post-war world
dominated, as he believed it would be, by Russia and America. Even per-
suading me, old dyed-in-the-wool Britisher that I was—'British to my Irish
core' was the description—that 'Pax Britannica', the British Empire, Sea
Power, all the cornerstones of my rather woolly political faith, would hold no
longer after the warring nations returned to their peaceful occupations.
'Nothing can be the same after this war. Don't look so blue, Chris. Your little
island will just have to change its rôle. It won't be so important, it may not
be so smug. It will have to loosen the reins, cease exploring and start to edu-
cate, and allow those pink blobs on the map to change to any colour they
please. I could believe it will be done gracefully; England is a pastmaster at
seeing the light just in time, and I could believe, too, that she will be helped
by all the richer countries having to provide massive support to the poorer
ones in order to help them to their nationhood. No charity about it; it is dangerous as well as unethical to be rich in a poor world.'

'Walked about the room looking at things.' I felt I was beginning to understand why Arnold looked thoughtful, and also why Peter had felt com-
pelled to try and rescue Adam regardless of the consequences, forgetting me
and forgetting the children. Living close to death I knew to be heightened
living. More than a friend, Adam had become a symbol, a clear and shining

symbol of the possible, of the might-have-been; he had been our future in some way and also our conscience. It was something therefore in himself perhaps, which Peter had tried to save, something on which we had pinned our hopes, something which at all costs must not be lost. There had to be a purpose, which gave us the right to live and there had to be the hope, in spite of any outward compromises we had made with a foul régime, that when the great moment came we would be found staunchly on the side of the angels.

I must have been very tired, for without my noticing it Arnold had taken up his tea cup, gone out of the room and closed the door. Without my noticing it darkness had fallen, and without my noticing it I was quite alone.

In the short five days that I was in Berlin, Peter's brother-in-law Reinhard Vogler came down from Hamburg bringing with him a breath of immensely comforting and respectable fresh air. He had decided to try his luck by putting in a good word for Peter at the Ministry of Justice. I knew that as a true Hamburg citizen he felt like a fish out of water in Berlin, but after his brush with officialdom when he was given a rude rebuff, he assured me that although he was a judge, he felt even less at home in the atmosphere of his Ministry.

Other friends were still around, though precious few: Hannes, Freda, Werner Traber, Lexi, but I knew they must be on the danger list and could do without a compromising visit from me. Racking my brains to find someone who was politically innocuous, I suddenly remembered von Brösigke, a handsome, lighthearted officer in the Cavalry SS, who had joined the set-up, I could swear, because the uniform suited him so admirably. Nazis and anti-Nazis, to him, were all just good chaps. In spite of his uniform he was the type who couldn't believe ill of anyone, a great man at a party, as innocent, one might say, as a new-laid egg. His good-heartedness had led him to help many who were in trouble, and many of his interventions had succeeded because one just couldn't disappoint such a sincere and likeable fellow. I rang him up and his reaction was true to form. Oblivious of the tapped telephone, he was loud in his indignation.

'What, Peter in prison, impossible! Good gracious, what the hell is going on. I've never heard such rot. Is there anything I can do? Wait, *Gnädige Frau*, we must meet.'

He told me that he was busy redecorating a little hunting lodge which he had inherited, somewhere east of Berlin. He asked me to come out and see it with him and help him perhaps with ideas.

With the Russians just outside Warsaw, hurtling westwards at incredible speed, I could think of many more fruitful ways of spending an afternoon, but he sounded a valuable ally and when I arrived, the little baroque hunting lodge was so lovely, and von B.'s enthusiasm so infectious, that I found myself offering suggestions which I realized later would have turned it into a very typical English manor house.

We were fetched from the station by a pony trap drawn by a pair of spanking cobs. An elderly coachman handed over the reins, covered our knees with a heavy fur rug and we bumped busily along through the flat, misty countryside. We wandered through the chilly, dusty rooms and an old manservant, obviously delighted at having the young laird home again, pulled back the heavy curtainings, brought out the silver and served us with tea and sandwiches in front of a blazing log fire.

Von Brösigke was a charming host and later brought out photograph albums to show me pictures of his family: faded picnic parties, posed about a table-cloth laden with eats, ladies in voluminous hats, and young men in boaters with heavy watch-chains adorning their waistcoats. Pickel-helmets galore and more of the old house as background to hunting scenes; portly huntsmen grasping their guns, and stag and wild boar stretched out in rows on the drive. A later volume showed wedding scenes, a smiling Hitler mixing with his guests. 'What a happy occasion that was,' von B sighed nostalgically, 'the Führer was in such good form,' and sure enough the bride looked lovely, the husband fond, and the groups of wedding guests well satisfied with themselves, as they toasted each other in doubtless French champagne. I looked at the date and place—Ober-Salzberg, 1943—the trees were in blossom, it was springtime I could see, it was also therefore—incredible as it may seem—a very short while after Stalingrad.

Before taking me to the station von Brösigke promised he would visit Peter as soon as he was transferred to some prison nearer Berlin. 'Such unheard of nonsense,' he repeated, 'Peter in prison. What the hell is happening anyway? Tell you what I'll do. I'll visit him in uniform. That'll show 'em. I can assure you, it will be a pleasure, *Gnädige Frau*, I'm allergic to policemen.'

Somehow I thought he would keep his word, for as he spoke his handsome face glowed with innocent zeal.

I only just got back to Rohrbach in time, for as I trudged up the valley road from the station I was overtaken by a motorcycle and sidecar. Such an unaccustomed sight made everyone pause in their work in the fields, and follow its progress down the track which led to the Mayor's house. There may have been nothing particularly menacing about the stiff figure in the green Homburg hat who climbed out of the sidecar and disappeared into the darkness of the Mayor's best front room, but there was certainly something most urgent in the manner in which the Mayor came running out of his doorway, grabbed his bicycle and started pushing it up the steep track to the road. There was also some embarrassment and at the same time a measure of relief in the look he gave me as he pedalled past and murmured, '*Grüss Gott, Frau Dr*, so you're back?'

I had not gone much further along the road before he returned posthaste, with Sepp pedalling behind him as swiftly as his ancient contraption could cover the ground. Yes, most certainly there was something up, for hardly had I reached the *Adler*, to be greeted with shouts of joy and hugs and kisses by my family, before Sepp passed the window on his way back to the shop. He was sweating profusely and did not stop to give us his usual cheery greeting.

In the evening though, he appeared at the window. 'May I talk to you a moment, Frau Dr,' he said, his kindly furrowed face looking unhappy and disturbed. 'Why of course, come in.' 'No, I won't come in,' he replied, 'it's easier said outside,' and when I joined him on the step, he moved away from the inn, down the road a little, to where there were no watching windows and only the misty fields stretched away to each side of us. 'I am going to tell you something which the Mayor and I think you should know,' he said. 'That fellow on the motorcycle came from Donaueschingen. He belongs to the Secret Police. He put you in our charge—you are under what he called "house arrest", Frau Dr, which means you must not leave the village. He asked us all about you, whether you had talked politics with us at all, and I can assure you we gave you a great reference. I told him how you worked with the peasants collecting stones off the potato patches, and your children helped with the herding, and how you felt almost more German than English. *Grosser Got*, we gave that little townsman a real earful.' 'That was good of you, Sepp,' I said, 'very good of you indeed. He didn't, I suppose, mention why my husband was in prison?' 'No—no,' he hesitated, 'just high treason was all he said it was—which reminds me, Frau Dr, he did say we were to give you no details as to what he had said to us,' he gave a short laugh, 'as if half the village didn't know at least who he was as soon as that motorcycle of his turned up the valley road. Anyway he told us that if we told you anything except that bit about house arrest we would be shot. The poor lower Baker got a bad fright when he said that, but we talked it over after he left and decided it was none of his business who we told. Stupid lowlander! Anyway, that's the way it is, and just don't tell anyone we have told you, and if you want to go to Furtwangen or any place to do some shopping, just let us know. Goodnight now, Frau Dr. And by the way, my wife told me to tell you there might be some white flour on the ration cards tomorrow, if you care to look in, and John's shoes—I'll try and have them ready for tomorrow too.'

The Unthinkable

Etty Hillesum

from *Letters from Westerbork*

Westerbork, 3 July 1943
Jopie, Klaas, my dear friends,

Here I am on the third tier of this bunk hurrying to unleash a veritable riot of writing, for in a few days' time it'll be the end of the line for my scribblings. I'll have become a "camp inmate," allowed to write just one letter a fortnight, and unsealed at that. And there are still a couple of little things I must talk to you about. Did I really send a letter that made it look as if all my courage had gone? I can hardly believe it. There are moments, it's true, when I feel things can't go on. But they do go on, you gradually learn that as well. Though the landscape around you may appear different: there is a lowering black sky overhead and a great shift in your outlook on life and your heart feels gray and a thousand years old. But it is not always like that. A human being is a remarkable thing. The misery here is really indescribable. People live in those big barracks like so many rats in a sewer. There are many dying children. But there are many healthy ones, too.

One night last week a transport of prisoners passed through here. Thin, waxen faces. I have never seen so much exhaustion and fatigue as I did that night. They were being "processed": registration, more registration, frisking by half-grown NSB men, quarantine, a foretaste of martyrdom lasting hours and hours. Early in the morning they were crammed into empty freight cars. Then another long wait while the train was boarded up. And then three days' travel eastwards. Paper "mattresses" on the floor for the sick. For the rest, bare boards with a bucket in the middle and roughly seventy people to a sealed car. A rucksack each was all they were allowed to take. How many, I wondered, would reach their destination alive? And my parents are preparing themselves for just such a journey unless something comes of Barneveld after all.

Last time I saw my father, we went for a walk in the dusty, sandy wasteland. He is so sweet, and wonderfully resigned. Very pleasantly, calmly, and quite casually, he said, "You know, I would like to get to Poland as quickly as possible. Then it will all be over and done with and I won't have to continue with this undignified existence. After all, why should I be spared from what has happened to thousands of others?" Later we joked about our surroundings. Westerbork really is nothing but desert, despite a few lupins and campions and decorative birds which look like seagulls. "Jews in a desert, we know that sort of landscape from before." It really gets you down, having such a nice little father, you sometimes feel there is no hope at all.

But these are passing moods. There are other sorts, too, when a few of us laugh together and marvel at all sorts of things. And then we keep meeting lots of relatives whom we haven't seen for years—lawyers, a librarian, and so on—pushing wheelbarrows full of sand, in untidy, ill-fitting overalls, and we just look at each other and don't say much. A young, sad Dutch police officer told me one transport night, "I lost two kilos during a night like this, and all *I* have to do is to listen, look, and keep my mouth shut." And that's why I don't like to write about it, either. But I am digressing. All I wanted to say is this: The misery here is quite terrible: and yet, late at night when the day has slunk away into the depths behind me, I often walk with a spring in my step along the barbed wire. And then time and again, it soars straight from my heart—I can't help it, that's just the way it is, like some elementary force—the feeling that life is glorious and magnificent, and that one day we shall be building a whole new world. Against every new outrage and every fresh horror, we shall put up one more piece of love and goodness, drawing strength from within ourselves. We may suffer, but we must not succumb. And if we should survive unhurt in body and soul, but above all in soul, without bitterness and without hatred, then we shall have a right to a say after the war. Maybe I am an ambitious woman; I would like to have just a tiny little bit of a say.

You speak about suicide, and about mothers and children. Yes, I know what you mean, but I find it a morbid subject. There is a limit to suffering; perhaps no human being is given more to bear than he can shoulder; beyond a certain point we just die. People are dying here even now of a broken spirit, because they can no longer find any meaning in life, young people. The old ones are rooted in firmer soil and accept their fate with dignity and calm. You see so many different sorts of people here, and so many different attitudes to the hardest, the ultimate questions . . .

I shall try to convey to you how I feel, but am not sure if my metaphor is right. When a spider spins its web, does it not cast the main threads ahead of itself, and then follow along them from behind? The main path of my life stretches like a long journey before me and already reaches into another world. It is just as if everything that happens here and that is still to happen were somehow discounted inside me. As if I had been through it already, and was now helping to build a new and different society. Life here hardly touches my deepest resources—physically, perhaps, you do decline a little, and sometimes you are infinitely sad—but fundamentally you keep growing stronger. I just hope that it can be the same for you and all my friends. We need it, for we still have so much to experience together and so much work to do. And so I call upon you: stay at your inner post, and please do not feel sorry or sad for me, there is no reason to. The Levies are having a hard time, but they have enough inner reserves to pull them through despite their poor physical state. Many of the children here are very dirty. That is one of our biggest problems—hygiene. I'll write again and tell you more about them. I enclose a scribbled note I began to write to Father and Mother, but didn't have to send; you might find some of it interesting.

I have one request, if you don't think it too immodest: a pillow or some old cushion; the straw gets a little hard in the end. But you are not allowed to send parcels weighing more than two kilos from the provinces, and a pillow probably weighs more than that. So if you happen to be in Amsterdam and should call at Pa Han's (please don't abandon him, and do show him this letter), you might perhaps send it from some post office there. Otherwise, my only wish is that you are all well and in good spirits, and send me a few kind words from time to time.

Lots and lots of love,
Etty

Sara Nomberg-Przytyk

"Friendly Meetings" from *Auschwitz: True Tales from a Grotesque Land*

A cold, penetrating rain had been falling for a few days. Such rains were not unusual in Auschwitz. I opened the gate of the infirmary very quietly so as not to disturb the performance and listened. "Plop, plop,"—the drops continued failing without a stop. Outside it was dark and quiet. The lights on the ramp of the station were out. It had been a few days since the last trainload of victims had arrived at Auschwitz. Perhaps, I thought, they would not bring any more victims here.

I sat down in the corner to watch the performance. It was Sunday. Since everything was at peace this day, Irena had organized a cultural evening in the infirmary. She had planned an evening of dancing—without men, of course. But then, it is possible to dance without men, too.

Irena was an actress. Although she was originally from Poland, she had lived in Paris some fourteen years before being shipped to Auschwitz. She was tall, strong, and straight. I remember that when I first met her it was hard for me to believe that she was an actress. Looking at her, you would absolutely never guess that she was an actress. The girls who knew her swore that once she got on the stage she changed so completely that you would never recognize her. She was particularly wonderful, they said, as a character actress.

In Auschwitz we often organized such friendly get-togethers. I remember that for the first few months of my stay here those get-togethers struck me as being indecent. How was it possible that we could sing while the sky above was red with the flames of the crematoria.

"How can you joke, dance, and tell stories," I asked, "when we are enveloped in a sea of suffering, pain, and tears?"

"You will get used to it. Then you will understand." So said the old prisoners.

One evening, as I was returning from the infirmary to the barracks for the night, I bumped into a group of girls from the *Leichenkomando*, whose job it was to load the dead into the trucks. One of them stood near a pile of corpses, the second near the truck, the third on a small stool, and the fourth on the platform of the truck. They were handing the dead to each other any old way: grabbing the corpse by the leg, or the arm, or the hair, and then swinging it onto the platform. I noted their indifference to the dead and tried to imagine what kind of women they had been a few years ago, when they loved and were loved in a world of normality. Every few minutes I could hear a sound—the thump of falling flesh and the cries of the women: "Hurry up. Why are you dawdling?"

One of the women started singing a song and immediately the rest of them joined in: "For a cup of flour, he kissed for an hour."

They sang to the melody of a German march. I descended on them, half choking:

"How can you sing a merry song in front of those skeletons?" I called out resentfully.

They looked at me in bewilderment, without the foggiest notion of what I was talking about.

"You'll get used to it," one of them said. Then, after a moment's silence, she added: "If you don't get used to it you'll drop dead."

I got used to it. After eight months in Auschwitz, I could look at the dead with indifference. When a corpse was lying across my path I did not go around it any more, I simply stepped over it, as if I were merely stepping over a piece of wood. I sang along with the others, and I laughed when I heard a good joke. I even told jokes myself. I even got used to the rats warming themselves in front of the stove like cats. I had imbibed all of the terrors of Auschwitz and lived. Then I really understood that my ability to adapt to just about anything was a most useful talent. Was this good or bad? It was difficult for me to know.

High on the ceiling a small light bulb was burning; we were sitting around, scattered all over the room. Some were sitting on the table, some were sitting on the floor. Marusia and Kwieta and all of the other Czechs were singing a beautiful youth song about those who "defy the wind." The words of the song said that only by swimming against the current could the strong achieve satisfaction. The French girls were singing French songs about Paris. I specialized in Russian songs. I sang without thinking about the red sky. Somebody recited a poem. Then, in hushed tones, we sang a prison hymn in German. The conductor of the orchestra, a Hungarian woman, was the main attraction. She had come to the camp with her violin; now she started playing Hungarian and gypsy melodies. We were sitting around, listening, as if bewitched. Suddenly the door of the infirmary opened with a loud crash, and there stood Hitler: moustache, hair, and a haughty, stupid expression. We all jumped up from our places, and Marusia even yelled "Achtung!" Hitler walked in with a long stride and an outstretched hand and kneeled in front of me. He set his hands beseechingly and whispered, "Maybe you would like to change places with me."

We all burst into joyous laughter. It was Irena. She was mocking my assertion that we had it better than Hitler because we had more of a chance of living through the war. Hitler would certainly not live through the war, but we might. She got up. We could not get over her impersonation. With the help of black shoe polish she had changed her face beyond recognition.

Now the girls started dancing to the accompaniment of the violin. Orli was standing next to me, pale and agitated.

"Has something happened?" I asked.

"Walk outside unobtrusively," Orli said, "so that nobody will notice."

We left the infirmary. It was raining without letup. The ramp was lighted up. The SS men were standing in front of the cars. We had been feeling happy because the transports were not arriving. Now the unloading of the people was starting again, but quietly, without the usual screaming. Nude men came out, so skinny that it was difficult to believe that those people were moving on their own power. They were, indeed, moving skeletons.

"Those are Russian prisoners," Orli whispered. "They were working someplace, and now, since they are incapable of working any more, they are being sent to the gas chambers."

They walked slowly under the cold rain. Some of them were swaying. They all went to the gas chambers. The lights on the station went out, the empty cars left, and we just stood there, outside.

"Let's not tell the girls anything. Let's not spoil their fun," Orli said quietly. We did not return to the infirmary. To sing and joke now was beyond our strength. After all, you could not get used to everything.

Charlotte Delbo

"Weiter" from *Auschwitz and After*

The SS at the four corners stake out limits not to be crossed. It was a large building yard. Everything that haunted us every night was assembled there: rocks to break, a road to pave, sand to excavate, handbarrows to transport the stones and sand, ditches to dig, bricks to carry from one pile to the next. Assigned to various teams together with Polish women, we exchanged sad smiles whenever our paths crossed.

Now that the sun was shining, it was not so cold. At the noon break, we sat down to eat on some building materials. Once we had downed our soup—it only took a few minutes, the longest time was spent waiting for its distribution, waiting in line in front of the canteens—we had a little time left before returning to the stones, sand, road, ditch and bricks. We squashed the lice at the open collars of our dresses. This is where they swarm the most. In view of their numbers, to kill a few hardly made any difference. It was our playtime. Sad. The midday break when we were able to sit down because the weather was fair.

Clustered in little groups of friends, we chatted. Each one spoke of her province, her home, invited the others to visit her. You'll come, won't you? You will come. We promised. We made so many trips.

"Weiter." The shout shatters the lull of our daydreams.

"Weiter." To whom is he speaking?

"Weiter."

A woman is walking towards the stream, her tin cup in hand, probably to rinse it out. She stops, hesitating.

"Weiter." Does he mean her?

"Weiter." There is a kind of mockery in the tone of the SS.

The woman hesitates. Must she really go farther? Could it be that to lean toward the stream is not allowed at this spot?

"Weiter," orders the SS more imperiously.

The woman draws back, stops again. Standing with the marsh behind her, everything about her questions: "Is it allowed here?"

"Weiter," shrieks the SS.

Then the woman begins to walk, upstream.

"Weiter."

A shot. The woman crumples.

The SS swings his gun back over his shoulder, calls his dog, walks toward the woman. Leaning over her body, he turns her over as one does game.

The other SS laugh from their posts.

She had gone beyond the limit by less than twenty steps.

We make a count of our group. Are we all here?

When the SS raised his gun and took aim, the woman was walking in the sun.

She was killed instantly.

It was one of the Polish women.

Some had not seen it and were wondering what happened. The others wonder if they had seen right but say nothing.

Elsa Morante

from *History: A Novel*

To all provincial authorities, to be carried out immediately, the following police order has been sent:

I—All Jews resident in Italian territory, even if granted special status, to whatever nation they may belong, must be sent to concentration camps set up for the purpose. All their property, real estate and other, must be immediately seized, until it can be confiscated by the Italian Social Republic, which will distribute it in the interest of indigent victims of enemy air raids.

2—All those born of mixed marriages who, in application of the existing racial laws, were recognized as members of the Aryan race, must be subjected to special surveillance by the police forces.

—Rome, 30 November 1943

This double ordinance, by which the Italians sanctioned the *Final Solution* already initiated by the Germans, covered the case of the widow Ida Mancuso née Ramundo, both in the first article (because she was an air-raid victim) and in the second (because an Aryan of mixed blood). But it doesn't seem to have had any practical effect on Ida, all the same. In fact, she received no benefit from the Jews' confiscated property. And, as for the second article, it's true, apparently, that in the course of the following season, after her transferral to a new temporary domicile, some policemen came to question the concierge about her situation. But the concierge-informer kept his information to himself; or at least, if he reported it to anyone, it was under the seal of secrecy. She never knew about it. And probably her file ended up lost in the subsequent annihilation of all destinies.

However, the double ordinance, which she happened to see at the beginning of December, meant for her that she was officially under special police surveillance from that moment. Her guilt was thus contemplated by the law, without ambiguity or compromise, and denounced to the world on the city walls: *Wanted, a certain Ida, alias Iduzza, of mixed race, mother of two children, the older a deserter and a partisan, and the second, a bastard of unknown father.* For Ninnarieddu, she wasn't too afraid: the moment she thought of him, she could see him, with his dancer's gait, his long, straight legs and his feet flung out, kicking aside any obstacle or tumult, her invulnerable son. But she was persecuted by horrible fears for Useppe. It was known that during the round-up of the Jews, the Germans had grabbed children, even babes in their mother's arms, flinging them into their funereal trucks, like rags into a rubbish pile; and that in certain villages, in reprisal or merely out of drunkenness, they had killed children, crushing them with tanks, or burning them alive, or slamming them against the walls. Few people, at that time, believed these reports, considered too incredible (though, to tell the truth—it must be reported—they were later confirmed by History and, indeed, represent only a small part of the reality). But Ida couldn't dispel those visions: so the streets of Rome and of the world for her seemed crowded with possible executioners of her Useppetto, her little pariah without race, underdeveloped, undernourished, poor valueless remnant. At times, not only the Germans and the Fascists, but all human adults seemed murderers to her; and she ran through the street, aghast, to arrive, exhausted, her eyes wide, in the big room, starting to call from the road "Useppe! Useppe!" and laughing like a sick little girl when the tiny voice answered her: "A' mà!"

The Nazi-Fascists, actually, still didn't dare show themselves too often in the slum. The October shootings hadn't sufficed to frighten the population of those huts drowned in mud and hunger. With winter, the attacks on bakeries and food trucks became more frequent. Bands of guerrillas were formed within the slum itself, and it was said that in the caves, in the hovels and little rooms where families of ten people slept, even under the beds, weapons were hidden, stolen back in September from army outposts and barracks. Even the young males, who in the rest of the city mostly remained hidden in the fear of raids, here displayed themselves defiantly, with hard, grim faces, in the courtyards and the holes and the garbage dumps of their outlying ghetto, among their worn and disheveled mothers, the wasted girls, the lice-ridden kids with their little bellies swollen from lack of nourishment. Ida avoided going too far away from the slum, so as not to leave Useppe alone; but to bring him something to eat, she forced herself to desperate exploits. Even the famous nest egg of savings sewn into the stocking had now been consumed in black-market shopping, and like the other kids', his little belly had also swollen slightly. Every time she went to the Bursary to draw her monthly pay, Ida felt her legs buckle beneath her, expecting the clerk to announce to her indignantly: "Wicked halfbreeds like you are no longer entitled to any salary!"

The big room had remained uninhabited only for a few days. At the beginning of December, once the news had spread that over there, at the end of that avalanche of mud and garbage, a roof was available, new lost creatures had begun to turn up, in whom Ida, with her confused prejudices, saw a threat rather than a protection. She was even more afraid to leave Useppe now in that company than she had been, before, to leave him alone.

Among the many newcomers, there happened to be the family of a little shopkeeper from Genzano, dazed with terror of air raids. Apparently some one of The Thousand had directed them here. The head of the family, a ruddy and corpulent man, who suffered from high blood pressure, had been seen only at their arrival, then he had rushed back to Genzano, where his shop had already been bombed out, but the house was still standing. The fact was that in a wall of the house he had secretly bricked up, for safe-keeping, all the money and valuables he had left, and for this reason he wanted to stand guard. Until one day, in a raid, which still left the house intact, he died of a heart attack, from fear. A relative came from Genzano to bring the news to the family, all women. And the room filled with screams and weeping. But after some argument, between sobs, the women, also overcome by terror of the bombings, left the relative the task of burying the dead man and watching the house; and they stayed where they were, in the room.

They were also obese, but pale; and the mother's legs were all swollen with varicose veins. They spent the day around a brazier, mourning, in total inertia and dejected silence. They were waiting for the arrival of the Allies, who, according to them, were at the gates, and then they would go back to Genzano, where, however, they no longer had a shop, or a man, nothing but that hypothetical, walled-up treasure. And they spoke of the imminent Liberation in spent voices, like enormous hens on a peg perch, saddened in the swelling of their feathers, reduced to waiting for the arrival of the master, to carry them off in a sack.

If Useppe approached the brazier, they pushed him away, saying in a whining voice, "Go back to your mamma, kid."

A woman from Pietralata also turned up, mother of one of the boys shot on October 22nd. When her son was alive, she had nagged him all the time because he came home late at night, until her son, exasperated by her constant yelling, had even beaten her, and she had also, in the past, reported him for this to the police. Now, every evening, she went wandering from one house to another because she was afraid to sleep at home, where she said her son's ghost came back every night to beat her. This boy of hers was named Armandino, and the Germans had arrested him before her eyes, after she too, that day as on previous occasions, had joined in the attack on the Fort, hoping to get some flour. Every now and then, during the night, she could be heard saying: "No, Armandino, no. Not your own mamma!" Often, in the daytime, she would boast of Armandino's beauty, famous in Pietralata for his resemblance to the actor Rossano Brazzi. And, in fact, she herself must also have been good-looking when young: she still had very beautiful long hair, but gray now, and lousy.

These new refugees in the big room had brought their own mattresses; and in addition, left by transient guests, there was some kapok scattered on the floor at the disposal of other temporary vagabonds. Carlo Vivaldi's pallet was occupied by a young man of whom Ida was especially afraid, as if of a werewolf. It's true he had made some improvements in the room, applying pieces of plywood to the broken windows, replacing the paper; but for the rest, he resembled not so much a man as some other starving mammal, of a nocturnal species. He was tall and muscular, but bent, and he had a cadaverous face, with protruding teeth. No one knew where he came from, or what his profession was, or how he had landed there; but from his speech, he seemed Roman. He also, if Useppe approached him, sent him away, saying: "Clear out, kid."

The days of The Thousand were past! The only one who occasionally paid any attention to Useppe was the mother of the executed boy; when it was dark, she would accompany him down to the latrine, if necessary, holding his hand as Carulina used to. And one evening, in helping him pull up his pants, touching his fleshless little ribs, she said to him: "Poor little bird, I have a feeling you won't make it, you won't grow up. You're not long for this world. The war slaughters kids."

She entertained him, too, with a game, or rather a fairy tale accompanied by mime, which she had already used with her own children when they were little. It was always the same, and it consisted of this: as a beginning, she tackled the palm of his hand, saying:

"Square, pretty square,
Here passed a crazy hare,"

and then, pulling up his fingers, one by one, beginning with the thumb, she continued:

"This caught him,
this killed him,
this cooked him,
this ate him,"

and reaching the little finger, she concluded:

"and this one was left all alone,
because for him there was none."

"Again," Useppe would say to her at the end of the story; and she would start over at the beginning, while Useppe would look at her intently, hoping that, one of these times, the crazy hare would manage to escape, leaving the

hunters empty-handed. But invariably the tale proceeded and ended always
in exactly the same way.

Mitsuye Yamada

Evacuation

As we boarded the bus
bags on both sides
(I had never packed
two bags before
on a vacation
lasting forever)
the *Seattle Times*
photographer said
Smile!
so obediently I smiled
and the caption the next day
read:

Note smiling faces
a lesson to Tokyo.

On the Bus

Who goes?
Not the leaders of the people
combed out and left
with the FBI.
Our father
stayed behind
triple locks.
What was the charge?
Possible espionage or

impossible espionage.
I forgot which.

Only those who remained
free in prisons
stayed behind.

The rest of us went to
Camp Harmony
where the first baby
was christened

Melody.

Harmony at the Fair Grounds

Why is the soldier boy in a cage
like that?
In the freedom of the child's
universe
the uniformed guard
stood trapped in his outside cage.
We walked away from the gate and
grated guard
on sawdusted grounds
where millions trod once
to view prize cows
at the Puyallup Fair.

They gave us straws to sleep on
encased in muslin ticks.
Some of us were stalled under grandstand
seats
the egg with
parallel lines.

Lines formed for food
lines for showers

lines for the john
lines for shots.

Curfew

In our area
was a block head
who told us
what's what
in a warden's helmet.

Turn off your lights
it's curfew time!

I was reading
with a flashlight
under my blanket
but the barracks boards
in the hot sun
had shrunk slyly
telling
bars of light

Off with your lights.

There must be no light.

In the Outhouse

Our collective wastebin
where the air sticks
in my craw
burns my eyes
I have this place to hide
the excreta and
the blood which
do not flush down
nor seep away.

They pile up
fill the earth.

I am drowning.

Inside News

A small group
huddles around a contraband
radio
What?
We
are losing the war?
Who is we?
We are we the enemy
the enemy is the enemy.

Static sounds and we
cannot hear.
The enemy is confused
the enemy is determined
and winning.

Mess hall gossips
have it that
the parents
with samurai morals
are now the children.

Hirabayashi Taiko

"Blind Chinese Soldiers"

On March 9, 1945, a day when by coincidence one of the biggest air raids
took place, the sky over Gumma Prefecture was clear. An airplane, which
might have taken off from Ota, flew along with the north wind.

Taking the road from Nashiki in the morning, I (a certain intellectual-turned-farmer) came down from Mount Akagi, where the snow in the valleys of the mountain was as hard as ice. From Kamikambara I took the Ashino-line train to Kiryu, transferred to the Ryoge-line, and got off at Takasaki. I was to transfer again to the Shingo-line to go to Ueno.

It was around four-thirty in the afternoon. Although the sky was still so light as to appear white, the dusty roofs of this machinery-producing town and the spaces among the leaves of the evergreen trees were getting dark. The waiting room on the platform was dark and crowded with people who had large bamboo trunks or packages of vegetables on their shoulders or beside them on the floor. It reverberated with noise and commotion.

After taking a look at the large clock hanging in front of me, I was about to leave the waiting room. Just at that moment, a group of policemen with straps around their chins crossed a bridge of the station and came down to the platform. Among them were the police chief and his subordinate, carrying iron helmets on their backs and wearing white gloves. The subordinate was talking about something with the station clerk who accompanied them, but it seemed that the word of the police chief, who interrupted their talk, decided the matter. The clerk crossed the bridge and then returned from the office with a piece of white chalk in his hand. Pushing people aside, he started drawing a white line on the platform.

I was standing in front of the stairway with one leg bent; I had sprained it when someone dropped a bag of nails in the crowded Ryoge-line train. The clerk came up to me, pushed me back aggressively, and drew a white line. As was usual in those days, the train was delayed considerably. The passengers, quite used to the arrogance of the clerks, stepped aside without much resistance and, to pass the time, watched what was happening with curiosity.

Shortly, a dirty, snow-topped train arrived. Before I noticed it, the policemen, who had been gathered together in a black mass, separated into two groups. They stood at the two entrances of the car that I was planning to board. The white lines had been drawn right there.

The car seemed quite empty, but when I tried to enter I found myself forcibly prevented by a policeman. I then realized that in the center of the car there was a young, gentle-looking officer sitting and facing another young officer who was obviously his attendant. With his characteristic nose, he was immediately recognizable as Prince Takamatsu.

With the strange, deep emotion that one might experience upon recognizing an existence hitherto believed to be fictitious, I gazed at this beautiful young man. My natural urge was to shout and tell everyone out loud, "The

Prince is in there. He's real!" Yet it was not the time, either for myself or for the other passengers, for such an outburst. Unless one managed to get into one of the cars—at the risk of life and limb—one would have to wait additional long hours; how long, no one knew.

I rushed to one of the middle cars immediately. Yet my motion was slowed by the wasteful mental vacuum that the shock of seeing the Prince had created. I stood at the very end of the line of passengers, looking into the center of the car and trying to see whether there was some way I could get in.

After glimpsing the pleasant and elegant atmosphere in the well-cleaned car with blue cushions, I found myself reacting with a particularly strong feeling of disgust to the dirtiness and confusion of this car. Shattered window glass, the door with a rough board nailed to it instead of glass, a crying child, an old woman sitting on her baggage, a chest of drawers wrapped in a large *furoshiki* cloth, an unwrapped broom—a military policeman appeared, shouting that there was still more space left in the middle of the car, but no one responded to his urging.

I gave up trying to get into this car and ran to the last car. There were no passengers standing there. A soldier, possibly a lower-ranking officer, was counting with slight movements of his head the number of the plain soldiers in white clothes who were coming out of the car. An unbearable smell arose from the line of the soldiers who, carrying blankets across their shoulders, had layers of filth on their skin—filth which one could easily have scraped off.

I was looking up at the doorway wondering what this could mean; then my legs began trembling with horror and disgust.

Looking at them carefully, I could see that all of these soldiers were blind; each one stretched a trembling hand forward to touch the back of the soldier ahead. They looked extremely tired and pale; from their blinking eyes tears were falling and their hair had grown long. It was hard to tell how old they were, but I thought they must be between thirty-five and fifty years old. On further examination, I observed that there was one normal person for every five blind men. The normal ones wore military uniforms which, although of the same color as Japanese uniforms, were slightly different from them. They held sticks in their hands.

Judging from the way they scolded the blind soldiers or watched how the line was moving, I guessed they must be caretakers or managers of the blind soldiers.

"*Kuai kuaide! Kuai kuaide!*" [Quickly, quickly] a soldier with a stick shouted, poking the soldier in front of him. I realized then that all the soldiers in this group were Chinese. I understood why, even aside from the feeling evoked by their extreme dirtiness, they looked strange and different.

All the soldiers who were led out of the car were left standing on the platform. There were about five hundred of them. I doubted my own eyes and looked at them again carefully. All of them half-closed their eyes as if it were too bright, and tears were dripping from every eye. It was certain that every one of them was blind.

The supervising soldiers who were not blind saluted suddenly, and a Japanese officer with a saber at his waist appeared from one of the cars.

"What about the others?" he asked, passing by a soldier who was busy counting the number of blind soldiers.

"They will come later, sir, on such and such a train," the lower officer answered.

"What on earth is this all about?" the sympathetic yet suspicious expressions of the passengers seemed to ask. A middle-aged woman even started crying, holding her hand-towel to her eyes. It was obvious that both the commander and the lower officer wanted to hide the blind soldiers from the passengers, but it took a long time to get the rest off the train, and the number of onlookers gathering behind the fence gradually increased.

At last those at the head of the line began climbing up the stairs of the station, while the train started moving slowly. I was standing on the steps of the car in front of the one which had just been emptied and was holding on with all my might. I could see the policemen who were guarding the soldiers whispering to each other.

"I guess they were used for a poison gas experiment or they are the victims of some sort of explosion," said a man with an iron helmet on his back, standing four or five persons ahead of me.

"They don't have to carry out poison gas experiments in the motherland," a man who appeared to be his companion objected. Following up the companion's comment, I asked a woman of about forty who was standing next to me,

"When did those soldiers get on the train?"

"Let's see, I think at around Shinonoi."

"Then they must have come from around the Nagoya area," I said to myself, although it did not give me a clue to understand anything.

Soon the passengers forgot about it and began to converse.

"I came from Echigo. I am on my way to Chiba with my daughter." The woman whom I had just come to know started talking in a friendly manner.

She told me that she was bringing her daughter to report for duty in the women's volunteer army and that her departure had been delayed for a week because her daughter had had an ugly growth on her neck. Since they could not get through tickets to Chiba, they would go as far as they could, then stay in the place they had reached, standing in line until they could buy tickets to continue their journey. They had come this far, she said, but the hardships they had been through were beyond description.

I had been offended a moment ago by the unconcerned way in which this woman had answered my question about the Chinese soldiers, but I now thought I could understand it. The Japanese were too involved in their own affairs to be moved by such an incident.

When the train left a station some time later, I went into the car which had been occupied by the Chinese soldiers, hoping to sit down and rest. I returned soon, however, because the smell there was intolerable.

The conductor came from the end of the train, announcing "Jimbobara next, Jimbobara next," as he passed among the passengers. By that time, the windows on the west side were burning with the rays of the setting sun, and the huge red sun was setting with the sanctity of the apocalypse. I realized that the car occupied by the Chinese had been taken away and that my car had become the last of the train.

Yes, there was the Prince, still in the car ahead of us, I remembered. But I was too tired to tell anyone.

After the war was over, I asked the merchants who had their shops in front of the Takasaki station whether they had seen the group of Chinese soldiers boarding the train again. They all said they had never seen them again. Perhaps they never returned from that place.

Kikue Tada

"The Scars Remain"

Hiroshima—a city proud of its abundant greenery, blue skies, and its seven rivers forming a beautiful delta—was converted in an instant to scorched earth by the atomic bomb. Even now, thirty-seven years later, I cannot forget the scenes I saw then, scenes beyond the power of pen or tongue to describe.

I was twelve in 1937, when the so-called China Incident occurred. Having been taught that dying for one's country was a great honor, I decided to become a nurse and tend soldiers on the battlefield. When the Pacific War began in December 1941, I had made the spirit of Florence Nightingale my own and become a nurse at the Ujina-machi Joint Army Hospital (currently the Hiroshima Prefectural Hospital). I was then sixteen years old.

Then, on August 6, 1945, the first atomic bomb to be used against human beings was dropped on my beloved city. Only a few minutes earlier a brilliant summer sun shone in the sky, people came and went in the streets, and children played under the trees. In one blinding flash all of this became a living hell.

I had gone to my family home in the country to be with my younger brother, who was to enter the navy at a place called Kure on August 6. I returned to the hospital on August 8, two days after the bombing. A stream of trucks was carrying the wounded to the hospital, but the hospital itself was in a shambles, having been hit by a blast of wind from the bomb. The ceilings had fallen, and all the windows were broken. Shattered glass lay everywhere. Because the wards were full, we cleared up the glass from the corridors and lobby and put them to use.

Treatment began with simply determining whether the patient was alive or dead. But there was really not much else we could do. The medical supplies were soon depleted, and we were reduced to brushing the patients' wounds with oil provided by the army. The most we could do for the dead, who lay everywhere at our feet, was to cover them with straw mats. Their bodies were horribly mutilated. Skin hung in tattered strips, and raw bloody wounds gaped like split pomegranates. They were often naked or nearly naked, and yet it was sometimes impossible to tell men from women.

The only food we had to offer them was mush made of flour and water, served in lengths of cut bamboo. There weren't enough nurses to hand-feed the immobile patients; we could only put the food by their sides and have them fend for themselves. In doing this, I asked myself if I was being true to my calling as a nurse. Was it not my duty to help people who could not help themselves? But I had no choice but to steel myself against these doubts and go on with my work.

Making our rounds we lifted up the straw mats covering patients to see whether they were alive or dead. The dead ones were unceremoniously hauled away on stretchers like so much baggage.

Day after day, under a blazing sun, B29s seemed never to tire of flying over the city. Formations of five or ten enemy planes flew over the hospital on their way inland. Each time they came, we hurried the living patients into air-raid shelters. To get out of the heat and into the cool of the shelter, many patients pushed and shoved their way in, only to die there. We walked over their bodies as we carried in other patients. Because it was our duty to stand guard, the nurses had to remain outside the shelters, where every day we watched fighter planes burst into flames and fall into the Seto Inland Sea. It was oddly like seeing war films.

Added to everything else was the constant fear that our white uniforms would make us easy targets for enemy gunners. Our duty to the patients, however, would not allow us to think of our own safety. Instead, between air raids we had to pull a seemingly endless number of bodies from the shelters with hooked poles of the kind used by construction workers, and then haul them to the cremation pit beside the hospital. This pit, which was big enough to hold a building, was fitted with a kind of grill—resembling the grills used in roasting fish—made of heavy steel beams. The bodies were piled on this grill, doused with gasoline, and burned. These cremations took place constantly, day and night.

With no electric lights of any kind, we went about our tasks at night under the illumination provided by the bluish cremation fire and by the flames of still burning houses. All this was ghastly enough, but we encountered even more gruesome sights when we made our rounds.

I recall a screaming baby trying to nurse at the breast of its already dead mother. Could there possibly be any scene more inhuman than this? And once, as I was making a check of the corridors, someone called out to me. Walking toward the voice, what I saw took my breath away—a person so horribly burned that it was impossible to tell whether it was a man or woman. "Nurse," the person said, "my train pass is in my pocket. Would you take it out and look at the photograph. Do I look like the picture?" The person was unable to move, but was apparently desperate to know the answer. From the pass I learned that she was a fourteen-year-old girl named Kazuko Fukuda, a second-year student in a girls' school. The photograph showed a clever-looking girl with bobbed hair. But no words could describe her appearance now. She was like a piece of raw meat from which skin dangled. But I blurted out, "Yes, yes, you look just like this. Very pretty!" Then in broken phrases she said, "My address is written there. Please get in touch with my mother. I can't die without seeing her."

I identified very closely with this poor girl, and wanted terribly to do something for her. After all, there was not that much difference in our ages. Shortly afterward the girl became too weak to talk. I poured a little water in her mouth, and was trying to determine whether she had swallowed it when I realized she was no longer breathing.

I had seen many people die, but no death has remained in my mind as vividly and as long as that of this girl, whose final words were spoken to me. I can still clearly picture her face, and from time to time she appears in my dreams. Even today, I am plagued by the question of whether her family ever received her remains.

A woman with a baby strapped to her back stalked like someone half mad through the corridor, lifting one straw mat after another and shouting, "No! This is not him! No, damn it. No!" Then she lifted the mat from a corpse that was burned black and whose lips were horribly swollen. Turning the body over and seeing a piece of clothing adhering to its back, she shrieked, "It's him! I know this pattern. It's him!" Weeping hysterically, she fell on the poor body that was so disfigured that even a wife of many years was unable to recognize it except by the pattern of a scrap of clothing. For a while I just stood there, wondering why such things had to happen.

The victims who were still alive three days after the blast were in pathetic condition. Their wounds had rotted and oozed black fluid. Maggots crawled around in the joints of their arms and legs; unable to speak, the patients could do nothing but watch the maggots moving about.

Since the day of the bombing, the nurses had lived in the courtyard under a mosquito net. In three or four days, some of the nurses, failing victim to overwork, ran high temperatures, developed diarrhea, and then collapsed. There was no alternative but to send them home. Feelings of frustration and anger became overpowering. On any number of days I thought I had reached my limit. But, renewing my vows as a nurse, I was determined to go on as long as there was an ounce of energy left in me.

Ambulatory patients, constantly calling for water, wandered about like sleepwalkers. Their bodies were painted over with iodine and mercurochrome, adding to their unearthly appearance. As nurses we should have been able to remain composed in front of such people, but sometimes it proved impossible to suppress a gasp of horror.

Though I was subjected to massive doses of secondary radiation while at the hospital, I still hoped to lead a normal, happy life, and eventually I got married. Not long afterward, however, I began suffering from damage to my liver, kidneys, and abdomen. I had two operations on my ovaries. I became feverish and nauseous. Unidentifiable growths, nine or ten centimeters in diameter, began appearing all over my body. Surgery only caused them to multiply. Because I was constantly in and out of the hospital, my husband and I got a divorce.

Physically frail and with two dear daughters to raise by myself, I sometimes thought of suicide. But each time the children encouraged me by saying we would be all right if we all worked together.

Then when it came time for my girls, whose upbringing had caused me such suffering and effort, to get married, I was always asked about the health prospects of children of atomic-radiation victims. The only thing I could say was that they were perfectly healthy at the present time. Even after their marriages, I worried about the children they would bear.

Of course, other people suffered horribly too. A friend of mind, a nurse at the Red Cross Hospital at the time of the bombing, had been trapped under a house and her face burned. She underwent plastic surgery a number of times, but in the end she herself broke off relations with the man she hoped to marry. She now lives alone and works in a hospital.

The aftereffects of the atomic bombing still persist. Five years ago I began suffering from cardiac insufficiency and angina pectoris. Each year, from about October to May, when the weather turns cold, I have severe attacks of pain in the chest that last for an hour or so. My blood pressure rises to 200 over 140. I suffer, but have no idea where to put the blame for the suffering.

Every year on August 6, great crowds of people gather in the Peace Park in Hiroshima. I wonder if they really understand what we victims feel. Can their prayers really contribute to worldwide peace? I have my doubts. But, as one of the few remaining victims of the bombing, I intend to go on telling my story as long as there is life left in me.

Victory, Occupation, and After

Doris Lessing

from *Landlocked*

Three days ago, on to the polished cement of the verandah had slid an official letter, bidding Mr. Quest to the Victory Celebrations for the Second World War (in Europe) as a representative of the soldiers of the First World War. Mr. Quest had been in a drugged sleep when the letter came. Mrs. Quest, long before he had woken up, had worked out a long and careful plan that would make it possible for her husband to attend. She yearned to be there, on that morning of flags and bands, her invalid husband—the work of so many years of devotion—beside her, his illnesses officially recognized as the result of the First World War. But she had been afraid he would refuse. In the past, he had always laughed, with a bitter contempt that had hurt her terribly. Or, if he had gone, it had been (or so it seemed) only for the sake of the angry nihilism he could use on the occasion after it was over.

In 1922 (was it?) she had stood by the Cenotaph in Whitehall with the handsome man who was her husband, and her soul had melted with the drums and the fifes and the flags of Remembrance Day. Afterwards Mr. Quest had indulged in days of vituperation about the generals and the government and the type of mind that organized Remembrance Days and handed out white feathers—he had been handed a white feather on the day he had put off his uniform after the final interview with the doctors who said he would never be himself again. "We are afraid you will never really be yourself again, Captain." He mocked everything that fed the tender soul of Mrs. Quest, who had always needed the comfort of anniversaries, ceremonies, ritual, the proper payment of respect where it was due.

But—and here comes something odd that Mrs. Quest was quite aware of herself. There was something in her that liked her husband's mockery, that needed it. Something older, more savage, more knowledgeable in the tidily hatted matron who let her eyes fill with tears at The Last Post waited for and needed the old soldier's ribaldry. Three days ago, when she had taken the official letter to him, she had expected him to laugh.

But he had lowered faded eyes to the government letter, and remained silent, his lips folding and refolding as if he was tasting something from the past. Then he looked up at his wife with a face adjusted to an appropriate humility (a look which appalled Mrs. Quest, so unlike him was it) and said in a voice false with proper feeling, "Well, perhaps if I wrap up, how about it?"

Mrs. Quest had been shaken to her depths. Perhaps for the first time she really *felt* what the nurse in her had always known, that hear husband really was not "himself." Not even intermittently, these days, was he himself, and for hours they had discussed in every painful detail how it could be possible for him to attend the ceremony, while his face preserved the terrifyingly unreal expression of a man who has given his all for his country and now submits in modesty to his country's thanks.

There were two main questions involved. One was, sleep or the absence of it. The other: Mr. Quest's bowels. But the problem was the same, in effect: it was impossible to predict anything. The point was, Mr. Quest's body had been so wrenched and twisted by every variety of drug, that drugs themselves had become like symptoms, to be discussed and watched. It was not a question of Mr. Quest's having taken so many grains of—whatever it was, which would have a certain effect. A sleeping draught, an aperient, might "work" or it might not, and if it did work, then it was unpredictably and extraordinarily, and information must be saved for the doctor, who would be interested scientifically in what surely must be unprecedented, from the medical point of view.

The Parade was at eleven, and would be over by twelve. During this hour Mr. Quest would be in a wheel chair with his medals pinned to his dressing gown—permission had been obtained for him to appear thus. But he must not fall asleep. And he must not . . .

They had discussed the exact strength of the dose appropriate to make Mr. Quest sleep all night yet wake alert enough to face the ceremony. It had been decided that seven-tenths of his usual dose would be right, if the doctor would agree to give a stimulant at ten o'clock. As for the bowels—well, that was more difficult. An enema at about nine-thirty would probably do the trick.

So it all had been planned and decided. And Mrs. Quest, last night, kissing her husband's cheek as he sank off to sleep already in the power of the drug that would keep him unconscious till nine next morning, had looked young for a moment, fresh—tomorrow she would be at the Parade, and she would be taken by Mrs. Maynard, who had been so kind as to offer them a lift.

For this, the Maynards' offer, Mr. Quest had been duly grateful, and had not made one critical comment. Yet he did not like Mrs. Maynard, he said she put the fear of God into him, with her committees and her intrigues.

Mrs. Quest had noted, but not digested, her husband's compliance. She had told Mrs. Maynard that they would be ready at ten-thirty. Mrs. Maynard had been "infinitely kind" about drugs and arrangements.

To get Mr. Quest to the Victory in Europe Parade had taken the formidable energies of one matron, and the readiness to be infinitely kind of another. But of course he wasn't there yet. He was still asleep.

Seven in the morning. Mrs. Quest, having decided that she might as well get into her best clothes, did nothing of the kind. She dressed rapidly in an old brown skirt and pink jersey. The bedroom she still shared with her husband was dim, and smelt of medicines, and he lay quite still, absolutely silent, while she banged drawers and rummaged in the wardrobe and brushed her hair and clattered objects on the dressing table. Partly, she was deaf, and did not know what noise she made. Partly, it was because it did not matter, "he would sleep through a hurricane when he had enough drugs inside him." Partly, this noise, this roughness of movement, was a protest against the perpetually narrowing cage she lived in.

When she was inside her thick jersey, and she felt warm and more cheerful, she went into the kitchen for the second time and told the cook to make some more tea. Letters lay on the kitchen table. Mrs. Quest trembled with excitement and took up the letter from her son in England and went back to the verandah. The sun was above the trees now, and sharp cool shadows lay across the lawns.

Mrs. Quest read the letter smiling. Before the end she had to rise to pin back a trail of creeper that waved too freely, unconfined, off a verandah pillar. She had to express her pleasure, her joy, in movement of some kind.

Jonathan, the young man convalescing in a village in Essex, had written a pleasantly filial letter, saying nothing of his deep feelings. He had been very ill with his smashed arm, had been frightened he would lose it. He did not want to worry his mother by telling her this, and so he chatted about the village, which was charming, he said; and the doctors and nurses in the hospital, who were so kind; and the village people—"really good types." He allowed his own emotions to appear for half a sentence, but in reverse, as it were: "Perhaps I might settle here, I could do worse!" What this meant was that he had a flirtation with the doctor's daughter in the village, and for an occasional sentimental half-hour thought of marrying her and living forever in this quiet ancient place that in fact spoke to nothing real in him. For he longed for Africa, and for a farm where he would have space "to be my-self"—as he felt it.

But before Mrs. Quest had read the letter twice, old daydreams had been revived. She had worked it all out: they—Mr. Quest and herself—would go to England and take a little cottage in the village where Jonathan would set-tle with his wife—for of course he had a girl, perhaps even a fiancée, the letter could mean no less!—and she and Mr. Quest would be done forever with this country where the family had known nothing but disappointment and illness. Besides, the English climate would be better for Mr. Quest, it might even cure him.

The servant brought tea, and found Mrs. Quest smiling out at her shrubs and lawns. "Nice morning," he ventured. She did not hear, at first, then she smiled: she was already far away from Africa, in a village full of sensible people where she would never see a black face again. "Yes, but it's cold," she said, rather severely, and he went back in silence to his kitchen.

When Mr. Quest woke up, she would tell him about going to England. She ached with joy. She had forgotten about the ugly dream, and the three days of miserable planning for the Parade. She was free of the patronage of Mrs. Maynard (now she was free, she acknowledged that Mrs. Maynard was patronizing). She would find her old friends and "when something hap-pened" (which meant, when her husband died—the doctor said it was a mir-acle she had kept him alive for so long) she would live with her old school friend Alice and devote herself to Jonathan's children.

At which point Mrs. Quest remembered the existence of her grand-daughter Caroline. Well, she could come and spend long holidays in England with her, Mrs. Quest, perhaps she should even live there, because the educa-tion was so much better there than in this country where there were no standards . . . as for Martha, well she said she was going to England too.

Her wings were beginning to drag. She remembered the dream. Her face set, though she had no idea of it, though she was planning happily for the Parade, into lines of wary resignation. She ought to go and dress properly. She stayed where she was, an old lady with a sad set face looking into a beautiful garden where a small dog pranced around a dry white bone. She sat, shivering slightly, for the cold was sharp, and thought—that she would give anything in this world for a cigarette.

The longing came on her suddenly, without warning. At the beginning of the war, when her son went into danger with the armies up North, Mrs. Quest gave up smoking. "As a sacrifice for Jonathan's getting through the war safely." Mrs. Quest did nothing if not "live on her nerves" and smoking was a necessity for her. It had been for many years. To give up smoking was more painful than she could have imagined. Yet, having once made the bargain with God, she stuck to it. She had not smoked, except for five anguished days when he was first wounded, and they had not been told how badly. Then no cigarettes for days, weeks, months. Today was Victory Day, the war was over (in Europe, anyhow) and she was now free to smoke? No, for the bargain she had made with God was that she would not smoke until he was home safely. Yes, but in his letter he had said he might stay in England for good? Therefore she was free, released from her part of the bargain? No, her conscience told her she was not. And besides, an old mine, or floating explosive of some kind might blow up the ship Jonathan came home in. She must not smoke yet.

Mrs. Quest went into the living room where a carved wooden box held cigarettes for visitors, and her hand went out to the lid. The small bell tinkled which meant that her husband was awake.

Immediately her spirits lifted into expectation: yes, it was just right. Eight o'clock in the morning, that meant she could talk, and gossip and coax him into wakefulness in good time for the car's arrival at ten-thirty.

When she reached the bedroom, it seemed that he was asleep again, his hand around the little silver bell. She fussed around for a while, looking at her watch, trying to make out from his face in the darkened room how he would feel when he woke.

Then he started awake, on a groan, and wildly stared around the room. "Lord," he said, "that was a dream and a half!"

"Well, never mind," said Mrs. Quest, briskly.

She moved to straighten the covers and help him sit up.

"Lord!" he exclaimed again, watching his dream retreat. "What time is it?"

"It's after eight."

"But it's early, isn't it?" he protested. He had already turned over to sleep again, but she said swiftly, "What would you like for breakfast?"

He lay seriously thinking about it, "Well, I had a boiled egg yesterday, and I don't think the fat if I had a fried egg . . . how about a bit of haddock?"

"We haven't got any haddock," she said. She realized he had forgotten all about the Parade, and from her spirits' slow fall into chill and resignation knew more than that, though she had not admitted it yet. She said brightly, "Well, if you remember, we had decided it would be better if you just had a bit of dried toast and some tea?"

He stared at her, blank. Then, horror came on to the empty face. Then it showed the purest dismay. Then came cunning. These expressions followed each other, one after another, each as clean and unmixed as those on masks for an actors' school. Mr. Quest, totally absorbed in himself, never thinking how he appeared to others, utterly unself-conscious in the way a child is— was as transparent as a child.

He said in a voice which he allowed to become weak and trembling, "Oh dear, I don't think I really feel up to all that."

"Well, never mind, it doesn't matter," she said. But her eyes were wet, her lips shook, and so she went out of the room so as not to upset him. Of course he was not going. He had never really been ready to go. How could she have been so ridiculous as to think he would? For three days she had allowed herself to be taken in . . . she stood in the stuffy little living room, trembling now with disappointment, her whole nature clamouring because of its long deprivation of everything she craved: the fullness of life, warmth, people, things happening . . . her body ached with lack and with loss. She had lit a cigarette before she knew it. She stood drawing in long streams of the acrid fragrance, eyes shut, feeling the delicious smoke trickle through her. But her eyes were shut, holding in tears, and she put down one hand to pat the head of the little dog. "There Kaiser, there Kaiser."

She thought: I'm breaking my bargain with God. Almost, she put out the cigarette, but did not. She went back into the bedroom where her husband was dozing. She looked quietly at the grey-faced old man, with his grey, rather ragged moustache, his grey eyebrows, his grey hair. A small, faded, shrunken invalid, that was her handsome husband. He opened his eyes and said in a normal, alert voice, "I smell burning."

"It's all right, go to sleep."

"But I do smell burning."

"It's my cigarette."

"Oh. That's all right then." And he shut his eyes again.

Wild self-pity filled his wife. She had not smoked through the war, except for those five days—could it be that Jonathan's arm had taken so long to heal because—no, God could not be so unkind, she knew that. She felt it. Yet now her husband, whose every mood, gesture, pang, look, she knew, could interpret, could sense and foresee before it happened—this man knew so little, cared so little for her, that he did not even remark when she had started to smoke again.

There was a long silence. She sat on the bottom of her unmade bed, smoking deliciously, while her foot jerked restlessly up and down, and he lay, eyes shut.

He said, eyes shut, "I'm sorry, old girl, I know you are disappointed about the Victory thing."

She said, moved to her depths, "It's all right."

He said, "But they're damned silly, aren't they, I mean, Victory Parades . . . in the Great Unmentionable, medals, that sort of thing, it was all just . . . I don't think I'll risk haddock, old girl. Just let me have a boiled egg."

She immediately rose to attend to it.

"Well don't rush off so. You're always rushing about. And you've forgotten my injection."

"No, I haven't. I've had a letter from Jonathan."

"Oh, have you?"

"Yes. He says his arm is clearing up at last." She could not bring herself to say: He'll be coming home soon, thus putting an end to her brief and, after all, harmless dream about England.

"He's a good kid. Nice to have him back again," said Mr. Quest, drowsily. He would be asleep again, unfed, if she did not hurry.

"When is Matty coming?"

"She was here last night, but you were asleep."

She boiled the egg, four minutes, took the tray in, gave him his injection, sat with him while he ate, chatted about Jonathan, gave him a cigarette and sat by while he smoked it, then settled him down for his morning's sleep.

She then telephoned Mrs. Maynard: so sorry, but he isn't well enough. Mrs. Maynard said it was too bad, but reminded Mrs. Quest that there was a committee meeting tomorrow night to consider the problems arising from Peace, and she did so hope Mrs. Quest could attend. Mrs. Quest's being again sprang into hopeful delight at the idea of going to the meeting. She had managed to attend two of them: the atmosphere of appropriately dressed ladies, all devoted to their fellow human beings, "the right kind of" lady, banded together against—but there was no need to go into what right-minded people were against—was just what she needed. But on the other evenings she had been invited, her husband had been ill, and she could not go. . . .

On the radio, the first stirrings of the Victory occasion could be heard. Horses' hooves. Drums—real drums, not a tom-tom. The commentator spoke of the brilliant day, and of the slow approach of the Governor and his wife.

Mrs. Quest heard this, saw it even, with a smile that already had the softness of nostalgia. This little town, this shallow little town, that was set so stark and direct on the African soil—it could not feed her, nourish her . . . an occasion where the representatives of Majesty were only "the Governor and the Governor's wife"—no, it wouldn't do. And the troops would have black faces or, at least, some of them would be black, and the dust clouds that eddied about the marching feet of the bands would be red. . . . Mrs. Quest was no longer in Africa, she was in Whitehall, by the Cenotaph, and beside her stood the handsome man who was her husband, and the personage who bent to lay the wreath was Royal.

The short hour of ritual was too short. Mrs. Quest came back to herself, to this country she could never feel to be her own, empty and afraid. Now she must go and wake her husband—because he couldn't be allowed to sleep *all* the time, he must be kept awake for an hour or so. He must be washed, and fed again and soon the doctor would come. And for the rest of that day, so it would be, and the day after, and the day after—she would not get to Mrs. Maynard's committee tomorrow night, and in any case, Mrs. Maynard did not want her, she wanted Martha.

Mrs. Quest went to the telephone and told Martha that Mr. Quest had been asking after his daughter, and why didn't she care enough for her father to come and visit him?

"But I was there last night."

"Well, if you haven't got time for your own father, that's another thing," said Mrs. Quest, and heard her own rough voice with dismay. She had not meant to be impatient with Martha. She reached for the box of cigarettes with one hand. The box was empty. She had smoked twenty or more that morning. If Jonathan's arm did not heal well, or if he was sunk coming home, then it would be her fault.

"I had a letter from Jonathan," said Mrs. Quest. "I think we might very well go and live in England now that the war is over. He's talking of settling in Essex."

Nothing, not a sound from Martha. But Mrs. Quest could hear her breathing.

The servant came into the room to say that it was time to cook lunch, what would she like? Mrs. Quest gestured to the empty box and pushed some silver towards him, with a pantomime that he must go and buy some cigarettes. Now, the nearest shop was half a mile away, and she was being unreasonable, and she knew it. She had never done this before.

She said loudly to Martha, "I said, did you hear me, we might go and settle in England?"

"Well, that's nice," said Martha at last, and Mrs. Quest, furious with the girl, looked at the servant, who was standing, holding the silver in his palm.

"See you tonight without fail," said Mrs. Quest, putting down the telephone. "What is it?" she said sharply to the man.

"Perhaps missus telephone the shop, I want to clean the verandah," said the servant.

"No missus will not telephone the shop, don't be so damned lazy, do as I tell you," said Mrs. Quest.

She could not bear to wait for the hour, two hours, three hours, before the shop could deliver. She had smoked not at all for five years, except for the few days when Jonathan was wounded, but now she would not wait an hour for a cigarette. "Take the young master's bicycle and go quickly," she ordered.

"Yes, missus."

That evening, Martha arrived to find her mother sitting on the verandah, hunched inside a jersey with a rug around her knees, smoking. Mrs. Quest had spent the afternoon in a long fantasy about how Martha joined Mrs. Maynard's ladies, but had to be expelled. Martha cycled up the garden at that moment when in her mother's mind she was leaving the Maynard drawing room in disgrace.

Mrs. Quest's mind ground to a stop. Actually faced with Martha she yearned for her affection. It was not that she forgot the nature of her thoughts; it was rather that it had never occurred to her that thoughts "counted."

Kathryn Hulme

from *The Wild Place*

You have to look through a block of ice to get the proper perspective on that first winter in Wildflecken. It has to be a clear block that does not distort the outlines of the twelve thousand Poles frozen in with the eighteen UNRRA men and women assigned to care for them. Surround that city-sized ice block with dense evergreen forests coated with frozen fog spun out glistening as far as eye can see and you have the fairy-tale world of Karl Grimm where we lived and labored for four snowbound months, minus of course the help of the fairies, whom History had displaced.

All life reduced to the stark simplicity of the supply line. Weekly boxcars of food and coal from Army depots in Würzburg appeared automatically in our railroad station, but the task of trucking the stuff one mile up our icebound hill to the warehouses haunted us before, during and after each operation. Often a thin glassy film of frozen fog lay over the cobbles, and until the pale sun came forth, not a thing could move on the deathtrap surface except the bedstead sleds our Poles had invented by sawing off the rounded tops of their iron beds and using these curved pieces as runners on their homemade inflexible flyers.

Food and fuels were the essentials of our supply anxieties but to round out our job a thousand other things were needed, and these we had to hunt for ourselves and take, when we found them, by any means including outright seizure, when barter with cigarettes and chocolate failed.

There was not, for example, a sewing machine needle in the whole of Germany—at least, not visible on any counter. Our Welfare had twelve sewing machines, the cornerstone for a sewing shop that would take our single women off the streets and give them useful employment if we could find needles for the machines. Londa and her French welfare girls went forth daily to scour cowtowns and villages within a radius of fifty miles.

Pedro was like a traveling salesman forever on the frozen road in quest of medicines and hospital equipment, following hints and rumors of some new dump of captured German medical supplies suddenly thrown open by Army to first-comers. When he returned to camp with such needed items as breast pumps, TB sputum cups and hypo needles, we feted him as for a birthday, after thawing him out.

Welding rod was another urgently needed item. Our Belgian engineer Jan discovered a broken snowplow and a welding machine side by side in an abandoned shed, but no welding rod. He became obsessed with the idea that the rod had to be somewhere in the camp. His calm Flemish nature altered in the weeks he hunted for it. He groped through unexplored warehouses until he was bleached like a snow man and wracked with frustration, and all the other objects he unearthed by the way—expected treasures such as diesel engines packed in grease, man-high drums of copper wire worth its weight in gold, hundreds of pairs of canvas snowshoes with flexible wood soles—brought no light of joy to his maniacal eyes.

Everyone developed the balmy faraway look of the old prospector. The multiple sweaters, socks and wool pants we wore to combat the zero days carried out the derelict impression. Then a nurse, prospecting for baby scales, discovered a cache of tanned sheepskins in a closed furrier shop in a distant town, which she thought could be had in exchange for lard. When Jan located his welding rod and got the snowplow mended, he returned to normal and went forth to barter for the nurse's find. And presently we were all walking around in great sheepskin jackets with pointed hoods, with the leather on the outside dyed brown (to differentiate us from the DP's in their white shepherd coats) and the fleece on the inside curling out from under the hoods like the white hair of the aged.

Each month another ten-thousand-box edition of Red Cross food parcels was laid down in our railroad station, and now we had another group than the tender little scouts to open these in the arctic wastes of the warehouse, where every tin that was touched stuck to the fingers in the searing cold. Tak Tak Schön had told us about the *Société de Culture Physique*, a group of some forty prisoner-of-war woman who had come to Wildflecken directly from Dachau, Buchenwald and Ravensburg and had been the camp's public women until a gifted Polish aristocrat had gathered them together in fierce possessive pride and created work for them to do to bring them back into society slowly and surely from lives that only she could understand, since she had been one with them in the concentration camp of Ravensburg. Before Ravensburg, the Countess told me, Madame Stanislawa had been a diplomaed engineer in Warsaw, a mathematician of repute and a belle of the old prewar society.

Madame Stanislawa marched her forty PW women to the food warehouse on a bitter December day when fine snow lay like sugar on the ground, every grain separate and dry. The women's tramping feet scuffed clouds behind their heels and the supply area looked like a smoking white battleground with those warrior women surging across it singing their brigade songs in voices from which all woman sounds had long since been tortured, raped and wept out. These were the women who had fought side by side with their men behind the Polish barricades, who had been captured by the Nazis, by the Russians and by Nazis again, as battle lines advanced and fell back, and who had been used by each conqueror as they passed from hand to hand. Their battered faces were charged with spirit as if release from their prisons had happened only yesterday.

Beside the boisterous column like a stern and watchful top sergeant walked the woman who had regenerated the group. Madame Stanislawa, Diplomaed Engineer, wore ski pants and a wool peasant blouse belted about a narrow waist. Her short cropped hair clung closely to a sculptured skull. Harsh lines of pain gave her face a forbidding look, until she spoke, and then her deep voice seemed to draw you behind the scenes, as it were, behind the pale unsmiling face and tragic eyes to the place where her single remaining emotion lived—her love for the tough unbeaten women whom she ruled with a hand of iron. They obeyed her like schoolgirls in love with their teacher.

The great warehouse drew audiences like a theater during the months the PW women worked there. Though the supply area was off limits to all except authorized employees, there was always a crowd of delighted Poles peering through the barred windows, and every truck that backed inside the warehouse to load up with the supplemental ration for that day had a dozen volunteer helpers aboard. The men who had come to look at their old flames at work were greeted with raucous shouts from the women and often a pointed remark that would send some hulking peasant hurrying out the door with red ears. There was continuous laughter and hoarse singing and a volume of production we had never seen before.

We gave the women broken packages of cigarettes to smoke and kept gallons of hot soup for them on the two iron stoves we had had installed. Londa brought from her clothing warehouse some dyed Wehrmacht ski jackets, originally destined for men workers but shrunk to woman size in the dyeing. Each time we thought of something else to do for her magnificent Magdalenes, Stanislawa walked away behind the stacked boxes so they would not see her face of joy.

Every day around four, as darkness was falling, Stanislawa gave the order to start burning the emptied Red Cross boxes. This was the wild finale for which all the men workers in the supply area waited. More than a thousand boxes were flung to the flames that leaped fifty feet high in the freezing dusk, a beacon that told the camp that another big *pakiety* day had ended. Snow fell through the roaring radiance and the women with their swollen red hands and shining faces pranced around their gigantic bonfire in rowdy release from their exacting toil. Then the first snowball would be thrown, spinning into the firelight from the outer circle where Polish guards and truck drivers clustered. The fight was on, tough man-girl roughhouse with bodies pinned down in snow and the air thick was should and cries and glistening missiles that exploded in white showers against shawled heads silhouetted by the blaze.

When Marcel came up with the taxi trucks, our wrestling warrior women climbed aboard and shook out their shawls demurely. Stanislawa made sure that all forty were safe in the two trucks before she climbed up with Marcel to lead her robust flock homeward to the rooms she shared watchfully with them.

Kay Boyle

"Fife's House"

Now summer was over, and the children would not be coming into the house any more; school had begun again. But in whatever community classrooms of the Zone the American children sat now, the sound of their voices lingered in this house, which had been built for people of another nationality. All summer, the children had come in from the other back yards, come down the hedge-lined pathway, where garbage cans marked "U.S. Property" stood at each gate, and in through the door that opened into the living room, where some petty official of the I. G. Farben works had sat in righteousness with his family once. Or if this door was closed, the children had climbed in across the window sills, some in child-size M.P. outfits bought at the Post Exchange, with handcuffs jangling at their belts, and others with strings or ribbons tied across their brows and a feather or two stuck upright at the back, warbling their Indian war cries as they came. They would mount the stairs looking for Fife, who was six that summer, sometimes half a dozen of them at a time and sometimes more—little girls in sun suits bought at Macy's or Bloomingdale's (or the Midwestern or Southern equivalent of these), or else picked from a Sears, Roebuck catalogue page, and little boys in faded corduroys and striped T shirts, coming barefoot or with soiled canvas sneakers on their feet, invading every corner of the Army-requisitioned house in their incurable sociability.

None of them had any last names, these children who crowded into the small, square rooms all summer. They were merely Linda, and Peggy, and Rosemary, and Joan, or else Douglas, and Michael, and Edwin, and Bill. And there were those who did not stay long enough in the block to be identified by any name—strangers in blue jeans or seersucker who came once or twice, in curiosity, to see Fife's crane work or to listen to his phonograph records before they moved away. But whoever they were or however long they stayed, they would come into the room where Fife's mother sat typing on her bed, and they would talk of the Stateside places that had been their homes once, and of the bikes and roller skates and the Flexible Flyers that had been theirs before they had had to come and live in Germany.

"Bluebells, cockleshells, evie, ivy, over," the children's voices would begin in the morning on the path, which ran the length of the block in back. These were the skipping-rope jumpers, and "Your mother, my mother, live across the way!" they would sing, skipping out the rhythm of it as they came. They and the M.P.s and the Indians would pass through the I. G. Farben official's living room and mount the stairs to where Fife's mother sat, and they would lean their tanned arms and place threw skipping ropes and their handcuffs on the papers scattered on the table by the bed, and her fingers would come to a halt on the typewriter keys. "Why is half of the ribbon black and the other half red?" Rosemary, or Linda, or Joan, might ask, and Fife would know the answer.

"The red is to write the exciting things with," he would say, "and the black is to write the ordinary things, like—you know, 'Once upon a time' or 'So the next day.'"

"Go to the end of the line, so we can hear the bell ring," the M.P.s or the Indians might plead, or they might ask for the carbon paper that was too worn to use any more.

The back yard of Fife's house was the same as every other back yard in the double block of identical two-story, attached house, except that the lilac bushes by the cement steps, and the sour-cherry tree in the middle of it, had grown taller than those in the other yards. It was perhaps that the official who had lived there once had been allocated a greater share of sunshine than the others, because of particular services he had rendered the chemical industry. But, however it was, only the sour-cherry tree in Fife's yard was strong enough to hold a rope swing on one of its branches, and right after breakfast the children would come to it, as noisy as starlings in the spring. They would fight for a turn on its plank seat and twist its rope into a spiral as they sat on it, for the pleasure of unwinding again in furious rapidity. These were the rope-swing swingers, and there were other groups that came. There were the doll-coach pushers, and the tricyclists, and those who drove their soapbox cars as far as the steps and parked them there before entering the house, calling out Fife's name as they came.

"Can Fife come out?" the voices would ask, and, loud and shrill in half a dozen voices, the "ack-ack-ack-ack" of antiaircraft fire would begin as Fife slid down the banisters, or down the rain pipe to the yard below.

Fife was small and slender and quick, and the back of his neck was burned dark by the sun. His eyes were blue, and in spite of the visions of Superman and Captain Marvel Jr. and the Man with the Automatic Brain that dwelled within them, they were as gentle and long-lashed as a poet's eyes. There were a few things that Fife owned with pride: a toy garage filled with partially or totally disabled trucks, trailers, and cars, and a Flit spray gun and an egg beater, both of which functioned imperfectly. But in a different class from these was a wristwatch his father had bought him in Switzerland, which was kept in a silk-lined box in his mother's bureau drawer. It had a delicate, copper-colored face, and a stop-watch gadget on its bevelled rim, and, besides hours and minutes and seconds, the days of the month unfolded on it, and the mutations of the moon were marked on it disk, in accordance with the rising and waxing and waning and setting of the true moon in the sky. On the occasions when Fife had worn it for a little while— on Sundays, and on his birthday once—it had hung cumbersome as a clock on his wrist, for it was made for a man, and only when he became twelve would it be his to keep and wear.

Fife could wail like a fire engine for unbroken periods of time, and he could imitate with distressing accuracy the whirring of the motor of a car that will not start. He could reproduce the whine of a dive-bomber as it dived, and the sound of airplane wings ripping, in full flight, from a fuselage. And he would reproduce these sounds, and others like them, over and over, as if they were music in his ears. So when the fish game was inaugurated, sometime in August, it brought a curious quiet to the yard and house. It began when Rosemary's father was transferred to Heidelberg, and Rosemary gave her goldfish to Fife before she moved away. This respite came in the hottest part of summer, and Fife and the other children drifted in nearly perfect silence through the living room and up the stairs toward the steady ticking of the mother's typing, their tanned arms in their T shirts weaving through the currents of this mutual vision while their mouths opened and closed, opened and closed, emitting no sound.

How many hours, or days, or weeks, the children might have continued to swim cannot be said, for hardly had this begun when, one afternoon, Fife found the German boy called Horst, and then everything was altered, and nobody came into the garden, and no one played the fish game any more.

It happened because the pathway that ran the length of the block behind the houses stopped short at the broken asphalt of a pavement, in a little clearing of parched, worn grass. And twice in the week the housemen rolled the garbage cans down the path to this clearing for collection, and twice in the week German children came in from the outer avenues and lifted the lids marked "U.S. Property," and went through the refuse that lay inside. Whenever this took place, Fife and the others gathered to watch the German children in envy as they sorted and selected, and carried away the things they wanted. And one afternoon a tall, strong boy in leather shorts was there for the first time among the others, salvaging the best from the stack of garbage cans. His name was Horst, and he was ten, Fife told his mother, having brought him in pride and awe, with a rucksack hanging on his shoulders, into her room, where she sat on the bed with the typewriter on her knees.

"He's got real deerhorn buttons on his pants," Fife said. There he stood before her, small, almost puny, beside the German boy, with his thin chest rising and falling fast. Horst's hair was flaxen, and it grew gracefully on his head. His cheeks were downy as peach skin in the summer light, and his long, bare arms and thighs were muscular and brown. "He says he'll be my friend," Fife said, and with these words the lineaments of the others—their blue jeans, their sun suits, and their familiar faces—were eased as drawings on a blackboard are erased. The voices of the skipping-rope jumpers droning "Evie, ivy, over" and the war cries of the Indians were heard only faintly and far away, through the window that stood open on the yard below. "His father shot the deer himself, and Horst helped him cut the horns off," Fife said, and the German boy's light eyes were fixed without emotion on him. "His father's a hunter," Fife said.

"What your father do?" Horst asked, saying it in a stubborn, untroubled English to him, and the mother, with her typewriter, might not have been in the room with them, for he did not look her way.

"Oh, he works in Military Government," Fife said, but this was of no importance and he went on quickly, "I'd like to go hunting," and he looked in shy, bleak hope now at the other boy.

"You get bullets, my father take you hunting," Horst said. He ran his thumbs inside the rucksack straps and jerked the full bag higher on his back. "My father need bullets. You get him bullets," he said, and Fife stood nodding his head in acquiescence before this figure of strength and comeliness that had taken shape before his eyes.

"Maybe Fife's a little too young to go hunting yet," Fife's mother said, but the words sounded frail and feminine in her own ears as she said them, the protest irrational and impotent.

Horst turned his head on his strong, sunburned neck, and he looked for the first time, and without any sign of interest, at her. "First time I go hunting, I'm four," he said.

This was the way it began, and in the days that followed the swingers no longer gathered at the swing behind the house, and the doll-coach pushers moved, two by two or in single file, in other directions. The Indian war cries sounded in the distance now, and the skipping-rope jumpers' voices said faintly, as if in sorrow, "Daisy, Daisy, touch the ground. Daisy, Daisy, turn around," but they did not come near. Fife's room was at the end of the hall, and Fife and Horst stayed there together, not playing on the floor with cars that wound up with a key, and not listening to the phonograph records, but talking in lowered voices, with circumspect pauses between their sentences, as old people talk. And on the second or third morning Fife came down the hall to his mother's room, coming quietly through the half-open door, and halted beside the bed.

"Look," he said, and he drew one finger along the painted metal of her typewriter. "That wristwatch you're keeping for me—it's my wristwatch, isn't it?"

"It's going to be yours," said his mother, and she went on typing, so that she need not see the tight white mark of pain around his mouth.

"Well, if it's mine, I can do what I want with it, can't I?" Fife said, but he still did not look into her face. "I told Horst about my wristwatch, and that's the kind of wristwatch he wants. If I give it to him, his father's going to take me hunting," he said.

"But you can't give something away that isn't yours yet," his mother said, and her fingers halted now on the typewriter keys. "You can't just skip five or six years like that. It's like trying to make Christmas come in the middle of summer."

"You told me Christmas comes in the middle of summer in Australia," Fife said.

That wasn't the end of it; it was nowhere near the end of it. In the afternoon, it was Horst himself who stood, bronzed and tall and handsome on the threshold of the room, looking Fife's mother in the eye. This time he wore black leather shorts, with edelweiss embroidered on the suède-like braces of them, and his blond hair gleamed as clear as light on the edge of the dim, shuttered room.

"I come for the vatch," Horst said. Behind him, small as one of the gnomes on his bibbed blue jeans, Fife lingered in the shadows of the hall.

"It doesn't belong to Fife yet," said the mother, and she slowly "X"ed out the last words she had written, for they were not the words she had wanted to set down. "He has to wait until he's older, and then he can do what he wants with it."

"O.K. I vait *bis* five o'clock," Horst said.

During this week in the summer when the children came no longer to the house, there was no language to speak to Fife in, for the substance of his being had seemed to change. He had entered an errant male world from which neither mother nor fellow countrymen could recall him, and in the early morning there was the sound of only one boy's footsteps coming up the stairs. Day after day, the two boys' voices murmured in Fife's room at the end of the hall, but it was only when the mother paused in her typing that she could hear the words they said. The argument may always have been the same one, for the bits and pieces of it were concerned with interchange and barter, and the mother heard Fife offer his Flit gun to Horst, and heard the gasp and wheeze of it as the German boy tried it, before the air pump jammed.

"It only jams every other time, not every time," Fife said in a low voice.

"I take the vatch instead," Horst said, and she heard him put the sprayer down.

Horst did not want the toy garage, or the cars that were in it, but it may have been that he considered for a moment the egg beater, which Fife kept under his pillow when he went to sleep, for the mother could hear the whirring of its flections. And then the sound of rotating ceased abruptly and there was silence in Fife's room and in the hall.

"When it sticks like that, all you have to do is turn the handle a little bit the other way. Like this," Fife said, and he seemed to be working with it. "It's a pretty good egg beater except for that one thing," he said.

"I don't vant it," said Horst, and the mother did not hear what he went on saying, for she had begun her typewriting again.

And then, at the end of the week, they made a final bid for the watch. They came to the mother's room, one bronze-limbed and flaxen-haired and tall, and the other almost dwarfed beside him in his shabby overalls.

"I wanted to show him my wristwatch," Fife said. "Just to show it to him."

"All right," said his mother, and she kept her eyes on the last line she had written. "Look at it quickly and then go away."

She did not have to turn her head to know how Fife would lift it from the silk-lined box. She could feel the delicacy and caution in his fingers as palpably as if he touched, not a cold gold shell in which the instants of life ticked brightly, mechanically, away, but the swift, impatient pulsing of her heart. She did not look up from the page before her until they had started toward the door.

"I vear it home tonight. I show my father," Horst said, and she saw that he had strapped it on his own brown wrist. "I bring it back O.K. tomorrow," he said.

"Look, Horst," said the mother, and now she set the typewriter aside, and she swung her legs in the blue silk housecoat down from the I. G. Farben official's varnished bed.

"He'll bring it back tomorrow. He just said he would," Fife said, but his dusty sandals wavered in pain and indecision on the shade-and-sun striped floor.

"Horst, I'm sorry. His father wouldn't like it," Fife's mother said.

"My father—" Horst began, but he did not go on with it. Instead, a look of fury came into his cold, light eyes. "That vatch not gold. I don't take it. I don't vant something phony," he said. He jerked the strap of it free of the buckle, and he tossed the wristwatch from him, toward where the mother sat upon the bed. It struck hard against the metal of the typewriter and fell upon the flowered cover with its coppery-colored gold face down. Once this was done, nobody moved, nobody seemed to draw breath in the room, and then Fife whirled on his dusty sandals, and he drove his fierce, small, unaccustomed fists into Horst's impervious flesh and bone.

That was the last time they saw Horst. He may have come back sometime in the evening of that same day, but that they never knew. It was known only that after dusk spirals of smoke began to rise in the hot, still air, each helix of it rising from each gate cut in the double hedgerow, and, standing at the open window, Fife's mother saw that the lids had been lifted and that flames were fanning, indolent and loose and golden, in the open garbage cans. There had been no outcry, no sound of footsteps rushing down the pathway, and yet these fires of rubbish burning had served as signals for assemblage. For now the children came out of their houses into the summer evening, came with watering cans and saucepans filled and splashing over as they ran across the grass. The skipping-rope jumpers and the rope-swing swingers and the soapbox drivers and the Indians crowded in ecstasy and disorder onto the common pathway, and, shouting and screaming, they fled from garbage can to garbage can, flinging the water they carried in upon the flames. The child-size M.P.s had fixed a garden hose to the faucet of one kitchen sink, and they played the jet that sprang from it onto the fires, while the others ran back through the yards, their voices piercing the evening air, to fill their receptacles again.

No bell had sounded out in summons, but after a moment Fife opened the door of his own silent room, and he came down the hall and crossed the threshold to where his mother stood.

"I can smell smoke, can't you?" he said, and he and his mother did not look into each other's faces yet but out across the lilac trees.

"Someone set fire to the garbage cans," his mother said, and Fife swung himself by his thin, braced arms onto the window sill.

"Golly, the whole row's burning!" he said, kneeling in wonder on the broad stone ledge.

Now the doll-coach pushers came hastening out, one behind another, the doll coaches careening crazily before them as they ran. The cushions, the covers, the dolls themselves—all the paraphernalia of motherhood—were gone, and the coaches carried tins of water. And with each slap of it cast on the flames it seemed to the mother that the hot, sore memory of Horst, and the features of his face, and the words he had said were extinguished. He was nowhere among the wildly leaping others as Fife stood up, holding with his hands to the iron ribs of the lifted blind, and moved on his rubber-soled sandals to the edge, and slid, calling their names out hoarsely as he went, down the rain pipe to the yard below.

Gwendolyn Brooks

"Gay Chaps at the Bar"

souvenir for Staff Sergeant Raymond Brooks and every other soldier

gay chaps at the bar

> . . . and guys I knew in the States, young
> officers, return from the front crying and
> trembling. Gay chaps at the bar in Los
> Angeles, Chicago, New York . . .
> Lieutenant William Couch
> in the South Pacific

We knew how to order. Just the dash
Necessary. The length of gaiety in good taste.
Whether the raillery should be slightly iced
And given green, or served up hot and lush.
And we knew beautifully how to give to women
The summer spread, the tropics, of our love.
When to persist, or hold a hunger off.
Knew white speech. How to make a look an omen.
But nothing ever taught us to be islands.
And smart, athletic language for this hour
Was not in the curriculum. No stout
Lesson showed how to chat with death. We brought
No brass fortissimo, among our talents,
To holler down the lions in this air.

still do I keep my look, my identity . . .

Each body has its art, its precious prescribed
Pose, that even in passion's droll contortions, waltzes,
Or push of pain—or when a grief has stabbed,
Or hatred hacked—is its, and nothing else's.
Each body has its pose. No other stock
That is irrevocable, perpetual

And its to keep. In castle or in shack.
With rags or robes. Through good, nothing, or ill.
And even in death a body, like no other
On any hill or plain or crawling cot
Or gentle for the lilyless hasty pall
(Having twisted, gagged, and then sweet-ceased to bother),
Shows the old personal art, the look. Shows what
It showed at baseball. What it showed in school.

my dreams, my works, must wait till after hell

I hold my honey and I store my bread
In little jars and cabinets of my will.
I label clearly, and each latch and lid
I bid, Be firm till I return from hell.
I am very hungry. I am incomplete.
And none can tell when I may dine again.
No man can give me any word but Wait,
The puny light. I keep eyes pointed in;
Hoping that, when the devil days of my hurt
Drag out to their last dregs and I resume
On such legs as are left me, in such heart
As I can manage, remember to go home,
My taste will not have turned insensitive
To honey and bread old purity could love.

looking

You have no word for soldiers to enjoy
The feel of, as an apple, and to chew
With masculine satisfaction. Not "good-by!"
"Come back!" or "careful!" Look, and let him go.
"Good-by!" is brutal, and "come back!" the raw
Insistence of an idle desperation
Since could he favor he would favor now.
He will be "careful!" if he has permission.
Looking is better. At the dissolution
Grab greatly with the eye, crush in a steel

Of study—Even that is vain. Expression,
The touch or look or word, will little avail.
The brawniest will not beat back the storm
Nor the heaviest haul your little boy from harm.

piano after war

On a snug evening I shall watch her fingers,
Cleverly ringed, declining to clever pink,
Beg glory from the willing keys. Old hungers
Will break their coffins, rise to eat and thank.
And music, warily, like the golden rose
That sometimes after sunset warms the west,
Will warm that room, persuasively suffuse
That room and me, rejuvenate a past.
But suddenly, across my climbing fever
Of proud delight—a multiplying cry.
A cry of bitter dead men who will never
Attend a gentle maker of musical joy.
Then my thawed eye will go again to ice.
And stone will shove the softness from my face.

mentors

For I am rightful fellow of their band.
My best allegiances are to the dead.
I swear to keep the dead upon my mind,
Disdain for all time to be overglad.
Among spring flowers, under summer trees,
By chilling autumn waters, in the frosts
Of supercilious winter—all my days
I'll have as mentors those reproving ghosts.
And at that cry, at that remotest whisper,
I'll stop my casual business. Leave the banquet.
Or leave the ball—reluctant to unclasp her
Who may be fragrant as the flower she wears,
Make gallant bows and dim excuses, then quit
Light for the midnight that is mine and theirs.

the white troops had their orders but
the Negroes looked like men

They had supposed their formula was fixed.
They had obeyed instructions to devise
A type of cold, a type of hooded gaze.
But when the Negroes came they were perplexed.
These Negroes looked like men. Besides, it taxed
Time and the temper to remember those
Congenital iniquities that cause
Disfavor of the darkness. Such as boxed
Their feelings properly, complete to tags—
A box for dark men and a box for Other—
Would often find the contents had been scrambled.
Or even switched. Who really gave two figs?
Neither the earth nor heaven ever trembled.
And there was nothing startling in the weather.

firstly inclined to take what it is told

Thee sacrosanct, Thee sweet, Thee crystalline,
With the full jewel wile of mighty light—
With the narcotic milk of peace for men
Who find Thy beautiful center and relate
Thy round command, Thy grand, Thy mystic good—
Thee like the classic quality of a star:
A little way from warmth, a little sad,
Delicately lovely to adore—
I had been brightly ready to believe.
For youth is a frail thing, not unafraid.
Firstly inclined to take what it is told.
Firstly inclined to lean. Greedy to give
Faith tidy and total. To a total God.
With billowing heartiness no whit withheld.

"God works in a mysterious way"

But often now the youthful eye cuts down its
Own dainty veiling. Or submits to winds.

And many an eye that all its age had drawn its
Beam from a Book endures the impudence
Of modern glare that never heard of tact
Or timeliness, or Mystery that shrouds
Immortal joy: it merely can direct
Chancing feet across dissembling clods.
Out from Thy shadows, from Thy pleasant meadows,
Quickly, in undiluted light. Be glad, whose
Mansions are bright, to right Thy children's air.
If Thou be more than hate or atmosphere
Step forth in splendor, mortify our wolves.
Or we assume a sovereignty ourselves.

love note
I: surely

Surely you stay my certain own, you stay
My you. All honest, lofty as a cloud.
Surely I could come now and find you high,
As mine as you ever were; should not be awed.
Surely your word would pop as insolent
As always: "Why, of course I love you, dear."
Your gaze, surely, ungauzed as I could want.
Your touches, that never were careful, what they were.
Surely—But I am very off from that.
From surely. From indeed. From the decent arrow
That was my clean naïveté and my faith.
This morning men deliver wounds and death.
They will deliver death and wounds tomorrow.
And I doubt all. You. Or a violet.

love note
II: flags

Still, it is dear defiance now to carry
Fair flags of you above my indignation,
Top, with a pretty glory and a merry
Softness, the scattered pound of my cold passion.
I pull you down my foxhole. Do you mind?

You burn in bits of saucy color then.
I let you flutter out against the pained
Volleys. Against my power crumpled and wan.
You, and the yellow pert exuberance
Of dandelion days, unmocking sun:
The blowing of clear wind in your gay hair;
Love changeful in you (like a music, or
Like a sweet mournfulness, or like a dance,
Or like the tender struggle of a fan).

the progress

And still we wear our uniforms, follow
The cracked cry of the bugles, comb and brush
Our pride and prejudice, doctor the sallow
Initial ardor, wish to keep it fresh.
Still we applaud the President's voice and face.
Still we remark on patriotism, sing,
Salute the flag, thrill heavily, rejoice
For death of men who too saluted, sang.
But inward grows a soberness, an awe,
A fear, a deepening hollow through the cold.
For even if we come out standing up
How shall we smile, congratulate: and how
Settle in chairs? Listen, listen. The step
Of iron feet again. And again wild.

The Cold War and Beyond

There **was hope** at the end of World War II for a more peaceful second half of the twentieth century. Recovery and rebuilding were going ahead and ambitious plans for economic aid to the defeated countries were very different from the punitive policies of blockade and reparations following World War I. The United Nations, founded in 1945, represented a stronger blueprint for true international order than the old League of Nations. Surely, humanity had learned its lesson from two world wars. Some even argued that with the development of nuclear weapons, war was now an impossibility.

Instead, as the century nears its end, at least thirty wars are being fought around the world, billions are spent yearly on weapons of mass destruction, nuclear missiles are still in place that could wipe out nations if not extinguish life on earth altogether, and more countries compete to become nuclear powers. Populations from Cambodia to Rwanda to Bosnia have suffered horrendous bouts of genocide. Doris Lessing in her "space fiction" novel *Shikasta* (1979) describes World Wars I and II as "First and Second Intensive Phases of the Twentieth Century War." Videos of a program called *Century of War* are advertised on television. Where there is peace, it has been called "militarized peacetime" by war scholar Cynthia Enloe.

The war literature of this period is no longer confined mainly to the West—it is worldwide. Communications have shrunk our world, bringing images of violence and war from every distant corner into our lives and living rooms. Writers, reporters, and photographers have risked their lives to cover wars around the world, to bear witness, often to elicit a response from other countries to intervene and stop the violence. At times the public is moved to ask for intervention; at other times it seems numbed by the endless parade of human misery.

The second half of the twentieth century has been dominated by a new kind of war, an ideological form of warfare that became known as the Cold War. This war essentially began before the end of World War II as the Allies raced the Soviet Union to divide Germany. In the first years after the war, the division between East and West hardened. The Soviet Union tightened its control over the Warsaw Pact countries behind the "iron curtain." The NATO countries continued preparing to resist Soviet moves towards expansion. A nuclear arms race began. The Russians soon had their own nuclear weapons and followed the United States in the development of hydrogen bombs with capacities thousands of times greater than the first atomic bombs dropped on Japan.

Although the forty-year-long Cold War with its nuclear arms race between the two superpowers arguably prevented a World War III, and the possibility of a major war in a Europe united in a Common Market and pledged to a common currency seems almost impossible today, hundreds of smaller wars have been fought. Most of them were in the developing countries, many of which were just emerging from colonial domination. The Cold War helped to nurture these wars when the United States and the Soviet Union armed and supported rival ideological factions within small countries to determine which system would control these countries, capitalism or communism. Policy in the United States adopted the "domino theory" postulating that if one country fell to communism, a series of others would follow. Both sides funneled money and arms into their satellites, often propping up dictators or even engineering coups to bring down leaders considered undesirable by one superpower or the other.

Two of these conflicts took place in Korea from 1950 to 1953 and in Vietnam from 1965 to 1978. Both involved defending the noncommunist south of the country against the communist north. Although the war in Korea was officially known as a United Nations police action and the war in Vietnam was never declared a war, both were major wars, mainly fought by the United States on the noncommunist side. Each war resulted in many thousands of military casualties and millions of civilian casualties and refugees. More bombs were dropped by the United States on the small country of Vietnam than had been used in both world wars.

The United States was deeply divided by the war in Vietnam—a war that seemingly could not be won and the reasons for which could not be explained to the public, a war in which young Americans acted in ways not usually associated with American behavior, epitomized by the My Lai massacre in which a whole village was exterminated, following the order, "Shoot everything that moves." Citizen protest reached new levels, influencing and restraining government actions, curtailing political careers.

Opposition to the war in Vietnam helped prepare for the next wave of citizen protest—against the nuclear arms race. In her 1959 introduction to *The Face of War*, Martha Gellhorn acknowledged that the history of warfare was irreversibly changed by the fact that a few leaders now held the power to destroy the world. Moreover, she wrote, "We need not even make war; only by preparing, by playing with our new weapons, we poison the air, the water, the soil of our planet, damage the health of the living, and weaken the chances of the unborn" (4). By 1988 when she reissued *The Face of War* with new articles on the more recent wars she had covered, Gellhorn wrote of how the nuclear accident at Chernobyl in the Ukraine in 1986 had contaminated the sheep in Wales where she lived.

In the United States, bomb shelters were built, children were taught to hide under their desks in schools, and the awareness of nuclear destruction shadows most memoirs of the 1950s and 1960s. Yet it was the 1980s that produced a worldwide protest against the continuation of a buildup, which had far exceeded the purpose of maintaining deterrence between the United States and the Soviet Union. Protesters organized in larger numbers than ever before and women in the enormous antinuclear movements in Germany and Italy as well as in the United States, Britain, and Japan, found their voices in alerting the world to the absurdity of threatening extinction as military policy. Opposition extended beyond the testing and development of nuclear weapons to nuclear power for creating dangerous wastes and threats to health. A women's ecological protest movement, allied with the Green movement, called for a more long-range, conservationist approach to development. Petra Kelly, a German Green party leader, wrote that "[w]omen all over the world are rising up, and infusing the anti-nuclear and peace movements with a vitality and creativity never seen before."

The Women's Peace Camp at Greenham Common was started when a few women decided to march from Cardiff, Wales to the United States missile base west of London. The deciding event was the 1979 NATO decision to bring cruise missiles to England, missiles that when equipped with nuclear warheads made Britain a target for nuclear destruction if the United States ever decided to use them. A similar phenomenon took place at the American base in Comiso, Sicily, where Italian women protesting nuclear missiles occupied the town center, which for centuries had been restricted to men. In the United States, American women formed a peace camp at Seneca Falls, historically linked to the suffrage movement.

Greenham women saw their lives at the base in a new light, explaining that traditionally men left home for war, but now women were leaving home for peace. Writer Caroline Blackwood came to Greenham partly to see why the women were so demonized in the press. She found instead a small, ragged collection of women living in wretched conditions, serene in their determination to awaken public opinion. Blackwood wrote, "Scorn and hostility could neither ruffle nor deter them, just as it never deterred the suffragettes when English society considered them pathetic, unfeminine figures of fun as they chained themselves to the railings" (36).

In the United States, the antinuclear movement was led by two women: Randall Forsberg, whose idea for a nuclear freeze became a national grassroots movement, and an Australian doctor Helen Caldicott, who organized doctors and women to work for nuclear disarmament. In her book *Missile Envy: The Arms Race and Nuclear War*, Caldicott described how she reached the decision to give up a promising career in medical research for disarmament work: "What was the use of keeping these children alive for another five, ten, or twenty years with meticulous and loving medical care when during this time they could all be vaporized in a nuclear war?" (6). As with the Greenham women, there were hostile reactions to women interfering in the areas of military policies. Yet thousands took up the work. Women, by challenging the nuclear arms race and the military-industrial complex that supported it, began to break down the historic barriers preventing them from having anything to say about war making.

A partial end to the nuclear arms race came with changes in the Soviet Union. Under Gorbachev's period of glasnost and perestroika—a new openness and reassessment of the past—the way was prepared for the collapse of the Soviet system. When the Berlin Wall came down in 1989, followed by the breakup of the Soviet Union, the prospects for global peace once again seemed hopeful. Plans were made for dismantling the nuclear arsenals and for forming structures such as a united Europe that would pursue economic rather than military goals. Hopeful trends towards democratization were visible around the world. But the expected era of peace and disarmament did not begin. Old ethnic and nationalistic conflicts, held down by the Cold War, now erupted. The former power bloc structure could not control these conflicts, neither could the post–Cold War European security measures nor the overly challenged peacekeeping resources of the United Nations.

In many ways, the savagery of these wars suggest a return to earlier times. Often fought with primitive weapons between closely related ethnic or national factions, these conflicts defy the efforts of outside mediation and can escalate to genocidal levels, as in the recent case of Rwanda. In the war in Bosnia, "ethnic cleansing," in which populations were systematically attacked, imprisoned, raped, executed, or forced to become refugees because of their religion or nationality, has meant a return to World War II atrocities in Europe, which Europeans had never expected to see again.

As the trend towards an ever greater civilian participation in warfare continued, women and their families suffered disproportionately. Civilian casualties rose steeply in comparison to military ones. In many of the civil wars that rage around the world, to be in the military can be the place of privilege. Food and other humanitarian relief from the outside world is controlled by the military and often relegated to their own use. Peacekeeping attempts, while increasing and often the only means for protecting, feeding, and providing a minimum of medical care to civilians, have not been able to adapt to or keep up with the horrendous conditions that unchecked military systems and "failed governments" have imposed on their populations.

Women in Korea and Vietnam

The "police" action in Korea began in 1950 and as Marguerite Higgins described in her *War in Korea*, U.S. troops were ill-prepared for the long and costly war they were going to fight there. Higgins had written about the end of the war in Europe and was determined to use her reporting skills in Korea. She narrowly missed being expelled from Korea, ostensibly because she was a woman. Another reason was her outspoken reporting on how badly the war was going for the United States. When China came into the war on the side of North Korea, the United States had to negotiate a withdrawal. Today, thousands of American soldiers are still stationed in South Korea to secure its border with North Korea, one of the world's few remaining communist countries.

In her next major book, *Our Vietnam Nightmare*, Higgins, whose French grandfather had died fighting in Vietnam to preserve it as a colony, recounted the diplomatic steps that led to U.S. involvement, including engineering the coup that killed South Vietnam's president, Ngo Dinh Diem. "How does it feel to be a murderer?" Higgins called the State Department to ask (qtd. in May 245).

Martha Gellhorn and Mary McCarthy agreed with Higgins that the Vietnam War was a nightmare, providing new reasons of their own. Gellhorn called it "a new kind of war" because it was described by U.S. officials as a war "for the hearts and minds of the people of South Vietnam." She went to cover the war, not to "learn about new techniques of warfare, nor ever again see young men killing each other on the orders of old men. Finally I went to South Vietnam because I had to learn for myself, since I could not learn from anyone else, what was happening to the voiceless Vietnamese people" ("The War in Vietnam" 224). After Gellhorn's articles were published in a British newspaper, she was denied a visa to return.

Mary McCarthy was much more outspoken in her opposition to the war. Asked by the *New York Review of Books* to go in 1966, she went "looking for material damaging to the American interest" (63). She, along with many other American artists and intellectuals, found the U.S. bombing of unprotected civilian populations intolerable and reminiscent of the Spanish Civil War and Guernica. Like Gellhorn, her curiosity was not in how the North Vietnamese conducted the war but how their people were able to stand up against the gigantic onslaught of U.S. military power. McCarthy was attacked for her position, even by opponents of the war who believed that visiting the enemy side would prolong the war.

The War Resisters' League sent a group of women to North Vietnam, including longtime peace activist Grace Paley, to arrange for the release of three U.S. bomber pilots. "There I saw war," she wrote, adding that having lived through World War II in America, she had never actually seen it. Her poem "That Country" expresses the idea very like Virginia Woolf's in *Three Guineas* that women can ignore nationalistic concepts for more inclusive ones.

Huong Tram's poem "The Vietnamese Mother" expresses the similarity of a mother's feeling in wartime with that of the "enemy" mother. The mother's generosity reflects the generosity that contemporary American visitors to Vietnam encounter—there is little anger against Americans. War is seen by the Vietnamese people as a function of governments, not their peoples.

Lady Borton, a Quaker, explained why she went to do relief work in Vietnam: "Like most Americans, I watched the war on television. . . . Each evening, Vietnamese refugees streamed across a flickering gray screen and into my living room. . . . [A]s I watched the TV war, I felt driven to learn the Vietnamese language so I could listen to those peasants" (6–7). Much of Borton's life has been dedicated to Vietnam; she has been back twice and continues to quote and translate the words of Vietnamese women, such as Huong Tram, as well as to write about her own experiences, most recently in *After Sorrow: An American among the Vietnamese*.

Once again, women writers demonstrated their consciousness of the wider effects of war and the inadequacy of purely military explanations for it. The legacy of this war is still felt in American society, questioning as it does many fundamental beliefs in U.S. military superiority and indeed the very validity of technological superiority prevailing against people who are defending their own territory. Vietnam produced an enormous amount of journalism, fiction, and poetry, followed in the 1970s and 1980s by a number of films.

This legacy continues to be explored by younger women writers, such as novelists Jayne Anne Phillips and Bobbie Ann Mason. Phillips's *Machine Dreams* (1984) and Mason's *In Country* (1985) show young women struggling to come to terms with a father's or a brother's death in that faraway conflict. The legacy of Vietnam is also explored by the women who served there, mostly as nurses. Lynda Van Devanter and others have asked that their war traumas be recognized and that nursing in forward MASH units be honored for the heroic and devastating experience it was.

Women in a Militarized World

Signs of a new awareness of the power of militarism in the Cold War world appeared in what women were writing. A new kind of women's war poetry emerged in America in the 1960s and 1970s. It was more than anti-war, it was anti-men. The effects of the second wave of the women's movement in the United States, combined with the increasing disillusion caused by Vietnam, resulted in a number of women poets blaming all men—not just those who fought or directed the war—for carrying out warfare on innocent populations. Women writers, identifying with women everywhere, included themselves as victims of men. As Adrienne Rich wrote in her poem "The Phenomenology of Anger" in 1972, while the woman is sleeping, the man is out there "burning the crops / with some new sublimate," or in "Trying to Talk with a Man," the woman in the desert "testing bombs" is talking of emergencies while the man counts the weapons, with eyes that "spell Exit" (*Poetry and Prose*). Kathleen Spivack in her series "The Jane Poems" equates atrocities committed by American soldiers in Vietnam with her own feelings about men: "jane runs through the street / with a rapist stalking / her, heavy booted. / . . . dropping his sperm on her like bombs" (30).

Canadian poet and novelist Margaret Atwood transforms the war of sexual politics between men and women into literal war between technology and humanism, a war which the women in her poems, seem to be losing, as in "At first I was given centuries." Atwood's poetry also explores the collective guilt women feel for universal suffering in a violent world. In "Solstice Poem," she writes, "Each fears her children sprout / from the killed children of others. / Each is right."

Muriel Rukeyser, who had gone to Spain and years later went to Vietnam, writes in one poem how "I lived in the first century of world wars. / Most mornings I would be more or less insane." She chose Käthe Kollwitz as the subject of her long poem on twentieth-century women's lives "held between wars." At the same time, she writes of the androgyny of the artist as Kollwitz expressed it. Many of the women poets writing about war also recognized their responsibility, their oneness with man: "The right hand holds the knife / The left hand dances," Atwood wrote.

Susan Griffin's long poem "Prayer for Continuation" weaves the threat of nuclear annihilation into the fabric of daily life, showing its destructiveness to that fabric. "How is it, / this woman asks, / the brilliant efforts of American scientists / have been put / to such destructive uses?" If "humanity had a day of birth," she questions, could it be facing a death? At the same time, her poem attempts to connect traditions of humane values which could negate these questions. These and other poems are an ultimate expression of the connection between the personal and the political which has characterized so much of women's writing in the twentieth century.

Women Making War

Many of the small wars in the last decades of this century were fought for a country's independence or for the overthrow of a repressive dictatorship. Women were involved at every level of these grassroots uprisings, often playing crucial roles in their success. The accounts they give show pride at being included. However, at a war or revolution's end, men usually reclaim both the power and the credit for what has happened, hence the importance of preserving these accounts and attempting to give these women a role in the rebuilding of their countries. The women in Ireland, for example, having championed peace through years of violence, are now demanding that they not be left out of the negotiations for the end of fighting. Women in South Africa who were leaders in the struggle to end apartheid are now trying to have some part in the new government. Israeli and Palestinian women are resisting the suppression of their efforts to bring about peace in the Middle East. In Algeria, rising fundamentalist forces have pushed back the rights of women to pre-Independence levels and in Afghanistan, after years of war, a militantly Islamic group has come to power and forbidden women to work or be educated.

The interview with Karla Ramirez, fighting as a guerrilla in El Salvador, indicates her willingness to fight and to die for a cause that is as intense for her as it is for the men she is with. Although from a middle-class background, Ramirez identifies herself with the landless peasants. Her idealism raises the question of what her future will be now that the revolution has ended.

Large governments wage war as well. Wars of intervention such as those waged by the United States in the small countries of Grenada and Panama continue to be options when the larger country's interests are seen to be threatened. Britain took action against Argentina in the Falklands War of 1982, and the United States took action against Iraq in the Gulf War of 1991. Both were short wars in which the smaller, aggressor countries were rapidly defeated or at least pushed out of the territory they had occupied.

British prime minister Margaret Thatcher was the driving force behind the Falklands campaign, describing it in her diary as the occasion for Britain to return to eminence as a world power. Thatcher did not favor a negotiated solution to this conflict, believing as she did that in cases of aggression, swift, armed action was essential. In the style of the great "warrior queens," Thatcher took responsibility for every aspect of the war, including its casualties.

American president George Bush, although leading a UN coalition, also saw the Gulf War as a reassertion of U.S. military power. There was talk at the time of ending the "Vietnam syndrome," the antimilitaristic feelings ascribed to the war in Vietnam. Molly Moore's account of the Gulf War shows American women involved as they never had been before. Forty thousand women took part in the war, thirteen died in action, two were taken captive out of a total of less than one hundred U.S. casualties. The public became accustomed to politicians referring to "our sons and daughters in the Gulf" and tearful photographs of soldier mothers saying goodbye to their infants. Moore showed how the rules barring women from combat were made invalid by the blurring of combat areas.

A contentious debate over women in combat continues in the United States even as the numbers of women entering the military rise sharply. Cynthia Enloe, in her book *Does Khaki Become You?: The Militarization of Women's Lives*, explores the continuing friction between the antifemale culture of militarism and the desire of women to find a secure place within it. In the United States, first the navy, and more recently the army, have been accused of sexually mistreating women. Around the world, fewer women take part in combat than formerly. The great question of whether women belong in or outside of the military system remains unanswered.

Children in War

There is no question, however, of how the many wars of this century affect children. The threat to them has grown steadily with the trend towards targeting populations and another trend—the increasing youth of soldiers. At the end of World War II, Germany sacrificed thousands of fourteen-year-olds in Hitler's last-ditch stand. Today, all over the world a gun and the guarantee of food lures boys as young as ten or eleven into armies. It is often the war literature of women that exposes the increasing violation of children.

As early as 1969, Palestinian poet Fadwa Tuqan described the young Arab boys, throwing their stones against the armed Israeli military in "Song of Becoming." Their actions preceded the official Palestinian uprising or Intifadah by eighteen years. More than one generation of boys has taken part in this struggle.

Israeli writer Dahlia Ravikovitch served in the army. In "One Cannot Kill a Baby Twice," she mourns the 1982 massacre of Palestinians in refugee camps. Israeli and Palestinian women have worked together for years to bring peace to the region.

Meena Alexander, an Indian writer who lives in the United States today, in "No Man's Land" shows women actively resisting the violence that destroys their children. Alexander's writings stress the effects of men's wars on women and children. In her introduction to *Blood into Ink*, Alexander writes of the struggle for women's rights that have accompanied these wars. Constant war and revolution in the Middle East have produced a women's literature barely known in the west today.

Argentinian Marta Traba writes here of two mothers, one whose child is missing, the other concerned that her child in Chile is also in danger. The "mothers of the disappeared" in Argentina continue their vigils to this day even though the dictatorship that existed when Traba wrote her novel has ended. The women carry photographs of their missing children, ask for information, and demand that those who caused their disappearance be punished instead of continuing to serve in the military and the government.

Lina Magaia, in "Madalena Returned from Captivity," writes from experience about the atrocities carried out by Mozambique soldiers against their own population after years of persecution under Portuguese rule. Magaia took an active role in rescuing children, adopting one into her own family.

In Margaret Drabble's novel *The Gates of Ivory*, a Cambodian mother reclaims one son when he is badly injured and relinquishes the son who fights somewhere far off, for whom and why she does not know. Drabble ends this novel with the image of this son: "He will march on, armed, blooded, bloodied, a rusty Chinese rifle at his back. Many have died and many more will die in their attempt to maim and capture him. He grows and grows, he multiplies. Terribly, he smiles. He is legion. He has not been told that he is living at the end of history. He does not care whether his mother lives or dies. He marches on. He is multitudes."

Women in Korea and Vietnam

Marguerite Higgins

from *War in Korea*

In the midst of the battle of Taejon, I received a personal blow that rocked me as rudely as if it had been a bullet. I received orders to get out of the Korean theater of war immediately. No one, including the officer who passed the message on to me, knew why.

Everyone jumped to the conclusion that I, like Tom Lambert of Associated Press and Pete Kalischer of the United Press, had been accused of writing stories "giving aid and comfort to the enemy."

In those weeks of defeat it was an agonizing period, emotionally and mentally, for front-line correspondents. We felt it our responsibility to report the disasters as we saw them. And we knew how passionately the guys who were doing the fighting wanted the "folks back home" to know what they were up against. But we frequently found ourselves called traitors by the brass at division, and especially the brass in Tokyo, for telling the brutal story about the licking our troops were taking.

I'd like to stress that there was never any quarrel between the press and officialdom on questions of purely military security. We were eager to keep out names of towns, camouflage tactical maneuvers, and, in short, co-operate in depriving the enemy of any information that might be of military help to him. We repeatedly asked, without success, for military censorship so that we would have uniform guidance. If we slipped—and I know I did in the first few days—it was because of ignorance or confusion. (Censorship was finally imposed seven months later. And then it went way beyond my concept of military censorship; in my opinion, it added up to psychological and political censorship.)

But in those early days officialdom's quarrel with us was over our reports on the bitterness and greenness of our troops and the humiliating mauling they were taking. Aside from accusing us of disloyalty, MacArthur's officialdom had the very real weapon of being able to throw us out summarily if we displeased them.

Like most newsmen, I deeply believe this: so long as our government requires the backing of an aroused and informed public opinion, so long as we are a democracy, it is necessary to tell the hard "bruising truth." It is best to admit panic among our soldiers and so bring home the great need for better training; it is best to admit that bazookas don't even tickle the big Soviet tanks and make known the urgent need for better and more weapons; it is best to tell graphically the moments of desperation and horror endured by an unprepared army, so that the American public will demand that it not happen again.

With these convictions, I and the rest of my colleagues quoted the Captain Healeys of the war ("You can't get a tank with a carbine"); told of the "whipped and frightened" GIs; took our rebukes; and hoped that officialdom's bark was worse than its bite.

But, as it turned out, my stories had nothing to do with my banishment. I was being thrown out on orders of Lieutenant General Walton H. Walker because I was a female and because "there are no facilities for ladies at the front."

The banishment-from-Korea edict came as very much of a last straw in what had been a frantic period, not just for me but for all correspondents. We never had any complaints about obtaining chow or a place to sleep; we could always scrounge for ourselves. The big hurdle was coping with headquarters and somehow, despite officialdom, getting the story out. We had, as a press corps, almost no co-operation in obtaining two essentials to our trade as war correspondents: transportation and communications. Keyes and I were the envy of the group because of our jeep, the one he had rescued from Seoul. For many months we had the only available vehicle. The rest of the press usually hitchhiked. Even during the brief days of victory it was easier to get a jeep out of the South Koreans, with their pitifully few vehicles, than from the Eighth Army, which had motor pools gorged with jeeps.

Despite the much-publicized 270 accreditations to the Korean war, there were never to my knowledge more than sixty-odd correspondents actually at the front at any one time, and the average was closer to twenty.

Hal Boyle, Associated Press columnist, whose long experience in World War II puts him in a better position to speak than I, said, "Never since, and including, the Civil War have correspondents had so few of the facilities vital to their trade."

Colonel Pat Echols, MacArthur's press chief, apparently regarded the press as natural enemies. He couldn't get rid of us completely, but he could make our reporting life very difficult. This headquarters attitude inevitably was reflected by the Army in Korea. The Air Force and the Marines, on the other hand, took the view, "Once our official business is clear, we'll give you what help we can." And that's all anyone asked.

One early rule that made us particularly angry was that the telephone could be used only from 12 to 4 A.M. or from 2 to 4 A.M. It didn't matter whether the line was completely free of military traffic at other hours; the arbitrary twelve-to-four rule would stick until another rule came along. We resented the drain on our energies made by what we viewed as unnecessary difficulties. We felt that the first call on our time should be coverage of the troops at the front.

At Taejon there had been crisis after crisis. The Army had cut off telephones again, and a new backlog meant that the only way to get a story out was to fly it personally to Japan.

Also, despite friendly reassurances from Keyes and Carl and Roy, I was sincerely worried about my job. I had heard nothing from the office since my colleague's warning that I would be fired if I stayed on in Korea. My state of mind was shaky and there was a continual, oppressive lump in the worry department located in my midriff.

So, as usual with bad things, the banishment edict could not have come at a worse time. I felt, of course, that it was highly unjust, and warranted a direct appeal to General MacArthur.

I had already been with the troops three weeks. Now, with an entire division in the line and more due to arrive, the worst had already been endured. Realizing that as a female I was an obvious target for comment, I had taken great pains not to ask for anything that could possibly be construed as a special favor. Like the rest of the correspondents, when not sleeping on the ground at the front with an individual unit, I usually occupied a table top in the big, sprawling room at Taejon from which we telephoned. The custom was to come back from the front, bang out your story, and stretch out on the table top. You would try to sleep, despite the noise of other stories being shouted into the phone, till your turn came to read your story to Tokyo. Then, no matter what the hour, you would probably start out again because the front lines were changing so fast you could not risk staying away any longer than necessary.

As for "facilities for ladies"—a euphemism employed by generals when they want to be delicate about latrines—nobody in Korea, including the Koreans, worried much about powder rooms. There is no shortage of bushes in Korea.

Bad language? Well, I'd already been at the front in World War II. And

I really didn't need a trip to our front lines to know how to fill in the dots and dashes in Hemingway's novels. The American Swearing Vocabulary is pretty limited, so far as I've observed. Nor do I think I inhibited the soldiers much, at least not much more than to make them lower their voices now and again. The niceties of language on a battle front just don't seem very important.

I telephoned General Walker in Taegu, and pleaded at the very least not to be yanked out of the story till a replacement could arrive. (My *Herald Tribune* colleague was then at sea to cover the 1st Cavalry's amphibious landing.) It was unfair, I argued, to deprive the *Herald Tribune* of coverage at this critical juncture in the Taejon battle. The answer was, "You'll have to leave." I told Walker I'd go "as soon as feasible."

On the afternoon of the edict a major tried to put me on the train leaving Taejon. But I had been entrusted by Keyes (also on the amphibious landing) with the jeep and was determined not to be separated from it. General Dean supported me in this, arguing that there was no need, after so many weeks of war, to give me a "bum's rush."

From then on, with my appeal to MacArthur still up in the air, I simply avoided headquarters and stayed at the front. In the succeeding days, rumor of my plight soon got around. A touching number of soldiers, from regimental commanders to privates first class, took the trouble to come to me and say, "We hope you can talk the general out of this." I believe they were sincere.

Their concern made me feel awful. There is very little that is not wasteful and dismal about war. The only clear, deep, good is the special kind of bond welded between people who, having mutually shared a crisis, whether it be a shelling or a machine-gun attack, emerge knowing that those involved behaved well. There is much pretense in our everyday life, and, with a skillful manner, much can be concealed. But with a shell whistling at you there is not much time to pretend and a person's qualities are starkly revealed. You believe that you can trust what you have seen. It is a feeling that makes old soldiers, old sailors, old airmen, and even old war correspondents, humanly close in a way shut off to people who have not shared the same thing. I think that correspondents, because they are rarely in a spot where their personal strength or cowardice can affect the life of another, probably feel only an approximation of this bond. So far as I am concerned, even this approximation is one of the few emotions about which I would say, "It's as close to being absolutely good as anything I know."

As more and more old front-line friends commiserated with me, I was increasingly aware of the feeling of kinship and of my emotional involvement in the war. It made the prospect of departure all the harder. The Reds had thrown me out of Seoul and it had been a long walk out. I wanted terribly to stick with this man's Army till we all walked back in. I was very much pleased one day when Colonel Stephens, trying to cheer me up, solemnly said, "I tell you what, Maggie, if they really try to throw you out as a correspondent, I'll hire you back for my rifle platoon."

Forty hours went by and still nothing from MacArthur. But there was one bright spot. My home office cabled that it was making strenuous efforts on my behalf. I was pleased and relieved. Their message was the first word since their original instructions to head for Korea, and it meant they supported me in my desire to stay at the front. It was one load off my mind.

By this time, July sixteenth, Taejon was tottering and almost all the rest of the correspondents had gone south with division rear echelon. I realized that a reversal of the edict apparently wasn't coming as quickly as I had hoped. The business of constantly dodging headquarters officialdom was very uncomfortable indeed. I decided to write my final front-line story and gradually go southward to Taegu. There I could plead my case personally with General Walker, who had said on the telephone that he would be glad to see me on my way through to Tokyo. . . .

That night I started for Taegu on a "hospital train" which consisted of unlit, filthy Korean passenger cars. I had wanted to take the jeep, but it developed that the Eighth Army was in an extra big hurry to get me out of the country. The train was due to leave at midnight.

It seemed we waited there for hours in that hot, stinking car as ambulance after ambulance disgorged its load of wounded. Silent and sullen, the litter patients and the walking wounded were crowded into the gloomy train. They were in the charge of a medic corporal. Stretchers were placed across the backs of the wooden benches. A gangrenous odor of untended wounds mingled with the car's own smell—that of a very old latrine. Many of the wounded tried to lie down on the floor and on the wooden seats. But we were so crowded there was no way for anyone to stretch out. The heat and fetid air made me agonizingly sleepy.

In the car, the bitterness in the face of the young boy across from me was such that I almost hesitated to speak to him. His misery gave me a deep sense of guilt that I was not wounded. I wanted to say, "Look, I'm not here because I want to be, but because a three-star general insisted on putting me on this train." Finally I said, "Could I get you some water?"

The kid—he must have been about eighteen—said, "No, ma'am." Then he asked the question I had heard all around the front: "How come you're up here if you don't have to be?"

I explained that I was a war correspondent, that this was a tremendous story in the United States, and that people wanted to know from firsthand observers how the GIs were doing.

"I hope you are telling them that this is nothing more than a perpetual Battle of the Bulge," he said.

A sergeant across the way, whose leg had been amputated, broke in, "Oh, for God's sake, quit griping. We finally won the Bulge battle, didn't we?"

Two wounded died that night. But they made no sound. I learned of it only on reaching Taegu, where the train paused en route to Pusan and their bodies were carried off.

At Eighth Army, I went straight to General Walker's aide, to ask for a date to see the general. He said Walker was at the front but that I could probably catch him around three that afternoon.

As I was very sleepy, I inquired of a military policeman about the newly established Eighth Army correspondents' billet and was referred to a captain of public relations, a rather tall, square-shouldered young man.

He greeted me with, "You're not going to any correspondents' billet. I'm taking you to the airstrip, and right now, if I have to call some military police. And you can write that down in your little notebook [which I did]. I know all about you. You're just trying to make some unpleasant publicity for the general."

"Am I under arrest?" I asked.

"Don't pull that stuff," he replied. "I know your publicity tricks. The general's orders are to take you to the airstrip, under escort, if necessary."

"Look," I said, "I came here to see General Walker. All I want is his okay to go back to the front. I've got a tentative date to see him after three."

"You're not going to see anyone," was the answer. "You're going to the airstrip."

It wasn't hard to figure out that there was no use arguing. I wrote a note to the head PIO protesting the expulsion, and that was that. Then the captain called a jeep and armed himself with a carbine. Two similarly armed soldiers joined us, and off we went. On the way to the field he further clarified his views on women correspondents.

When I arrived in Tokyo that night I learned that General MacArthur had rescinded the expulsion order some twelve hours earlier. It must have been just about the time the captain was packing me off to the field.

Responding to a cable from Mrs. Ogden Reid, president of the New York *Herald Tribune*, MacArthur messaged: "Ban on women in Korea being lifted. Marguerite Higgins held in highest professional esteem by everyone." It was a very welcome change.

I've been asked a lot about the advantages and disadvantages of being a woman in my profession, especially in a war. I think the biggest disadvantage is that you are a target for all sorts of stories, most just exasperating, but some very vicious. The fact that they are untrue has nothing to do with quashing them. You just have to toughen the area between your shoulder blades and prepare for a lot of darts thrown in that direction.

Each time I'd go back to Tokyo, Carl would fill me in on the latest crop of Maggie Higgins stories. Once, very discouraged, I complained bitterly about them to Jimmy Cannon, columnist for the New York *Post*.

He said, "If the *Racing Form* sent a race horse to cover the war, he wouldn't be any more of an oddity than you are. That horse's activities would be the subject of all sorts of stories, and nobody would care how true they were so long as they were good stories. You're in the same fix and you'd better just quit worrying about what you hear."

I think Jimmy's advice was exactly right.

If you offer any competition in the highly competitive daily newspaper world, some male colleague—especially if he had just got a "where were you?" from his home office on one of your stories—is going to say that you got that story only because you have a very nice smile. Even if you got the information from the boss's female secretary and not from the boss, there is nothing you can do about it.

Some of the men correspondents in Korea had a distinct objection to female invasion of the field of war corresponding. Walter Simmons of the Chicago *Tribune* wrote in a news article, "Women correspondents in Korea are about as popular as fleas." This hostility was certainly shared at first by others, especially at the opening of the war. But it was never manifested in anything other than a few nasty comments now and again, and these came mainly from the Tokyo contingent rather than from the front-line correspondents.

At the actual war front a woman has equal competitive opportunities. Essentially it comes down to being in the combat area at the crucial time and having the stamina to do the jeeping and hiking necessary to get to where you can file your story.

Of course GIs whistle and wolf-call as you jeep past a convoy on a road. But when the shelling and the shooting starts, nobody pays any attention.

They are too busy fighting and dodging bullets. No one has offered me his foxhole yet. And they didn't have to. I early developed a quick eye for protective terrain and can probably hit a ditch as fast as any man.

I recently received from Robert Worth Bingham, president of the Louisville *Courier-Journal*, a clipping about me from his editorial page. It said, in part: "Miss Higgins shows no desire to win a name as a woman who dares to write at the spot where men are fighting. Her ambition is to be recognized as a good reporter, sex undesignated . . . An envelope in our newspaper library's clipping file is labeled: Higgins, Marguerite—Newsman. We believe Miss Higgins would like that."

The Louisville *Courier-Journal* was very right.

Martha Gellhorn

"A New Kind of War"

September 1966

U.S. troops, upon arrival in South Vietnam, are read an indoctrination lecture of 30 mimeographed pages which is earnest, clear, and laudably humane. The following paragraphs seem best to sum up the whole:

"You and I know that we are here to *help* the people and the Government of South Vietnam. We know what our mission is: we are here to help save this valiant little country, and with it all of South-East Asia, from Communist aggression and oppression. In doing so, we will strengthen the security of the United States itself. And you and I know that we can't accomplish this mission without the support of the Vietnamese people. Everything we do to help win their support will help to shorten and win this war; and anything we do to alienate them will only weaken our effort at its most vital point. . . .

"From everything I've said, it should be plain to see that we're in a new kind of war. And the name of this new game is much, much more than just 'Kill VC' (Vietcong). We've got to kill VC all right; but there's a lot more to it than that. To really and truly and finally win this war, we must help the Government of South Vietnam win the hearts and minds of the people of South Vietnam."

In its simplest terms, this is the American doctrine in Vietnam; and though my contacts with any U.S. officials, civilian or military, were brief and glancing, I had the impression that all sincerely believed it, especially the central tenet: Americans are in Vietnam to help the people and they are helping the people. (The lecture defines "the people" as the peasants, 80 percent of the population of the country.)

The new port and old provincial capital of Qui Nhon was once a pretty seaside resort for the French rulers and a native fishing village with a population of 20,000. The population now is said to be 200,000. Statistics on the Vietnamese are honest guesses at best; too often they are propaganda nonsense. Qui Nhon is a huge U.S. military supply dump, shrouded in red dust from the grinding wheels of army transport, and suffocated in heat like glue. There are the usual tent cities of the soldiery, the claptrap bars and laundries and shops that spring up wherever Americans go, the resort hotels and villas turned into headquarters, messes and billets, and everywhere the shacks of refugees built of anything from paper to sheet of rolled beer tins. It is estimated that 72,000 refugees are huddled in the town limits but no one can keep count of the increasing hordes of uprooted peasants.

Each of the provincial capitals in South Vietnam has a free hospital for civilians. The Qui Nhon provincial hospital is crowded to bursting with wounded peasants, men, women and children of all ages, none of whom would be alive were it not for the New Zealand surgical teams which have served in this hospital since 1963. Those doctors and nurses are beyond praise.

A New Zealand doctor, who had more important work to do, led me on a fast tour of the promises. Four big two-storey buildings are connected by covered walks; each floor is a single ward. But the wounded peasant pour in day after day and week after week and the narrow cots, packed close together, are filled two to a bed, sometimes three to a bed; it is luxury to have a cot to yourself. In some wards the wounded also lie in stretchers on the floor, and outside the operating room and in the recovery room the floor is covered with them. Everything smells of dirt, the mattresses and pillows are old and stained; there are no sheets, of course, no hospital pajamas or gowns, no towels, no soap, nothing to eat on or drink from. The Vietnamese Government allows a free food ration for one meal per day for 287 patients; there are 500 patients. Far from home, often homeless by now, the relatives of the wounded must somehow provide what is needed, cook for and feed and wash and nurse their own. So the jammed wards are further jammed by grandparents caring for tiny children, teenagers caring for parents, a vast conglomeration of the semi-starved looking after the desperately hurt. Everyone, healthy and wounded alike, is thin; fragile bones and tight skin, and the controlled faces, the tormented eyes.

As the doctor walked quickly through the wards, the people spoke to him in Vietnamese which he does not understand. He smiled the warm, loving smile he reserves for his patients, patted an arm, and soothed and encouraged them in a language they do not understand. "We're very proud of him," said the doctor, stopping by the cot of an old man, aged in fact 61. "Took bomb bits out of his brain, chest and abdomen. He'll live; I even think he'll be quite normal." Farther down the ward, he waved amiably at a young man with a shock of stiff black hair, a narrow naked torso and a leg in plaster. "Yes, that's a handcuff," the doctor said. It looked like a leather bracelet chaining the wounded man to his cot. "Vietcong. We have quite a few. Fine people, rather better educated than the rest, cheerful, make the people laugh, good influence in the ward."

"Like to show you something," said the doctor, and we raced along the covered walk to the end of the hospital where a small smoke-blackened cavern was the hospital kitchen, flanked by six latrines. Four were boarded up, totally blocked by excrement; two open doors showed overflowing mounds of filth. "Facilities for the families," the doctor said.

Across the way there was a handsome building, rather like a roomy seaside villa, and I thought perhaps the doctors lived in it. "Put up by US AID for the relatives of the patients," the doctor said. "Marvelous dining room, screened, never used; they take food to their wounded and eat whatever's left over, squatting on the floor the way they always have. Bedroom—maybe 30 could sleep in it cheek by jowl, but there are about 600 relatives here, and they sleep on the floor beside their own people, have to, who else is to look after the patients at night? There's a fine bathroom over there, too, with two toilets, now locked. Solid feces. That big building is the storeroom for medicines. AID spent $2 million on fixing up this hospital."

I got an interpreter and went round the wards asking plain factual questions. The old are pitiful in their bewilderment, the adults seem locked in an aloof resignation, the children's ward is unbearable. No one protests or complains. We big overfed white people will never know what they feel.

A boy of 15 sat on his cot with both legs in plaster casts. He and his little brother had gone to the beach to mend nets; a Vietnamese patrol boat saw them and opened up with machine gun fire; his little brother was killed. The boat then pulled in to shore to see what it had bagged and found two children. The American adviser got the living boy to the nearest town, where a helicopter picked him up. His mother and older brother made their way here by motor-boat to nurse him. He is lucky; he has only been in this appalling place for two and a half months and will some day walk again. He said he did not know the beach was forbidden; that was his only comment.

The tiny children do not cry out in pain; if they make any sound it is a soft moaning; they twist their wounded bodies in silence. In the cot by the door is a child burned by napalm. He is seven years old, the size of a four-year-old of ours. His face and back and bottom and one hand were burned. A piece of something like cheesecloth covers his body; it seems that any weight would be intolerable but so is air. His hand is burned, stretched out like a starfish; the napalmed skin on the little body looks like bloody hardened meat in a butcher's shop. ("We always get the napalm cases in batches," the doctor had said. And there's white phosphorus too and it's worse because it goes on gnawing at flesh like rat's teeth, gnawing to the bone.) An old man, nearly blind with cataract, was tending this burned child, his grandson. The napalm bombs fell a week ago on their hamlet, he carried the child to the nearest town, and they were flown here by helicopter. The child cried with pain all that week, but today he is better, he is not crying, only shifting his body to try to find some way to lie that does not hurt him.

In theory, the peasants are warned of an air attack on their hamlet, by loud-speaker or leaflets 48 hours in advance, but as the military say, this is not always possible. Obviously I did not canvass the country, but I found no case in the hospitals I visited where this timetable was kept. In the areas called Free Air Strike Zones, or some such jargon, there is no warning and the people can be bombed at will day or night because the area is considered entirely held by Vietcong, and too bad for the peasants who cling to their land which is all they have ever known for generations. In this child's hamlet, the people were warned to leave by loud-speaker from the air in the night; but no one in Vietnam moves readily by night and besides, in the dark and the haste and the fear, how could they take with them their possessions which they value fiercely just because they have so few.

That night, the boy and his grandfather, his mother and older brother got away from the hamlet with two of their four buffaloes. The buffaloes were their only capital, their fortune, without the buffaloes they could not cultivate their fields. At first light, many of the peasants crept back to the hamlet to rescue more of their livestock and household goods. The old man, too blind to go alone, took the child with him to try to find their remaining two buffaloes. But the jet fighter-bombers came at once. The two buffaloes were killed by napalm, the old man said, and so were many of the people, and many were burned. No damages for lost property, death or wounds will be paid to these people, though the whole business of damages to civilians looks like another of the many dreams on mimeographed paper which characterize this war. But damages, if ever paid, are only paid for accidents; these people were warned, their hamlet was destroyed as an act of war.

The old man was penniless, of course; he was given 300 piastres, before coming here with the child, in part a contribution from the local authority, partly a gift from neighbors. Three hundred piastres is less than 14 shillings, less than $2.00. He had now 100 piastres left to feed himself and the child. One cannot know what will happen when that runs out; it is no one's duty to worry about him. In principle, a refugee gets 7 piastres a day from the Government for about a month; 7 piastres is a sum too small to describe in our terms, and will not buy one kilo of rice. The little boy's father had already been killed in the Vietnamese army; his mother and older brother are somewhere in a refugee camp.

Another child, also seven years old, had been burned in the same hamlet. His mother stood over his cot helplessly. The child was in acute pain; she had covered him with a light cloth and kept fanning the small body as if she could cool that wet, blood-red skin. She too had gone back to save more things from her house, cooking pots, rice, clothing. She said that the Vietcong overran their hamlet—which means that, in some force, guerrilla fighters moved into the area—in April, but were long gone; why destroy their houses and their possessions and their children now in August?

The Vietnamese are a beautiful people, especially the children. The most beautiful child in this ward was a little boy who looked about five years old, with plaster on both his legs to the hips. He and two little girls sat on the tile floor which is cooler, resting their heads against the side of a cot. They simply sat, motionless and silent; the girls were also in plaster, a leg, an arm. The boy's eyes were enormous, dark, and hopelessly sad; no child should have such eyes. The mother of the little girls, who had been wounded by our artillery, told the boy's story: he and his mother were going back to their hamlet from the town market in a minibus, the midget-sized tin trucks pulled by a Lambretta scooter which are the transport of the poor in this country. The bus was mined by the Vietcong. The child's mother was killed, and many of the others in the bus. His father had brought the child here, given this woman money to buy food and care for his son, and returned to his hamlet because he had to; there were other children at home.

If this hospital were unique it would be dreadful enough but there is every reason to assume that all the provincial hospitals are the same, crowded with non-combatants, under conditions suitable to the Crimean war. No Ministry keeps a record of civilian wounded, at least those who are able to reach a hospital. No official tries to discover from the survivors the number of civilian dead. But if any neutral harmless-looking observers went through the provincial hospitals and asked the people how they were wounded and who else in their family was killed, I believe they would learn that we, *unintentionally*, are killing and wounding three or four times more people than the Vietcong do, so we are told, on purpose.

We are not maniacs and monsters; but our planes range the sky all day and all night and our artillery is lavish and we have much more deadly stuff to kill with. The people are there on the ground, sometimes destroyed by accident, sometimes destroyed because Vietcong are reported to be among them. This is indeed a new kind of war, as the indoctrination lecture stated, and we had better find a new way to fight it. Hearts and minds, after all, live in bodies.

Mary McCarthy

from "Hanoi"

In Hanoi, because of the war, the population goes to work at six in the morning. The stores open at five or even four. Few people eat at home any more or in restaurants. They take their meals in the government canteens, turning over their rationing tickets. An exception was Mr. Phan of the Peace Committee, a gourmet, who did his own cooking, his wife being either at work in a government office, in one of her two evening classes, or at committee meetings. He profited from trips to the country to shoot birds to bring home; so, in fact, did the driver.

It was plain that life in Hanoi was austere and strenuous, though every effort was made to lessen this for the foreign visitor, who was regarded as a weaker vessel. The indulgences of the West were known to the North Vietnamese by repute, though their travel had usually been confined to attending congresses in Communist countries. They would apologize for the inconvenience caused by the alerts—an excess of courtesy when speaking to an American, I felt. They were solicitous about one's health, how one had slept, whether one was tired. Our tour of the recent bomb sites in the city required a 7:00 A.M. departure from the hotel, and they excused themselves for this. "We are sorry about it, but that way it is safer." The bombers, they told us, seldom arrived before 9:00 A.M. "You mean the pilots have to have a hot breakfast first," I said ironically. "We do not know the explanation," they replied. "But we have observed that this is the case." It did indeed appear to be so, as a general rule, in the countryside as well as in the city. In my notes I have marked down only one early-morning alert: at 5:45 A.M. on March 21.

For an overnight trip, you waited till late afternoon to start. Preparations were methodical. First, you were given time to rest in your room. Then a light supper was ordered in the dining room for precisely four-thirty. Your guides from the Peace Committee (it was never clear whether they themselves had eaten or whether they ever rested) were distressed, almost alarmed, if you protested at eating so early, having finished lunch at about two—luckily, I am docile about sitting down to table when told to. At the destination, you would be fed again—fed and fêted. Wherever you went, there would be basins of hot water and towels for you to wash up; I was never invited to wash so often as in North Vietnam. And, when we stopped en route, young Mrs. Chi of the Peace Committee whispered: "Would you like to make water or shit?"

Each departure, smacking of danger, was an adventure. Shortly before six, the baggage waiting in the hotel lobby was carried out to the cars. In Vietnam, it gets dark about seven, all year round. By the time we went through the military checkpoint at the city limits (all automobiles entering or leaving the city are checked, but not bicycles or pedestrians), it was dusk, and trucks and military vehicles, which had been parked by the roadside, had begun moving, too, like sleepers awaking and stretching. This crepuscular stirring at nightfall, when good people should be preparing for bed, was full of excitement, half-childish, as though you were in a dense forest when the owls and other night creatures came into their own, and the effect was enhanced by the sibilant leaves of the camouflage. Gradually, headlights blinked on, the big trucks using only one, like the Cyclops. Lanterns hung over the tables of little country inns; a dim crowd of working people was waiting by the road's edge. "A bus stop." Under cover of darkness, the country was resupplying.

Respecting that cover, I never asked exactly what was in the trucks or where the convoys were going. I did not want to feel like a spy. Indeed, I had a strong desire not to observe any movement of men or vehicles that might have a military or political significance. I tried to restrict myself to innocent questions and speculations, such as "Was that thunder and lightning or a bomb?" This inhibition extended to observing my companions and attempting to study their attitudes and behavior, in the manner of a social scientist. A poor approach for a reporter, but I suspect it was rather general and dictated by courtesy to a people whose country was being invaded not only by fleets of bombers but also by reconnaissance planes, monitoring every pigsty and carp pond, while in the South, below the DMZ, North Vietnamese prisoners were being interrogated, their documents, little poems, and diaries read and studied by military intelligence and U.S. political scientists, hopeful of penetrating the medulla of North Vietnamese resistance to find evidence of homesickness, malnutrition, disillusion, war fatigue.

Nevertheless, I could not help noticing an awesome lot of military traffic, any more than I could help seeing that the car I was riding in was a Volga and that the car ahead, bearing another guest of the Peace Committee, was an old Peugeot, and the car ahead of that, bearing the doctor and the photographer (guests of the government, when traveling, must be accompanied by a doctor), a Warszawa.

Nor could I wholly disconnect the intelligence apparatus within my own head, which registered the evident fact that my companions were Communists, that they were sometimes guarded in their conversation and quick to correct a doctrinal error or slip on the part of a compatriot, as when, in the Museum of Art, the director, a gray-haired painter, while making some point about a fifteenth-century Vietnamese landscape with figures, had referred in a derogatory way to the Chinese, meaning plainly, I thought, "the cruel Mings," and the Peace Committee guide, with a sharp cough, interposed, "The Chinese feudal oppressors," lest we think we had heard a slur on the People's Republic of China. The embarrassing point of this little episode, in terms of political constraint, apparent to any Westerner, including a non-Party Russian, a Czech, or a Hungarian, was probably lost on our young guide, who must have felt simply that he had covered, with smiling rapidity, a tense moment, instead of, on the contrary, causing one.

He was a nice person, Mr. Van, modest, kind, amused at himself, with a startled harelike look, always dressed, when we went to the country, in a rather sporty cloth cap and scarf. I wished he had not had to do that or to nod to us with boyish satisfaction, like a senior approving a junior recitation, when the museum director promptly echoed, "Certainly; the Chinese feudal oppressors." But I did not blame him, really. I blamed the United States. If we had not been bombing his country, Mr. Van might be a free, or at least a freer, spirit, instead of an anxious chaperon fearful that his charges might draw an "improper" conclusion.

Grace Paley

"That Country"

This is about the women of that country
sometimes they spoke in slogans
They said
    We patch the roads as we patch our sweetheart's trousers
    The heart will stop but not the transport
They said
    We have ensured production even near bomb craters
    Children let your voices sing higher than the explosions
                    of the bombs
They said
    We have important tasks to teach the children
    that the people are the collective masters
    to bear hardship
    to instill love in the family
    to guide for good health of the children (they must
    wear clothing according to climate)
They said
    once men beat their wives
    now they may not
    once a poor family sold its daughter to a rich old man
    now the young may love one another
They said
    once we planted our rice any old way

now we plant the young shoots in straight rows
so the imperialist pilot can see how steady our
hands are

In the evening we walked along the shores of the Lake
of the Restored Sword

I said is it   true?   we are sisters?
They said, Yes, we are of one family

Huong Tram

"The Vietnamese Mother"

One night in late 1965
A Vietnamese mother received a letter
From her beloved child
In the battlefield
Telling her of his first memories of war.
He'd seen a young American soldier
Agonizing
As he let out his last sigh.
"Oh Mama!" the American had cried.
Tears filled the Vietnamese mother's eyes.

Seven years later
Waiting for her son's letter
Her hair now white
When a letter finally arrived. But
Not his handwriting this time.
Strange feelings
Her heart tightens
A friend of his writes
"Oh Mama!" he cried before he died
Bathed in moonlight.

Day after day
She reads the few letters since 1965
Again and again she cries
For her lost son
And for an unknown American mother
Who lost her beloved child.

(Translated by Phan Thanh Hao with Lady Borton)

Lady Borton

from *Sensing the Enemy*

An Island on the Mainland

Radio News from Trengganu. 2:30 P.M. Prepare for new arrivals: sixteen survivors of a pirated boat that left Vietnam with seventy-six on board.

Radio News from Trengganu. 4 P.M. Washed ashore on the mainland: three bodies and one head.

The sixteen survivors came on *Black Gold* just at sunset. They stood along the deck railing, staring at us as the World War II landing craft inched along-side the mooring barge. Their faces were drawn, exhausted, their hair stiff with salt. One man had blood seeping through a bandage that was wrapped around his brow. He touched his wife's shoulder. A teenage boy stood alone, his eyes glazed as he stared over the rail.

The entire camp turned out to meet the survivors. Hands reached out to help them cross the gangplank from the mooring barge to the jetty. Empty-handed, the new arrivals stayed close to each other during the long walk down the jetty to the beach.

A few nights later I went to wake a patient who was to make the journey to the mainland hospital for observation. Hai was a woman in her fifties who had a cardiac condition as well as a goiter that rose like a hill from her neck. She lay asleep on a cot at the far end of the Bidong general ward. Her gray hair was thin at the temples. When she inhaled, I could just see in the dim light the tip of her gold tooth. Her toothless seven-year-old granddaughter slept curled inside Hai's arms. I touched Hai's shoulder gently, trying not to wake the sleeping child.

Just as Hai and I reached the jetty, the generator hesitated, then quieted. All along the beach, fluorescent lights flickered as the camp settled into moon dappled darkness. At the end of the jetty, waves lapped against *Red Crescent 2* bobbing at her creaking lines. *RC 2* had to leave deep in the night in order to reach the treacherous Trengganu River channel by high tide at dawn.

Hai, who'd decided to travel without the usual family member as escort, peered into *RC 2*'s cabin. There, three Malay boatmen slept flopped over each other like fish in a hold, sarongs loose around their hips, their chests bare.

"*Sợ quá.*—Fearful," Hai said. She stepped backward and clutched her sack of possessions. Her fingers picked at the sack's woven pink twine.

"I'll go with you," I said. I awakened the captain, who cast off and cranked the engine.

Hai and I sat forward in the bow, our blouses billowing in the breeze. As *RC 2* eased into the darkness, the rubbish barge with its wafting odor of rotting garbage merged with the beach. The shore receded into darkness. Soon even Bidong's volcanic cone disappeared. The breeze stiffened. We shivered and turned up our collars.

"Would you rather ride in the cabin?" I asked.

Hai shook her head. The wind lifted a strand of gray hair escaping from the bun at the nape of her neck.

"Maybe they have a blanket." I grasped the winching boom and scrambled aft to the cabin.

The captain stood near his sleeping crew as he rolled the helm slowly to starboard and back to port. I gestured toward a blanket behind him. He stayed the helm with his toe and reached for it. Offering a life jacket, he made a pillow with his hands and mimicked a snore, then laughed, the stub of his cigarette wagging on his lip.

In the bow, Hai and I stuffed the life jacket behind our backs. We draped the blanket over us and leaned back against the bulwark.

"Perhaps you fear the sea after your trip from Vietnam," I said, pulling the blanket closer around my shoulders. I was grateful that it enclosed Hai's warmth too.

"No. We had water. And no pirates." Hai touched her goiter. "But—but the sea makes me long for Vietnam." She looked eastward toward the moon. As far as one could see, moonlight glittered in patterns like silver flying fish gliding over the waves.

Nestling like rice bowls, Hai and I curled around each other and slept. We awakened when the sky was gray-orange. Ahead lay the Trengganu

River estuary with great swells thrusting between sand spits. A crew member scrambled forward and stood gazing intently on either side of the hull's stem. He signaled with his hands, and the captain maneuvered *RC 2* through the snaking channel. On one shoal listed the Singapore tanker that had run aground months before; on the other rested ribs from the wrecked Vietnamese boat.

Malaysian craft left the river as we slipped in. Nets piled their bows, while astern, bare-chested fishermen stood smoking in bright orange sarongs. Once through the estuary, *RC 2* eased into the Trengganu jetty. We climbed onto the pier as a Chinese cyclo driver pedaled up, ringing his bell. He raised the trishaw's accordion top when Hai and I climbed inside. The muscles of the driver's calves bulged taut as he pedaled uphill through the Chinese market. Merchants were sliding back their iron gates and arranging displays of chopsticks and woks, shrimp and garlic.

At the hospital, an orderly led us to the women's ward, a long stucco building under the flame trees. "*Đẹp quá!*—So beautiful!" Hai said as we entered the ward. Wildly patterned curtains fluttered in windows along the walls. The beds had mattresses and the sheets were stark white. The women who stared from row upon row of beds all wore stark white overshirts and green sarongs.

A Malay nurse brought Hai a set of hospital clothes. She showed her how to hold one end of the sarong against her abdomen, wrap the material around her hips, fold the other end and tuck it in at her waist. She pointed to the bathroom and then to Hai's *quần*.

In Quảng Ngãi we used to call *quần* "slimy slacks." These loosely fitting satin trousers, commonly worn by Vietnamese peasants, had a slippery texture. The satin felt cool, and the black color was practical. On Bidong I wore my old *quần* with barbed-wire nicks from daily use ten years before in Quảng Ngãi; sometimes in the States I had worn them when I needed to be dressy.

Hai glanced at her satin trousers and set the net bundle aside on her bed. With two hands she politely accepted the garments. She touched her goiter and looked around the ward at the women in green sarongs, who watched her as she walked down the long aisle between the rows of beds. When Hai returned, she held her *quần* in one hand and with the other anxiously clutched the bright green tuck at her waist. She looked back and forth at the rows of beds from which Malay, Indian and Chinese occupants watched her. She sat on her own cot and stared bleakly at the floor.

"*Hai ơi! Hai ơi!*" Bidong patients called out. They were peering between the flowered curtains in the windows.

Hai looked up and laughed, her gold tooth shining.

The Bidong patients invited Hai to the hospital canteen, where they bought her coffee and sweet rolls with ringgit given them by a Malaysian patient of Chinese ethnic origin. They asked her question after question about news of the island.

While on the mainland a week later, I stopped by the hospital to see Hai. It was evening. Children played tag in the hospital courtyard while women in green sarongs chatted nearby. Three goats walked past me, their hooves clattering on the concrete walkway. In the women's ward, Hai brimmed with news. The doctors had discharged her. Her gold tooth brightened her smile as she touched her goiter and asked for transport to Bidong.

Women in a Militarized World

Margaret Atwood

"At first I was given centuries"

At first I was given centuries
to wait in caves, in leather
tents, knowing you would never come back

Then it speeded up: only
several years between
the day you jangled off
into the mountains, and the day (it was
spring again) I rose from the embroidery
frame at the messenger's entrance.

That happened twice, or was it
more; and there was once, not so
long ago, you failed,
and came back in a wheelchair
with a moustache and a sunburn
and were insufferable.

Time before last though, I remember
I had a good eight months between
running alongside the train, skirts hitched, handing
you violets in at the window
and opening the letter; I watched
your snapshot fade for twenty years.

And last time (I drove to the airport
still dressed in my factory
overalls, the wrench
I had forgotten sticking out of the back

pocket; there you were,
zippered and helmeted, it was zero
hour, you said Be
Brave) it was at least three weeks before
I got the telegram and could start regretting.

But recently, the bad evenings
there are only seconds
between the warning on the radio and the
explosion; my hands
don't reach you

and on quieter nights
you jump up from
your chair without even touching your dinner
and I can scarcely kiss you goodbye
before you run out into the street and they shoot

Muriel Rukeyser

"Käthe Kollwitz"

I

Held between wars
my lifetime
                among wars, the big hands of the world of death
my lifetime
listens to yours.

The faces of the sufferers
in the street, in dailiness,
their lives showing
through their bodies
a look as of music
the revolutionary look
that says   I am in the world

to change the world
my lifetime
is to love to endure to suffer the music
to set its portrait
up as a sheet of the world
the most moving the most alive
Easter and bone
and Faust walking among the flowers of the world
and the child alive within the living woman, music of man,
and death holding my lifetime between great hands
the hands of enduring life
that suffers the gifts and madness of full life, on earth, in our time,
and through my life, through my eyes, through my arms
    and hands
may give the face of this music in portrait waiting for
the unknown person
held in the two hands, you.

II

Woman as gates, saying:
"The process is after all like music,
like the development of a piece of music.
The fugues come back and
                          again and again
interweave.
A theme may seem to have been put aside,
but it keeps returning—
the same thing modulated,
somewhat changed in form.
Usually richer.
And it is very good that this is so."

A woman pouring her opposites.
"After all there are happy things in life too.
Why do you show only the dark side?"
"I could not answer this. But I know—
in the beginning my impulse to know
the working life

had little to do with
pity or sympathy.
I simply felt
that the life of the workers was beautiful."

She said, "I am groping in the dark."

She said, "When the door opens, of sensuality,
then you will understand it too. The struggle begins.
Never again to be free of it,
often you will feel it to be your enemy.
Sometimes
you will almost suffocate,
such joy it brings."

Saying of her husband: "My wish
is to die after Karl.
I know no person who can love as he can,
with his whole soul.

Often this love has oppressed me;
I wanted to be free.
But often too it has made me
so terribly happy."

She said: "We rowed over to Carrara at dawn,
climbed up to the marble quarries
and rowed back at night. The drops of water
fell like glittering stars
from our oars."

She said: "As a matter of fact,
I believe
          that bisexuality
is almost   a necessary factor
in artistic production; at any rate,
the tinge of masculinity within me
helped me
          in my work."

She said: "The only technique I can still manage.
It's hardly a technique at all, lithography.
In it
      only the essentials count."

A tight-lipped man in a restaurant last night saying to me:
"Kollwitz?   She's too black-and-white."

III

Held among wars, watching
  all of them
  all these people
  weavers,
  Carmagnole

Looking at
  all of them
  death, the children
  patients in waiting-rooms
  famine
  the street
  the corpse with the baby
  floating, on the dark river

A woman seeing
  the violent, inexorable
  movement of nakedness
  and the confession of No
  the confession of great weakness, war,
  all streaming to one son killed, Peter;
even the son left living; repeated,
  the father, the mother; the grandson
  another Peter killed in another war: firestorm;
  dark, light, as two hands,
  this pole and that pole as the gates.

What would happen if one woman told the truth about her life?
  The world would split open

IV / Song : The Calling-Up
  Rumor, stir of ripeness
  rising within this girl
  sensual blossoming
  of meaning, its light and form.

  The birth-cry summoning
  out of the male, the father
  from the warm woman
  a mother in response.

  The word of death
  calls up the fight with stone
  wrestle with grief with time
  from the material make
  an art harder than bronze.

V / Self-Portrait
  Mouth looking directly at you
  eyes in their inwardness looking
  directly at you
  half light   half darkness
  woman, strong, German, young artist
  flows into
  wide sensual mouth meditating
  looking right at you
  eyes shadowed with brave hand
  looking deep at you
  flows into
  wounded brave mouth
  grieving and hooded eyes
  alive, German, in her first War
  flows into
  strength of the worn face
  a skein of lines
  broods, flows into
  mothers among the war graves
  bent over death

facing the father
stubborn upon the field
flows into
the marks of her knowing—
Nie Wieder Krieg
repeated in the eyes
flows into
"Seedcorn must not be ground"
and the grooved cheek
lips drawn fine
the down-drawn grief
face of our age
flows into
Pieta, mother and
between her knees
life as her son in death
pouring from the sky of
one more war
flows into
face almost obliterated
hand over the mouth forever
hand over one eye now
the other great eye
closed

Susan Griffin

"Prayer for Continuation"

I.

There is a record
I wish to make here.
A life.
And not this life alone
but the thread
which keeps shining

like gold floss woven into cloth
which catches your eyes
and you are won over.

Kyrie Eleison
Baruch a toh
Hosana   adonai
Omne Padme   Gloria
Nam Myo-Ho
Renge Kyo
Galan
galancillo.
Do you love
this world?

Where is the point I can enter?
Where is the place I can touch?

Let me tell you
I am so serious
and taking aim
like a woman with a bow
eyes looking silently
at each space between the trees
for movement.

2.

I cannot begin now.
I do not wish to write these numbers
on this page here.
224 warheads destroy
every Soviet city with a population
over 100,000.
But once I begin writing
the figures do not stop.
A 20 megaton
bomb, a firestorm rages over
3,000 acres.

A 1,000 megaton bomb
destroys
California,
Nevada, Utah, Oregon,
Puget Sound.
Destroys.
California.

3.

Thirty-seven days from my
fortieth birthday. I have
gone up and down this coast
so many times I could trace
the shape of it for you
with my hands, up
into the high cold trees, down
to warm water and
the sprawling city
where I was
born, 1943.
In that year
while I slept
not entirely wanted
in a still room
behind Venetian blinds
somewhere in a foreign language
babies were set on fire.
Their cries did not wake me.
Only I breathed in the dust
of their deaths.

4.

It is my love I hold back
hide
not wanting to be seen
scrawl of hand
writing
don't guess

don't guess at my
passion
a wholly wild and raging
love for this world.

5.

   (Home)
   If you look in this block
   in the North of California
   you will find a house
   perhaps a century old
   with the original wood shingles
   dark from years of sun
   and fine old joints: the men
   who made them are dead, the attic
   made into a bedroom now, the
   linoleum added in 1955.
   Twenty years ago
   I lived there, a student
   studying the history of
   Western Civilization, reading John Milton,
   looking out the attic window
   at a cement sidewalk
   which was before just a
   dirt path
   and Spanish, and was before
   perhaps, a forest or a
   meadow, a field,
   belonging to the Ohlone
   who have all,
   even their children,
   even all traces of who they were,
   perished.

6.

   This is the world I was born into.
   Very young I learned
   my mother and my father

had a terrible sorrow.
And very young
I learned this sorrow from them.

7.

The mind is vast
what we know small.
Do you think we are not all
sewn together?
I still argue with her
grit my teeth trying to feel
the pain that riddled her body
the day they told her
she would never walk.
I try to enter her mind
the night she took her own life.

Cells have memory!
I shout to her.
Science gave you
an unnecessary despair.

8.

Nor do they argue
nor do they understand
nor do they know
but still it is so.
And there are structures of
unknowing
we call disbelief.

9.

Every American city
with a population above
25,000
targeted.
A bomb with the

explosive power
of 20 million tons of TNT.
80 per cent of all cancers.
How is it,
this woman asks,
the brilliant efforts of
American scientists
have been put
to such destructive uses?

10.

It is not real, they tell us,
this home we long for
but a dream of a place
that never
existed.
But it is so familiar!
And the longing in us is
ourselves.

. . . .

22.

Kyrie Eleison
Baruch a toh adonai
Omne Padme
New rules
take the place of the old.
Be Here Now
is the lesson.
But I do not want to be.
I am one hundred years away
into the future.
My heart aches wondering.
Will this old tree grow even bigger?
Will its roots threaten the foundation of
                  this house?
Will there be a daughter of a
     daughter of a daughter

a son? And what is the
look in their eyes? Tell me
what you see there. And
do you like to watch
them as they walk across
fields.

Fields?

Women Making War

Karla Ramirez

"El Salvador"

I grew up in the capital of San Salvador. My family was not poor and so it was not until high school that I met all different kinds of people, many very poor girls and boys. The house I had grown up in was not very big, but we had everything we needed. Suddenly I was going to the houses of my friends, and I thought it was impossible for anyone to live the way they did.

I remember one friend I had whose mother made tortillas for a living. I saw her little brothers playing in the dirt, with no clothes on, eating whatever they found on the ground. I saw many people like that around me, and then when I went to the country to do social work, I saw what life was like for the farmers. It was a life of poverty and hardship. That's why I started fighting. It wasn't for myself but for my people and what was happening to them.

When I went to the University, I studied anaesthesiology, which I liked. I thought I could someday work in a hospital and help the poor; but, when I was eighteen years old, I learned what it was I had to do instead. At first I wasn't in the B.P.R. (Popular Revolutionary Bloc), but I worked with them. There was a lot of repression of young people and students in the capital because they knew we had the heart to fight. After awhile I met more people in the group, and they found in me the feelings they were looking for, and so I was allowed to join. We used to go to B.P.R. meetings in the morning, to the University in the afternoon, and we studied at night.

Our group is clandestine. The military doesn't know who is in it, so they kill some people who are members, and they also kill some who aren't members just because they suspect them of belonging. The first thing the government forces do if they capture anyone in the B.P.R. is torture them to get information. What you have to do is to endure it and keep your mouth shut. You already know what you are supposed to say and what you cannot. And then they kill you.

I think about being captured sometimes, but I'm not afraid. When I think about it, I pray, "Please God, don't let me talk. If they torture me, please give me the strength to keep quiet." Many of our people have died because of someone talking. I have many people behind me, around me, and they can't die because of me.

I always did whatever my leader told me to do. In the beginning, we would go out on the streets at night and put posters on the lamp posts. We knew the government forces suspected us and were following us. You are taught to recognize when the police or the military are following you, and after awhile you feel their presence on the street or in a store. You learn to be like an animal with an animal's nose and ears.

I had a girlfriend who was in the B.P.R. with me. One night we were studying together for a test we had at the University the next day. When I went to take the test the next morning she wasn't there. I was too upset to take the test. I went to my compañeros and we started looking for her, but we couldn't find her. Three days later they found her body lying on the ground beside a street.

I drove with some friends to where the body was. There were many people standing around it, but I could see right away that it was my friend. I can't explain to you how I felt. What do you feel when you look at your best friend and her head has been cut off? She was almost seven months pregnant, and they had cut open her stomach and put her dead baby between her legs, and then they had put her head inside her stomach where the baby had been. We had felt that her baby would be another son of the revolution; now he was dead, too.

All I could think of was who could do something like that? I wanted a gun at that moment and I wanted to go to the police and kill every single one of them. The military does things like that every day. They don't just kill one person a day, they kill hundreds. Thousands and thousands of people have been killed, and not just quickly with a bullet. They rape women, they torture, they do everything you can imagine. They come out of nowhere and knock on your door at night and take people away in trucks. You have to watch them take away your family, and often you don't know why because they haven't even done anything the government thinks is wrong.

Many people are missing and their families don't know if they're dead or alive or in jail. There's a mothers' committee of women whose children have disappeared, and they have the faith to keep searching for them. They ask the military, "Please, just tell us if they are still alive." But the government doesn't care for their feelings. Thousands and thousands of people have died like that, taken away and killed and buried somewhere, and their family will never know what happened or where they are buried.

One night the military took away my cousin, who was eighteen. We never knew why. Sometimes they take pictures of the corpses, however, and so that is how I know what they did to him: they burned him to death with torches. That was another reason I had to fight.

In 1980, I realized I had to go to the mountains and help the compañeros to fight and to help with the wounded. At first I was scared to go because I thought about what could happen to me and also because I had a baby son just four months old. I didn't know anything about living like the compañeros, but when they told me what it was for, what I could contribute there, I no longer thought only about myself. It was hard to get away from all the things I was used to having, but you have to separate from all that. Now I don't miss those things at all.

Members of the organization came to my house at about five o'clock, when it was still dark. I took my *mochila*, my backpack, and went with them. My husband understood why I had to go. He was in the organization, too, but he had to stay in San Salvador. My mother was very upset about my leaving because she knew it was dangerous work, but she was also upset because I left my baby with her. She was forty-six years old and also in the organization, along with my father, and it was going to be hard for her to go to the meetings now that she had to take my baby along. It was very, very hard to leave him. I cried. But I knew what I did was for my baby, and not only for him, but for everybody, because for me everybody is my son.

I had been breast-feeding him, so I had to take a breast pump with me into the mountains to take the milk out. In Latin America the people are very modest, but I had to learn not to care about doing that in front of my compañeros. It is really so beautiful to live in common with the people. Some women gave birth in the mountains and didn't have much milk, so I gave my milk to them for their babies. We didn't have enough food there, and babies get so hungry.

Sometimes I would think, "Is this truly what I have to do? To leave my baby and come here?" Sometimes, in the beginning, I got confused.

Early on you learn all about the struggle and you meet your compañeros, but you don't learn any names. He is just your compañero, and she is just your compañera. That's the only way you know them, because if the military would take you away later, and they did things like pull off your fingernails and cut your fingers off or put nails through your hands, how do you know whether or not you could keep quiet?

In the mountains I learned how to crawl so the enemy couldn't see me coming close, and I learned to roll along the ground to avoid the bullets. I learned to climb, to protect myself, and to hide from the enemy. I learned to use all kinds of weapons, including the M-19. It was hard to carry and hard to learn how to open it and clean it and then assemble it again very fast. You had to know exactly how many seconds it took to clean your weapon because sometimes you don't know if the enemy is nearby or not and you have to be prepared always.

It's beautiful being there. The feeling in the camp is often happy. You can listen to the music of your people, you can pick fruit or make tortillas with your compañeros and sit together and eat. Usually the cooking is done by women from the countryside, poor people who come to live with us. They usually do the things we don't have time to do, like cooking and washing. They do it, not because they are our maids, but because they know they are our compañeros.

The first mission I had was to stop a convoy of weapons along the highway. Every time there is a convoy we have to stop it because most of our weapons come from the military.

There were twenty-five of us on my first mission. We went down the mountain on foot in the amount of time we had been told to take. You know the soldiers will start shooting right away and you have to be prepared for that.

When I saw that first convoy coming, I felt the hair on my skin stand up, I was so scared. But when they came close enough for me to see them, then I didn't feel any fear. When the soldiers saw us they wanted to run away, but we had them surrounded and they had to fight.

I have fought many times, but that first time was not easy. I had to keep in mind that these are people who had killed someone in my family, and as long as I kept thinking that, I knew I could kill them. While I was waiting, I thought, "I cannot, cannot." Then, when the convoy came, I knew I could. There is no choice but to kill, you have to demonstrate to your compañeros that you can. You know everybody is scared. If you ran away, others might do the same and it would be your fault.

It is hard to kill someone. I have to keep my compañeros in mind, a special, very human feeling, and then I can do it. I have cried sometimes for what I have had to do. Compañeros will say, "Don't. You do not need to demonstrate to your compañeros what you are feeling." But sometimes you can't stand it. You are human. Men would cry too, sometimes, but no one would say anything to them about what they were feeling because they would be embarrassed. When I cry all those things that make me feel bad seem farther away, and I feel much better. I pray, "God, what can I do? I have to do this because there is no other way to make people understand that this struggle has to be." I make myself strong by thinking about my cousin and my girlfriend, but most of all I think about my son. I think about all the people who are waiting for the liberation of our country, and that every time I fight I help to win that struggle.

Sometimes we take prisoners, but we do not kill anyone after we have taken control of the weapons. We do not feel that they have to die just to die. Often they are boys just sixteen or seventeen years old, and we feel like they could be our brother or our compañero and that sometime later they might join us. Many of them do.

I stayed in the mountains for five months the first time and went on twenty missions. We didn't only fight, but went into the towns and took control of them so we could speak to the people, to give them the conscience to help us. We know there are people who don't understand us. They are not educated and have been told lies. However, many people leave the towns with us and go to the mountains. It's hard to take care of the children, especially since we have to move from place to place, but we can't leave them behind. They want to be with us; they don't want to go home, even the very little children. Even five-year-olds want to learn how to fight with guns, but we don't train them until they are ten. We have to be aware when they're ready for certain things.

In our group there are about two hundred and fifty women and almost seven hundred men. There is really no difference between us. A woman can become a leader the same as a man and do everything a man can do.

We all hold the same desire in our hearts. We only want to have justice, and liberty. We want to have our own houses and enough money to live on. Fourteen families in my country have everything, and there are people who are dying because they don't have enough food or medicine. How can you feel nothing when a child is dying because he can't get a shot to cure his tuberculosis? When you plant a seed and care for it, why when it grows up can't you keep it to feed your child?

I think the feeling I have is the same feeling that many women have, and if they have my feeling then they should go ahead and not be afraid to die to change things. If you die you leave behind your heart to the people who follow, to your child who comes after you.

Margaret Thatcher

from *The Downing Street Years*

By now, my thoughts were again on what was happening in the Falklands. Our troops had struck out against other Argentine positions. There had been no Argentine counter-attack. Major-General Moore had arrived to assume command of all land operations and the 5th Infantry Brigade (5 Brigade), reinforcing our troops on the islands, had landed on 1 June. The main problem was to transport enough equipment and ammunition forward in preparation for the final assault on the ring of mountains which protect Port Stanley.

President Reagan arrived in Britain on Monday evening on an official visit and I met him at the airport. The next day he was due to speak to Members of both Houses of Parliament. But it is the terrible losses we suffered at Bluff Cove which are etched on my mind for that day. The landing ships, *Sir Tristram* and *Sir Galahad*, full of men, equipment and munitions, had been sent round to Bluff Cove and Fitzroy in preparation for the final assault on Port Stanley. The clouds cleared while the ships were still unloading the Rapier missiles which would protect them from air attack and the Argentinians scored hits on both. *Sir Galahad* had not discharged its troops and the result was great loss of life and many survivors were left with terrible burns. The Welsh Guards took the brunt of it. As on all these occasions, the natural reaction was 'if only'—above all, if only the men had been taken off and dispersed as soon as they arrived then nothing like this number of casualties would have been suffered. But the losses would have been even greater were it not for the heroism of the helicopter pilots. They hovered close to the burning oil slicks around the ship and used the draught from their rotors to blow life rafts full of survivors away from the inferno into which they were being drawn.

Again, there were almost insuperable problems in releasing news of casualties. Rumours of very large numbers were spread by the Argentinians. Families were frantically worried. But we decided to hold up details of the numbers lost—although of course (as always) relatives were individually informed. We knew from intelligence that the Argentinians thought that our casualties were several times worse than they were and that they believed this would hold up our attack on Port Stanley. The attack on Mount Longdon, Two Sisters and Wireless Ridge was due to begin on Friday night. Surprise was vital.

I hoped against hope that our worst losses were behind us. But early on the morning of Saturday 12 June the No. 10 duty clerk came up to the flat with a note. I all but seized it from him, expecting it to say that the attack on the mountains around Port Stanley had begun. But the news was very different. I kept the note, which reads:

> HMS *Glamorgan* struck by suspected Exocet missile. Ship is in position 51/58 South. Large fire in vicinity of hangar and in gas turbine and gear room. Power still available. Ship making ten knots to the South.
>
> —MoD as yet have no details of casualties and wouldn't expect them for several hours. They will keep us informed.

Glamorgan had been bombarding the Argentine positions in Port Stanley and on the hills around before the forthcoming battle. She had in fact been hit by a land-based Exocet while on her way out of the area.

How bitterly depressed I was. At moments like this I felt almost guilty at the comfort, protection and safety in No. 10 while there was so much danger and death in the South Atlantic. That day was the Trooping of the Colour for the Queen's birthday. For the only time that I can remember the ceremony was marred by a downpour of rain. It was unpleasant for the Guards, but with the news so bad and the uncertainty so great, it seemed appropriate. I wore black, for I felt that there was much to mourn. John Nott arrived shortly before I was to take my place on the stand. He had no further news. But he thought he would have been told if the attack had not started. Afterwards, dripping wet, the guests, including Rex and Mrs Hunt, dried out before the fires in No. 10 as best we could.

Shortly before 1 o'clock we heard that all our military objectives had been achieved. But there had been a stiff battle. Two Sisters, Mount Harriet and Mount Longdon had been secured. The plan had been to press on that night to take Mount Tumbledown, still closer to Port Stanley, but the troops were tired and more time was needed to bring up ammunition, so it was decided to wait. I went up to Northwood that afternoon to hear precisely what was happening. There was better news there about *Glamorgan*; her fires were under control and she was steaming at 20 knots.

More than ever, the outcome now lay in the hands of our soldiers on the Falklands, not with the politicians. Like everyone else in Britain, I was glued to the radio for news—strictly keeping to my self-imposed rule not to telephone while the conflict was underway. On my way back from Chequers to No. 10, that Sunday (13 June), I went via Northwood to learn what I could. What was to turn out to be the final assault was bitterly fought, particularly at Mount Tumbledown where the Argentinians were well prepared. But Tumbledown, Mount William and Wireless Ridge fell to our forces, who were soon on the outskirts of Stanley.

I visited the islands seven months later and saw the terrain for myself, walking the ground at first light in driving wind and rain, wending my way around those grim outcrops of rock which made natural fortifications for the Argentine defenders. Our boys had had to cover the ground and take the positions in thick darkness. It could only have been done by the most professional and disciplined of forces.

When the War Cabinet met on Monday morning all that we knew was that the battle was still in progress. The speed with which the end came took all of us by surprise. The Argentinians were weary, demoralized and very badly led—as ample evidence at the time and later showed. They had had enough. They threw down their arms and could be seen retreating through their own minefields into Stanley.

That evening, having learnt the news, I went to the House of Commons to announce the victory. I could not get into my own room; it was locked and the Chief Whip's assistant had to search for the key. I then wrote out on a scrap of paper which I found somewhere on my desk the short statement which, there being no other procedural means, I would have to make on a Point of Order to the House. At 10 p.m. I rose and told them that it had been reported that there were white flags flying over Port Stanley. The war was over. We all felt the same and the cheers showed it. Right had prevailed. And when I went to sleep very late that night I realized how great the burden was which had been lifted from my shoulders.

For the nation as a whole, though the daily memories, fears and even the relief would fade, pride in our country's achievement would not. In a speech I made in Cheltenham a little later, on Saturday 3 July, I tried to express what the Falklands spirit meant:

We have ceased to be a nation in retreat. We have instead a newfound confidence—born in the economic battles at home and tested and found true 8000 miles away . . . And so today we can rejoice at our success in the Falklands and take pride in the achievement of the men and women of our task force. But we do so, not as at some flickering of a flame which must soon be dead. No—we rejoice that Britain has rekindled that spirit which has fired her for generations past and which today has begun to burn as brightly as before. Britain found herself again in the South Atlantic and will not look back from the victory she has won.

Molly Moore

from *A Woman at War: Storming Kuwait with the U.S. Marines*

I was relieved to be living in a tent inhabited by people other than public affairs officers and reporters. All the military services worked a little too hard at keeping reporters segregated from real troops when we went to the field.

"We have about two hundred people working here," Shotwell said. "But we have so few women they all sleep in the same tent. It's just easier that way. General Boomer's busy now, but he wants to see you later this afternoon. Until then, we'll help you get settled in."

Shotwell stopped at the edge of a row of about a dozen railcar boxes which had been lined up side by side in the sand. He pointed to the first box.

"This is where I live." A small cardboard sign taped to the metal door read: "PAO."

"You're welcome to write your stories here," he offered. "We have a word processor and electricity. Oh, and we also have a cot for you. Sorry it's one of the old wooden ones, but it's the only thing we could find."

"I'm sure it will beat sleeping on the dirt," I assured him.

"I'll take you over to the women's tent," he said, heaving my rucksack on his shoulder. I left my computer in the railroad boxcar and grabbed the cot and my duffel bag. We followed a wide roadway banked by high sand berms on both sides, turned onto a narrower path, and stopped.

"It's supposed to be somewhere around here," Shotwell said with a perplexed look on his face. "I've never actually been there myself."

We walked around the next sand berm. Shotwell looked even more confused. "I know it's around here somewhere. Hey, Corporal," he shouted, hailing a young Marine walking in our direction. "Know where the WMs' tent is?"

The Marines had an annoying way of referring to women Marines as WMs.

"I think it's just over that berm over there," he replied.

We climbed the sand wall and looked down into a pit with a lone tent. We slid down the back side of the berm and approached the front flap.

"Knock, knock," said Shotwell in a loud voice, the standard way troops announced their presence outside a tent.

No response. "Why don't you look inside," he suggested.

I ducked through the flap. It was like no other tent I'd visited anywhere in the desert. It didn't smell like dirty socks or look like a locker room. Cots were lined nearly on each side. Cardboard boxes containing personal belongings were tucked meticulously beneath each cot. A bouquet of dried roses hung on the canvas wall above one of the cots.

I poked my head out. "This looks like it. I'll just find a spot to leave my stuff and meet you back at your place."

In most military camps, a tent's inhabitants are related by job type or military unit. Because the Marine Corps—unlike the Army—generally assigns men and women to separate sleeping areas and because there were so few women assigned to Boomer's camp, the entire female population fit inside one tent.

It was large and uncrowded, with about seven cots in the space normally reserved for twice that number. I didn't want to stake a claim without authorization. Past experience taught me how territorial tentmates could be. I was piling my gear in a corner when one of the residents returned.

"Hi, you must be the reporter they told us about," the woman greeted me.

"Uh-oh. You've been warned," I replied, introducing myself. "I hope you guys don't mind an intruder."

"No. We're never here anyway. We all work different schedules. You won't bother us a bit. You can set up your cot in that corner where you have your stuff. We just got another new woman yesterday. She's from the Army. She's the cot next to you there."

"Thanks."

"Sure. See you later. I'm due back on duty." She disappeared through the flap. A second later her head reappeared. "By the way, the head's just

over the back berm and down to the left. And if you're interested, women's
shower hours are from four to four-fifteen today."

"Short hour," I replied.

"That's if we have any water at all today. Haven't had any for the last
three days."

I waved my thanks. At least the latrine was conveniently located.

I unfolded my cot, and after a few minutes of tugging and kicking, I had
a bed. I leaned my rucksack against the edge of the cot as a makeshift night-
stand. Within arm's reach were pockets with a flashlight and a contact-lens
case so I wouldn't wake up everyone else if I stumbled into the tent late at
night.

While I unpacked, some of my bunkmates darted in and out during
breaks in their shifts. I began to piece together a picture of the family that
occupied my desert home.

Most of the women worked in secret intelligence operations, which
were among the first assignments opened to women since the jobs usually
didn't involve front-line combat positions. But because of the changing
shape of the modern battlefield, these women were closer to the front lines
than tens of thousands of male troops and officers in Saudi Arabia. Each
woman worked in a different intelligence unit.

The women had been thrown together in the past few weeks, as the Marine forward command post leapfrogged across the desert, closer and closer
to the front lines. They had learned to survive as a family, sharing everything from intelligence information to CARE packages from home.

Specialist 4 Michele Curtis-Matthews, "C.M." to her tentmates, was
a thirty-three-year-old Army intelligence specialist on loan to the Marine
Corps to help identify targets photographed by the Army's experimental
Joint Surveillance Target/Attack Radar System (JSTARS), which had been
rushed to Saudi Arabia even though it was still in the developmental stage.
To the untrained eye, the photographs looked like lines of headlights against
a navy-blue background. To Michele, they signified convoys of trucks or
tanks or armored personnel carriers.

C.M., the most gregarious member of the tent family, had long blond
hair which she wore pulled back into a ponytail, thick, expressive eyebrows,
and an infectious laugh. Her father had been a Green Beret in Vietnam and
she'd married an "SF," a member of the Army's secret special operations
forces. Her husband was now on an undisclosed mission somewhere on the
Arabian Peninsula; even she didn't know precisely where.

C.M., who had taken on the role of tent mother, offered me her coffee-pot, which the women used to heat water to wash their hair. "I also have baby powder," she offered. "On days when there's not enough water, you just brush it through your hair and it gets all the oil out."

I was impressed with their ingenuity. My shoulder-length brown hair, which I occasionally trimmed with fingernail scissors in front of the hotel bathroom mirror, stayed so filthy in the desert that I tied it in a ponytail and would go for days without taking off my hat.

C.M. was also the master scrounger. When the women went too many days without a turn at the showers, she'd cut a deal with the men who operated the generators that ran the showers: four Snickers bars for five minutes of shower time for her tent. Not just any Snickers would do, however.

"I have American Snickers," she boasted. "There's a big difference. Saudi Snickers taste like shit."

C.M. rummaged through the cardboard box she kept tucked beneath her cot. She unwrapped a plastic package and handed me a round, nut-covered candy. "My mother sends me great stuff. She lives in Germany and sends me German chocolates."

She paused and wrinkled her nose. "She also sent me disposable panties. She heard we had no place to do laundry."

Meanwhile, her father, a Vietnam vet, had sent her to war with condoms. " 'Rubbers?' I said. I couldn't believe he was saying that. But he told me I'd need them to protect the end of my M-16 rifle from sand and dirt. And he was right."

"Yeah," I replied. "The Brits ordered half a million camouflage-colored condoms for their troops for the same purpose."

In turn, C.M. told me, when the women troops—after much complaining—finally began receiving tampons through the military supply system, they donated them to the male reconnaissance teams who manned the border observation posts. If the men were shot during a chemical attack, they could use the tampons to plug a bullet wound while medics decontaminated their bodies.

"If they get shot through their chemical suit they can immediately stop the flow of blood with the tampons," C.M. explained. "It's clean and it's sterile."

After testing the latrine, I gave myself a walking tour of the camp. No one had come right out and told me, "The ground war is starting in the next couple of days," but it just seemed implicit. Fighter jets, bombers, and aerial-refueling tankers roared overhead every few minutes. The kabooms of bombing raids rumbled across the desert and vibrated through the tents and railcar boxes of the encampment.

I saw several handwritten notices tacked to poles along the main paths of the encampment: "Prayers before the Storm. Tonight. 7:30. Chapel of the Breach." The Chapel of the Breach was about fifteen steps from the public affairs box. It was the camp church, a large tent filled with a dozen rows of wooden benches. "Chapel of the Breach" was carved into a large wooden board that hung over the entrance. The Catholic priest and the Protestant minister who tended the headquarters flock took the name from the Marines' mission of breaching the minefields.

Just outside the church was a large canvas bag suspended between three poles lashed together tepee-style. A cardboard sign commanded: "Wash hands only." I'd only been at the camp a few hours and already felt gritty. I walked to the water bag, pulled one of the levers, and let a trickle of water run over my hands. I glanced around idly as I stood up and spotted a man about ten feet away urinating into a hole in the sand wall behind the chapel. Our eyes met at about the same instant. I quickly looked in the opposite direction and walked away as briskly as I could.

I should have been used to those kinds of encounters by now; they'd occurred at just about every camp I'd visited since August. In the walled encampments near the front, the engineering crews routinely compensated for the shortage of wooden latrines by shoving pipes into the sand berms. The resulting toilet was commonly referred to as a "piss hole." Even though the environment left little room for modesty, it never failed to embarrass me every time I came upon a man using one of them.

As an outsider, and a female outsider at that, I got the usual stares I'd come to expect. The residents on our end of the compound seemed very friendly. The row of rail container boxes—called Con-X boxes—made up a little community. Camouflage nets were strung over the boxes, creating a canopy that also covered the wide path in front of the offices. It had the feel of a communal front porch. To complete the effect, several men positioned folding chairs outside their front doors.

The camp doctor occupied the box next to the public affairs office. Country music blared from the radio on his desk. He introduced himself as Captain Jerry R. Crim, the staff surgeon. "We're getting ready for a chemical class, you should sit in on it," he suggested.

I didn't need a second invitation. I'd heard the lecture about half a dozen times already, but the proximity to G-day warranted a refresher course. I joined the group of two dozen men in a semicircle outside the doc's front door.

A barrel-chested sergeant appeared to be the chief instructor.

"You may hear some alarms going off this afternoon," he began. "Don't get worried. It's a test of a new $260,000 piece of equipment designed to detect certain agents. We have it set for biological germs—anthrax and botulism. It is supposed to give you a three-hour warning.

"How do you know if you've been infected? With anthrax, the symptoms won't start for two or three days. The first thing you notice are little black dots appearing on your skin. You have hours or maybe only minutes to live at that point. You'll feel like you have a cold congestion. Then you can't breathe. When you're that bad, you're probably gonna die.

"Botulism is more interesting. If you hear the alarm, give yourself first aid immediately. The only symptom of botulism is choking and dying."

He held up a package of large white capsules. "This is Cipro. It will help protect you against some biological warfare agents, specifically anthrax and botulism. You should take one of these every twelve hours."

He waved a package of small white tablets in a plastic case. They looked like a month's supply of birth-control pills. "These are your NAPPs pills— nerve agent pyridostigmine pretreatment tablets. As of six a.m. Friday you should have started taking them. You take them every six hours. One Marine took twenty-one pills at once. Don't do that."

It was now Saturday afternoon. I wondered if it was too late for me to start the dosage.

The sergeant reached inside his gas-mask pouch and pulled out the dreaded atropine injector.

"Symptoms that you've contacted chemical agents: headache, runny nose, nausea, vomiting."

Shit, I thought. That's how I've felt most of the time I've been in Saudi Arabia. How am I supposed to tell the difference?

At the first signs of nerve agents, the sergeant said, we should pull the two small injectors out of our pouch and jab them into our thighs. He raised a needle that looked better suited to treating bulls than humans.

"This one is for when things get really bad. Remove the gray safety cap by pulling it out. Do not touch the black end of the injector until you are ready to inject. Place the black end of the injector against the mid-outer thigh. Don't jab it into the side close to the bone. The needle could break off."

I could almost hear the snap of the broken needle.

"Push the injector hard against the thigh. Inject it through your clothing. It's going to sting a little bit." He paused. "Actually, it's going to sting quite a bit. Wait ten seconds, then remove the needle with one quick pull.

"These are not gonna kill you," he promised. "Already Marines are proving that." I'd heard several reports of Marines who'd accidentally injected themselves by sitting on their gas-mask pouches.

The corpsman then went through a demonstration of how to cut a contaminated chemical suit off a colleague and how to clean your gas-mask hood, boots, and gloves with a solution of water and 5 percent bleach.

"The Army, Navy, and Air Force will not transport anyone who has not been cleaned up," he warned. "One of the problems you're going to run into: people will already be in convulsions. You know they're gonna die. You can't decontaminate them. They have to be set aside."

"Another problem," interrupted Crim, the surgeon. "Two-thirds of the casualties who come in have not been gassed at all, but think they have."

By this point, the symptoms of botulism, nerve agents, and mustard gas were washing over me in alternate waves of nausea, headaches, and lung congestion. As soon as the session had ended, I knocked on the doctor's door. "I need to raid your medicine cabinet."

Children in War

Fadwa Tuqan

"Song of Becoming"

They're only boys
who used to frolic and play
launching rainbowed kites
on the western wind,
their blue-red-green kites
whistling, leaping,
trading easy laughter and jokes
duelling with branches, pretending to be
great heroes in history.

Suddenly now they've grown,
grown more than the years of a normal life,
merged with secret and passionate words,
carried love's messages like the Bible or Quran,
to be read in whispers.
They've grown to become trees
plunging deep roots into earth,
stretching high towards the sun.
Now their voices are ones that reject,
that knock down and build anew.
Anger smouldering on the fringes of a blocked horizon,
invading classrooms, streets, city quarters,
centering on squares,
facing sullen tanks with streams of stones.

Now they shake the gallows of dawn
assailing the night and its flood.
They've grown more than the years of a life
to become the worshipped and the worshippers.

When their torn limbs merged with the stuff of our earth,
they became legends,
they grew into vaulting bridges,
they grew and grew, becoming
larger than all poetry.

(Translated from the Arabic by Naomi Shihab Nye [with the help of
Salma Khadra Jayyusi])

Dahlia Ravikovitch

"One Cannot Kill a Baby Twice"

Upon sewage puddles in Sabra and Shatila
Where you delivered masses of people
Considerable masses
From the world of living to the world of truth.

Night after night.
First they shot
Then they hung
At last they slaughtered with knives.
Terrified women appeared in urgence
Above a sand hillock:
"They slaughter us there,
In Shatila."

A refined trail of a newborn moon was hung
Above the camps.
Our soldiers illuminated the place with lightening shells
Like daylight.
"Go back to the camp, march!" the soldier commanded
The yelling women from Sabra and Shatila.
He had orders to follow.
And the children were already laid in dung puddles
Their mouths wide open
Calm.

Nobody will hurt them anymore.
One cannot kill a baby twice.

And the moon's trail became bigger and bigger
Until it turned into a complete coin of gold.

Our sweet soldiers
They asked nothing for themselves,
How strong was their desire
To return home in peace.

Meena Alexander

"No Man's Land"

The dogs are amazing
sweaty with light
they race past the
dungheaps

Infants crawl
sucking dirt from sticks
whose blunt ends
smack elder flesh
and ceaseless bloodiness

The soldiers though
are finally resting
by the river
berets over their noses.

Barges from the north
steam past nettles
cut stalks of blackthorn
and elder, olive trees
axed into bits

Women wash their thighs
in bloodied river water,
over and over
they wipe their flesh

In stunned
immaculate gestures
figures massed with light.

They do not hear
the men
or dogs or children.

Marta Traba

from *Mothers and Shadows*

The two women walk one behind the other because of the narrow pavement and the odd person sitting out on the doorstep with legs protruding, in time-honoured indifference to the passers-by. She would rather have gone down another street, Florida for example, but Elena presumably wanted to avoid the risk of bumping into someone she knew. She looked down the first side-street towards the port, and with a twinge of nostalgia recognised the distant outlines of the ships at anchor. It was as if she'd flashed back to the childhood days when ships and ports dizzied her with an attraction nothing else could equal, rescuing her from the urban greyness of Buenos Aires. They went on walking in silence till they came out into the square.

She stopped short, dazzled by the whiteness of that vast, bleak, open space, with its ludicrous obelisk sticking up in the middle. 'It must be the light reflecting on the paving stones,' she thought, confronted by a stream of images in which she crossed the square again and again, first as a child and then as a girl. She began to make her way falteringly across the horrid square, squinting at the blinding light. When finally she opened her eyes wide, she saw the sun was still high overhead, in an unblemished sky without a hint of cloud. She felt irritated by that conjunction of blue and white, evoking the national colours and flag. Argentine nationalism was, it seemed, doomed to belong to the category of the kitsch. Give her the tropics any day, with their stormy skies perpetually rent by the play of warring elements. She noted that a handful of people, no more than that, were dotted around the middle of the square. But something felt wrong. She looked and looked again, trying to work out what was out of place in that provincial square whose every detail she knew so well. Her eyes went from the Cabildo to the Cathedral, and back again. The Casa Rosada, as unspeakably hideous as ever, was blocking the view of the river. When would they pull that pink monstrosity down? Everything was as it had always been, drab, bare and ugly. And then it hit her; apart from the groups of women arriving for the demonstration, there was nobody in the square. No sightseers were standing around, no school children or men going about their daily business were hurrying across it, no old people were sunning themselves on the park benches. There were no street vendors anywhere to be seen. 'I'm going mad like the other women,' she thought, and looked round the square again, surveying it inch by inch. The gathering in the middle of the square was growing; women on their own or arm-in-arm were streaming out of the side-streets. 'I can't believe it,' she said to herself again. 'Why is there no one here?' She turned round and saw four women coming towards her, knotting their scarves under their chins. On the comer behind them, a little girl was tying her scarf round her neck. She looked up at the windows overlooking the square. No one was looking out. With a puzzled frown, she took her white scarf out of her bag and put it on. Elena was watching the demonstration grow from the pavement at the edge of the square. But her mind was completely taken up with the fact that, at half past four in the afternoon, there was not a single person there except for the women taking part in the demonstration. Elena took Victoria's photograph out of her handbag and started to study it; it looked somewhat the worse for wear, though she did her best to flatten it out and straighten the corners. She felt embarrassed to ask if she could have a look at it. From what she could make out, it seemed that Victoria was standing on a beach though wearing a polo-neck sweater and trousers. Did she have her hands in her pockets? But Elena lowered the photo and started to walk towards the centre of the square. In the fraction of a second that she was left stranded not knowing quite what to do, a woman dashed past with a bundle of duplicated lists and handed her one. It went on for twenty-three pages; she felt an urge to count the names and started to run her forefinger down the columns to work out how many names were on each page. She'd got to the forty-fifth line when someone stopped at her el-bow and said: 'You needn't bother to count them, sister, there are about a thousand names down here, but the actual number who've disappeared is much higher than that. We've only just started compiling the lists. The job is complicated by the fact that a lot of people are unwilling to give the full names and ages, or the parents' names and phone numbers.' She shrugged her shoulders and walked on. She felt annoyed with the woman for calling her 'sister' and poking her nose into what was none of her business, but she took another glance at the list. Only now did she notice the ages; they mostly ranged from fifteen to twenty-five; she went on going through it page by page. A woman of sixty-eight, another of seventy-five. She shuddered. A four-month-old baby, a two-year-old girl, another of five, a brother and sister of three and four. The list in her hand began to quiver. How can a four-month-old baby disappear? The entry read: Anselmo Furco, four months, disappeared on . . . Parents: Juan Gustavo Furco, 23, Alicia, 20, also miss-ing. It was followed by the name, address and telephone number of the grandparents. A violent lurch in the pit of her stomach made her grope for the nearest wall to lean against. Someone came up to her and said: 'Come on now, you mustn't give up.' They steered her back to the square. She felt bet-ter in the open air and looked around her. So these were the Madwomen of the Plaza de Mayo . . . The number of women was incredible and so was the silence; apart from the rapid footsteps and muffled greetings, there was not a sound. Not a single prison van, not a single policeman, not a single army jeep was in sight. The Casa Rosada looked like a stage set, with thick curtains drawn across its windows. There were no grenadier guards on sentry duty at the gates either. It was the realisation that the grenadier guards were not there that gave her a sudden, terrifying insight into the enemy's machina-tions: *every Thursday, for the two to three hours during which the demonstration took place, the Plaza de Mayo was wiped off the map.* They couldn't fire on the women or lock them all up. It would have undermined the concerted effort they'd made to project a carefree image of 'the Argentina I love'. Their ploy was simply to ignore them; to ignore the existence of the square and of the madwomen stamping their feet. Had they arrived at that degree of sophisti-cation? And why not, if the same sophistication operated at the level of tor-tures and abductions? A developed nation does things properly.

She was beginning to give way to despair; more questions flooded into her head. What about the people who regularly passed through the square at that time of day? What about the bank clerks? What about the crowds permanently gathered on the corner by the Cabildo? Where the devil were they? What about the priests and parishioners who every afternoon without fail went to pray in the Cathedral? Did they sneak out of the back door or stay waiting inside in the dark? What about the people who at that precise moment had to get an important document signed at the solicitor's offices bordering the square? How had they managed to get such a motley collection of people, who couldn't possibly have come to a joint agreement, to melt into thin air? What had provoked this reaction of blind terror in each and every one of them? Or were they unanimously shunning this vast array of desperate women because it brought them face to face with a grief that words could not convey? And the same cowards who would not risk setting an immaculately shod foot in the square would loudly proclaim, contented citizens all, that they were avid football fans, that they ate meat every day, that they holidayed at Mar del Plata whenever the fancy took them, that they wouldn't dream of missing a Sunday on the beach despite all those dreadful rumours—put around by the enemies of the fatherland—of bodies floating in the River Plate. Or did they sleep uneasily at night?

Meanwhile more and more women kept on arriving; by now the square was so packed they were spilling out into the roadway. She lost sight of Elena and knew there was no point trying to look for her in such a crowd, but she plunged into it all the same, edging her way forward as best she could.

'Did I tell you I've got some terrible photos a friend took there one Thursday? If I'd known we were going to talk about it I'd have brought them with me. To be honest, I never really understood why you went back to Buenos Aires. Anyway, you wouldn't want to look at my pictures if you saw it for yourself. There's another group here that's printing copies of all the photographs in their records. That's an even more gruesome sight. But the photos of the missing children are important, because they've been known to turn up in other countries. It's a kind of hell we're living in.'

And what a hell, Dolores! A new man-made version, such as no one ever imagined. Without a word or command being uttered, the women raised the photographs above their heads. Why, when there was no one there to see them? I expected that, with so much handling and fondling, those childlike faces would soon be disfigured past the point of recognition. Near me, an old woman was holding up a cheap studio portrait with both hands. The girl was smiling stiffly, her head tilted to one side, no doubt obeying the photographer's instructions. She was sitting with her legs crossed, an organdie dress covering her knees. Another woman was holding a passport photograph in the palm of her hand, shielding it as if it were an egg she'd just that minute hatched; she raised it gingerly and started to wave it from side to side; she couldn't stop shaking and the tears were streaming down her face, but she kept her lips tightly pressed together. A woman right next to me took out of her handbag a tiny picture in an oval frame. She looked at me and smiled apologetically. The only photos she had of him were taken when he was a child, if only she'd known . . . I asked her how old he was now. 'He'll be twenty next month. We were so proud of him. We were going to hold a party to celebrate.' She could barely finish the sentence, but she pulled herself together, sighed and raised the tiny frame as high as she could, along with all the other photographs. I started to feel uncomfortable just standing there with nothing to hold up. I raised the list with both hands and waited expectantly. Was that it? Just this coming together to share one's silent grief with the silent grief of others?

And that was when it started, Dolores, I can't explain to you what it was that happened. How can I find the words? I could say that suddenly someone started to shout and everyone started shouting and in a matter of minutes the whole square was one single shout. But that wouldn't begin to tell you what it was like. There are so many people shouting all over the place . . . And you'll probably smile if I tell you I started to shout as well, though it had nothing to do with me, and I've no idea what I shouted, I couldn't understand a word of what the other women were shouting either, because it was as if the words were severed from one another by the sobbing and howling. Every now and then I thought I heard the words 'Where are they?', 'Where are they?' but it may have been my imagination. And yet they must have been voicing some demand that served as a focus for the general mood of anger, because the crowd of women surged forward like a tide. They continued to advance, we knocked into one another, stumbling over each other's feet. The chaos was indescribable as hundreds of sheets of paper were tossed into the air. I did exactly the same as the madwomen, and I couldn't begin to tell you what I felt; it was as if someone was trying to rip my insides out and I was clinging on to them for all I was worth. But that's not it, either. I can't be sure it was really like that. I keep groping for the words but it's useless. I heard an alarming whirring sound overhead and ducked instinctively; it soon dawned on me it was the pigeons flapping their wings in terror as they flew round and round, not knowing where to settle. They went on wheeling frantically, feathers flurrying, beaks snapping furiously. I collided head-on with a girl who was groaning, she can't have been more than twenty. Who had she lost? Her baby, her husband, her parents? I couldn't see the crumpled photo she was clutching with both hands. I thought I glimpsed a snatch of Elena's jacket in the middle of a circle of women and I elbowed my way towards her. She was part of a chorus chanting in unison, and this time I could clearly hear the words 'Where are they?', 'Where are they?' She had her back to me, but she didn't turn round even when I put my hand on her shoulder and shook her. Then I shouted her name. You say you knew her well, Dolores, but at that moment you'd never have recognised her. I'd grown up with her but she was a complete stranger to me. I wish I could forget that twisted face, that gaping, howling mouth and, even worse, her skin, that delicate skin of hers, discoloured with purple blotches. She wasn't holding Victoria's photo up in the air but was clasping it to her chest with both hands, huddling over it; an old woman cowering in the face of death. I put my arm round her and started to chant with her. Until everything began to quieten down. The madwomen began to drift away. Three women of indeterminate age were trying to calm another woman who was shaking her clenched fist at the Casa Rosada. They started to straighten their jackets, smooth their blouses, resettle their handbags on their arms; they tidied their hair and looked around for the best way out of the square. The crowd thinned out, revealing the paving stones strewn with stencilled sheets. I felt completely stunned, I needed more time to recover. I lost sight of Elena again. It was only a matter of minutes before the square had emptied itself. A woman took a packet out of her bag and started to throw bits of bread to the pigeons, but they were still chary; they kept skidding on the bits of paper and taking off again in panic, leaving the food. I felt like kicking the pigeons, but I took pity on the woman; how many times had she come to feed them with her missing son or daughter?

I crossed over to the opposite pavement and, looking up at the sky, saw that the pigeons were reassembling in flying formation and winging their way back to their usual perch on the obelisk. My friend was waiting for me on the corner of the Calle San Martín; her pale pointed face was calm and serene.

She must have noticed something alarming in my expression, because she gaped at me as if about to say something. Then she shook her head. 'Don't let it upset you like that, don't let it upset you like that,' she murmured and now it was her turn to put her arm round me. But I did something awful, really awful, I'll never forgive myself for it.

'What did you do?' the girl asked, putting down the blazer she was about to put on.

'I broke away from her and ran out into the middle of the road shouting how was I supposed to feel, for Christ's sake, how was I supposed to feel, and why didn't those bastards hiding behind the curtains come out into the open; I was ranting and raving like a maniac, while she stood there going red as if I'd slapped her in the face.'

Dolores sat watching her cigarette go out in the ashtray.

'I created a real scandal. And do you think anyone came out to see what was going on, do you think anyone looked out of the window? Not a soul.'

'I'm sorry,' Elena said. 'I'm really sorry.'

But I wasn't sorry; what I was feeling was completely different, horribly different. I told Elena I was going back to the square. She glanced at me briefly without a word, then turned on her heels and went back home, presumably. The square was still empty, or almost empty, I don't remember exactly. I sat down on a bench, muttering 'How am I supposed to feel, for Christ's sake, how am I supposed to feel?' over and over again, till I'd said it so many times it started to lose its force. I was distracted by the sight of an old man doing his utmost to get a little boy he was holding by the hand to touch a pigeon. I looked around me and realised why I'd returned to the square, I'd returned to watch the rats slinking back once they'd sensed that danger was over. Now the whole square was full of rats loitering or scurrying around. More and more rats kept pouring in and out of the side-streets. I looked over at the Cathedral and saw the steps lined with rats. But were they really rats? Disgusting, stinking, cowardly rats? Ought they to be exterminated like vermin? I looked at the little boy chasing the pigeons. I looked at the Casa Rosada, two grenadier guards were on sentry duty. At that point I leant my head against the back of the iron bench and began to weep, silently, so no one would notice.

The girl put her blazer on and went to look out of the window.

'It's got dark,' she said. 'The last thing I wanted was to go home in the dark.'

But something else was obviously on her mind. As they turned to face each other at the front door, she clutched her by the arm.

'I don't know how one's supposed to feel about it either. All I know is that you have to find some kind of breathing space. Because if you don't have room to breathe, you'll be dead as well. And the worst of it isn't that you'll be dead but that you'll have added another corpse to their collection.'

Lina Magaia

"Madalena Returned from Captivity"

Madalena has returned, a child of fourteen suffering from rickets because of malnutrition. Fourteen years ago her father had been arrested far away in Cabo Delgado, on the plateau, by puppets of the Portuguese political police, PIDE, and sent to Machava. From the tough Kadjamangwana prison in Machava he was sent as an unpaid labourer to Maragra, the sugar factory, where he courted a woman. From this love affair came Madalena.

Madalena was kidnapped by armed bandits near Maluna, where she was visiting relatives. For weeks and months, Madalena lived in a bandit base. The child was made forcibly into a woman for the bandits.

Madalena trembles. Talking to her is the commander of the force that found her in the bush when they were searching for bandits.

Madalena has lice all over her head, her body and her clothing. The commander orders them to cut her hair and find her a place to bathe. Madalena trembles.

The commander takes her, with her head shorn and her face washed, to the brigade commander. Others present include the local militia chief, who has known Madalena for more than a decade.

Madalena trembles and holds her legs tightly together. She remains standing. She stares with eyes moist with tears that refuse to flow at the group of people watching her. She continues to tremble.

The brigade commander askes, 'How do you feel, child?'

She looks at the ground without replying. She tries to open her mouth. Then the tears are released and they run down her lean cheeks. Madalena's throat is covered with streaks of ingrained dirt. Her hands end in nails that are overgrown and dirty, reminiscent of wretchedness and jiggers. Madalena has jiggers in her feet.

The brigade commander tries to soothe her. 'So, why are you crying, child? Aren't you happy to be going home? Don't you want to talk about what happened to you?'

Among the people surrounding the brigade commander is a woman whom Madalena knows. The commander turns to her and suggests, 'You talk to her. You women may understand each other.'

The woman is startled. She eyes Madalena and thinks, 'What does he want of the child? What could she possibly say at this moment?'

However, she asks, 'Madalena, how did you escape?'

She replies, 'It was when the soldiers attacked the big base. We were in a small base. The bandit chief ran away from the big base and came to the one we were in. The other bandits were afraid of him and hid us. There was me, Toneca and Elisa . . . '

She can't go on but it is obvious she wants to say more. The woman smiles at her and says, 'Do you know where Toneca and Elisa are?'

'No, I don't,' she replies. 'They told us to run into the bush when their chief arrived. We were running together at the beginning, but when we heard shots behind us I hid. We had agreed to escape to our homes . . . I don't know what happened to my friends afterwards.'

'But why were they afraid of their chief?' the woman asks.

'Because they were our husbands and they said they were afraid that the chief would want to keep us for himself.'

'So you had a husband? What was his name?'

Madalena begins to shake even more. She purses her lips and remains in shameful silence. She is petrified with fear.

After a while she speaks. 'There were lots. One of them was named Armando. He made me call him uncle.'

The brigade commander issues an order to the woman, 'Take the child home. Make sure she sees a doctor. She must be carrying all kinds of disease.'

The woman has one more question for Madalena:

'Were there many people at the base, apart from the bandits?'

'Yes. Men, women and children. I don't know how many. The bandits drank a lot of hooch every day, and when they were drunk, they would pick out someone to kill—with a knife, or a bayonet, or hatchet or even with a pestle.'

More tears flowed down Madalena's lean cheeks. 'And they made us watch. I know some of the people they killed. We were kidnapped at the same time.'

The brigade commander repeats his order: 'Take the child home. Don't forget to ask the doctor to examine her.'

Madalena's home is in the Maragra first neigbourhood, an area inhabited mostly by the Maconde community. These people from the plateau far away in the Cabo Delgado more than fourteen years earlier had responded to the call to defend their country and to free it from colonial rule. They were arrested on the plateau in Cabo Delgado, brought to Machava prison and then sold to Maragra. Today they live freely with their families.

They reach Madalena's house. The local militia commander knocks at the door of the community secretary. He passes on the news.

Though there is no telephone or radio, almost everyone hears the news at the same time. They surge out of their houses, some bare-chested, some wrapped in blankets, the women wearing cloths on their heads to shield themselves from the intense cold cast by the dew. In the midst of them is Madalena's maternal grandmother. She is old, ages old, with wrinkles on her face, wrinkles on her arms, folds on her throat, emaciated legs seemingly unable to bear the weight even of her own thin body. On her head she wears a scarf that scarcely hides the cotton that her hair has become with the passage of time. She is crying. 'Nwananga mina! Nwananga mina u buyile! Yo nwananga . . . ' ('My child! My child, you've come back! Oh, my child . . . ')

And she falls on to the dew-soaked ground.

Madalena is sobbing.

Out of a hut comes a woman with one eye blinded by a cataract, and she whispers, 'Bernardo, Bernardo my beloved? When will you come back?' (Bernardo is in Maputo.) 'How shall I find you to tell you that your daughter has returned?' She embraces Madalena and weeps. Many of the women are also weeping. All of a sudden someone begins a song. A song of the people.

The woman with the blind eye whispers again, this time to Madalena, 'My child, you've come back . . . '

Someone starts to dance. Then everyone dances—except for Madalena's mother and grandmother. Madalena remains in the centre of the circle made by the dancers, but she doesn't dance. She sobs . . .

The militia commander and the woman who have escorted Madalena are hugged and kissed by many of those present. Someone tells Madalena, 'Don't cry any more. They will never find you again.'

Margaret Drabble

from *The Gates of Ivory*

Mme Akrun watches the dust of the departing car, and then she goes back into her hut and rubs the pink words off the blackboard. Liz is right to guess that she has changed. She has relinquished Mitra. His shadow no longer haunts her. She has let him go. He must take his own chance, wherever he may be. Los Angeles, Toronto, Siem Reap, Hong Kong, Gravesend. He is on his own now. She returns no more to the clearing in the forest. She has other preoccupations now.

It is not time alone that has accomplished this. She had begun to believe that time would never heal her, for she had not wished to be healed. She had hoped that her own hope would keep Mitra alive, and with the dirty needle of hope she had picked at her memories, had infected them and kept them as a running sore. She had watched others around her deal with their memories in this way, and in others. Some, like her daughter Sok Sita, had lost their wits. Some had cauterized the past with rage, and lived off anger and hatred. Some had been arrested as by a flow of burning lava in postures of bowed submission, of cowed despair: and now crawled around, bent and deformed. Some of the young fed off film-star dreams of escape. Playing ping-pong, they chattered of visas and papers that would never come. Some plotted revenge. Some went back across the border to join the resistance. Some lived for the moment, learning camp ways, learning to wheedle and exploit and profit, to scavenge and trade. Even here, there were objects to sell and recycle, there were unexplained arrivals of snakeskin and pig meat and musical instruments. Of late, a new supply of small carvings had begun to appear on the market. A lizard, a fish, a flower, a crocodile: antique or fake, who cared? They fetched a price.

Some despair and some cultivate their gardens. Mme Akrun and her colleagues water the red lilies and the marigolds with water provided by the United Nations and recycled from washtubs and cooking pots. There are no crops here, for this is bad land. Life here is neither urban nor rural. It is a parody of the town, a parody of the village.

Time has passed, but it is not the passing of time or the birth of a grand-child that has closed the wound of Mitra.

Mme Akrun tidies up her meagre worn text books, shuts and locks the drawer of her desk, hangs the key on its string round her neck, collects the placatory offerings of the large white woman from London, and sets off to-wards her home down the dusty red path, nodding and smiling to friends and colleagues as she goes, a respectable matron, honoured amongst her fellows.

She had not thought it would turn out this way. She had not thought that it would be her youngest son, Kem, who would rescue her from the lingering death-grip of the ghost of Mitra.

This place is neither town nor country. This time is neither peace nor war.

When Kem had gone missing, at first she had refused to respond. In her heart she felt nothing, to her community she said nothing. So many go missing. Now the photographer and his friend from England have gone missing.

One more, one less, who cares? After Mitra's loss, how could she care? Kem had gone over the border with the bandit called Lek Let, with the men with guns. She said to herself that she would never see him, would never hear from him again. He was well lost, the bad boy, the delinquent, the drug-addict, the bitter child of No Man's Land. Let him call himself a resistance fighter. What did it matter? He was lost.

So she told herself, as day succeeded day. She would send no messages after him, as she had sent after Mitra. She would not alert the Red Cross, the United Nations Border Relief, the camp commanders. She would wait for her heart to turn to stone. And hour by hour, it petrified.

Mme Akrun smiles, waves. There is Chin Sokha on his bicycle, there is Mme Yan's youngest grandchild, there is the mad monk, there is one-armed Proap Am beating tin cans into cooking vessels, there is the secretary of the Khmer Women's Association with his new Panama hat.

She had waited for the triumph of nothing, for the victory of indifference. And when the news came that Kem had been found, that he was lying in the camp hospital, she had gasped with distress to feel that she could still feel distress.

She had not wanted to go near him. She was told he was mortally ill. He had been blown up by a mine, he was in pieces, he would surely die, rumour had told her with vindictive relish. If only she could stay away until it was all over!

But she was drawn, she was pulled. A hook had entered her guts, and she was pulled. She could not force herself to stay away. The hook was lodged in some soft nerveless hidden tissue, and, although she could not feel it, she could not resist it. It tugged her, towards the bamboo shack that called itself a hospital, towards the camp beds with their rows of injured and their buzzing flies. Resentment and foreboding dragged her back and made her as heavy as lead as she approached. Her feet slurred and stumbled. She did not want this confrontation. But on she went.

She could not at first identify her son amongst the maimed and the sick. Where was he, which was he, was he dead and buried already, was he that hunched shape with the bandaged skull, was he that heap of rags? And then she saw him. He was sitting, propped up, in the middle of the row, awaiting her visit, his face hot with pain, his brow damp, his eyes and nostrils distended, his breath short and quick. His eyes were searching for her, and when they caught her, he in hope reached out a hand, and then in despair, in submission, let it drop. She paused, frozen, the blood drumming in her ears. The moment lasted for ever. He continued to look towards her. It was his pain that filled her. It flowed from him to her until she was drowned in it, flooded by it. She could see that his face was full of doubt, he expected chastisement, rejection. She could not move. She tried to move towards him, but she staggered as though under a great burden, as she had staggered through the undergrowth with his feverish seven-year-old body in her arms. She was suffocating, she would die. His eyes had dropped from hers, but he made one last effort, and cried out. 'Mother!' he called. 'Mother!'

And she made it to his bedside, and collapsed there against his mattress in the dust.

They had taken off his leg. The stump, brutally bandaged, struck at her and her own flesh bled. She shut her eyes, and moaned, and shook her head. All of her past and of his seemed to be gathered up here in retribution, in reproach. She had abandoned and betrayed him, and now he would die, her little one, her baby, he would die in terrible pain.

'Mother,' he whispered. 'Little mother.' He dared to touch her hair.

And so they had been reunited. She had wept and wept. He had comforted her. He too had wept. He had become her son. He had been returned to her, and she had forgiven him.

He did not die. She watched over him, tended him, endured with him each pang and each spasm. The pain persisted, and stubbornly she partook of it. She was driven away by hospital orderlies, and she returned with offerings. Hour by hour, inch by inch, she regained him, as she tried to make amends.

As she sat by Kem's bedside, the plaintive ghost of his brother Mitra slipped quietly away into the shades of the jungle. Mitra was forgotten. Kem was her salvation.

Gradually, the pain diminished. She wept bitter tears of joy when he was fitted with a wooden leg tipped with old rubber from a blown tyre. She smiled and wept as he practised staggering round the hospital compound, to the cheers and jeers of his fellow-amputees. And when he was allowed home, she killed the fatted chicken and bought pig meat and cooked a feast for the prodigal son. Ah, such an evening, such happiness! Sok Sita giggling nervously, and Am Nara at last vastly pregnant, and her son-in-law Chut Pek, and her friend Mme Yan and Yan's family, a whole reception committee for Kem's return. There was rejoicing and hope and excitement. Now they were reunited, now their luck would change!

And the good luck is still with her, thinks Mme Akrun, as she walks homewards through the throng of bicycles. Kem remains sweet of nature. He is transformed, he is humble, he is grateful. He is safe, he is good, she knows where he can be found at any time of night or day. He occupies himself, he has even started to study a little, he is learning English. He will be pleased with the magazines that the Englishwoman brought, with their news of the outside world, with their advertisements for aftershave and car telephones and tennis rackets and Wedgwood china. He can no longer wander off in bad company. He is no use to the guerrillas or to the bandits now. He cannot play at soldiers any more. He is her darling, her favourite, her little one. She is reborn as Mother. Her family is complete once more. She is happy. She walks towards him as he sits waiting in his bamboo prison, with her head held high, with the step of a young girl. It has been hard, but Kem is her reward.

Selected Bibliography
Contributors
Sources and Credits
Index

SELECTED BIBLIOGRAPHY

Women's War Literature

Aldrich, Mildred. *A Hilltop on the Marne*. Boston: Houghton Mifflin, 1915.

Arnow, Harriette. *The Dollmaker*. New York: Avon Books, 1972.

Bagnold, Enid. *A Diary Without Dates*. New York: William Morrow, 1935. London: Virago, 1978.

———. *The Happy Foreigner*. London: Virago, 1987.

Barker, Pat. *The Eye in the Door*. London: Penguin, 1993.

———. *The Ghost Road*. London: Penguin, 1995.

———. *Regeneration*. London: Penguin, 1992.

Bauman, Janine. *Winter in the Morning: A Young Girl's Life in the Warsaw Ghetto*. New York: Free Press, 1986.

Becker, Elizabeth. *When the War Is Over*. New York: Simon and Schuster, 1986.

Blackwood, Caroline. *On the Perimeter*. London: Flamingo, 1984.

Bogan, Louise. *What the Woman Wrote: Selected Letters of Louise Bogan, 1920–1970*. Edited by Ruth Limmer. New York: Harcourt Brace Javanovich, 1973.

Borton, Lady. *After Sorrow: An American among the Vietnamese*. New York: Viking, 1995.

Boston, Anne, ed. *Wave Me Goodbye: Stories of the Second World War*. London: Penguin, 1989.

Bourke-White, Margaret. *Shooting the Russian War*. New York: Simon and Schuster, 1942.

Brittain, Vera. *Testament of Youth*. New York: Viking Penguin, 1978.

———. *Wartime Chronicle: Diary, 1939–1945*. London: Victor Gollancz, 1989.

Burdekin, Katherine. *Swastika Night*. Old Westbury, N.Y.: Feminist Press, 1985.

Colette. *Earthly Paradise: An Autobiography*. Edited by Robert Phelps. New York: Farrar, Straus, and Giroux, 1994.

Cornum, Rhonda. *She Went to War: The Rhonda Cornum Story*. Novato, Calif.: Presidio, 1992.

Cowles, Virginia. *Looking for Trouble*. New York: Harper, 1949.

Didion, Joan. *A Book of Common Prayer*. New York: Simon and Schuster, 1977.

———. *Democracy: A Novel*. New York: Simon and Schuster, 1984.

———. *The Last Thing He Wanted*. New York: Alfred A. Knopf, 1996.

———. *Salvador*. New York: Simon and Schuster, 1983.

Donhoff, Marion. *Before the Storm: Memories of My Youth in Old Prussia*. Translated by Jean Steinberg. New York: Alfred A. Knopf, 1990.

Duras, Marguerite. *The War: A Memoir*. New York: The New Press, 1986.

Filipovic, Zlata. *Zlata's Diary: A Child's Life in Sarajevo*. New York: Viking, 1994.

First, Ruth. *117 Days*. New York: Monthly Review Press, 1989.

Flanner, Janet. *An American in Paris: Profile of an Interlude Between Two Wars*. New York: Simon and Schuster, 1940.

——. *Paris Was Yesterday, 1925–1939*. New York: Viking, 1972.

Frank, Anne. *The Diary of a Young Girl*. Translated by B. M. Mooyaart. New York: Bantam Books, 1993.

Gellhorn, Martha. *The Face of War*. New York: Grove/Atlantic, 1988.

——. "The Russians." In *The Face of War*. New York: Grove/Atlantic, 1988.

——. "The War in Spain." In *The Face of War*. New York: Grove/Atlantic, 1988.

——. "The War in Vietnam." In *The Face of War*. New York: Grove/Atlantic, 1988.

Ginzburg, Eugenia. *Into the Whirlwind*. Translated by Paul Stevenson and Manya Harari. London: Collins Harvill, 1989.

Ginzburg, Natalie. *The Little Virtues*. London: Carcanet, 1985.

Grenfell, Joyce. *The Time of My Life: Entertaining the Troops, Her Wartime Journals*. London: Hodder and Stoughton, 1989.

Hall, Radclyffe. *Miss Ogilvy Finds Herself*. New York: Harcourt Brace, 1934.

——. *The Well of Loneliness*. London: Virago, 1982.

Hartley, Jenny, ed. *Hearts Undefeated: Women's Writing of the Second World War*. London: Virago, 1995.

Hassell, Fey von. *A Mother's War*. New York: Berkley, 1992.

Hayslip, Le Ly. *When Heaven and Earth Changed Places*. New York: Doubleday, 1989.

Hellman, Lillian. *An Unfinished Woman: A Memoir*. Boston: Little, Brown, 1969.

Hershman, Marcie. *Tales of the Master Race*. New York: HarperCollins, 1991.

Higgins, Marguerite. *Our Vietnam Nightmare*. New York: Harper and Row, 1965.

Higonnet, Margaret R. *Lines of Fire: Women's Writers of World War I*. New York: Dutton, 1998.

Hollingsworth, Hilda. *Places of Greater Safety*. Berkeley: Zenobia Press, 1993.

Holtby, Winifred. *The Frozen Earth and Other Poems*. London: Collins, 1935.

Jacobs, Helen Hull. *"By Your Leave, Sir": The Story of a Wave*. New York: Dodd, Mead and Co., 1943.

Johnson, Georgia Douglas Camp. *Bronze: A Book of Verse*. Boston: B. J. Brimmer Co., 1922.

Kanda, Mikio, ed. *Widows of Hiroshima: The Life Stories of Nineteen Peasant Wives*. New York: St. Martin's, 1989.

Khalifah, Sahar. *Wild Thorns*. London: Al Saqi Books, 1985.

Klein, Yvonne M., ed. *Beyond the Homefront: Women's Autobiographical Writing of the Two World Wars*. Washington Square: New York University Press, 1997.

Kyi, Aung San Suu. *Freedom from Fear and Other Writings*. Edited by Michael Aris. New York: Viking, 1991.

Larsen, Wendy Wilder, and Tran Thi Nqa. *Two Women and Vietnam*. New York: Perennial Library, 1987.

Laska, Vera, ed. *Women in the Resistance and in the Holocaust: The Voices of Eyewitnesses*. Westport, Conn.: Greenwood, 1983.

Levertov, Denise. *Out of the War Shadow: An Anthology of Current Poetry*. New York: War Resisters' League, 1967.

Luce, Clare Boothe. *Europe in the Spring*. New York: Alfred A. Knopf, 1940.

Macaulay, Rose. *Letters to a Sister*. New York: Athæeneum, 1964.

——. *Non-Combatants and Others*. London: Methuen, 1986.

Mack, Louise. *A Woman's Experiences in the Great War*. London: T. Fisher Unwin Ltd., 1915.

Marchant, Hilda. *Women and Children Last: A Woman Reporter's Account of the Battle of Britain*. London: Victor Gollancz, 1941.

Matthews, Caroline Twigge. *Experiences of a Woman Doctor in Serbia*. London: Mills and Boon, 1916.

McCarthy, Mary. *The Seventeenth Degree*. New York: Harcourt Brace Jovanovich, 1974.

McCullers, Carson. *Reflections in a Golden Eye*. New York: New Directions, 1950.

Meiselas, Susan. *Nicaragua, June 1978–July 1979*. Edited by Claire Rosenberg. New York: Pantheon, 1981.

Menchu, Rigoberta. *I, Rigoberta Menchu: An Indian Woman in Guatemala*. Edited by Elisabeth Burgos-Debray. Translated by Ann Wright. London: Verso, 1984.

Nelson, Alice Dunbar. *The Works of Alice Dunbar Nelson*. New York: Oxford University Press, 1988.

Nwapa, Flora. *Wives at War and Other Stories*, Nigeria: Tana Press Ltd., 1980.

Owings, Alison. *Frauen: German Women Recall the Third Reich*. New Brunswick, N.J.: Rutgers University Press, 1993.

Panter-Downes, Mollie. *London War Notes*. Edited by William Shawn. London: Addison Wesley Longman, 1972.

Pargeter, Edith. *She Goes to War*. London: Headline House, 1989.

Piercy, Marge. *Gone to Soldiers*, New York: Summit, 1987.

Porter, Katherine Anne. *Pale Horse, Pale Rider: Three Short Novels*. New York: Harcourt Brace, 1939.

Randall, Margaret. *Sandino's Daughters: Testimonies of Nicaraguan Women in Struggle*. Vancouver: New Star Books, 1981.

Rathbone, Irene. *We That Were Young*. London: Virago, 1988.

Rein, Natalie. *Daughters of Rachel: Women in Israel*. New York: Penguin, 1980.

Rich, Adrienne. *Adrienne Rich's Poetry and Prose: Poems, Prose, Reviews, and Criticism*. New York: W. W. Norton, 1993.

——. *Poems: Selected and New, 1950–1974*. New York: W. W. Norton, 1974.

Russ, Joanna. *The Female Man*. New York: Bantam Books, 1975.

Saywell, Shelley. *Women in War*. New York: Penguin, 1986.

Scholl, Inge. *The White Rose: Munich 1942–1943*. Translated by Arthur R. Schultz. Hanover, N.H.: Wesleyan University Press, 1983.

Schwertfeger, Ruth. *Women of Theresienstadt: Voices from a Concentration Camp*. Oxford: Berg, 1989.

Scrivener, Jane. *Inside Rome with the Germans*. New York: Macmillan, 1945.

al-Shaykh, Hanan. *The Story of Zahra*. London: Quartet, 1986.

Sinclair, May. *Journal of Impressions in Belgium*. New York: Macmillan, 1915.

——. *The Tree of Heaven*. New York: Macmillan, 1918.

Smith, Winnie. *American Daughter Gone to War*. New York: William Morrow, 1992.

Sontag, Susan. "Godot Comes to Sarajevo." *New York Review of Books*, 21 Oct. 1993, 52–59.

Spark, Muriel. "The First Year of My Life." In *Collected Stories of Muriel Spark*. New York: Penguin, 1994.

Spivack, Kathleen. *The Jane Poems*. Garden City, N.Y.: Doubleday, 1974.

Stein, Gertrude. *Wars I Have Seen*. New York: Random House, 1945.

Stobart, Mrs. St. Clair. *The Flaming Sword in Serbia and Elsewhere.* London: Hodder, 1916.

Sutherland, Christine. *Monica: Heroine of the Danish Resistance.* New York: Farrar, Straus, and Giroux, 1990.

Szymusiak, Molyda. *The Stones Cry Out: A Cambodian Childhood, 1975–1980.* New York: Hill and Wang, 1986.

Tate, Trudi. *Women, Men and the Great War: An Anthology of Stories.* Manchester: Manchester University Press, 1995.

Thompson, Dorothy, ed. *Over Our Dead Bodies: Women Against the Bomb.* London: Virago, 1983.

Tobias, Sheila. "Armed and Dangerous." *Ms. Magazine.* Aug. 1988, 63–67.

Van Devanter, Lynda. *Home Before Morning.* New York: Beaufort Books, 1983.

Vassiltchikov, Marie. *Berlin Diaries, 1940–1945.* New York: Vintage, 1988.

Waddington, Mary King. *My War Diary.* New York: Charles Scribner's Sons, 1917.

Warner, Sylvia Townsend. *A Garland of Straw.* New York: Penguin, 1943.

Wesley, Mary. *The Camomile Lawn.* London: Macmillan, 1984.

Wolf, Christa. *Accident: A Day's News.* Translated by Heike Schwarzbauer and Rick Takvorian. London: Virago, 1989.

———. *Cassandra: A Novel and Four Essays.* Translated by Jan van Heurick. New York: Farrar, Straus, and Giroux, 1984.

———. *What Remains and Other Stories.* New York: Farrar, Straus, and Giroux, 1993.

Zucker-Bujanowska, Liliana. *Liliana's Journal: Warsaw 1939–45.* New York: Dial Press, 1980.

Works on Women's War Literature

Accad, Evelyne. *Sexuality and War.* New York: New York University Press, 1990.

Benstock, Shari. *Women of the Left Bank.* Austin: University of Texas Press, 1986.

Berry, Paul, and Alan Bishop, eds. *Testament of a Generation: The Journalism of Vera Brittain and Winifred Holtby.* London: Virago, 1985.

Braybon, Gail, and Penny Sommerfield. *Out of the Cage: Women's Experiences in Two World Wars.* London: Pandora, 1987.

Cambridge Women's Peace Collective. *My Country Is the Whole World: An Anthology of Women's Work on Peace and War.* London: Pandora, 1984.

Cooke, Miriam. *War's Other Voices: Women Writers on the Lebanese Civil War.* Cambridge: Cambridge University Press, 1988.

———. *Women and the War Story.* Berkeley: University of California Press, 1996.

Cooke, Miriam, and Angela Woollacott, eds. *Gendering War Talk.* Princeton, N.J.: Princeton University Press, 1993.

Cooper, Helen M., Adrienne Auslander Munich, and Susan Merrill Squier. *Arms and the Woman: War, Gender, and Literary Representation.* Chapel Hill: University of North Carolina Press, 1989.

Fryth, Jim, and Sally Alexander. *Women's Voices from the Spanish Civil War.* London: Lawrence and Wishart, 1991.

Gilbert, Sandra M., and Susan Gubar, eds. *Letters from the Front.* Vol. 3 of *No Man's Land: The Place of the Women Writers in the Twentieth Century.* New Haven, Conn.: Yale University Press, 1994.

———. *The Norton Anthology of Literature by Women: The Tradition in English*. New York: Norton, 1985.

———. *Sexchanges*. Vol. 2 of *No Man's Land: The Place of the Women Writers in the Twentieth Century*. New Haven, Conn.: Yale University Press, 1989.

———. *The War of the Words*. Vol. 1 of *No Man's Land: The Place of the Women Writers in the Twentieth Century*. New Haven, Conn.: Yale University Press, 1988.

Gioseffi, Daniela, ed. *Women on War: Essential Voices for the Nuclear Age*. New York: Simon and Schuster, 1988.

Goldman, Dorothy, ed. *Women and World War I: The Written Response*. New York: St. Martin's, 1993.

Heinemann, Marlene E. *Gender and Destiny: Women Writers and the Holocaust*. New York: Greenwood, 1986.

Higonnet, Margaret, et al., eds. *Behind the Lines: Gender and the Two World Wars*. New Haven, Conn.: Yale University Press, 1987.

Honey, Maureen. *Creating Rosie the Riveter: Class, Gender and Propaganda During World War II*. Amherst: University of Massachusetts Press, 1984.

Jeffords, Susan. *The Remasculinization of America: Gender and the Vietnam War*. Bloomington: Indiana University Press, 1989.

Macdonald, Sharon, Pat Holden, and Shirley Ardener. *Images of Women in Peace and War*. Madison: University of Wisconsin Press, 1988.

Marcus, Jane. Afterword, "Corpus/Corps/Corpse: Writing the Body in/at War," to *Not So Quiet . . . : Stepdaughters of War* by Helen Zenna Smith. New York: Feminist Press, 1989.

Marshall, Catherine. *Militarism Versus Feminism: Writings on Women and War*. London: Virago, 1987.

Matthews, Irene. "Women, Writing, and War." Ph.D. diss. University of Michigan, 1990.

Muir, Kate. *Arms and the Woman*. London: Sinclair-Stevenson, 1992.

Reilly, Catherine, ed. *Chaos of the Night: Women's Poetry and Verse of the Second World War*. London: Virago, 1984.

———. *Scars Upon My Heart: Women's Poetry and Verse of the First World War*. London: Virago, 1981.

Richler, Mordecai, ed. *Writers in World War II*. New York: Vintage Books, 1993.

Rittner, Carol, and John K. Roth. *Different Voices: Women and the Holocaust*. New York: Paragon House, 1993.

Scarry, Elaine. *The Body in Pain: The Making and Unmaking of the World*. New York: Oxford University Press, 1985.

Schweik, Carol. *A Gulf So Deeply Cut: American Women Poets and the Second World War*. Madison: University of Wisconsin Press, 1991.

Sheridan, Dorothy, ed. *Wartime Women: An Anthology of Women's Wartime Writing for Mass-Observation 1937–45*. London: Mandarin, 1991.

Theweleit, Klaus. *Male Fantasies*. Translated by Stephan Conway. Minnesota: University of Minnesota Press, 1987.

Tylee, Claire M. *The Great War and Women's Consciousness: Images of Militarism and Womanhood in Women's Writings, 1914–1964*. Iowa City: University of Iowa Press, 1990.

Wagner, Lilya. *Women War Correspondents of World War II*. Westport, Conn.: Greenwood, 1989.

Women, War, and Peace

Adam-Smith, Patsy. *Australian Women at War*. Victoria: Nelson, Melbourne, 1984.

Addams, Jane. *Newer Ideals of Peace*. New York: Macmillan, 1907.

Alonso, Harriet. *Peace as a Women's Issue: The U.S. Movement for World Peace and Women's Rights since 1820*. Syracuse, N.Y.: Syracuse University Press, 1992.

Anderson, Bonnie S., and Judith P. Zinsser. *A History of Their Own: Women in Europe from Prehistory to the Present*. Vol. 2. New York: Harper and Row, 1988.

Bennett, Olivia, Jo Bexley, and Kitty Warnock, eds. *Arms to Fight, Arms to Protect*. London: Panos, 1995.

Buck, Pearl. *Of Men and Women*. New York: John Day, 1941.

Cock, Jacklyn. *Colonels and Cadres: Women and War in South Africa*. Cleveland: Pilgrim Press, 1993.

Elshtain, Jean Bethke. *Women and War*. New York: Basic Books, 1987.

Elshtain, Jean Bethke, and Sheila Tobias, eds. *Women, Militarism, and War*. Savage, Md.: Rowman and Littlefield, 1990.

Enloe, Cynthia. *Bananas, Beaches, and Bases: Making Feminist Sense of International Politics*. Berkeley: University of California Press, 1990.

——. *Does Khaki Become You?: The Militarization of Women's Lives*. London: Pandora, 1988.

Fraser, Antonia. *The Warrior Queens*. New York: Alfred A. Knopf, 1989.

Hartmann, Susan M. *The Home Front and Beyond: American Women in the 1940's*. Boston: Twayne, 1982.

Holm, Jeanne. *Women in the Military: An Unfinished Revolution*. Novato, Calif.: Presidio, 1982.

Howes, Ruth H., and Michael R. Stevenson, eds. *Women and the Use of Military Force*. Boulder, Colo.: Lynne Rienner Publishers, 1994.

Isaksson, Eva, ed. *Women and the Military System*. New York: St. Martin's, 1988.

Jones, Lynne, ed. *Keeping the Peace: A Women's Peace Handbook*. London: The Women's Press, 1983.

Keil, Sally Van Wagenen. *Those Wonderful Women in Their Flying Machines*. New York: Rawson, Wade, 1979.

Koonz, Claudia. *Mothers in the Fatherland: Women, the Family, and Nazi Politics*. New York: St. Martin's, 1987.

Kraft, Barbara S. *The Peace Ship*. New York: Macmillan, 1978.

May, Antionette. *Witness to War: A Biography of Marguerite Higgins*. New York: Penguin, 1985.

Peters, Cynthia, ed. *Collateral Damage: The "New World Order" at Home and Abroad*. Boston: South End Press, 1989.

Price, Alan. *The End of the Age of Innocence: Edith Wharton and the First World War*. New York: St. Martin's, 1996.

Randall, Mercedes M. *Improper Bostonian: Emily Greene Balch*. New York: Twayne, 1964.

Reardon, Betty. *Sexism and the War System*. New York: Teachers College Press, 1985.

Rowbotham, Sheila. *Women, Resistance, and Revolution: A History of Women and Revolution in the Modern World*. New York: Vintage, 1974.

Ruddick, Sara. *Maternal Thinking: Towards a Politics of Peace*. Boston: Beacon, 1989.

Rupp, Leila J. *Mobilizing Women for War: German and American Propaganda 1939–1945*. Princeton, N.J.: Princeton University Press, 1978.

Schneider, Dorothy, and Carl J. Schneider. *Into the Breach: American Women Overseas in World War I*. New York: Viking, 1991.

Schreiner, Olive. *Woman and Labour*. London: Virago, 1978.

Soderbergh, Peter A. *Women Marines in the Korean War Era*. Westport, Conn.: Praeger, 1994.

Stiehm, Judith. *Arms and the Enlisted Woman*. Philadelphia: Temple University Press, 1989.

———, ed. *It's Our Military Too!: Women and the U.S. Military*. Philadelphia: Temple University Press, 1996.

———, ed. *Women and Men's Wars*. New York: Pergamon, 1983.

Stiglmayer, Alexandra. *Mass Rape: The War Against Women in Bosnia-Herzegovina*. Lincoln: University of Nebraska Press, 1994.

Summers, Anne. *Angels and Citizens: British Women as Military Nurses, 1888–1914*. London: Routledge and Kegan Paul, 1988.

Swerdlow, Amy. *Women Strike for Peace*. Chicago: University of Chicago, 1993.

Vickers, Jeanne. *Women and War*. London: Zed Books, 1993.

Weitz, Margaret Collins. *Sisters in the Resistance: How Women Fought to Free France, 1940–1945*. New York: John Wiley and Sons, 1996.

History of War in the Twentieth Century

Arendt, Hannah. *On Revolution*. New York: Penguin, 1990.

Caldicott, Helen. *Missile Envy: The Arms Race and Nuclear War*. Rev. ed. New York: Bantam Books, 1986.

Cohn, Carol. "Sex and Death in the Rational World of Defense Intellectuals." *Signs* 12, no.4 (1987): 687–718.

Cohn, Ilene. *Child Soldiers: The Role of Children in Armed Conflict*. New York: Oxford University Press, 1994.

Cruttwell, C. R. M. F. *A History of the Great War*. London: Granada, 1982.

Fitzgerald, Frances. *Fire in the Lake: The Vietnamese and the Americans in Vietnam*. Boston: Little, Brown, 1972.

Fussell, Paul. *The Great War and Modern Memory*. New York: Oxford University Press, 1975.

———. *Wartime: Understanding and Behavior in the Second World War*. New York: Oxford, 1989.

Gallagher, Carole. *American Ground Zero: The Secret Nuclear War*. Cambridge: MIT Press, 1993.

Gilbert, Martin. *The Second World War: A Complete History*. New York: H. Holt, 1989.

Goodwin, Doris Kearns. *No Ordinary Time: Franklin and Eleanor Roosevelt: The Home Front in World War II*. New York: Simon and Schuster, 1994.

Hooker, John. *Korea, The Forgotten War*. North Sidney, NSW: Time-Life Books, 1989.

Johnston, Carla B. *Reversing the Nuclear Arms Race*. Cambridge, Mass.: Schenkman Books, 1986.

Keegan, John. *The Face of Battle*. New York: Viking, 1976.

———. *The Second World War*. New York: Penguin, 1989.

Myrdal, Alva. *The Game of Disarmament: How the United States and Russia Run the Arms Race*. New York: Pantheon, 1976.

Silber, Laura, and Allan Little. *The Death of Yugoslavia*. New York: Penguin, 1995.

Solo, Pam. *From Protest To Policy: Beyond the Freeze to Common Security*. Cambridge, Mass.: Ballinger, 1989.

Tuchman, Barbara. *The Guns of August*. New York: Macmillan, 1962.

Young, Marilyn B. *The Vietnam Wars*. New York: HarperCollins, 1991.

CONTRIBUTORS

Jane Addams (1860–1935) founded Hull House, the first U.S. settlement house, in Chicago in 1889. She opposed American entry into World War I and was the first head of the Women's Peace Party. She was elected president of Women's International League for Peace and Freedom, a post she kept for life. She won the Nobel Peace Prize in 1931.

Anna Akhmatova (1889–1966) was born in Odessa. She worked as an editor in St. Petersburg, later becoming one of the best-known Russian poets of the century. Her husband was executed, and her work was banned for many years.

Meena Alexander (1951–) was born in India and educated in India, North Africa, and Great Britain. She now lives in New York and teaches at Hunter College. In addition to her poetry, she has written a novel and critical studies on Mary Wollstonecraft, Dorothy Wordsworth, and Mary Shelley.

Margaret Atwood (1939–) was born and raised in Ottawa, Ontario, and has published many volumes of poetry and criticism. Her novels include *Surfacing*, *The Handmaid's Tale*, and *Life Before Man*. Atwood is active in PEN and Amnesty International.

Christabel Bielenberg (1911–) was born in England and became a German citizen. Her husband was involved in the plot to assassinate Hitler. Bielenberg moved to Ireland with her husband and children after the war. She wrote *The Road Ahead*, a sequel to *The Past Is Myself*, in 1988.

Louise Bogan (1897–1970) became the poetry critic for the *New Yorker* in 1931, her job for thirty-eight years. Her memoirs were published posthumously in the *New Yorker* in 1978.

Mary Borden (1886–1968) equipped and ran an award-winning field hospital for the French army in World War I. She wrote *Sarah Gay* (1931), a novel about a nurse for whom war represented freedom as opposed to marriage. She also wrote *Journey Down a Blind Alley* in 1946 about a hospital venture in World War II.

Lady Borton worked with the American Friends Service Committee in Vietnam from 1969 to 1971. She went to North Vietnam during the war and returned in 1980 to work with Vietnamese boat people. In 1990, she again went to Vietnam, working as the only foreigner allowed by the Vietnamese government to live among villagers.

Elizabeth Bowen (1889–1973) nursed shell shock victims of World War I in Dublin.

In London during World War II, Bowen wrote for the Ministry of Information. Her wartime short stories were collected in *The Demon Lover*. She also wrote a novel about war in London, *The Heat of the Day*, in 1948.

Kay Boyle (1902–1992) wrote many stories on fascism and a series of novels with war and occupation as subjects. Boyle taught at San Francisco State University and was active in civil rights and antiwar work. She went to Cambodia in 1966 in protest against the Vietnam War.

Vera Brittain (1896–1970) joined the Volunteer Aid Division (V.A.D.). Two fiancés and a brother were killed in World War I. She later married and had two children. She is the author of twenty-nine books, including *Testament of Youth* from which the television series was created.

Gwendolyn Brooks (1917–) is the first African American woman to receive the Pulitzer Prize in poetry, for *Annie Allen* in 1949. In 1993, the Center for Black Literature and Creative Writing was established at Chicago State University, where Brooks holds the Gwendolyn Brooks Chair.

Bryher (Annie Winifred Ellerman [1894–1983]) was a companion to poet Hilda Doolittle (H.D). She married writer Robert McAlmon in New York in 1921. With her financial backing, McAlmon was able to become major publisher of modernist works in Paris, including several of Bryher's books. After helping Jews escape Hitler, Bryher was barely able to escape herself to England in 1940.

Willa Cather (1873–1947) was a magazine editor, but she left her job as managing editor at *McClure's* to write full time in 1912 when her first novel was serialized in the magazine. She based *One of Ours*, for which she won the Pulitzer Prize, in part upon her experiences in France before the war and the letters of a nephew who was killed.

Colette (1873–1954) nursed in Paris during the early part of World War I before smuggling herself to the front to join her husband. She reported from Venice and Rome during the second year of war. During World War II, she lived in Paris for the major part of German occupation, writing about the occupation in *Paris from My Window*. In 1945, she was elected to the Academie Goncourt.

Frances Davis (1889–1993) was brought up in a utopian community in the United States and began writing for a newspaper in her teens. During the Spanish Civil War, she risked her life to smuggle articles by male writers into France until she was hired to report for the *London Daily Mail*. She was injured by shrapnel, which resulted in a serious infection and forced her to return home.

Charlotte Delbo (1913–1985) was involved in the French Resistance. She was sent to Auschwitz in 1943 for producing anti-German leaflets. Of the 230 other French women involved in underground activities, forty-nine returned, Delbo among them. She is the author of numerous plays and essays and the

Auschwitz and After trilogy: *None of Us Will Return* (1965), *Useless Knowledge* (1970), and *The Measure of Our Days* (1970).

Ding Ling (1904–1985) was born in China. Influenced by Western writers, she became a nationally recognized writer in 1928. Her first husband was executed by the Nationalists. She was persecuted during the Cultural Revolution, exonerated in 1978, and continued to write until her death.

Margaret Drabble (1939–) was born in Sheffield, England, and published her first novel in 1962. Since then she has had a steady production of successful novels along with works of biography and literary criticism.

Dorothy Canfield Fisher (1879–1958) did relief work in France during World War I. Her novel *The Deepening Stream* (1930) portrays Paris during that war. She wrote many novels, collections of short stories, and works on education.

Martha Gellhorn (1908–1998) was a war correspondent during the Spanish Civil War. She met Ernest Hemingway in Spain and was married to him for five years. She lived mostly an expatriate life. She wrote novels and short stories about war but was most successful with her articles, collected under the title of *The Face of War.*

Susan Griffin (1943–) was born in Los Angeles. Her first book of poetry in 1976 won an award for radio drama. She has also published *Woman and Nature: The Roaring Inside Her* (1978), a long prose poem exploring women's place in world, and more recently she published *The Chorus of Stones: The Private Life of War* (1992).

H.D. (Hilda Doolittle [1886–1961]) was a pioneer in the imagist school of poetry. With her companion Bryher, she was instrumental in arranging Freud's escape to London when the Germans occupied Austria. H.D. lived through World War II in London from which came the trilogy: "These Walls Will Not Fall," "Tribute to Angels," and "The Flowering of the Rod."

Marguerite Higgins (1920–1966) was sent to London in 1944 as a reporter for the *Herald Tribune.* She was in Paris in March 1945 and went to the front two months later. She reached Buchenwald a few hours after its liberation. She worked in Berlin during the airlift and was the first woman correspondent to go to Korea. She died of an infection contracted while she was in Vietnam.

Etty Hillesum (1914–1943) was a linguist and a psychologist. She began writing her diary at age twenty-seven. She could have stayed out of Westerbork, the transit camp in northeastern Holland, because she was a member of the Jewish Council. However, she chose to stay with her parents and her younger brother, and they were all transported to their deaths at Auschwitz.

Kathryn Hulme (1900–1981) was the deputy director of the United Nations Relief and Rehabilitation Administration and the International Refugees Organization field teams following World War II, which led to her book *The Wild Place.* A character appearing in that book also was in *The Nun's Story*

(1956), which was the winner of numerous awards and was made into a film.

Käthe Kollwitz (1867–1945) was born in Koenigsberg, East Prussia. Her youngest son Peter died in World War I, and her grandson Peter died in World War II. Kollwitz became an important artist in the 1920s. Under the Hitler regime, she was forbidden to teach or to exhibit art.

Gertrud Kolmar (1894–1942) worked as an interpreter and a postal censor in World War I. Her sister was able to get to Switzerland in 1938, but Gertrud stayed in Berlin and sent her poems to her sister. She wrote of concentration camps as early as 1933 in "Im Lager." Kolmar died in Auschwitz some time after February 1942.

Ellen La Motte (1873–1934) was a nurse at Johns Hopkins, met Mary Borden, and was able to nurse at the front during World War I. After her work at the front, she went to China where she worked in an anti-opium campaign and wrote *The Ethics of Opium.*

Mary Lee (1891–1982) went overseas from June 1917 to July 1919 with the American Expeditionary Force. She was a reporter for the *New York Evening Post* until 1923, continuing with freelance work for the *New York Times Sunday Magazine* and *Atlantic* magazine. *It's a Great War!* won a contest for the best war novel, but the prize was refused when it was discovered the author was a woman; eventually, the prize was split between Lee and a male writer.

Doris Lessing (1919–) lived in Southern Rhodesia. After experiencing World War II in Rhodesia, she left her husband and two of her three children to move to London where she began a series of novels, *Children of Violence.* War is also a major subject of her "space fiction" novels, which include *The Marriages Between Zones Two, Three, and Five.*

Amy Lowell (1874–1925) published her first book of poetry, *A Dome of Many-Colored Glass,* in 1912. Her lifelong companion was actress, Ada Russell Dwyer. In England during World War I, Lowell was close to Ezra Pound and H.D. and with them defined the poetic movement known as imagism. Lowell was awarded the Pulitzer Prize posthumously.

Lina Magaia is from southern Mozambique. She interviewed victims of what she calls "not a civil war" but "genocide perpetuated by armed men against defenseless populations" and put their stories in her book, *Run for Your Life.* Magaia is particularly concerned with child victims of war.

Olivia Manning (1908–1980) traveled through many British war zones during World War II with her husband, a British council lecturer. She worked as a press officer in Bucharest, Athens, Cairo, and Jerusalem. These experiences led to her two most popular works, *The Balkan Trilogy* and *The Levant Trilogy,* televised as *The Fortunes of War.*

Katherine Mansfield (Kathleen Beauchamp [1888–1923]) was determined to re-create her New Zealand childhood in her writing after her younger brother was killed in World War I one month after getting to France. She is best known for her contributions to the development of short story form. A friend of D. H. Lawrence and Virginia Woolf, she married critic J. Middleton Murry.

Mary McCarthy (1912–1989) was raised by different relatives after the death of her parents in the influenza epidemic in 1918. Her childhood and education were recorded in *Memories of a Catholic Girlhood* (1957). She also wrote the best-selling book *The Group*. McCarthy was politically active and controversial, especially in her opposition to the Vietnam War.

Charlotte Mew (1870–1928) began publishing in 1894 with a short story. Soon a successful poet with a certain notoriety as a "new woman," she followed her female lover to Paris. During World War I, Mew worked with wives of volunteers who did not know how to collect allowances and later with the War Office. She committed suicide in 1928.

Edna St. Vincent Millay (1892–1950) gained attention and fame early with her long poem "Renascence" in 1912, which led to her being able to go to Vassar. She got a job with *Vanity Fair* writing articles in Paris in 1921 and stayed abroad for two years. She won a Pulitzer Prize in 1923 for *The Harp-Weaver and Other Poems*.

Molly Moore graduated from Georgetown University and began working for the *Washington Post* in the 1980s. As a senior military correspondent, she was the only reporter to accompany a senior commanding general in the Gulf War.

Elsa Morante (1918–1985) began writing at age thirteen and published her first short stories in the 1930s. She married Alberto Moravia and both became prominent members of the Roman literary scene. She is described as a magic-realist.

Toni Morrison (1931–) was born in Lorain, Ohio, attended Howard University, received a masters degree from Cornell, and taught English for a number of years before publishing *The Bluest Eye* in 1970. She holds an endowed professorship at Princeton. Her novel *Beloved* received a Pulitzer Prize in 1988, and she was awarded the Nobel Prize for Literature in 1993.

Sara Nomberg-Przytyk (1915–) comes from a Hasidic background. Her grandfather was a teacher and rabbi. After the German invasion of Poland, she fled to eastern Poland and was deported in 1943, first to Stutthof concentration camp, then to Auschwitz. She returned to Poland after the war to marry and practice journalism.

Iris Origo (1902–1988) was an Anglo-American who married an Italian aristocrat. She and her husband took over and restored a neglected Tuscan estate, becoming responsible for the lives, health, and education of fifty tenant farmers and their families. Between 1943 and 1944 their area became a battle-gound. She was the author of historical and literary studies including *The Merchant of Prato*.

Grace Paley (1922–) is a lifelong New Yorker, whose parents were Jewish immigrants from the Ukraine. She published her first short stories in 1960. An activist for peace and social change, she was often jailed for taking part in demonstrations against the war in Vietnam and the nuclear arms race.

Dorothy Parker (1893–1967) was best known for her humorous poems, which got her a job in advertising and then led to her position at *Vanity Fair* as a drama critic. She became a member of the famous Algonquin Round Table. Going to Spain during its civil war was "the proudest thing" she had ever done. She was blacklisted along with her husband, Alan Campbell, in the 1940s.

Emmeline Pethick-Lawrence (1867–1954) founded a girl's club in London. She married Labor minister Fred Lawrence in 1901, joined the Suffrage Society, and served six prison terms, which she wrote about in *Why I Went to Prison*. She ran for office, reported on atrocities by British soldiers in Ireland, and continued working for women and peace all her life.

Dahlia Ravikovitch (1936–) was born in Tel Aviv and served in the Israeli army. She studied English literature at Hebrew University and is the author of several books of poems; a collection of short stories, *Death in the Family*; and two books of poetry for children. She is the winner of several literary prizes.

Muriel Rukeyser (1913–1980) was born in New York, where she spent most of her life and started a literary magazine with Elizabeth Bishop and Mary McCarthy. She was devoted to the search for justice, went to Spain during its civil war, and later protested the Korean and Vietnam Wars. Her poetry and feminism are major influences on younger women poets.

Elizabeth Shepley Sergeant (1881–1955) was wounded in France during World War I while observing the front as a journalist. She was a close friend of Willa Cather and wrote *Willa Cather: A Memoir* in 1953.

Mary Lee Settle (1918–) went to England in 1942 to join the Women's Auxiliary Air Force. She has traveled widely and written many articles and novels since her war experience. Her novels include the Beulah series set in West Virginia. In 1995, she wrote *Choices*, which covers wars from the Spanish Civil War through World War II.

Helen Zenna Smith (Evadne Price [1896–1985]) was a freelance journalist and also wrote children's books, romances, plays, and films. She was a correspondent during World War II.

Gertrude Stein (1874–1946) lived abroad as a child with her German-Jewish family before settling in Oakland, California. She studied at Radcliffe before going on to medical school at Johns Hopkins. In 1904, she moved to Paris with her brother Leo, where they collected and encouraged the work of modern painters. She lived through both world wars in France, writing *Wars I Have Seen* in 1945.

Kikue Tada (1925–) became a nurse at age sixteen in 1941 when the war between Japan and the United States began and was working at an army hospital in Hiroshima when the nuclear attack occurred.

Hirabayashi Taiko (1905–1972) moved to Tokyo from the country and studied English while working as a telephone operator. She became politically active in the proletarian movement for which she was imprisoned. She contracted tuberculosis, and "Blind Chinese Soldiers" was one of the first stories written after her recovery. She traveled and spoke in other Asian countries during her later years and won prizes for women's literature in Japan.

Margaret Thatcher (1925–) attended Oxford during World War II, where she became president of the Oxford University Conservative Association. She married Denis Thatcher and became a lawyer. She was elected to Parliament in 1959, became a cabinet minister in 1961, and prime minister in 1979. She was reelected twice more, serving eleven years in all.

Dorothy Thompson (1893–1961) had her first job with a suffrage organization. Lecturing led to journalism, and she was made Central European bureau chief for a New York newspaper. Her second marriage in 1928 was to Sinclair Lewis from whom she was divorced in 1942. She protested the rise of fascism and was expelled from Nazi Germany in 1934. Her column "Let the Record Speak" in the New York *Herald Tribune* was syndicated around the country and made her name a household word.

Marta Traba (1930–1983) was born in Buenos Aires, Argentina, studied art in Rome and Paris, and became a major art critic in Latin America. She lived mostly outside of Argentina in other South American countries, in the United States, and in France. Her writing exposed the regimes in Argentina, Uruguay, and Chile, which oppressed their populations with systematic torture, "disappearance," and exile. She was killed in a plane crash near Madrid.

Huong Tram (Phan Thanh Hao [1952–]) lived in Hanoi during the Vietnam War and the Christmas bombing in 1972, as she says, "sharing the same war experience as others in her generation." She joined the Foreign Language Publishing House. A well-known poet and novelist as well as editor, translator, and journalist, she has translated three of her novels.

Fadwa Tuqan (1917–) was born in Nablus, Palestine. Her early poems were about love. After the war of 1967, she wrote increasingly about Israeli occupation of the West Bank, describing Palestinian resistance in the years before the Intifadah.

Elizabeth Vaughan (1905–1957) studied journalism and sociology before leaving the United States to teach at the University of the Philippines, where she met her husband, an American engineer. The Vaughans lived a prosperous colonial life until the Japanese invaded. After Vaughan's return to the United States, she published several studies on communities suffering imprisonment, including *Community under Stress* and *An Internment Camp Culture.*

Rebecca West (Cicily Fairfield [1882–1983]) went to London at age sixteen to try the stage before beginning to write under the pen name of a radical feminist in an Ibsen play. At twenty, she began an affair with H. G. Wells and had a son by him in 1914. Her first novel *The Return of the Soldier* was published in 1918, and she had a lifelong career as both a journalist and a novelist.

Edith Wharton (1862–1937) came from a wealthy New York family. Her first book was a collaboration with an architect, *The Decoration of Houses.* Her fame began with *The House of Mirth* in 1905; she won a Pulitzer Prize for *The Age of Innocence* in 1920. She lived mostly in France, especially after her divorce, and she died there shortly before the outbreak of World War II.

Virginia Woolf (1882–1941) was educated at home and became a founder of the Bloomsbury group of artists. She married Leonard Woolf, also a writer, and together they ran the Hogarth Press, bringing many authors to Britain for the first time, including James Joyce and Sigmund Freud. She had a lifelong battle with depression. War was a subject and theme in much of her work, including *Jacob's Room, To the Lighthouse, Three Guineas,* and *Between the Acts.*

Mitsuye Yamada (1943–) was born in Kyushu, Japan, but was raised in Seattle until World War II when her family was removed to an internment camp in Idaho. She is a professor of English and has published two books of poetry, *Camp Notes and Other Poems* and *Desert Run: Poems and Stories.* She is the chair of Amnesty International's Committee on International Development and a founder of Multicultural Women Writers.

SOURCES AND CREDITS

Part One. The Great War

Nina Macdonald. "Sing a Song of War-Time" from *War-Time Nursery Rhymes*. Routledge and Kegan Paul Ltd. Reprinted by permission of Routledge and Kegan Paul Ltd.

Rebecca West. "The Cordite Makers" from *The Young Rebecca: Writings of Rebecca West, 1911–1917*. Edited by Jane Marcus. New York: Viking, 1982. Reprinted by permission of the estate of Rebecca West.

Vera Brittain. Excerpt from *Chronicle of Youth: The War Diary, 1913–1917* by Vera Brittain, edited by Alan Bishop. Copyright © 1981 by the Literary Executors for the Vera Brittain Estate. Reprinted with the permission of Vera Brittain's literary executor, Paul Berry; William Morrow and Company, Inc.; and Victor Gollancz Ltd.

Edith Wharton. Excerpt from *Fighting France: From Dunkerque to Belport*. New York: Charles Scribner's Sons, 1915.

Mary Borden. "Conspiracy" from *The Forbidden Zone* by Mary Borden. Copyright 1930 by Doubleday, a division of Bantam Doubleday Dell Publishing Group. Used by permission of Doubleday, a division of Bantam Doubleday Dell Publishing Group, Inc.

Ellen La Motte. "Women and Wives" from *The Backwash of War: The Human Wreckage of the Battlefield as Witnessed by an American Hospital Nurse*. New York: Putnam, 1916.

Colette. "Verdun, December–January, 1915" from *Earthly Paradise: An Autobiography* by Colette, edited by Robert Phelps. Copyright © 1966 and renewed 1994 by Farrar, Straus & Giroux, Inc. Reprinted by permission of Farrar, Straus & Giroux, Inc. and Reed Consumer Books, Ltd.

Helen Zenna Smith. Excerpt from *Not So Quiet . . . : Stepdaughters of War*. New York: Feminist Press, 1989. Reprinted by permission of the Feminist Press.

Dorothy Canfield Fisher. "A Honeymoon . . . Vive L'Amerique" from *Home Fires in France*. New York: Henry Holt, 1918.

Amy Lowell. "In the Stadium" from *Pictures of the Floating World*. Boston: Houghton Mifflin, 1919.

Willa Cather. Excerpt from *One of Ours* by Willa Cather. Copyright 1922 by Willa Cather and renewed 1950 by Edith Lewis, Executrix of the Estate of Willa Cather. Reprinted by permission of Alfred A. Knopf Inc. and Virago Press.

Mary Lee. Excerpt from *It's a Great War!* Boston: Riverside Press/Houghton Mifflin, 1929.

Elizabeth Shepley Sergeant. Excerpt from *Shadow-Shapes: The Journal of a Wounded Woman*. Boston: Houghton Mifflin, 1920.

Gertrude Stein. Excerpt from *The Autobiography of Alice B. Toklas* by Gertrude Stein. Copyright © 1933 and renewed 1961 by Alice B. Toklas. Reprinted by permission of Random House, Inc. and the estate of Gertrude Stein.

Käthe Kollwitz. Excerpt from *The Diary and Letters of Kaethe Kollwitz*. Edited by Hans

Part Two. Between the Wars

Part Three. World War Again

Part Four. The Cold War and Beyond

INDEX

Sayre P. Sheldon, a graduate of Radcliffe College and Boston University, teaches at Boston University, where she has developed courses in American literature and women's studies. The founding president of Women's Action for Nuclear Disarmament (WAND), she continues to serve as a national board member to the organization under its current name, Women's Action for New Directions. She has represented WAND at national and international conferences including the fourth United Nations Conference on Women in Beijing. Her written work includes many articles on both literature and disarmament.